EPISTEMIC FREEDOM IN AFRICA

Epistemic Freedom in Africa is about the struggle for African people to think, theorize, interpret the world and write from where they are located, unencumbered by Eurocentrism. The imperial denial of common humanity to some human beings meant that in turn their knowledges and experiences lost their value, their epistemic virtue. Now, in the twenty-first century, descendants of enslaved, displaced, colonized and racialized peoples have entered academies across the world, proclaiming loudly that they are human beings, their lives matter and they were born into valid and legitimate knowledge systems that are capable of helping humanity to transcend the current epistemic and systemic crises. Together, they are engaging in diverse struggles for cognitive justice, fighting against the epistemic line that haunts the twenty-first century.

The renowned historian and decolonial theorist Sabelo J. Ndlovu-Gatsheni offers a penetrating and well-argued case for centring Africa as a legitimate historical unit of analysis and epistemic site from which to interpret the world, while simultaneously making an equally strong argument for globalizing knowledge from Africa so as to attain ecologies of knowledges. This is a dual process of both deprovincializing Africa, and in turn provincializing Europe. The book highlights how the mental universe of Africa was invaded and colonized, the long-standing struggles for 'an African university', and the trajectories of contemporary decolonial movements such as Rhodes Must Fall and Fees Must Fall in South Africa. This landmark work underscores the fact that only once the problem of epistemic freedom has been addressed can Africa achieve political, cultural, economic and other freedoms.

This groundbreaking new book is accessible to students and scholars across Education, History, Philosophy, Ethics, African Studies, Development Studies, Politics, International Relations, Sociology, Postcolonial Studies and the emerging field of Decolonial Studies.

Sabelo J. Ndlovu-Gatsheni is Executive Director of the Change Management Unit (CMU) in the Principal and Vice-Chancellor's office at the University of South Africa (UNISA), and Professor of African Political Economy at the Thabo Mbeki African Leadership Institute (TMALI) at the same institution. Previously, he headed the Archie Mafeje Research Institute for Applied Social Policy (AMRI). He is the author of 14 books, including *Coloniality of Power in Postcolonial Africa: Myths of Decolonization* (2013), *Empire, Global Coloniality and African Subjectivity* (2013) and most recently *The Decolonial Mandela: Peace, Justice and the Politics of Life* (2016).

Rethinking Development

Rethinking Development offers accessible and thought-provoking overviews of contemporary topics in international development and aid. Providing original empirical and analytical insights, the books in this series push thinking in new directions by challenging current conceptualizations and developing new ones.

This is a dynamic and inspiring series for all those engaged with today's debates surrounding development issues, whether they be students, scholars, policy makers and practitioners internationally. These interdisciplinary books provide an invaluable resource for discussion in advanced undergraduate and postgraduate courses in development studies as well as in anthropology, economics, politics, geography, media studies and sociology.

A full list of titles in this series is available at: www.routledge.com/Rethinking-Development/book-series/RDVPT. Recently published titles include:

Learning and Volunteering Abroad for Development
Unpacking Host Organisation and Volunteer Rationales
Rebecca Tiessen

Communicating Development with Communities
Linje Manyozo

Learning and Volunteering Abroad for Development
Emerging Economies and Development
Jan Nederveen Pieterse

Disability and International Development
A guide for students and practitioners
David Cobley

Numeracy as Social Practice
Global and Local Perspectives
By Keiko Yasukawa, Alan Rogers, Kara Jackson and Brian V. Street

Communication in International Development
Doing Good or Looking Good?
By Florencia Enghel and Jessica Noske-Turner

Epistemic Freedom in Africa
Deprovincialization and Decolonization
Sabelo J. Ndlovu-Gatsheni

EPISTEMIC FREEDOM IN AFRICA

Deprovincialization and Decolonization

Sabelo J. Ndlovu-Gatsheni

LONDON AND NEW YORK

First published 2018
by Routledge
2 Park Square, Milton Park, Abingdon, Oxon OX14 4RN

and by Routledge
711 Third Avenue, New York, NY 10017

Routledge is an imprint of the Taylor & Francis Group, an informa business

© 2018 Sabelo J. Ndlovu-Gatsheni

British Library Cataloguing-in-Publication Data
A catalogue record for this book is available from the British Library

Library of Congress Cataloging-in-Publication Data
A catalog record has been requested for this book

ISBN: 978-1-138-58857-8 (hbk)
ISBN: 978-1-138-58859-2 (pbk)
ISBN: 978-0-429-49220-4 (ebk)

Typeset in Bembo and Stone Sans
by Florence Production Ltd, Stoodleigh, Devon, UK

For my children:
Vulindlela Kings, Thandolwenkosi Jacqueline,
Nobuntu Anaya

CONTENTS

ILLUSTRATIONS

Figure

Tables

FOREWORD

Optimism for Afro-futurism

Toyin Falola

UNIVERSITY DISTINGUISHED PROFESSOR, JACOB AND FRANCES SANGER MOSSIKER
CHAIR IN THE HUMANITIES AT THE UNIVERSITY OF TEXAS AT AUSTIN AND
HONORARY PROFESSOR, UNIVERSITY OF CAPE TOWN

In his last year on earth, providing one of his very last testaments, Frantz Fanon, the most prominent anti-colonial intellectual of the twentieth century, made one of the most profound statements of that era: 'For Europe, for ourselves and for humanity, we must turn over a new leaf, we must work out new concepts, and try to set afoot a new man.' Yes!

Professor Sabelo J. Ndlovu-Gatsheni is, I am most certain, responding to this revolutionary call, turning over a new leaf, providing new concepts, and empowering new men and women to liberate the African continent. A highly successful scholar, Professor Ndlovu-Gatsheni has given the entire project of decoloniality the relevance and respect it deserves.

There was much jubilation two years ago when Professor Ndlovu-Gatsheni was selected as one of the best scholars of decoloniality in the world by a French news agency. What a proud moment! This book consolidates his stature as a preeminent scholar of decoloniality. He is one of the most celebrated scholars to have guided us in understanding our weakened intellectual reality. He is the one to turn to in order to understand various crucial concepts: dimensions of epistemological decolonization (provincializing Europe while deprovincializing Africa); Africanizing knowledge; decolonial critiques of existing knowledge; ecologies of knowledges; and the nativist approach to knowledge. The book teaches us a great deal about a variety of concepts: 'provincializing' and 'deprovincializing', distinction between 'epistemic freedom' and 'academic freedom', subalternity, African existential philosophy, creolization, coloniality of being, coloniality of power, coloniality of knowledge, dismemberment, re-membering, delinking, moving the centre, colonialism of special type, African personality, Negritude, Ethiopianism, Pan-Africanism and many others.

As we follow him on the journey of concept articulation, we are introduced into the larger world of ontology, epistemology and pedagogy. He teaches us, and at the same time, is humanizing us to be sensitive to the application of knowledge to development. He challenges us to reclaim the intellectual tradition of leading African politicians-cum-intellectuals who have contributed to the philosophy of liberation.

In anchoring his vibrant analyses to the past of Africa, and the imagination of its futurism, Professor Ndlovu-Gatsheni draws on the work of leading African theorists, ranging from the humanist to the revolutionary, figures like the psychiatrist-political philosopher like Frantz Fanon, leading spokespeople of change, anti-colonial activists, civil rights champions, socialist thinkers and many more. In the long roll call are pioneers like Edward Wilmot Blyden, pathfinders such as Cheikh Anta Diop, scholars of the left like Dani W. Nabudere and Samir Amin, critical thinkers like Catherine Odora Hoppers, globalists like Ali A. Mazrui, and political leaders like Kwame Nkrumah and Nelson Mandela.

The cast is noted for its varied ideas of black upliftment and black consciousness such as the idea of Negritude by Leopold Sedar Senghor and the aftermath by Kwame Nkrumah. This distinguished crowd was passionate about Africa, and profoundly critical of the colonial and postcolonial state. They confronted issues of racial domination, nationalism, development, political stability, among others.

Professor Ndlovu-Gatsheni goes further in four chapters to focus on distinguished scholars with definitive contributions. Their lives, careers and works are situated in the context of African crises and the possibilities of recovery. One is the chapter on Professor Mahmood Mamdani whom Professor Ndlovu-Gatsheni praises for his ability to rethink Africa, focusing on his major ideas. As he explains, Mamdani is able to privilege Africa's 'internal historical dynamics'; explain the workings of the colonial state and its contentious political identities; and projects the possibilities of civil societies as engines of growth. In summarizing the totality of Mamdani's achievement, he concludes that 'the significance of Mamdani's academic and intellectual interventions is that they speak directly and consistently to the long-standing question of locus of historicization and theorization of Africa so as to liberate knowledge from the snares of extraversion and coloniality'.

Professor Ndlovu-Gatsheni equally identifies the contributions of Nelson Mandela, praising him for not focusing on criminal prosecutions but the promotion of 'political justice' that can transform society. With maturity, he analyses the plusses and minuses of Mandela as a thinker and leader, reaching a most compelling conclusion: 'What hit Mandela's conception of politics was its dependence on the goodness of human beings, including those who had been irreparably corrupted by colonialism and apartheid to the extent of falling from humanity itself'. He notes also the contributions of Ali. A. Mazrui on the invention of Africa, concepts of 'triple heritage', and the promotion of a new identity called 'Afrabia' to unite Africa with parts of the Middle East. On the economy, he praises him for advancing the idea of decolonizing modernity through five processes of indigenization, domestication, diversification, horizontal interpenetration and vertical counter-penetration.

The issues that Professor Ndlovu-Gatsheni addresses, in very absorbing ways, are complex, focused around intriguing figures who propose ideas of great intellectual significance. As the chapters move into the second half of the book one begins to see that decoloniality is not just an academic exercise, but also one of human concern. Africa is not a tragic figure, as portrayed by its enemies. Rather, as he argues, the continent was raped. Addressing the issues around that rape is a decolonial project. Overcoming that rape is a decolonial project. Admitting the psychic disorder among the leaders who brutalize their own people and who steal money, to me, is also a decolonial project.

This book, I assert, is one of great revelation: once Africa decolonizes, its future trajectory would be great. Africans, he argues, must understand the interconnections between the coloniality of power, knowledge and development. He argues that as African scholars package knowledge, they must insist on six critical elements: deracialization, detribalization, depatriachization, decorporatization, deimperialization and democratization.

He insists that a set of the ideas that various scholars have articulated can be drawn to support those six elements. On this there is no dearth of knowledge, suggesting that the works of the following scholars be compulsory readings in schools: Paulin J. Hountondji, Oyeronke Oyewumi, Bagele Chilisa, Jacques Depelchin, Mahmood Mamdani, Achille Mbembe, Francis Nyamnjoh, Thandika Mkandawire, Issa Shivji, Peter Ekeh, Toyin Falola, Neville Alexander, Ngugi wa Thiong'o, Yirga Gelaw Woldeyes, Amilcar Cabral, Molefi Asante, Kenneth Kaunda and Nelson Mandela. These scholars, he points out, have contributed to our understanding of epistemic freedom, epistemological decolonization, decolonizing the university, Africanity, cognitive justice, the national question, the meaning of freedom and decolonial pedagogy for African futures. He does not ignore non-African thinkers, and he makes a strong case for intellectual alliances, drawing ideas from Edward E. Said, William E. B. Dubois, Marcus Garvey, Lewis R. Gordon, Michael-Rolph Trouillot, Ashis Nandy, Paulo Freire, Julia Suárez-Krabbe, Dipesh Chakrabarty, Nelson Maldonado-Torres, Ramon Grosfoguel, Walter D. Mignolo, Anibal Quijano, Edouard Glissant, Enrique Dussel, Gurminder K. Bhambra, An Yuontae, Kuan-Hsing Chen and many others. He praises the contributions of Immanuel Wallerstein, Bonaventura de Sousa Santos, Amy Allen and others for continuing with the tradition of the critique of Eurocentrism from inside Europe.

His advocacy includes the vibrant practical measures needed to move Africa forward: deprovincialization of Africa; the construction of 'Africanity' as a trans-space, trans-time, trans-geographical, and trans-cultural phenomenon. I support his commitment to always look inward for home grown ideas. Similarly, I endorse his recommendation that African universities must become the sites of decolonial ideas. I salute his courage in praising the generation of students who struggle for decolonization, and organizing around the great slogan of 'Rhodes Must Fall'.

Among those who have witnessed the failure of postcolonial Africa, few have written with the power and brilliance of Professor Ndlovu-Gatsheni who has dedicated himself to both the intellectual and practical project of decoloniality. This book, like his previous others, remains among the most serious and radical indictments of both colonialism and postcolonialism. It is indeed a work of good sense and judgement, a sophisticated analysis of the epistemology of the South, and a landmark text in the fields of coloniality and postcoloniality. I will not challenge his consistent claim that it is possible to start the imagination of Africa's future from the scratch by building on a long list of thinkers/activists, as I understand this as a clear expression of his frustration with the collective failure of the continent.

The book identifies the challenges without taking away hope; it analyses failures without accepting defeat; and our distinguished author deftly disagrees with some views without disparaging those who make them. His sense of rage at Africa's rape does not lead to despair and despondency but to optimism.

ACKNOWLEDGEMENTS

I wrote this book during a very hectic time in my professional life. At the end of 2015, I received an unexpected letter from the Vice-Chancellor of the University of South Africa (UNISA), Professor Mandla Makhanya, offering me the position of Director in the newly established Change Management Unit (CMU) located in his office. My directorate was to deal with transformation of scholarship in the context of the rising student demands for decolonized education. I accepted the offer in December 2015 and joined CMU in January 2016. In South Africa, the years 2015–2016 were the most hectic as they witnessed the boiling point of student demands for free, quality and decolonized higher education. CMU was expected to actively drive the implementation of transformation of the university. My specific position was to drive the epistemological decolonization strand of transformation. This made me think deeply about knowledge, the very idea of the university, curriculum and pedagogy from a decolonial perspective. The idea for this book emerged as I was busy with my new position at CMU – an administrative position that had very limited space for scholarly research and writing. Despite this constraint, I convinced myself that this was an important book and that the transformation agenda we were driving as CMU had to be informed by research and well thought-out ideas.

I would, therefore, like to express my most sincere gratitude to Professor Mandla Makhanya for granting me 3 months sabbatical (January–March 2017) that enabled me to concentrate on research and writing some of the chapters of this book. I also extend my thanks to Professor Greg Cuthbertson (the Executive Director of CMU) for allowing space to writing while doing the work of the unit. My colleagues Dr Malekutu Bopape (Director: Culture at CMU) and Professor Vuyisile Msila (Director: Leadership in Higher Education at CMU) contributed immensely to the refinement of most of the ideas contained in this book through daily conversations.

I acknowledge the opportunity to present and discuss aspects of my thoughts on epistemic freedom and decolonization of the university at the London School of Economics and Political Science (LSE), Annual Barcelona International Summer School on Decolonizing Knowledge, Power and Being; Annual UNISA Decoloniality Summer School, University of KwaZulu-Natal (UKZN), Central University of Technology (CUT), Tshwane University of Technology (TUT), University of Western Cape (UWC), University of Johannesburg (UJ), University of Fort Hare (UFH), University of the Free State (UFS) and Nelson Mandela University (NMU).

However, it was an unexpected communication from Helena Hurd (Routledge Editor – Development Studies) after reading an abstract of a keynote address that I was invited to deliver at HDCA Conference in Cape Town South Africa, which opened the way to discuss the prospects of considering Routledge as a publisher for this book. The communication further galvanized me into working more consistently on the book manuscript. I would, therefore, like to thank Helena for considering my book proposal and accepting it in record time. With the acceptance of the book proposal I had no option but to complete the writing of the book manuscript. My thanks also go to Matthew Shobbrook at Routledge who not only sent me the final version of the signed publication contract but also briefly discussed the possibility of submitting the manuscript earlier than 30 May 2018.

The members of the Africa Decolonial Research Network (ADERN), particularly Professor Morgan Ndlovu (Department of Development Studies-UNISA), Professor Tendayi Sithole (Department of Political Science-UNISA), Dr William Mpofu (Centre for Diversity Studies-Wits University), Dr Eric Nyembezi Makoni (University of Johannesburg), Dr Last Moyo (independent Researcher) and Dr Blessed Ngwenya (Department of Communication Science-UNSA), have been one of the most reliable intellectual communities with which I have been privileged to work, to constantly bounce ideas and receive comments. The same is true of Professor Charisse Burden-Stelly (USA), Professor Ramon Grosfoguel (USA), Professor Nelson Maldonado-Torres (USA), Professor Finex Ndhlovu (Australia) and Professor Siphamandla Zondi (Department of Political Sciences-University of Pretoria) – they have been always available to read and provide comments on my work. Last but not least, my sincere gratitude is extended to my wife, Pinky Patricia Nkete, with whom I have shared most of the ideas contained in this book from the time of the conception to the publication of this book.

I, however, take full responsibility for the content of this book.

1

INTRODUCTION

Seek ye epistemic freedom first

Epistemic Freedom in Africa: Deprovincialization and Decolonization is a study of the
politics of knowledge in general and specifically of African struggles for epistemic
freedom. As a result of the long-term consequences of modernity, enslavement
and colonialism, African people have been reproduced as agents in a Eurocentric
history. What exist today as conventional 'philosophy of history' and academic
discourse of history produced within modern universities is still normatively
Eurocentric, neo-Enlightenment, neo-Hegelian, neo-Marxist, neo-modernist
and Habermasian. In this context thought about historical change is still hostage
to resilient linear social-evolutionary notions of 'transitional' shifts (Bhambra
2007: 24).

A major consequence of this Eurocentric thinking is that what is today known
as 'African history' has been 'subsumed to the ideological parameters and
periodization of the general framework, be it colonial, nationalist, or Marxist'
(Bhambra 2007: 25). This point was delivered more emphatically by Dipesh
Chakrabarty (2007: 27) when he argued: ' "Europe" remains the sovereign, theoretical subject of all histories, including the ones we call "Indian," "Chinese,"
"Kenyan," and so on.' It was perhaps this reality that provoked the African historian E. S. Atieno-Odhiambo (2002: 14) to pose the question: 'Can African
historians recapture this historical space and reintroduce an African philosophy of
history that emphasizes African autonomy?' Atieno-Odhiambo (2002) pushed for
a paradigm shift 'from African historiographies to an African philosophy of history'.
In an earlier publication, Atieno-Odhiambo (1996: 31) eloquently expressed the
epistemic quandary haunting the so-called 'African history':

> Has the time come to question the unitary acceptance of the hegemonic
> episteme which posits that the discipline of history uniquely belongs to
> Western civilization? Alternatively, can Africans articulate an African gnosis

that stands independently of these western traditions in our study of African history? Need African epistemes be intelligible to the West? Need the study and practice of history be tied to the guild of historical study at the universities? Is there still the lingering possibility than any one of us working within the western mode can have the arterial bypass surgery that may still be the viaduct upstream to the African reservoir of history?

At another level, Amy Allen (2016: 44) correctly critiqued Eurocentric notions of 'macrohistory' in these revealing words: 'If global unity and capacity to make history are themselves historical developments that have emerged relatively recently, then they cannot be made the premises of an understanding of history as *a whole*.' Hence the urgent need for epistemic freedom, which restores to African people a central position within human history as independent actors. This epistemological concern is fundamentally decolonial. As a people, Africans were always there in human history. They were never creatures of 'discovery'. Africans were always present ('presence Africaine'). Africans were never absent. Africa was never a *tabula rasa* (Dark Continent). Africans always had their own valid, legitimate and useful knowledge systems and education systems. This is the decolonial tale at the centre of this book. The foundation of this decolonial tale is well articulated by the Wole Soyinka who had this to say about Africa:

> The African continent appears to possess one distinction that is largely unremarked. Unlike the Americas or Australasia, for instance, no one actually claims to have 'discovered' Africa. Neither the continent as an entity nor indeed any of her later offspring – the modern states – celebrates the equivalent of America's Columbus Day. This gives it a self-constitutive identity, an unstated autochthony that is denied other continents and subcontinents. [. . .] Africa appears to have been 'known about', speculated over, explored both in actuality and fantasy, even mapped – Greeks, Jews, Arabs, Phoenicians, etc., took their turns – but no narrative has come down to us that actually lays personal claim to the discovery of the continent. Ancient ruins, the source of a river, mountain peaks, exotic kingdoms, and sunken pyramids, yes, but not the continent itself – as in the case of the Americas. Hundreds have ventured into, explored, and extensively theorized over the continent, but no one has actually claimed to have discovered her.
> (Soyinka 2012: 27)

Soyinka challenged the colonial paradigm of 'discovery' and highlighted Africa's primordial existence. This means that Africa has a long history that pre-dated its encounter with Europe. It also means that such a primordial entity had and has its own rich knowledge that kept it alive. What is explored in this book is not only how Africa in particular and the rest of the Global South in general became victims of genocides, epistemicides, linguicide and cultural imperialism, but also the trajectories of struggles for epistemic freedom that were provoked and ensued.

Thus, conceptually speaking, the book delves deeper into such concepts as 'the epistemic line' as the problem of the twenty-first century; the perennial problem of 'silences' of African voices and problematic African archives enabled by the 'Europeanization' of the world on the one hand and the subalternization of Africa on the other hand; and the imperative of 'rethinking thinking' during the current age of epistemic and systemic crisis.

The epistemic line

If the 'colour line' was indeed the major problem of the twentieth century as articulated by William E. B. Du Bois (1903), then that of the twenty-first century is the 'epistemic line'. The 'epistemic line' cascades from the 'colour line' because denial of humanity automatically disqualified one from epistemic virtue. The epistemic line is sustained by what Boaventura de Sousa Santos (2007) termed 'abyssal thinking' – an imperial reason that reduced some human beings to a sub-human category with no knowledge. This means that the epistemic line is simultaneously the ontological line.

Thus the triple processes of provincializing Europe, deprovincializing Africa and epistemological decolonization which frame this book constitute a drive for a restorative epistemic agenda and process that simultaneously addresses ontological and epistemological issues haunting Africa. The definitive entry of descendants of the enslaved, displaced, colonized and racialized peoples into the existing academies across the world, proclaiming loudly that they are human beings, their lives matter, and that they were born into valid and legitimate knowledge systems, enabled the resurgence of long-standing struggles for epistemic freedom. Thus epistemic freedom speaks to cognitive justice. Epistemic freedom is fundamentally about the right to think, theorize, interpret the world, develop own methodologies and write from where one is located and unencumbered by Eurocentrism. Samir Amin (2009) depicted Eurocentrism as one of the great ideological deformation of our time. Epistemic justice is about liberation of reason itself from coloniality.

Africa is one of those epistemic sites that experienced not only colonial genocides but also 'theft of history' (see Goody 2006), epistemicides (killing of indigenous people's knowledges) and linguicides (killing of indigenous people's languages) (see Ngugi wa Thiong'o 2009a; Ngugi wa Thiong'o 2009b). Therefore, African people's epistemic struggles are both old and new. They are old in the sense that they emerged at the very time of colonial encounters. They are new in the sense that they are re-emerging within a context of a deep present global systemic and epistemic crisis. What is projected here is epistemological decolonization as a double task of 'provincializing Europe' and 'deprovincializing Africa'. The processes of 'provincializing' and 'deprovincializing' are inextricably linked as they speak to how what appears on a global scale as European thought could be claimed as human heritage rather than a thought from one geographical centre. 'Provincial-izing' is a process of 'moving the centre' to borrow a concept from Ngugi wa Thiong'o (1993). 'Moving the centre' is understood in a double-sense:

I am concerned with moving the centre in two senses at least. One is the need to move the centre from its assumed location in the West to a multiplicity of spheres in all the cultures of the world. The assumed location of the centre of the universe in the West is what goes by the term Eurocentrism [. . .] The second sense is even more important [. . .]. Within nearly all nations today the centre is located in the dominant social stratum, a male bourgeois minority. [. . .] Moving the centre in the two senses – between nations and within nations – will contribute to the freeing of the world of cultures from the restrictive walls of nationalism, class, race and gender.

(Ngugi wa Thiong'o 1993: xvi–xvii).

In this sense, 'provincializing Europe' is meant to confront the problem of overrepresentation of European thought in knowledge, social theory and education, which resulted in what the European historian John M. Headly (2008) celebrated as 'the Europeanization of the World'. To 'provincialize Europe' is fundamentally to 'de-Europeanize' the world. De-Europeanization of the world entails what Kuan-Hsing Chen (2010) depicted as 'deimperialization'. Chen (2010: vii) defined deimperialization as movement that demanded (ex)-imperial powers to genuinely reflect on 'their imperial histories and the harmful impacts those have had on the world'. This is a fundamental decolonial demand of which political decolonization of the twentieth century failed to deliver. The process of 'de-Europeanizing' is here rendered as 'deprovincializing Africa' – an intellectual and academic process of centring of Africa as a legitimate historical unit of analysis and epistemic site from which to interpret the world while at the same time globalizing knowledge from Africa. Such a move constitutes epistemic freedom as that essential prerequisite for political, cultural, economic and other freedoms.

Epistemic freedom is different from academic freedom. Academic freedom speaks to institutional autonomy of universities and rights to express diverse ideas including those critical of authorities and political leaders. Epistemic freedom is much broader and deeper. It speaks to cognitive justice; it draws our attention to the content of what it is that we are free to express and on whose terms. Cognitive justice as defined by Boaventura de Sousa Santos (2014) is premised on recognition of diverse ways of knowing by which human beings across the globe make sense of their existence. Epistemic freedom is about democratizing 'knowledge' from its current rendition in the singular into its plural known as 'knowledges'. It is also ranged against overrepresentation of Eurocentric thought in knowledge, social theory and education. Epistemic freedom is foundational in the broader decolonization struggle because it enables the emergence of the necessary critical decolonial consciousness.

In Africa, decolonization has generally been understood to have begun with 'political decolonization' predicated on seeking the 'political kingdom first'. However, the current struggles for epistemic freedom have provoked a need for rethinking of the decolonial trajectories. While it is true that political, economic, cultural and epistemological aspects of decolonization were and are always inextricably intertwined, we have to be cognisant of the fact that the 'sequencing' arose from a practical strategic logic of struggles against colonialism, which privileged attainment of political sovereignty first. In the co-constitution of political, economic, cultural and epistemological decolonization, epistemic freedom should form the base because it deals with the fundamental issues of critical consciousness building, which are essential pre-requisites for both political and economic freedom. This point was highlighted by E. Mveng (1983: 141): 'if political sovereignty is necessary, the scientific sovereignty is perhaps more important in present-day Africa'. Mveng (1983: 141) elaborated that 'The West agrees with us today that the way to Truth passes by numerous paths, other than Aristolean Thomistic logic or Hegelian dialectics. But social and human sciences themselves must be decolonized'. Paulin J. Hountondji (1996: 107) also emphasized the need for epistemic freedom when he argued that:

> We must be ambitious for Africa and for ourselves; we must be careful not to nip in the bud the unparalleled promise of our history or to prune it prematurely. We must on the contrary open it up, liberate it [. . .]. Beyond all facile solutions, beyond all myths, we must have courage to make a fresh start.

Hountondji (2002: 103) went on to articulate some of the key aspect of the African struggles for epistemic freedom:

> The struggle against intellectual extraversion presupposes the creation, in Africa, of an autonomous space for reflection and theoretical discussion that is indissolubly philosophical and scientific. Only such a space can enhance an effective participation of African peoples – and not just some individuals of African origin – in the debates about them. That will be the condition for intellectual freedom.

But in the search for epistemic freedom, knowledge cannot be reduced to 'philosophical' and 'scientific' forms only. Recognition of various forms of knowledge and knowing is called for in decolonization. Hountondji (2002: 104) elaborated that the task of epistemic freedom is 'that of organizing in Africa an autonomous debate that will no longer be a far-flung appendix to European debates, but which will directly pit African philosophers against one another'. To Hountondji (2002: 139), the base for sustainable epistemic freedom lies in formulation of 'original set of questions' and he elaborated on this point this way:

> The creation of an autonomous body of thought had to begin with the effort to formulate original set of questions, not out of a search for novelty for its own sake, but out of a concern for authenticity, of a desire to be oneself by freely asking questions that one spontaneously asks oneself and by

trying to raise them to a higher level of formulation, rather than by passively accepting the questions that others ask themselves or ask us from their own preoccupations.

What is also necessary for the success of epistemic freedom according to Hountondji (2002: 139) is the 'change of audience' by African researchers 'to consider his or her African public as his or her prime target'. All these moves speak to the necessary processes of deprovincializing Africa and 'provincializing Europe'. Suffice to say deprovincializing Africa addresses marginality and peripherality of Africa in the knowledge and education domain through recentring it. Chakrabarty, who introduced and popularized the concept of 'provincializing Europe', seemed to be concerned about how the 'Restern world' could claim what has been known as European ideas and thought. This is indeed another important way of subverting and confronting the problem of Eurocentrism as an enabler of Western epistemic hegemony. Chakrabarty (2000: xiv) highlighted how 'universalistic thought was always and already modified by particular histories'.

While this is indeed a valid intervention, there is still the need to stretch the concept of 'provincializing Europe' into a decolonial perspective where it has to directly address the problem of 'coloniality of knowledge' which took the form of 'invasion of the mental universe' of the colonized world (see Ngugi wa Thiong'o 1986; Quijano 2007). This analysis takes us to the concept of epistemological decolonization, which is meant to deal with problems and consequences of the 'metaphysical empire' such epistemicides, linguicides, cultural imperialism and alienation. At the centre of epistemic freedom is demythologizing of both the idea of Europe as a teacher of the world and the idea of Africa as a pupil (Ngugi wa Thiong'o 1986). With specific reference to demythologizing Africa, Hountondji posited that:

> The search for intellectual freedom presupposes a 'demythologizing' of the idea of Africa. The 'dominant, mythological conception of Africanness' had to be demolished, and re-established the simple, obvious truth that Africa is above all a continent, and the concept of Africa an empirical and geographical concept and not a metaphysical one'.
>
> (Hountondji 2002: 126)

Jean Comaroff and John L. Comaroff (2012: 1) also highlighted a decolonial epistemological move of decentring the Global North as the centre of knowledge and recentring the Global South. This is how they pondered on this deprovincializing strategy:

> But what if, and here is the idea in interrogative form, we invert that order of things? What if we subvert the epistemic scaffolding on which it is erected? What if we posit that, in the present moment, it is the global south that affords privileged insight into the workings of the world at large?

The Comaroffs posited these key epistemological questions as part of pushing for deprovincializing the 'Global South' within a historical and epistemic context in which 'Western enlightenment thought has [. . .] posited itself as the wellspring of universal learning, of Science and Philosophy [. . .], it has regarded the non-West – variously known as the ancient, the orient, the primitive world, the third world, the underdeveloped world, the developing world, and now the global south – primarily as a place of parochial wisdom, of antiquarian traditions, of exotic ways and means' (Comaroff and Comaroff 2012: 1). It is within this terrain that the current assertions of epistemic freedom emerged but they became accentuated in the twenty-first century because the 'Global North' 'after five centuries of "teaching" the world, it lost the capacity to learn from the experience of the world' (Santos 2014: 19). This inability of the 'Global North' to learn from the rest of the world emerged from invented white supremacy that underpinned colonialism and imperialism (Santos 2014: 19). It has delivered a double crisis – systemic and epistemic.

It was during the heydays of colonialism that Africa was reinvented as a site of 'darkness' bereft of any knowledge beyond superstitions. But the reality of today is that what has existed as 'Western, Eurocentric critical tradition' is exhibiting clear signs of exhaustion (Santos 2014: 19). The exhaustion manifests itself in various forms that Santos (2014: 19) summarized as: 'irrelevance, inadequacy, impotence, stagnation, paralysis'. The epistemic crisis is also expressing itself in terms of what Santos (2014: 33) depicted as 'loss of critical nouns'. He elaborated that:

> There was a time when Eurocentric critical theory 'owned' a vast set of nouns that marked its difference from conventional or bourgeois theories. These nouns included socialism, communism, revolution, class struggle, dependency, alienation, fetishism of commodities, and so on. In the past thirty years the Eurocentric critical tradition seems to have lost 'its' nouns and now distinguishes itself from conventional or bourgeois theories by the adjectives it uses to subvert the meaning of the proper nouns it borrows from such theories. Thus, for instance, if conventional theory speaks of development, critical theory refers to alternative, integral, inclusionary, democratic, or sustainable development; if conventional theory speaks of democracy, critical theory proposes radical, participatory, or deliberative democracy.
>
> (Santos 2014: 33)

At another level, such African leading philosophers as Hountondji (1997) have noted that, even though today, mainly because of globalization, there is increasing talk of a global economy of knowledge, such globalized knowledge still has an identifiable centre from which it cascades and circulates. That centre is Europe and North America. A long-standing asymmetrical division of intellectual labour sustains epistemic hegemony. In this context African scholars have largely functioned as 'hunter-gatherers' of raw data as well as 'native informants'. Europe and North America have remained sites of processing of raw data into concepts and theories. These concepts and theories are then consumed in Africa. Africa remains a large laboratory for testing of concepts and theories.

This explains why many African students continue to make great treks to Europe and North America for education, even though the dream of 'one country one university' has long been realized by Africa. African scholars continue to seek affirmation and validation of their knowledge in Europe and North America. This affirmation and validation take the form of publication in the so-called international, high impact and peer-reviewed journals. Europe and North America constitute the 'international' and the rest of the world is 'local'. Consequently, international, high-impact and peer-reviewed journals, and internationally respected publishing houses and presses are those located in Europe and North America. Highly ranked universities are located in Europe and North America. Taken together, these realities confirm the existence of epistemic hegemony. The signature of epistemic hegemony is the idea of 'knowledge' rather than 'knowledges'.

Contextualizing African struggles for epistemic freedom

Resurgent struggles for epistemic freedom are provoked by the reality of continued entrapment of knowledge production in Africa within Euro-North American colonial matrices of power. Since power and knowledge are inextricably intertwined, control of the domain of knowledge generation and knowledge cultivation remain very important for the maintenance of asymmetrical global power structures in place since the dawn of Euro-North American-centric modernity. This is why Walter D. Mignolo (2007: 463) articulated epistemic decolonization as an expansive movement targeting the 'geo-political location of theology, secular philosophy and scientific reason and simultaneously affirming the modes and principles of knowledge that have been denied by the rhetoric of Christianisation, civilisation, progress, development, market democracy'.

The broader discursive context of epistemic struggles is what became known as 'modernity'. Gurminder K. Bhambra (2007: 1) correctly noted that 'Modernity is the dominant frame for social and political thought, not just in the West, but across the world'. She went further to explain two key assumptions that underpinned modernity '*rupture* and *difference* – a temporal rupture that distinguishes a traditional, agrarian past from the modern, industrial present; and a fundamental difference that distinguishes Europe from the rest of the world' (Bhambra 2007: 1). Bhambra's intellectual intervention is very important because it challenges 'the continued privileging of the West as the "maker" of universal history and seek to develop alternatives from which to begin to deal with the questions that arise once we reject this categorization' (Bhambra 2007: 2).

If anything called 'universal history' exists in the first place, it can only do so as a sum total of diverse human histories. Seeking to move beyond the trap of what Immanuel Wallerstein (1997) termed 'anti-Eurocentric-Eurocentrism',

Bhambra contested the very idea of Europe, particularly the 'facts' of 'specialness of Europe' in human history (Bhambra 2007: 2–3). She defined Eurocentrism (that leitmotif of modernity) as nothing other than 'the belief, implicit or otherwise, in the world historical significance of events believed to have developed endogenously within the cultural-geographical sphere of Europe' (Bhambra 2007: 5). The second important intervention of Bhambra is:

> The ideas of difference and rapture that form debates about modernity should be regarded as 'interpretative categories', whereby the 'unity' and 'integrity' of specific experiences are created by abstraction from wider interconnection.
>
> (Bhambra 2007: 7)

Bhambra (2007: 10) proceeded to pose an important epistemological argument: 'The historicity of the human condition, whereby we are born into pre-existing conversations regarding our pasts and our presents, necessarily shapes the positions from where we think and argue.' To Bhambra, the colonial encounter, which was far from being 'an encounter and more a conquest, domination, and enslavement of peoples and forms of life [. . .] is constitutive of the very disciplines that express or seek to understand modernity' (Bhambra 2007: 16). She proposed: 'What is required is a more thoroughgoing analysis of the underlying assumptions upon which discourses and practices come to be premised' (Bhambra 2007: 21).

Building on the work of Sanjay Subrahmanyam (1997, 2005), Bhambra concluded that the escape route from the trap of a Euromodernity is to project 'connected histories' as a departure point because such an approach 'allows the deconstruction of dominant narratives at the same time as they are open to different perspectives and seek to reconcile them systematically both in terms of reconstruction of theoretical categories and in the incorporation of new data and evidence' (Bhambra 2007: 33). Cascading from this analysis, one key aspect of decolonial epistemic struggles of the twenty-first century is to correct the distorted human relationships that emerged from the social classification of human species and their racial hierarchization. This 'reinvention' of the human by other humans has had long-term implications for knowledge, education and social theory.

Also, what emerged clearly from this engagement with the ubiquitous modernity is that to gain a deeper understanding of the essence of the struggles for epistemic freedom, it is important to appreciate the entanglement of knowledge in imperial/colonial economy and politics. A clear understanding of entwinement of knowledge in both economic and epistemic extraversion is very important. The work of Samir Amin (1968) introduced the concept of 'extraversion' from a political economy perspective. Extraversion is to turn a previously functioning, stable and alive economy upside down so as to lose its self-sustaining stamina through destabilization of its internal coherence (Amin 1974). It goes further to entail subordinating such an economy to the whims and needs of global capital and minority bourgeois ruling classes (Amin 1973). The result is what became known as 'underdevelopment', which arose during the forcible integration of African subsistence economies into the global capitalist market through such devices as enslavement and colonization (Amin 1990). Hountondji (1996) extended the concept of economic extraversion and applied it to the domain of knowledge and coined 'intellectual extraversion'. He explained that:

> I found an approach that situated the production of knowledge in the general context of production *tout court* and that examined North/South relations in the field of science and technology on this basis illuminating and heuristically fruitful
>
> (Hountondji 2002: 255)

Just as economic extraversion resulted in economic dependence, intellectual extraversion resulted in scientific dependence. Both situations provoked struggles for 'delinking'. Just as economic dependence produced a situation of 'growth without development', scientific dependence produced knowledge without invention. Intellectual extraversion is indeed an 'analysis of the scientific and technological relations of production on an international scale; and a critique of the actual functioning of research in the periphery as it relates to the world of knowledge controlled and managed by the rich countries of the North' (Hountondji 2002: 161). Hountondji went on to explain the process of epistemic freedom in these useful words:

> To learn anew to be free intellectually and politically, *that* to me was the current requirement. This liberty presupposes the reassessment of the status that had been worked out, the paradigms that had been established, and the canons of thought that had been developed for us. Shutting ourselves up in our cultural past – a purely apologetic relation to our heritage – would respond exactly to what is expected of us. In this regard, nothing will be more Euro-centred than a febrile nationalism that would be content to hold up the treasures of African culture to the face of the world by congealing them, mummifying them, freezing them in their muggy eternity.
>
> (Hountondji 2002: 190)

Here, Hountondji is offering both pathways to be pursued in search of epistemic freedom and is also warning us about the dangers of degenerating into nativism in our struggles for epistemic freedom.

Having framed the context of the struggles for epistemic freedom, it is important to understand the trajectories of this struggle since it has a long history. The history of knowledge generation and knowledge cultivation in Africa began with what Falola termed the 'traditional intellectuals/traditional elites' that comprised priests, kings, chiefs, magicians, praise poets and merchants of the pre-colonial era (Falola 2001: 56). These people produced mainly oral knowledge that drove pre-colonial African societies. The advent of colonialism became very brutal to these African knowers. Kings were attacked, defeated, captured and decapitated. The decapitated heads of African kings were taken and transported overseas to decorate European museums. Some were buried with their head-up-side-down as a symbolic act of signifying the death of the African world. Yet others were exiled to very cold islands as part of dismembering them from their societies.

Ngugi wa Thiong'o (2009a) argued convincingly that 'dismemberment' was part of colonial technology of planting European memory. He gave the example of Waiyaki wa Hinga who actively led his Gikuyu people against British colonialism. He was eventually captured and removed from the centre of his people only to be 'buried alive' at 'Kibwezi, head facing the bowels of the earth – in opposition to the Gikuyu burial rites' requirements that the body face Mount Kenya, the dwelling place of the Supreme Deity' (Ngugi wa Thiong'o 2009a: 3). Informed by Cartesian philosophy, European colonialists targeted heads of African kings because to them the heads carried knowledge and memory. They had to be cut from the bodies as part of the broader process of dismemberment. The knowledgeable African women were simply discredited as witches. Remember that in Indo-Europe itself knowledgeable women had been burned alive accused of being witches during a period that Ramon Grosfoguel has correctly termed 'the four genocides/epistemicides of the long 16th century' (see Grosfoguel 2013: 73–90).

Those who survived death together with magicians were discredited as demon possessed and subjected to forcible and violent conversion to Christianity. Conversion was itself a form of epistemicide. Achille Mbembe (2015: 213–214) distilled five features Christianity as a monotheistic system with God as its apex symbolizing 'fantasm of the One'. The first feature is *primacy* (god who signified only himself and is the genesis). The second is *totalization* (condensation of sovereignty that is against plurality of gods). The third is *monopoly* (suppression of other forms of worship/incompatibility with worship of other gods). The fourth is *omnipotence* (divinity and its supreme essentiality). The fifth is the *ultimate* (alpha and omega) (see Mbembe 2015: 214–215). Mbembe defined the epistemic implications of 'conversion' in these informative words:

> [T]he act of conversion is also involved in the destruction of worlds. To convert the other is to incite him or her to give up what she or he believed. Theoretically, the passage from one belief system to another ought to entail the submission of the convert to the institution and authority in charge of proclaiming the new belief. In actuality, every conversion has always been, if only covertly, an operation of selection has always required, on the part of the convert, an exercise of judgement. Further, it is also assumed that the person who is converted agrees to accept, in everyday life, the practical consequences of this submission and of this transfer of allegiance. [. . .] By divesting himself or herself of previous beliefs, the neophyte is supposed to have shifted his or her centre of gravity. A test or ordeal of defamiliarization and disorientation, conversion distances the convert from family, relatives,

language, customs, even from geographical environment and social contacts – that is, from various forms of inscription in a genealogy and an imaginary.

(Mbembe 2015: 228–229)

Mbembe elaborated on the essence and meaning of 'conversion' that:

Therefore, from a theological point of view, conversion is supposed to move from death to life – or, in any event, to the promise of life. This tend to suggest that conversion always involves an act of destruction and violence against an earlier state of affairs, an accustomed state for which one seeks to substitute something different. This act of violence and destruction is always carried out in the name of a specific materiality, one that claims to oppose a system of truth to an order of error and falsehood.

(Mbembe 2015: 229–230)

Fundamentally, according to Mbembe (2015: 231), 'conversion always presupposes an entry into the time of the other'. Conversion is a mechanism of epistemicide. On the graveyard of African indigenous knowledges, colonialism planted European memory. The church and the school played a major role in the planting of European memory including imposition of colonial languages. What is often ignored in the analysis of the impact of missionary education on Africa is that by the time the colonialists were conquering and colonizing Africa in the nineteenth century, already Europe, where they came from, was distancing itself from theological thought. It has been undergoing intensive secularization since the dawn of Enlightenment. For them to then come to Africa and introduce 'education for salvation' was part of the broader colonial process of desocializing African people out of their cultural and historical context into zombies of colonialism.

Ngugi wa Thiong'o (1986: 16) emphasized that 'the most important area of domination was the mental universe of the colonized, the control through culture, of how people perceived themselves and their relationship to the world'. The missionary church and the colonial school were meant to establish effective mental control. Ali A. Mazrui (1978) documented how the establishment of mission boarding schools was meant to separate African children from the influence of their parents and the home environment and how this process eventually influenced a new class formation in Africa. The French colonizers became famous for their 'cultural arrogance' whereas the British became well known for their 'racial arrogance' and all these 'arrogances' combined to degrade the very humanity and cultures of Africa (Mazrui 1978: 11).

Christianization constituted a form of education and an epistemicide simultaneously. It is not surprising that the earliest group of educated Africans consisted of Christianized ex-slaves. At the time of abolition of slavery some of these educated Christianized ex-slaves were shipped back to Africa and they founded Sierra Leone and Liberia as independent republics within a colonized continent. These early Africans had imbibed Western thought and experienced

Western lifestyles from the traumatic experiences of bondage, colonial schools, mission schools and churches (July 1968). Their activism and struggles were limited to what Mazrui (1978: 12) termed 'rebellious emulation'. They had not yet developed decolonial or anti-colonial consciousness necessary for tearing away from colonialism and Christian missionary thought. Mazrui (1978: 16) correctly noted that the influence of Western education became that of 'psychological deruralization' to the extent that the educated African 'became in a fundamental sense a misfit in his own village'. Dramatizing the negative influence of colonial education on Africans, Ngugi wa Thiong'o (1986: 9) argued that:

> Berlin conference of 1884 was effected through the sword and the bullet. But the night of the sword and the bullet was followed by the morning of the chalk and the blackboard. The physical violence of the battlefield was followed by the psychological violence of the classroom.

It is not surprising that the early African educated elite, which comprised of evangelists, bishops, reverends, nurses and teachers, were deeply seduced by the salvationist and civilizationist promises of colonial education and that being fluent in colonial languages such as French and English was part of acquisition of knowledge itself. Mazrui (1978) provided a catalogue of the benefits of gaining colonial education within a fast-changing colonial environment where anything African had to die unless it was of benefit to the project of colonialism. The most poignant change and benefit took place at the centre of new class formation. This is how Mazrui (1987: xiii) put it:

> The colonial impact transformed the natural basis of stratification in Africa. Instead of status based on, say age, there emerged status based on literacy. Instead of classes emerging from the question 'who owns what?', class formation now responded to the question 'who knows what?'

The seeds of scientific and intellectual dependency are rooted in the seductive nature of colonial education as well as the epistemicides, linguicides and alienations it committed. As correctly stated by Ngugi wa Thiong'o (1986: 11): 'The language of my education was no longer the language of my culture.' The long-term consequence of colonial education has been the distortion of African consciousness as colonial education was deliberately meant to 'obscure reality and force a certain perception of reality' consonant with the colonial project (Ngugi wa Thiong'o 2012: 30). Frantz Fanon captured the epistemicidal nature of colonialism very well when he wrote:

> Colonialism is not satisfied merely with holding a people in its grip and emptying the brain of all form and content. By a kind of perverse logic, it turns to the past of oppressed people, and distorts, disfigures, and destroys it.
>
> (Fanon 1968: 210)

The key consequence of this process is alienation. Ngugi wa Thiong'o captured the essence of alienation in these revealing words:

> The colonial process dislocates the traveller's mind from the place he or she already knows to a foreign land. It is a process of continuous alienation from the base, a continuous process of looking at oneself from the outside of self or with the lenses of a stranger. One may end up identifying with the foreign base as the starting point, from self to other selves. [. . .] This colonization of the cognitive process was the everyday experience in a colonial classroom anywhere.
>
> (Ngugi wa Thiong'o 2012: 39)

Emerging from this alienating terrain, modern African intellectualism has never been a simple one of enjoyment and a mere professional vocation. The activist aspect is embedded through and through. It has taken the formats of empiricism, ideological interventions and activism simultaneously. What is disturbing, though, is that despite the fact that African intellectuals have produced numerous books and journal articles speaking directly on pertinent issues of epistemic freedom and development, these works have not succeeded in replacing those of Western theorists such as Michael Foucault, Antonio Gramsci, Max Weber and Karl Marx, even within African academies. African intellectual productions have not yet assumed dominance in the field of global knowledge in the way that Marx, Derrida and Foucault are doing currently. The African academy has remained a site of inculcation of Western knowledge, values, ways of knowing and worldviews that are often taught as universal values and scientific knowledge. The African continent is still stuck with the problem of 'the place that Western thought occupies in non-Western discursive formations' (Diawara 1990: 56).

Thandika Mkandawire (1995: 2) sought to understand and explain the ideological orientation of African intellectuals and logic behind their emphasis on different issues affecting Africa and he developed the notion of 'three generations' of African intellectuals. The first generation of African intellectuals were the first to occupy academic positions in the universities at the time of attainment of political independence. Many of them became ardent supporters of African nationalism and uncritical celebrators of political independence. The second generation of African intellectuals comprised African scholars that were produced during the hey-day of the Marxist and neo-Marxist schools of thought, and some of them were products of African universities themselves.

What was distinctive about this group was their faithful adherence to Marxist and political economy thought. They supported African nationalism and were anti-imperialist. They were at the same time critical of the neo-colonial direction that the postcolonial state was taking. The third generation of scholars became the current young academics, most of whom were produced by African universities as well as non-African institutions and have imbibed neoliberal, postcolonial and postmodernist thought. Most of them became critical of African nationalism, particularly its antipathy towards democracy and its disdain for human rights. But the categorization of African intellectuals into three generations is not cast in stone, as ideological persuasions and intellectual traditions 'criss-crossed' the generations easily and tendentiously.

There are also common experiences that characterized African intellectual interventions across the three generations. For instance, Peter N. Thuynsma explained why issues such as socialism and development have pre-occupied the African mind and African struggles for freedom. He stated:

> Africanists have never been able to afford scholarship for its luxury. In whatever field, we have worked with an unwritten command *to tell our people about our people.* We have had to work our way out from under a number of historical boulders rolled over us by foreign interests (emphasis in the original source).
>
> (Thuynsma 1998: 45)

No wonder that African intellectual interventions have often sounded deeply polemical, if not aggressive. Falola explained why:

> Reading the works of Africans or listening to their lectures, you may form an impression that they are polemical or defensive, bitter or apologetic. Yes, you are right! However, you need to know the reason for this. Scholarship in Africa has been conditioned to respond to a reality and epistemology created for it by outsiders, a confrontation with imperialism, the power of capitalism, and the knowledge that others have constructed for Africa. The African intelligentsia does not write in a vacuum but in a world saturated with others' statements, usually negative about its members and their continent. Even when this intelligentsia seeks the means to intrude itself into the modern world, modernity has been defined for it and presented to it in a fragmented manner.
>
> (Falola 2001: 17)

Even though African people have continued to be major consumers of ideas generated in the West and tested on the African soil and on African minds, some African scholars began to engage and critique Western epistemology from an Afrocentric perspective. For instance, Archie Mafeje had this to say:

> Afrocentrism is nothing more than a legitimate demand that African scholars study their society from inside and cease to be purveyors of an alienated intellectual discourse [. . .] [W]hen Africans speak for themselves and about themselves, the world will hear the authentic voice, and will be forced to come to terms with it in the long-run [. . .] If we are adequately Afrocentric the international implications will not be lost on others.
>
> (Mafeje 2000: 66)

Claude Ake added his voice to the debate on the decolonization knowledge when he argued:

> Every prognostication indicates that Western social science continues to play a major role in keeping us subordinate and underdeveloped; it continues to inhibit our understanding of the problems of our world, to feed us noxious values and false hopes, to make us pursue policies which undermine our competitive strength and guarantee our permanent underdevelopment and dependence. It is becoming increasingly clear that we cannot overcome our underdevelopment and dependence unless we try to understand the imperialist character of Western social science and to exorcise the attitudes of mind which it inculcates.
>
> (Ake 1979: 12)

At the centre of the African search for self-knowing are six core concerns and demands: complete African self-rule, self-regeneration, self-understanding, self-definition, self-knowing and self-articulation of African issues after centuries of domination and silencing. While Achille Mbembe (2002) tried to caricature these legitimate African concerns as nativism and Afro-radicalism, these aspirations form a core part of the quest for freedom, development and identity in a world still dominated by Western particularistic world views that have been universalized and globalized.

Black scholars from the Diaspora like Molefi Asante (1988) have questioned and critiqued Eurocentrism even more consistently than those African intellectuals based on the continent. Asante is well known for his consistent and systematic push for 'Afrocentricity' not only as a direct challenge to Eurocentricity but as another epistemology that takes Africa as it departure point. Afrocentricity is 'the belief in the centrality of Africans in post-modern history' and a 'critical perspective placing African ideals at the centre of any analysis that involves African culture or behaviour' (Asante 1987).

Within the continent such scholars as Dani W. Nabudere have also been very vocal on issues of epistemological decolonization. Nabudere's *Afrikology, Philosophy and Wholeness: An Epistemology* (2011) boldly and directly confronted the limits of Eurocentrism and traced the historiography of African epistemology from the 'Cradle of Humanity', which is Africa. Nabudere emphasized that all sources of knowledge were valid within their historical, cultural and social contexts. He used the term 'Afrikology' to refer to an Africa-focused epistemology that fully took into account African history, culture and context. Nabudere argued:

> The construction of the science of Afrikology therefore directly flows from the need for Africans to redefine their world, which can enable them to advance their self-understanding and the world around them based on their cosmologies. [. . .]. Afrikology must proceed from the proposition that [it] is a true philosophy of knowledge and wisdom based on African cosmologies because it is *Afri-* in that it is inspired by ideas originally produced from the

Cradle of Humankind located in Africa. *It is not Afrikology because it is African* but it is *Afri-* because it emanates from the source of the Universal system of knowledge in Africa.

(Nabudere 2011: 17–18)

But why is it difficult to break from the colonizer's model of the world and the epistemology it produced? Ashis Nandy's book *The Intimate Enemy: Loss and Recovery of Self under Colonialism* (1983) provided part of the answer. His concept of an 'intimate enemy' speaks to colonialism as that enemy that invades and resides in one's heart, mind and body. Intimate enemies consistently survive through processes of naturalizing and routinizing themselves as part of camouflaging so as to claim non-existence. Nandy vividly described how colonialism existed and operated as an 'intimate enemy' that worked on the psychology of both colonized and colonizing societies. The concept of 'intimate enemy' captured accurately the reality of colonialism's 'colonization of the minds in addition to bodies and it releases forces within the colonized societies to alter their cultural priorities once for all' resulting in internalization of Eurocentrism ('The West is now everywhere, within the West and outside; in structures and minds') (Nandy 1983: xi). For Nandy:

[T]he drive over men is not merely a by-product of a faulty political economy but also of a world view which believes in the absolute superiority of the human over the nonhuman and the subhuman, the masculine over the feminine, the adult over the child, the historical over the ahistorical, and the modern or progressive over the traditional or the savage. It has become more and more apparent that genocides, ecodisasters and ethnocides are but the underside of corrupt sciences and psychopathic technologies wedded to new secular hierarchies, which have reduced major civilizations to the status of a set of empty rituals. The ancient forces of human greed and violence, one recognises, have merely found a new legitimacy in anthropocentric doctrines of secular salvation, in the ideologies of progress, normality and hyper-masculinity, and in theories of cumulative growth of science and technology.

(Nandy 1983: x)

Nandy also highlighted how deceitful colonialism is as an 'intimate enemy'. It presents itself as bringing about civilization, progress and development as it subverts and destroys the order it found. Thus the colonialism that is invoked in Nandy's (1983: xi) work is one 'which survives the demise of empires'. As a strategy of defeating colonialism, Nandy (1983: 3) posits: 'Perhaps that which begins in the minds of men must also end in the minds of men'. This is because 'colonialism is first of all a matter of consciousness and needs to be defeated ultimately in the minds of men' (Nandy 1983: 63). This is why this book is focused on epistemic freedom that speaks directly to both technologies of dismemberment and the struggles for what Nandy (1983) termed 'recovery of self under colonialism'. Nandy's analysis resonates with that of Ngugi wa Thiong'o, which emphasizes the process of decolonization of the mind as the first article of freedom and documents various African and Africa Diasporic initiatives aimed at 'recovery of self under colonialism' in order to 're-member' Africa after centuries of 'dismemberment' (Ngugi wa Thiong'o 2009a, 2009b).

Silences as epistemicides

A struggle for epistemic freedom is ranged against silences as an imperial/colonial technology of dismemberment. The first silence cascaded from the very Eurocentric idea of history and the philosophy of history. The epistemic problem that emerged out of this development was termed 'historicism' by Chakrabarty (2007). The problem of 'historicism' defied even Marxist critique of bourgeois society and capital, and was in fact reproduced by Marx through his stagist conceptions of human history. The problem of historicism is fundamentally that of Cartesian and Enlightenment reason as they spoke to what is knowledge and transcendence over the so-called irrationalities and superstitions. Here was born the Eurocentric idea of history 'as the rational-secular discipline' (Chakrabarty 2007: 237). At the centre of this idea of history was the 'spirit of science', 'rational outlook', 'free enquiry' and faith in 'progress' (Chakrabarty 2007: 237).

From the ideas of 'rapture' and 'difference' as constitutive technologies of colonization of time emerged the problematic paradigm of difference as well as the monolingual language of social science that obliterated the realities of plural ways of being human and knowing. At the centre of 'historicism' is the story of Europe as a 'macrohistory' of the human. Furthermore, this was the basis for 'irrational' rationality within history as a knowledge system. This 'irrationality' manifested itself through overrepresentation of Europe if not outright dominance in historical knowledge. The long-standing consequence of historicism was to subordinate and subsume all human histories within the Western episteme and to reduce all diverse histories into mere episodes within an assumed 'universal transcendental history with a capital 'H'. This is why Allen (2016: 25), building on the work of Latin American decolonial theorists, called 'for the specific project of rethinking the relationship between history and normativity that is necessary if critical theory is to be decolonized'. She concluded:

> [C]ritical theory stands in need of decolonization insofar as its strategy for grounding normativity relies on the notion of historical progress; thus, if critical theory is to be decolonized, it will have to find another strategy for grounding normativity and another way of thinking about progress.
>
> (Allen 2016: 36)

Historicism as an epistemicide affected the rest of the colonized part of the world. The Caribbean scholar Edouard Glissant has systematically critiqued the Eurocentric idea of history and philosophy of history from the vantage point of the Caribbean black societies:

History is a highly functional fantasy of the West, originating at precisely the time when it alone 'made' the history of the world. If Hegel relegated African people to the ahistorical, Amerindians peoples to the prehistorical, in order to reserve History for European peoples exclusively, it appears that it is not because these African or American peoples 'have entered History' that we can conclude today that such a hierarchical conception of the 'march of history' is no longer relevant.

(Glissant 1999: 61)

Because of the impact of the slave trade and the experience of the 'middle passage', the Caribbean terribly suffers from what Glissant (1999: 63) has termed 'nonhistory'. Like all other victims of the epistemicide known as 'historicism', Glissant (1999) consistently worked to undermine and unmask the notion of a coherent, progressive and linear history ('from the shame of Fallenness to the glory of cosmic Perfection') (see Introduction by Dash 1999: xxviii). The Caribbean just like Africa fell on the margins of such a conception of history. To Glissant the totalizing imperative of 'a transcendental History (with a capital H)' resulted in the reproduction of a Hegelian 'division of History into ahistory, prehistory and History' (see Introduction by Dash 1999: xxix). This Eurocentric rendition of history into a singular 'macrohistory' had had a deadly effect on Africa, Latin America, the Caribbean and Asia.

With specific reference to Africa, it was actually Terence Osborne Ranger, the British liberal Africanist historian, who posed the question of how 'African' is 'African history' as he reflected on methodology and methods as well as thematic concerns cascading from Western historiography and their sufficiency as tools for researching and narrating African history' (see Ranger 1968, Atieno-Odhiambo 2002). He posited that there was need

to examine whether African history was sufficiently Africa; whether it had developed the methods and models appropriate to its needs or had depended upon making use of methods and models developed elsewhere; whether its main themes of discourse had arisen out of the dynamics of African development or had been imposed because of their over-riding significance in the historiography of other continents.

(Ranger 1968: x)

The debate was picked up by the Kenyan historian Bethwell Allan Ogot in the 1970s and he called for a development of 'philosophy of history of Africa' (Ogot 1978: 33). He elaborated:

We have struggled hard to reject a conceptual framework which is Western both in its origins as well as its orientations. But we have not yet succeeded in evolving an autonomous body of theoretical thinking. Herein lies the root of our cultural dependence.

(Ogot 1978: 33)

The challenge of silences in African history in particular and African Studies in general has also been at the centre of the work of the Congolese historian Jacques Depelchin in recent years. In his book entitled *Silences in African History: Between the Syndromes of Discovery and Abolition* (2005: xi), Depelchin highlighted what he described as 'the Herculean task of producing historical knowledges for a group of people who were seen by the hegemonic other as lacking history/sense of history'. Understood from the perspective of silences, the epistemic struggle is a direct confrontation with the Columbian-Hegelian-Conradian-Hugh Trevor Ropian imperial/colonial discourse, not of simple silencing but exclusion.

To deeply appreciate the importance of the struggle for epistemic freedom, it is important to understand the discursive terrain of politics of knowledge, particularly such key elements as 'subject-positions, institutional practices, systems of exclusion, epistemes, and so forth' (Allen 2016: 213). Political decolonization of the twentieth century did not delve deeper into the complexities of the knowledge terrain, hence it failed to deliver epistemological decolonization (Depelchin 2005: xii). For those people who endured enslavement, colonialism, capitalist exploitation, cultural imperialism, forced religious conversion, gender and race discrimination as well as political domination and repression, silences constitute facts of their lives (Depelchin 2005). Depelchin's analysis confronted epistemic violence in its various guises and manifestations including those embedded in research techniques and methodologies as well as in 'syndromes of discovery and abolition'. Depelchin had this to say:

> The syndrome of abolition can be clearly seen in the words and actions of the 'abolitionists' who fought to end slavery, crediting themselves as the ones to realise its inhumanity; as if those oppressed by slavery had not already been aware of this.
>
> (Depelchin 2005: 6)

Broadly speaking, according to Depelchin (2005: 12), African history has undergone two forms of silencing: 'denial' of existence right up to the 1960s and 'recognition' since then. Depelchin posited:

> In reality, however, it was the former which continued to dominate, but under a different form. The apparent paradigmatic shift – from denial to recognition – can be revealed as false by showing that the affirmation was paralleled by a systematic silencing of questions, themes and/or conceptualizations. So, in reality, what took place was a redefinition or reformulation of denial.
>
> (Depelchin 2005: 12)

Depelchin also confronted the dominant narrative of 'discovery' that dominated in the story of the unfolding of modernity, imperialism and colonialism. He argued that 'Nothing is "discovered" until such "discovery" can become part of the arsenal of the reproduction of the superiority of the discoverers' (Depelchin 2005: 13).

The theme of silencing of the past is also the subject of the Michael-Rolph Trouillot's classic book *Silencing the Past: Power and the Production of History* (1995) in which he distilled and delineated four major moments of silencing of history in general:

> Silences enter the process of historical production at four crucial moments: the moment of fact creation (the making of *sources*); the moment of fact assembly (the making of *archives*); the moment of fact retrieval (the making of *narratives*); and the moment of retrospective significance (the making of *history* in the final instance).
>
> (Trouillot 1995: 26)

Trouillot underscored these four moments of silencing the past as he grappled with the silenced significance of Haitian Revolution of 1791–1804 that is always overshadowed by the histories of French and American Revolutions. The importance of the Haitian Revolution for Africa in particular and humanity in general is that it confronted racism, slavery and colonialism very early in the annals of modern global history. Fundamentally, the Haitian Revolution was a heroic struggle organized and prosecuted by black people whose humanity was denied and who were reduced to commodities and enslaved, and inferiorized as slaves. To Trouillot (1995: 82) the Haitian Revolution was subjected to a major silence known as the 'unthinkable' ('that for which one has no adequate instruments to conceptualize'). He elaborated on this point this way:

> The Haitian Revolution did challenge the ontological and political assumptions of the most radical writers of the Enlightenment. The events that shook up Saint Dominique from 1791to 1804 constituted a sequence for which not even the extreme political left in France or in England had a conceptual frame of reference. They were 'unthinkable' facts in the framework of western thought. [. . .] The unthinkable is that which one cannot conceive within the range of possible alternatives, that which perverts all answers because it defies the terms under which the questions were phrased. In that sense, the Haitian Revolution was unthinkable in its time: it challenged the very framework within which proponents and opponents had examined race, colonialism, and slavery in the Americas.
>
> (Trouillot 1995: 82–83)

The Haitian Revolution signified a radical paradigmatic shift in the very conceptions of the human and in other ways. It directly challenged the colonial discourse of doubting the humanity of those people they reduced to slaves that made slave-owners to propagate a false view of obedient 'Negros' who do not think and for whom revolt was impossible. The reality of the Haitian Revolution spearheaded by the enslaved did not coincide with deeply held Eurocentric colonial and racist discourses of an enslaved people who could not imagine freedom. The Haitian Revolution broke the philosophical, epistemological and ontological Western ethno-beliefs.

Trouillot (1995: 88) correctly designated the Haitian Revolution as that moment, which is located 'at the limits of the thinkable'. Not only the slave-owners but even the philosophers of Europe could not think of black enslaved people organizing themselves and establishing solidarity that was capable of producing a coordinated and successful revolution. Hence, attempts were made to blame outsiders/non-existent agitators as the brains behind the revolution. Even the victory of the black slave is trivialized through emphasis on how the diseases not the actions of the black enslaved people made the revolution successful ('The Haitian Revolution appears obliquely as part of medical history') (Trouillot 1995: 99). Black racial pride and black agency was unthinkable.

The Haitian Revolution is relevant for any history of black people not only because it led to the collapse of a system of slave trade but because it produced the first independent black-ruled republic of Haiti. It challenged most of what Europeans had told themselves and believed in. Trouillot (1995: 107) concluded: 'The silencing of the Haitian Revolution is only a chapter within a narrative of global domination.' The major lesson is that the silencing of the Haitian Revolution was reproduced on a world scale and it was sustained by genocides, epistemicides, linguicides as well as outright 'theft of history' to use Jack Goody's (2006) terminology.

Silences also arise from what Amy Allen (2016) has termed the 'normative foundation of critical theory'. Focused on how the Frankfurt School, which despite its claims to be critical, was silent on racism, slavery, imperialism and colonialism, Allen set out to explain the sources of this 'quietude'. In fact, Allen is building on the work of Edward E. Said who 1993 criticized the Frankfurt School in these piercing words:

> Frankfurt School critical theory, despite its seminal insights into the relationships between domination, modern society, and the opportunities for redemption through art as critique, is stunningly silent on racist theory, anti-imperialist resistance, and oppositional practice in the empire.
>
> (Said 1993: 278)

Said posited that the 'silence' was never an oversight but 'a motivated silence' (Allen 2016: 1). It was a silence that emerged from ideas of 'blithe universalism', which had normalized notions of racial inferiority of other people and routinized subordination of other cultures to those of Europe. Allen (2016: 2) has noticed that despite Said's critique of 1993, the Frankfurt School 'remains all too silent on the problem of imperialism'. In search of explanation for this silence, Allen (2016) ventured into the 'normative foundations of critical theory' as practiced by the members of the Frankfurt School. Her discovery has been that there are core Eurocentric normative beliefs on social evolution, historical progress, development and emancipation, which form the base of critical theory (Allen 2016: 3). This is how she explained it:

> Thus, they [members of Frankfurt School] are [. . .] deeply wedded to the idea that European, Enlightenment modernity – or at least certain aspects or features thereof, which remain to be spelled out – represent a developmental advance over premodern, nonmodern, or traditional forms of life, and, crucially, this idea plays an important role in grounding the normativity of critical theory for each thinker. In other words, both Habermas and Honneth are committed to the thought that critical theory needs to defend some idea of historical progress in order to ground its distinctive approach to normativity and, thus, in order to be truly critical. *But it is precisely this commitment that proves to be the biggest obstacle to the project of decolonizing their approaches to critical theory.*
>
> (Allen 2016: 3, my emphasis)

The epistemic limits of the Frankfurt School and the blindness of its critical theory to those key concerns affecting the 'non-Western' world, haunts the entire Western thought and make the theorists fail to hear and comprehend the core aspects of struggles for epistemic freedom cascading from the Global South.

Rethinking thinking

The epistemic and systemic crisis that is haunting the world today, calls for rethinking thinking itself. Catherine Odora Hoppers and Howard Richards in their *Rethinking Thinking: Modernity's 'Other' and the Transformation of the University* (2012: 8) articulated the essence of 'rethinking thinking' this way:

> The casting of light at last onto subjugated peoples, knowledges, histories and ways of living unsettles the toxic pond and transforms passive analysis into a generative force that valorises and recreates life for those previously museumised. [. . .] it is a process of engaging with colonialism in a manner that produces a program for its dislocation. This dislocation is made possible not only by permitting subalterns direct space for engaging with structures and manifestations of colonialism, but also by inserting into discourse arena totally different meanings and registers from other traditions. [. . .] The task for rethinking thinking is therefore precisely this: to recognize the cultural asphyxiation of those numerous 'others' that has been the norm, and work to bring other categories of self definition, of dreaming, of acting, of loving, of living into the commons as matter of universal concern.

Hoppers and Richards (2012) delved deeper into the constitutive make-up of such disciplines as law, economics, education, and natural science in their endeavour to rethink them. They posited:

> Law, like economics, science and education, is a box. These boxes consti-
> tute four pillars of modernity. Law protects the propertied; science valorises
> a mechanistic worldview over holistic cosmologies; economics upholds a
> metaphysics that justifies survival of the fittest over the metaphysics of
> sharing that governs a large majority of livelihoods in the world; education
> refuses to recognize and build on the knowledge that the children from
> non-western systems of thought have. Among the four boxes, circuits of
> fragmentation and dehumanization are masked and rationalized.
>
> (Hopper and Richards 2012: 45)

Building on this argument, Hoppers and Richards (2012: 50) emphasized the
need to change the rules that constitute the disciplines of law, education, science
and economics as part of setting afoot a new thinking in the knowledge domain.
Rethinking thinking, in their analysis, entailed rectification of the problem of
'epistemological disenfranchisement' (Hoppers and Richards 2012: 84). This is
necessary because knowledge constitutes the 'software' of coloniality.

Rethinking thinking is fundamentally a decolonial move that requires the
cultivation of a decolonial attitude in knowledge production. It is informed by a
strong conviction that all human beings are not only born into a knowledge
system but are legitimate knowers and producers of legitimate knowledge.
Rethinking thinking is also a painstaking decolonial process of 'learning to unlearn inorder to re-learn' as well as an opening to other knowledges and thinkers
beyond those from Europe and North America that have dominated the academy
in the last 500 years (Tlostanova and Mignolo 2012). This 'learning to unlearn'
entails the painstaking and difficult process of 'forgetting what we have been
taught, to break free from the thinking programs imposed on us by education,
culture, and social environment, always marked by the Western imperial reason'
(Tlostanova and Mignolo 2012: 7).

Rethinking thinking also calls for what Lewis R. Gordon (2006) has rendered
as 'shifting the geography of reason'. It is not only relevant for the Caribbean
world where the Caribbean Philosophical Association (CPA) has adopted it as a
motto. The imperative to shift the geography of reason arises from the reality of
dismemberment of black people from the human family, which raises the
fundamental problematic of 'what it means to be human after the restrictions
placed on such a concept by modern conquest and colonization' (Gordon 2006:
12). Shifting the geography of reason means a number of decolonial moves. In the
first place, it challenges the imperial/colonial historiographical tendency of making
European and North American historical experience the template of measuring
other historical experiences and that Europe and North America are the only
repositories of rational thinking. In the second place, it challenges the Hegelian
idea of an Africa that existed outside the geographical reach of reason. In the third
place, shifting the geography of reason challenges the old Cartesian view of
knowledge as an individual possession and restores the situatedness of knowledge

in communities and civilizations (intersubjective character of knowledge) (Nisbett 2003: Banchetti-Robino and Headley 2006).

Rethinking thinking speaks to unthinking some of the presumptions of knowledge that has been polluted by Eurocentrism so as to escape from what Paulin Hountondji (1990) termed 'scientific dependence' and Syed Hussein Alatas (1969; 1974) described as 'the captive mind'. This rethinking thinking becomes urgent not only in the context of liberating the colonized from Eurocentricism and colonization of the minds but because of the exhaustion of what Immanuel Wallerstein (1999: 4) terms 'nineteenth century social science'. He elaborated:

> It is quite normal for scholars and scientists to rethink issues. When important new evidence undermines old theories and predictions do not hold, we are pressed to rethink our premises. In that sense, much of nineteenth-century social science, in the form of specific hypotheses, is constantly being rethought. But, in addition to rethinking, which is 'normal', I believe we need to 'unthink' nineteenth-century social science, because many of its presumptions – which, in my view, are misleading and constrictive – still have far too strong a hold on our mentalities. These presumptions, once considered liberating of the spirit, serve today as the central intellectual barrier to useful analysis of the social world.
>
> (Wallerstein 1999: 4)

The situation becomes worse when African scholars are dependent on an exhausted intellectual tradition and social science that is no longer useful in the analysis of the social world in general and African experience in particular. Hountondji (1990: 10) distilled 13 'indices of scientific dependence'. The first is dependence on technical apparatuses made in Europe and North America. The second is dependence on foreign libraries and documentation centres for up-to-date scientific information. The third is what he termed 'institutional nomadism, a restless going to and fro' European and North American universities. The fourth dependence manifests itself as 'brain drain'. The fifth is importation of theory from the North to enlighten the data gathered in the South. The sixth dependence is aversion to basic research and sticking to the colonial ideology of instrumentality of knowledge. The seventh problem is in choice of research topics that is determined by interests of the North where knowledge is validated (Hountondji 1990: 12).

The eighth dependence is confinement to territorial specializations in which African scholars are often reduced to native informants. The ninth form of dependence is that African scholars are engaged in scientific research that is of direct service to coloniality. The tenth issue relates to research into indigenous knowledge that eventually is disciplined to fit into the modes of Western science. The eleventh challenge is that of linguistic dependence on six European languages (English, French, German, Spanish, Italian and Portuguese) in teaching and research. The twelfth index of scientific dependence is lack of communication among African scholars as most prefer 'a vertical exchange and dialogue with scientists from the North than horizontal exchange with fellow scholars from the South' (Hountondji 1990: 13). The final index of dependence manifests itself through reproduction of mediocrity that makes it justifiable to look for competent scholars in the North (Hountondji 1990: 13).

This analysis takes us to the consideration of the deeper intellectual and epistemological crisis. Issa G. Shivji clearly defined the African intellectual/epistemological crisis as manifested by the fact that:

> The majority of African intellectuals have pretty well accommodated mainstream thought. This includes former militant nationalists and radical socialist intellectuals. The metamorphosis of the African intellectual from a revolutionary to an activist, from critical political economist to post-modernist, from a social analyst to a constitutionalist liberal, from anti-imperialist to a cultural atavist, from a radical economics professor to a neo-liberal World Bank spokesperson, from an intellectual to a consultant is blatant, unrepentant, and mercenary.
>
> (Shivji 2003: 19)

Mamdani (2011: 5) clearly identified the African intellectual challenge for the twenty-first century as that of questioning and unpacking the foundations of the prevailing Euro-American intellectual paradigms which have turned the dominant Western experience into a model under which research is conceived as nothing other than a demonstration that non-Western societies around the world either conform or deviate from that model. What is needed is to take the struggle for decolonization to a higher level, informed by a decolonial epistemology focused on unpacking the constitutive negative aspects of Western modernity as the broader terrain within which coloniality and Euro-American epistemologies were generated.

What is promising though in the domain of struggles for epistemic freedom is that younger African scholars have not given up the liberatory agenda of rethinking thinking and even unthinking some ideas introduced on Africa by colonialism and hegemonic Eurocentric thinking. For example, the Nigerian decolonial feminist sociologist Oyeronke Oyewumi (1997)'s work helps us to rethink thinking on gender and the 'woman question'. She took African society and context seriously and eloquently demonstrated empirically and theoretically how Oyo history in West Africa underwent three process of 'patriarchalization' through masculinization of the *alaafin*, 'feminization of certain positions, whereby the society-wide influence of females in power has been narrowed to an undefined interest, distinct from the rest of the community', and 'genderization' through invention of an essentialized category of 'woman' and 'man' that did not exist prior to colonialism in the Oyo-Yoruba society of Nigeria. Oyewumi (1997)'s work is one of the best and convincing testaments of how the very process of 'writing history' of Africa has been informed by hegemonic Western thought and its analytical categories such as 'biological determinism', centrality of 'bodies' as well as privileging of sense of sight (visual) over other sense to the extent of globalizing ideas of 'worldview' over 'world sense'.

Oyewumi (1997)'s work directly confronted the silencing impact of imposition of Western gender categories on Africa particularly the Yoruba of Nigeria. In African studies, there is a general concern with how history writing has tended to privilege 'his story' over and above 'her story' in capturing human experiences across space and time. Oyewumi (1997) complicated this rather simplistic approach of merely adding the experiences of women to a world of knowledge that wrongly assumed the universality 'gender' and 'woman' categories as trans-cultural and transhistorical. Oyewumi (1997: ix) posited 'The woman question is a Western-derived issue – a legacy of the age-old somatocentricity of Western thought. It is an imported problem, and it is not indigenous to the Yoruba'. In Oyewumi's work one finds a robust, meticulously research and convincingly argued and first-rate case of 'rethinking thinking' on gender in particular and African thought in general. For instance, Oyewumi boldly revealed:

> As the work and my thinking progressed, I came to realise that the fundamental category 'woman' – which is foundational in Western gender discourses – simply did not exist in Yorubaland prior to its sustained contact with the West. There was no such pre-existing group characterised by shared interests, desires, or social position. The cultural logic of Western social categories is based on an ideology of biological determinism: the conception that biology provides the rational for the organization of the social world. Thus this cultural logic is actually a 'bio-logic.' Such categories like 'woman' are based on body-type and are elaborated in relation to and in opposition to another category: man; the presence or absence of certain organs determines social position.
>
> (Oyewumi 1997: ix–x)

The significance of Oyewumi's work is that it intervened robustly on the sociology of knowledge in general in the process directly challenging the dominant Western thought while at many levels retrieving and anchoring African thought. In the first place, Oyewumi (1997) challenges the idea of 'gender' as the first article of faith in thinking about any society and its organization. She questioned the Western idea of the universal subordination of women and even rejected the universalization of the category 'woman' because in the Yoruba society 'there were no women – defined in strictly gendered terms – in that society' (Oyewumi 1997: xi–xiii).

According to Oyewumi (1997) there is urgent need for careful historical and sociological research on Africa that is not informed by existing analytical categories borrowed from Europe and America. She identified some of the key problems of history, theory and methodology that are themselves colonized. Oyewumi (1997: x–xi) identified the core components of Western thought as privileging not only 'body-based categories' but the sense of sight in its interpretation of human phenomena. She elaborated on this problem this way:

> In African studies, historically and currently, the creation, constitution, and production of knowledge have remained the privilege of the West. Therefore, body-reasoning and the bio-logic that derives from the biological determinism inherent in Western thought have been imposed on African societies. The presence of gender constructs cannot be separated from the ideology of biological determinism. Western conceptual schemes and theories have become so widespread that almost all scholarship, even by Africans, utilizes them unquestioningly.
>
> (Oyewumi 1997: x)

One of her points is that African scholars must be conscious of the fact that 'all concepts come with their own cultural and philosophical baggage, much of which becomes alien distortion when applied to cultures other than those from which they derive' (Oyewumi 1997: xi). Oyewumi (1997: xi) posed the fundamental question: 'What are the relationships between, on the one hand, bio-anatomical distinctions and gender differences as part of social reality and, on the other hand, gender constructs as something that the observer brings to a particular situation?' Her response based on her meticulous sociological research on the Yoruba society is:

> The Yoruba case provides one such different scenario; and more than that, it shows that the human body need not be constituted as gendered or be seen as evidence for social classification at all times. In precolonial Yoruba society, body-type was not the basis of social hierarchy: males and females were not ranked according to anatomic distinction. The social order required a different kind of map, not a gender map that assumed biology as the foundation for social ranking.
>
> (Oyewumi 1997: xii)

Oyewumi is not in any way creating the impression of a golden age of Yoruba society that was a domain of pristine village democracies cascading from absence of any form of hierarchization. She revealed:

> Yoruba society was hierarchically organized, from slaves to rulers. The ranking of individuals depended first and foremost on seniority, which was usually defined by relative age. Another fundamental difference between Yoruba and Western social categories involves the highly situational nature of Yoruba social identity. In Yoruba society before the sustained infusion of Western categories, social position of people shifted constantly in relation to those with whom they were interacting; consequently, social identity was relational and was not essentialized.
>
> (Oyewumi 1996: xiii)

Oyewumi launched a daring intellectual challenge to the existing feminist discourses even revealing a fundamental contradiction in their understanding of such concepts as gender (social construction) and sex (biological construction). The contradiction if not feminist paradox is here: in the very celebrated 'funda-mental assumption of feminist theory is that women's subordination is universal' which universality of 'gender asymmetry suggests a biological basis rather than a cultural one, given that the human anatomy is universal whereas cultures speak in myriad voices' (Oyewumi 1997: 10). Oyewumi proceeded to unpack this paradox in this manner:

> That gender is socially constructed is said to mean that the criteria that make up male and female categories vary in different cultures. If this is so, then it challenges the notion that there is a biological imperative at work. From this standpoint, then, gender categories are mutable, and as such, gender then is denaturalized.
>
> (Oyewumi 1997: 10)

Oyewumi's point is very important for rethinking thinking on Africa because it revealed how:

> In fact, the categorization of women in feminist discourses as homogeneous, bio-anatomically determined group which always constituted as powerless and victimized does not reflect the fact that gender relations are social relations and, therefore, historically grounded and culturally bound. If gender is socially constructed, then gender cannot behave in the same manner across time and space. If gender is a social construction, then we must examine the various cultural/architectural sites where it was constructed, and we must acknowledge that variously located actors (aggregates, groups, interested parties) were part of construction. We must further acknowledge that if gender is a social construction, then there was a specific time (in different cultural/architectural sites) when it was 'constructed' and therefore a time before which it was not. Thus, gender, being a social construction, it is logical to assume that in some societies, gender construction need not have existed at all.
>
> (Oyewumi 1997: 10)

At another level, this generalization about powerless, disadvantaged and victimized women across the world might be taken to be another form of silence in which the world of the Yoruba society is ignored. But Oyewumi is careful not to challenge one generalization while creating another based on one case study. She is very clear on this:

> Although it is clear that findings of this study are applicable to other African societies, I hesitate to apply them broadly, primarily because I do not want to fall into the common trap of erasing a multitude of African cultures by

making facile generalizations, a process that results in unwarranted homogenization. The erasure of African cultures, a major defect of many studies on Africa, motivates my efforts not to make a simplistic general case about Africa from the Yoruba example.

(Oyewumi 1997: xiv)

What is important about Oyewumi's work is that in her critique of Western-centric 'body-reasoning' approaches to society that carried gender differentiation as a major lens, she revealed how 'scholars create gender categories', how any simplistic and uncritical deployment of gender lens 'necessarily write gender into that society' under study and how 'In actuality, the process of making gender visible is also a process of creating gender' (Oyewumi 1997: xv). Thus she concluded her in these wise words:

The present book has cleared the way for asking first-order, foundational questions about gender and difference in Yoruba society. It has shown that our interest in gender in Yorubaland cannot be divorced from the West's domination of both the constitution of the academy/scholarship and the socio-political and economic world spheres. Ultimately, this study raises the question of whether it is possible to have independent research questions and interests given the Western origins of most disciplines and continued Western dominance of the world, for now.

(Oyewumi 1997: 179)

Rethinking thinking cannot be realized without decolonizing methodology and research. It is here that the impressive work of Linda Tuhiwai Smith (1999) and Bagele Chilisa (2012) become indispensable. Smith and Chilisa's work takes us into the depth of the 'sacred' field of research and methodology and they excavate the dirty colonial history embedded in the very activities of researching. While Smith brought the world of the indigenous people of New Zealand into the world of research, Chilisa brought the world of the indigenous people of Africa into the world of research. It was Smith (1999) who bold declared that 're-search' was the most 'dirtiest' word because it involved enquiring into the secrets and scared lives of those who were its objects.

Chilisa (2012: xv) departs from the questions of 'social justice' and 'human rights' arising from the very research process. The convergence of Smith and Chilisa's work is on the call for decolonizing research methodologies as a process towards achievement of epistemic freedom by those peoples such as women, minorities, indigenous people, and formerly colonized, whose knowledges remain marginalized. They both delved deeper into cultures, philosophies, histories and power dynamics embedded in research and methodology.

Chilisa's work highlighted how mainstream research conducted on those societies considered being 'non-Western' still ignored other ways of knowing and other knowledge systems. This means that the struggles of decolonizing and indigenizing research methodologies form an important part of the broader struggles for epistemic freedom. Chilisa (2012: 3) argued:

> Social science research needs to involve spirituality in research, respecting communal forms of living that are non-Western and creating space for inquiries based on relational realities and forms of knowing that are predominant among non-Western Other/s still being colonized.

Chilisa formulated a useful definition of decolonization from the perspective of research:

> Decolonization is thus a process of conducting research in such a way that the worldviews of those who have suffered a long history of oppression and marginalization are given space to communicate from their frames of reference. It is a process that involves 'researching back' to question how the disciplines – psychology, education, history, anthropology, sociology, or science – through an ideology of Othering have described and theorized about the colonized Other, and refused to let the colonized Other name and know their frame of reference.
>
> (Chilisa 2012: 14)

Understood from a research and methodological perspective, decolonization entails 'deconstruction and reconstruction', that is, 'destroying what has wrongly been written – for instance, interrogating distortions of people's life experiences, negative labelling, deficit theorizing, genetically deficient or culturally deficient models that pathologizes the colonized Other – and retelling the stories of the past and envisioning the future' (see Smith 1999; Chilisa 2012: 17). At the centre of this process is 'recovery and discovery' (Chilisa 2012: 17).

Decolonization is also about attainment of 'self-determination and social justice', that is, seeking 'legitimacy for methodologies embedded in histories, experiences, ways of perceiving realities, and value systems' on the one hand and on the other, giving 'voice to the researched and moves from deficient-based orientation' to 'reinforcing practices that have sustained the lives of the researched' (Chilisa 2012: 17–18; see also Smith 1999). Chilisa's work articulated what she termed 'a postcolonial indigenous research paradigm' as 'a framework of belief systems that emanate from the lived experiences, values, and history of those belittled and marginalised by Euro-Western research paradigms' (Chilisa 2012: 19). To Chilisa (2012: 20): 'A postcolonial indigenous research is thus informed by relational ontologies, relational epistemologies, and relational axiology.'

Organization of the book

The core chapters of the book are constructed around major African intellectual and political thinkers. The emphasis is on how such intellectuals and political thinkers advanced the struggles of epistemic freedom. Featured in this book are such African intellectuals and political thinkers as Cheikh Anta Diop, Edward Wilmot Blyden, Frantz Fanon, Dani W. Nabudere, Cathrine Odora Hoppers, Paulin J. Hountondji, Oyeronke Oyewumi, Bagele Chilisa, Jacques Depelchin, Mahmood Mamdani, Achille Mbembe, Samir Amin, Francis Nyamnjoh, Thandika Mkandawire, Issa Shivji, Peter Ekeh, Ali A. Mazrui, Leopold Sedar Senghor, Kwame Nkrumah, Toyin Falola, Neville Alexander, Ngugi wa Thiong'o, Jean Comaroff and John L. Comaroff, Yirga Gelaw Woldeyes, Amilcar Cabral, Kenneth Kaunda and Nelson Mandela among many others. Some are dealt with in the introductory chapter as they provide invaluable concepts usable in framing the debates on epistemic freedom and others are included in the core chapters of the book.

The choice of African thinkers was not random. It was determined by the relevance of their intellectual and political thought and interventions to the core themes of the book. The core themes of the book range from epistemic freedom, epistemological decolonization, decolonizing the university, Africanity, cognitive justice, national question, meaning of freedom, decolonial pedagogy to African futures. Therefore, such African thinkers as Edward Wilmot Blyden, who was among the first people to fight for 'an African university', could not be ignored in a book dealing with struggles for epistemic freedom. Mamdani's work which emphasized the historical legitimacy of Africa as a unit of analysis and revolted against writing African history by analogy is very important in understanding issues of epistemic freedom. Because epistemic and ontological questions are inextricably intertwined, the expansive archive of Ali A. Mazrui who persistently argued for the invention of open Africanity predicated on the 'triple heritage' and abolition of continental boundaries became very useful.

Who would ignore the useful work of Ngugi wa Thiong'o who has consistently written and fought for the decolonization of the African minds and Leopold Sedar Senghor who argued for a 'planetary negritude' as part of deprovincializing Africa? The global icon Nelson Rolihlahla Mandela, who introduced a new politics founded on the 'will to live' rather that the 'will to power' as well as innovative conception of justice predicated on the survival of both perpetrators and victims, advanced our thinking on 'the political' in Africa. Oyeronke Oyewumi's decolonial feminist sociological work revolutionized our understanding of the problems of using Western thought in understanding African reality and demonstrated empirically and theoretically how the 'woman question' emerged as an imposition on such societies as the Yoruba of Nigeria. Bagele Chilisa's interventions in the 'sacred' field of methodology and research, boldly making a convincing case for use of indigenous research methodologies, cannot be ignored in any work concerned with epistemic freedom. Toyin Falola, that indefatigable African historian of our era who has researched, written and published in almost every aspect of African society and has directly contributed to the epistemic struggles of 'Africanizing knowledge', cannot fail to find a space in this book.

Because struggles for epistemic freedom are not confined to Africa, the insights of leading African scholars are opened up to dialogue with other thinkers mainly from the Global South and the African Diaspora such as Edward E. Said, William E. B. Dubois, Marcus Garvey, Molefi Asante, Lewis R. Gordon, Michael-Rolph Trouillot, Ashy Nandy, Paulo Freire, Julia Suárez-Krabbe, Dipesh Chakrabarty, Nelson Maldonado-Torres, Ramon Grosfoguel, Walter D. Mignolo, Anibal Quijano, Edouard Glissant, Enrique Dussel, Gurminder K. Bhambra, An Yuontae, Kuan-Hsing Chen and many others. The integration of this scholarly tradition is inevitable because the struggles for epistemic freedom are planetary and many African Diaspora intellectuals have contributed immensely to the advancement of black struggles for epistemic freedom. The work of such progressive Western scholars as Immanuel Wallerstein, Boaventura de Sousa Santos, Amy Allen and others cannot be ignored in any book that deals with the question of epistemic freedom. This is because they continue the tradition of critique of Eurocentrism from inside Europe. But part of deprovincializing Africa entails avoiding pitfalls of epistemic xenophobia, nativism and ghettoization of knowledge that characterizes some of the previous studies that have sought to debunk the hegemony of Euromodernist epistemologies.

The book is organized into ten thematic chapters. This introductory chapter sets the decolonial tone for the book and opens the canvas on the meanings and debates on 'provincializing' and 'deprovincializing' as well as 'epistemic freedom' versus 'academic freedom'. Beyond the definitional scope, the chapter provides a detailed review of some of the key epistemic challenges facing Africa today. The chapter makes a case for the primacy of epistemic freedom within the trajectories of decolonization. Epistemic freedom is an essential pre-requisite for other freedoms (political, economic and cultural). While political, economic and epistemic decolonization were inextricably intertwined, the privileging of seeking the political kingdom that was emphasized in the decolonization of the twentieth century has proven to be problematic unless it is underpinned by strong epistemic freedom, which generates a necessary decolonial attitude and decolonial consciousness needed for sustenance of political and economic freedom.

The second chapter defines the key contours of the decolonization of twenty-first century (otherwise known as decoloniality), in the process introducing not only the key nomenclatures of decolonization but also fleshing out the idea of three empires (physical, commercial–military–non-territorial and metaphysical) that provoked three trajectories of decolonization (political, economic and epistemological). It proceeds to layout the three units of analysis (power, knowledge and being) that underpin and propel decoloniality. At the same time, the chapter brings into creative dialogue and complimentarity the decolonial ideas and concepts cascading from different epistemic sites such as Latin America, Caribbean, Asia, Africa and African Diaspora to enrich the epistemic struggles, which are taking a planetary course and scope. Thus, such concepts as subaltern, African existential philosophy, creolization, coloniality of being, coloniality of power, coloniality of knowledge are brought into dialogue with African ones such as neo-colonialism, dismemberment, re-membering, delinking, moving the centre, colonialism of special type, African personality, Negritude, Ethiopianism, Pan-Africanism and many others.

The third chapter addresses triple issues of ontology, epistemology and pedagogy. Its tone is philosophical as it articulates three ontological-oriented understandings of the 'human' (re-humanizing, humaning and posthumanism) and their inter-connections with epistemology. It proceeds to flesh-out a decolonial attitude as a necessity for epistemological decolonization. Six dimensions of epistemological decolonization (provincializing Europe while deprovincializing Africa; African-izing knowledge; decolonial critique of existing knowledge; adding to the existing knowledge; ecologies of knowledges and the problematic nativist approach to knowledge) are distilled and explained. It proceeds to explain the necessity of decolonial pedagogy. This approach enables the chapter to delve deeper into challenges of decolonizing teaching and learning while laying-out a re-education/re-socialization programme predicated on decolonization of the very normative foundations of dominant critical theory so as to 'rethink thinking itself' and unleashing the painstaking process of 'learning to unlearn in order to relearn' as a key and necessary response to colonial desocialization and dehumanizing processes.

The fourth chapter is focused on the important theme of reconstitution of the political as a decolonial move. Can't we begin with a decolonial appreciation of how the Biblical shift from the 'old testament' to the 'new testament' with Jesus Christ of Nazareth leading the offensive against old Judaic/Abrahamic/Roman Christendom's inflexible laws and traditions as the key symbolic if not ecclesiastic representation of a reconstitution of a new order entails? Eurocentric hegemonic and imperial thought spoiled the very constitution of the political in a fundamental way. The process of spoliation of the very constitution of the political involved fetishism of power, which culminated in the lodging of the paradigms of difference and war as well as the will to power into the centre of the very idea of politics.

Chapter 4 highlights what can be gained through a decolonial reconstitution of the political. It launches reclamations of the intellectual and political thoughts of such leading African thinkers and freedom fighters as Patrice Lumumba, Leopold Sedar Senghor, Amilcar Cabral, Kenneth Kaunda and Nelson Mandela that are constitutive of the decolonial/anti-colonial archive. These leading African politicians-cum-intellectuals contributed to the transformation of the 'constitution of the political' from the 'will to power' and the paradigm of war *(homo polemos)* to the 'will to live'. Mandela in particular emerges as a philosopher of liberation, which is planetary in its reach as it turned-upside down such standing conception of politics as the 'will to power', and worship at the altar of war (paradigm of war).

Mandela's anti-apartheid politics inaugurated a decolonial shift from the Nuremberg template of transitional justice predicated on criminal prosecutions to new political justice which privileged political transformation of societies emerging from war. While Mandela's vision and ideas are today facing their most difficult testing times in South Africa, they continue to be positively embraced by many as progressive and innovative. Chapter 4 posits that a combination of global imperial designs and white South Africans who were never prepared to share their colonial loot failed Mandela rather than Mandela failing to lead South Africa into a better future. What hit Mandela's conception of politics was its dependence on the goodness of human beings, including those who had been irreparably corrupted by colonialism and apartheid to the extent of falling from humanity itself.

The fifth chapter is specifically focused on the topical theme of invention and reinvention of Africa by Africans themselves as a key aspect of epistemic freedom and contribution to deprovincialization of Africa. It underscores the identity known as 'Africanity' as a trans-space, trans-time, trans-geographical and trans-cultural phenomenon. The discussion is centred on the expansive archive of Ali. A. Mazrui. Three key areas of intervention – the invention of Africa, contested meaning of Africanity, and the concomitant complex question of the African condition frame the chapter. As part of Mazrui's contribution towards deprovincializing Africa, he introduced the concepts of 'triple heritage' and the idea of the abolition of the Red Sea in his push for a new identity called 'Afrabia'. At the economic level, Mazrui advanced the idea of decolonizing modernity through five processes of: indigenization, domestication, diversification, horizontal interpenetration and vertical counter-penetration.

The sixth chapter is focused on the contributions of the Ugandan political scientist Mahmood Mamdani to the intellectual and academic tasks of rethinking Africa. Mamdani's intellectual and academic work set out to establish 'the historical legitimacy of Africa as a unit of analysis' and to transcend colonial historiographical practice of writing African history 'by analogy'. What is captured here are five contributions to rethinking thinking on Africa by Mamdani. The first is his decolonial approach to the study of Africa, which privileged internal historical dynamics. The second is his analysis of how colonial power worked and how it impinged on and shaped African resistance and generated postcolonial dilemmas. The third is his thesis on how colonial rule invented very problematic political identities which are today haunting contemporary Africa's nation-building and state-making processes. The fourth is his concept of 'actually existing civil society' that is opposed to the abstract/programmatic conceptions of civil society in Africa. The fifth is his rearticulation of transitional justice beyond the traditional post-1945 Nuremberg template. The significance of Mamdani's academic and intellectual interventions is that they speak directly and consistently to the long-standing question of locus of historicization and theorization of Africa so as to liberate of knowledge from the snares of extraversion and coloniality.

The seventh chapter focuses on understanding pre-colonial indigenous knowledge systems and the education systems they enabled. The case study of Ethiopian indigenous education and the Ethiopian indigenous education system is very important because Ethiopia is the only African country that managed to successfully repel and resist military colonial conquest and direct colonial administration. But at the same time Ethiopia provides an ironic if not tragic situation of a country that was never colonized but progressively colonized itself with foreign institutions and ideas while dismissing its rich indigenous knowledge and even indigenous schools. The chapter continues to articulate the long-standing but unfinished struggles for an African university while at the same time making sense of the African decolonial efforts aimed at reconstitution of the university across time. A triple genealogy of the 'university in Africa' emerges: namely the pre-colonial African/Arab/Muslim intellectual tradition, the Western imperial/colonial modernity and the anti-colonial nationalist liberatory developmentalism predicated on the idea of one country one university emerges poignantly in this chapter. Conceptually, the chapter locates the struggles for an 'African university' within the broader context of African struggles for epistemic freedom, the search for modern African identity and autonomous African development. Its importance lies in careful historicization of the emergence and trajectories of higher education institutions in Africa. This task is necessary at a time of resurgent demands for decolonization of universities in the twenty-first century, proving beyond doubt the incompleteness of the African decolonial project.

The eighth chapter shifts the focus to the important case study of South Africa and is specifically concerned with the unresolved national question. The rich work of Neville Alexander and his wide-ranging ideas provided the stepping-stone and ideal entry point into the complexities of the national question in South Africa. What the chapter provides is a deep historicization of the national question, tracing it from its pre-colonial lineage that is often ignored and consistently highlighting the areas of divergence and conflict in the various imaginations of post-apartheid South Africa. It concludes with a reflection on idea of South Africa as a difficult liberal experiment in which the triple imperatives of the National Democratic Revolution (NDR), decolonization and liberal constitutionalism are in deep tension.

South Africa is chosen as a case study because it is today one of the highly volatile sites of multiple struggles including that spearheaded by students which demands decolonization in a country which was said to have gained political independence in 1910. South Africa is located in a strategic region of Southern Africa and is one of those sites that were imagined on the image of Europe despite its location at the Southern-most tip of Africa. It is, therefore, important to understand the very idea of South Africa and why it has been consistently generating so many conflicts. The national question is framed by the broader intersecting context of modernity, colonialism, decolonization and postcolonialism. The national question is a perennial challenge in Africa in general and South Africa in particular. It haunted colonialism (as the native question), African nationalism and decolonization (as a racial and colonial question), and 'postcolonialism' (as nation-building and state-making). It has re-emerged today as constitutive element of epistemological decolonization.

The ninth chapter turns to the most recent struggles for decolonization of South African universities in particular. The chapter locates and theorizes the Rhodes Must Fall movements within a broader context of a broader epistemic and systemic crisis engulfing the modern world. Thus it provides details on the three phases of African anti-colonial protests of 1950s and 1960s; the anti-austerity and limits of reform protests of 1980s and 1990s, and the current 'Africa Uprisings' as it opens the canvas for contextualizing specific South African context mediated by the 'paradigm of difference' and practices of 'impossibility of co-presence'. As the last outpost of the empire to shed off juridical colonialism known as apartheid, South Africa is indeed racing against time in its attempts to decolonize power, knowledge and being.

The university in South Africa became a key site of decolonial struggles in 2015. What began as Rhodes Must Fall targeting Cecil John Rhodes's statue at the University of Cape Town (UCT) quickly expanded into broader demands for cognitive justice, change of curriculum, decommissioning of offensive colonial/apartheid symbols, right to free, quality and relevant education, cultural freedom, and overall change of the very idea of the university from its Western pedigree ('university in Africa') to 'African university'. Even more importantly the demands of Rhodes Must Fall not only expanded to the centre of the empire (Britain) where the students at the premier Oxford University also protested against the presence of Rhodes's statue at Oriel College. When read together with such other movements as 'Why is My Curriculum White?' in the United Kingdom and 'Black Lives Matter' in the United States of America, Rhodes Must Fall became part of planetary struggles for epistemic freedom and life itself.

The tenth chapter pulls together the lines of arguments raised in this book and grapples with the difficult question of how can Africans create African futures within a modern world system structured by global coloniality as it concludes the book. What are restated are the interconnected and intertwined challenges of coloniality of power, knowledge and being as constitutive elements of global coloniality that makes it difficult for Africans to create their own futures. It highlights that an analysis of both the constitution and workings of modern global power is an important intellectual task because global coloniality has direct implications on African initiatives aimed at creating African futures. No African futures without epistemic freedom. Decolonization of the twenty-first century compared to that of the twentieth century has to gesture into the future that is predicated on '6-ds': deracialization, detribalization, depatriachization, decorporatization, deimperialization and democratization.

Conclusion

Indeed the whole world is experiencing the deep and catastrophic effects of double crisis. The crisis is both systemic and epistemic. The epistemic part has led to the reopening of the basic epistemological question and set in motion planetary epistemic struggles that are simultaneously unmasking what has been concealed by Eurocentric epistemology while searching for new knowledges capable of taking the world out of the epistemic crisis. The planetary nature of the epistemic and systemic crisis manifested itself recently in the form of what became known as the 'global financial crisis'. It took the world by surprise, including Europe and North

America who have paraded themselves as alert to anything that could potentially disturb the legacy of capitalist modernity. The crisis destabilised the epistemological confidence of the Euro–North American world. Modern institutions such as the banks, stock markets and the entire global financial system nearly lost credibility.

The current environmental/ecological crises rocking the modern world are another indicator of the epistemic crisis as well as the systemic crises that remind us of the catastrophic failures and vulnerabilities of the modern world system that has been caught off guard. What the world is facing is a broad 'civilizational crisis' which loudly proclaims that modernity has produced many modern problems for which it has no modern solutions. Consequently, it would be naïve for peoples of the Global South in general, and Africa in particular, to continue looking to Europe and North America for usable knowledge, relevant ideas, critical theories and solutions to modern problems. This is why this book calls for intensification of African struggles for epistemic freedom as a way of rehabilitating the entire world from the current systemic and epistemic crisis.

References

Ake, C. 1979. *Social as Imperialism: The Theory of Political Development*. Ibadan: Ibadan University Press.

Alatas, S. H. 1969. 'The Captive Mind and Creative Development'. In K. B. Madhava (ed.), *International Development*. New York: Oceania Publications, pp. 39–49.

Alatas, S. H. 1974. 'The Captive Mind and Creative Development'. *International Social Science Journal*, 36(4), pp. 691–699.

Allen, A. 2016. *The End of Progress: Decolonizing the Normative Foundations of Critical Theory*. New York: Columbia University Press.

Amin, S. 1968. *Le developpement du capitalisme en Cote d'Ivoire*. Paris: Minuit.

Amin, S. 1973. *Neo-Colonialism in West Africa*. Translated by Francis McDough. New York: Monthly Review Press.

Amin, S. 1974. *Accumulation on a World Scale*. Translated by Brian Pearce. New York: Monthly Review Press.

Amin, S. 1990. *Delinking: Towards a Polycentric World*. Translated by Michael Wolfers. London: Zed Books.

Amin, S. 2009. *Eurocentrism: Modernity, Religion, and Democracy: A Critique of Eurocentrism and Culturalism*. New York: Monthly Review Press.

Asante, M. K. 1987. *The Afrocentric Idea*. Philadelphia, PA: Temple University Press.

Asante, M. K. 1988. *Afrocentricity*. Trenton, NJ: Africa World Press.

Atieno-Odhiambo, E. S. 1996. 'Democracy and the Emergent Present in Africa: Interrogating the Assumptions'. *Africa Zamani*, 3(2), pp. 27–42.

Atieno-Odhiambo, E. S. 2002. 'From African Historiographies to an African Philosophy of History'. In T. Falola and C. Jennings (eds), *Africanizing Knowledge: African Studies Across the Disciplines*. New Brunswick and London: Transaction Publishers, pp. 13–63.

Banchetti-Robino, M. P. and Headley, C. R. 2006. 'Introduction: Charting the Shifting Geography of Reason'. In M. P. Banchetti-Robino and C. R. Headley (eds). *Shifting the Geography of Reason: Gender, Science and Religion*. Newcastle, UK: Cambridge Scholars Press, pp. 1–9.

Bhambra, G. K. 2007. *Rethinking Modernity: Postcolonialism and the Sociological Imagination*. New York: Palgrave Macmillan.

Chabal, P. and Daloz, J-P. 1999. *Africa Works: Disorder as Political Instrument*. Oxford, UK: James Currey.

Chakrabarty, D. 2007. *Provincializing Europe: Postcolonial Thought and Historical Difference*. Second Edition. Princeton, NJ: Princeton University Press.

Chen, K-H. 2010. *Asia as Method: Toward Deimperialization*. Durham, NC and London: Duke University Press.

Chilisa, B. 2012. *Indigenous Research Methodologies*. Los Angeles, CA, London and New Delhi: Sage.

Comaroff, J. and Comaroff, J. L. 2012. *Theory from the South or, How Euro-America Is Evolving Toward Africa*. Boulder, CO and London: Paradigm.

Dash, J. M. 1999. 'Introduction'. In Glissant, E. *Caribbean Discourse: Selected Essays*. Translated and with An Introduction by J. Michael Dash. Third Edition. Charlottesville, NC: University Press of Virginia, pp. xi–xlv.

Depelchin, J. 2005. *Silences in African History: Between the Syndromes of Discovery and Abolition*. Dar es Salaam: Mkuki na Nyota Publishers.

Diawara, M. 1990. 'Reading Africa through Foucault: V. Y. Mudimbe's Reaffirmation of the Subject'. *October*, 55, pp. 65–96.

Du Bois, W. E. B. 1903. *The Souls of Black Folk*. New York: Dover Publications.

Falola, T. 2001. *Nationalism and African Intellectuals*. New York: The University of Rochester Press.

Fanon, F. 1968. *The Wretched of the Earth*. New York: Grove Press.

Glissant, E. 1999. *Caribbean Discourse: Selected Essays*. Translated and with an Introduction by J. Michael Dash. Third Edition. Charlottesville, NC: University Press of Virginia.

Goody, J. 2006. *The Theft of History*. Cambridge, UK: Cambridge University Press.

Gordon, L. R. 2006. 'Foreword'. In M. P. Banchetti-Robino and C. R. Headley (eds), *Shifting the Geography of Reason: Gender, Science and Religion*. Newcastle, UK: Cambridge Scholars Press.

Grosfoguel, R. 2013. 'The Structure of Knowledge in Westernized Universities: Epistemic Racism/Sexism and the Four Genocides/Epistemicides of the Long 16th Century'. *Human Architecture: Journal of the Sociology of Self-Knowledge*, xi(1), Fall, pp. 73–90.

Headley, J. M. 2008. *The Europeanization of the World: On the Origins of Human Rights and Democracy*. Princeton, NJ and Oxford, UK: Princeton University Press.

Hoppers, C. O. and Richards, H. 2012. *Rethinking Thinking: Modernity's 'Other' and the Transformation of the University*. Pretoria: UNISA Press.

Hountondji, P. J. 1990. 'Scientific Dependence in Africa Today'. *Research in Africa Literatures*, 21(3), pp. 5–15.

Hountondji, P. J. 1996. *African Philosophy: Myth and Reality: Second Edition*. Translated by Henri Evans. Bloomington, IN: Indiana University Press.

Hountondji, P. J. 2002. *The Struggle for Meaning: Reflections on Philosophy, Culture, and Democracy in Africa*. Athens: Ohio University Research in International Studies Africa Series No. 78.

Hountondji, P. J. 2007 (ed.). *Endogenous Knowledge: Research Trails*. Translated by Ayi Kwesi Armah. Dakar: CODESRIA Books.

July, R. W. 1968. *The Origins of Modern African Thought: Its Development in West Africa During the Nineteenth and Twentieth Centuries*. London: Faber & Faber.

Mafeje, A. 2000. 'Africanity: A Combative Ontology'. *CODESRIA Bulletin*, 1, pp. 66–67.

Mamdani. M. 2011. 'The Importance of Research in a University.' *Pambazuka News*, 526, pp. 1–12.

Mazrui, A. A. 1978. *Political Values and the Educated Class in Africa*. Berkeley and Los Angeles, CA: University of California Press.

Mbembe, A. 2002. 'African Modes of Self-Writing'. *Public Culture*, 14(1), pp. 239–273.

Mbembe, A. 2015. *On the Postcolony*. Johannesburg: Wits University Press.

Mignolo, W. D. 2007. 'Delinking: The Rhetoric of Modernity, the Logic of Coloniality and the Grammar of De-Coloniality', *Cultural Studies*, 21(2–3), pp. 449–514.

Mkandawire, T. 1995. 'Three Generations of Africa Scholars: A Note'. *Transformation*, 28, pp. 143–144.

Mveng, E. 1983. 'Recents Developments de la Theologie Africaine'. *Bulletin of African Theology*, 5(9), pp. 138–156.

Nabudere, D. W. 2011. *Afrikology: Philosophy and Wholeness: An Epistemology*. Pretoria: Africa Institute of South Africa.

Nandy, A. 1983. *The Intimate Enemy: Loss and Recovery of Self Under Colonialism*. New Delhi: Oxford University Press.

Ngugi wa Thiong'o. 1986. Decolonizing the Mind: The Politics of Language in African Literature. Oxford, UK: James Currey.

Ngugi wa Thiong'o. 1993. *Moving the Centre: The Struggle for Cultural Freedoms*. Oxford, UK: James Currey.

Ngugi wa Thiong'o. 2009a. *Re-Membering Africa*. Nairobi, Kampala, Dar es Salaam: East African Educational Publishers.

Ngugi wa Thiong'o 2009b. *Something Torn and New: An African Renaissance*. New York: Basic Civitas Books.

Ngugi wa Thiong'o. 2012. *Globalectics: Theory and the Politics of Knowing*. New York: Columbia University Press.

Nisbett, R. 2003. *The Geography of Thought: How Asians and Westerners Think Differently . . . and Why*. New York: The Free Press.

Ogot, A. 1978. 'Three Decades of Historical Studies in East Africa, 1949–1977'. *Kenya Historical Review*, 6(1–2), pp. 22–33.

Oyewumi, O. 1997. *The Invention of Women: Making an African Sense of Western Gender Discourses*. Minneapolis, MN and London: University of Minnesota Press.

Quijano, A. 2007. 'Coloniality and Modernity/Rationality.' *Cultural Studies*, 21(2–3), (March/May), pp. 168-178.

Ranger, T. O. 1968. 'Introduction'. In T. O. Ranger (ed.). *Emerging Themes in African History*. Nairobi: East African Publishing House, pp. i–xxxv.

Ranger, T. O. 1976. 'Towards Usable Past'. In C. Fyfe (ed.), *African Studies Since 1945*. Harlow, UK: Longman, pp. 17–24.

Said, E. E. 1993. *Culture and Imperialism*. New York: Vintage.

Santos, B. de S. 2007. 'Beyond Abyssal Thinking: From Global Lines to Ecologies of Knowledges'. *Review*, xxx(1), pp. 45–89.

Santos, B. de S. 2014. *Epistemologies of the South: Justice Against Epistemicide*. Boulder, CO and London: Paradigm.

Shivji, I. G. 2003. 'The Rise, the Fall, and the Insurrection of Nationalism in Africa'. Keynote Address Delivered at CODESRIA East African Regional Conference, Addis Ababa, Ethiopia, 29–31 October.

Smith, L. T. 1999. *Decolonizing Methodologies: Research and Indigenous Peoples*. London and New York: Zed Books.

Soyinka, W. 2012. *Of Africa*. New Haven, CT and London: Yale University Press.

Subrahmanyam, S. 1997. 'Connected Histories: Notes Towards a Reconfiguration of Early Eurasia'. *Modern Asian Studies*, 31(3), pp. 735–762.

Subrahmanyam, S. 2005. *Explorations in Connected Histories: Mughals and Franks*. Oxford, UK: Oxford University Press.

Terreblanche, S. 2014. *Western Empires, Christianity, and the Inequalities Between the West and the Rest 1500–2010.* Johannesburg: Penguin Books.

Thuynsma, P. N. 1998. 'On the Trial of Christopher Okigbo'. In O. H. Kokole (ed.), *The Global African: Portrait of Ali Mazrui.* Trenton, NJ: Africa World Press.

Tlostanova, M. V. and Mignolo, W. D. 2012. *Learning to Unlearn: Decolonial Reflections from Eurasia and the Americas.* Columbus, OH: The Ohio State University Press.

Trouillot, M-R. 1995. *Silencing the Past: Power and the Production of History.* With a New Foreword by Hazel V. Carby. Boston, MA: Beacon Press.

Wallerstein, I. 1997. 'Eurocentrism and Its Avatars: The Dilemmas of Social Science'. *New Left Review*, 226, November–December, pp. 93–104.

Wallerstein, I. 1999. 'Introduction: Why Unthink?' In I. Wallerstein (ed.), *Unthinking Social Science: The Limits of Nineteenth Century Paradigms.* Cambridge, UK: Polity Press, pp. 1–26.

2

NOMENCLATURE OF DECOLONIZATION

Introduction

'Coloniality is not over, it's is all over' declared Walter D. Mignolo (2016) in a conversation with Aryan Kaganof. Coloniality is a description of the persistence of colonialism beyond dismantlement of its direct administrative structures (Quijano 2000). This way, coloniality differs from postcolonialism as it is not an 'after' of colonialism. Long before Anibal Quijano coined the concept of 'coloniality', the leading Pan-Africanist leader and intellectual Kwame Nkrumah (1965) articulated this persistence of colonialism in terms of 'neo-colonialism', again a continuation rather than an 'after'. It is this survival of coloniality on a global scale (as global coloniality), which has provoked the resurgence of decolonization in the twenty-first century. This resurgence has taken the form of what the Latin American decolonial theorists have named as decoloniality. Decoloniality is a collective name for all those anti-slavery, anti-racism, anti-colonialism, anti-capitalism, anti-patriarchy, anti-Eurocentric hegemonic epistemology initiatives and struggles emerging in different geo-political sites haunted by coloniality in its physical, institutional, ideational and metaphysical forms (Mignolo 2000; Quijano 2000; Grosfoguel 2007; Maldonado-Torres 2007). The 'de' as opposed to the 'post' underscores and embraces many temporalities as it critiques imperial linear conception of time (Mignolo 2014: 21).

Ngugi wa Thiong'o (1986) and Chinweizu (1987) highlighted how colonialism lingered on the minds of the colonized like a nightmare long after its administrative/juridical presence has been dismantled. What Ngugi wa Thiong'o and Chinweizu understood as 'colonization of the mind' has direct implications for struggles for epistemic freedom. How can a people with colonized minds even think of freeing themselves from colonial invasion of their mental universe? This reality makes the decolonization of the twenty-first century, which is confronting coloniality within the domain of knowledge, very complex and difficult.

Because decolonization struggles have re-emerged centuries after dismantlement of physical colonialism, they have elicited intense debates over their definition, meaning and essence. Five broad imperatives dictate that we define decolonization of the twenty-first century and flesh-out its key contours as a necessary intellectual, ethical, epistemic and political movement. The first is that the key site and flashpoint of current decolonial struggles is the university. A university has never been a site of consensus. It is always a site of dissensus over definition, meaning and implications of concepts, ideas and theories. The second imperative is that this decolonization of the twenty-first century is one of the most misunderstood and caricatured intellectual movements especially by those who are beneficiaries of the current status quo of coloniality. Most of its critics though do not display any sign of having read the rich literature on decoloniality and its expansive decolonial archive.

The third imperative is that there are those even among scholars who strongly believe that the decolonization struggles belonged to the past and that they delivered a postcolonial world in the twentieth century and even a post-racial world in the twenty-first century. As articulated by David Theo Goldberg (2015), the election of Barack Obama as the first black president of the United States of America in November 2008 was given as a sign of the birth of a postcolonial and post-racial world (see also Tesler and Sears 2010). Even the celebrated African scholar, Ali A. Mazrui (cited in Adem 2014) was enchanted by the election of Obama to the extent of shifting his research thrust from Africa to Islamophobia, which he depicted as escalating compared to Negrophobia, which in his estimation was deescalating. Unbeknown to those who hailed the election of Obama as a signal of the end of racism, was that he was going to be succeeded by Donald Trump, an alt-right nationalist, racist, patriarchal and xenophobic politician who has proven beyond doubt that we are very far from a post-racial world. Even before Obama left office, there were escalating incidents of killing of black Americans by the police, which provoked the rise of such movements as 'Black Lives Matter' (Goldberg 2015).

The fourth imperative is the genuine need for clarity on concepts, theories and ideas cascading from the field of decolonization if we are to implement genuine and sustainable decolonial change. The fifth imperative is that (ex)-sites of colonialism such as Latin America, Asia, Caribbean, Africa and the African Diaspora continue to generate and produce decolonial concepts as they grapple with the long-term consequences of colonial experience. The challenge is not to reproduce the imperial/colonial paradigm of difference but to build interconnectedness of concepts and movements ranged against slavery, racism, colonialism, apartheid and patriarchy.

Connected histories and sources of decolonial nomenclatures

The paradigm of difference is a leitmotif of coloniality. It sustains the fiction of a separate human species with distinct cultures and societies. It valorizes geographical separations. Decoloniality is the opposite. It highlights human interconnections.

This approach enables a better framing and embracement of different decolonial currents emerging from different geo-political sites and different historical periods. It also enables a transcendence of the divisive epistemic xenophobia that fails to take into account the planetary nature of the struggles for epistemic freedom. Kwame Nimako (2014: 61) emphasized the idea of connected histories and connected social thought which he defined as 'Africana intellectual tradition' and he concluded:

> There is a distinctive Africana intellectual tradition that flows from Africa's history in relation to Europe. This tradition finds its expression differently in different locations, and in different historical periods. Like all intellectual traditions, the Africana intellectual tradition describes phenomena, but unlike other traditions, it is corrective and prescriptive in context and historical, structural, and development in content. The common thread that runs through the intellectual and political tradition I have articulated [. . .] is 'race', humiliation, slavery, colonialism and memory. And these are the phenomena that continue to shape this tradition as we enter further into the twenty-first century.
>
> (Nimako 2014: 61)

At another level, Achille Mbembe (2017: 2) engaged with the question of blackness in modern world history and contextualised it in 'three critical moments'. The first moment is dated from the fifteenth through to the nineteenth century and it was marked by the reduction of African men and women 'into human-objects, human commodities, human money' (Mbembe 2017: 2). This process, which became known as the 'Transatlantic Slave Trade', constituted an unprecedented humiliation and dehumanization of a people of Africa. The second moment according to Mbembe (2017: 3) 'corresponded with the birth of writing near the end of the eighteenth century, when Blacks, as beings-taken-by-others, began leaving traces in a language all of their own and at the same time demanded the status of full subjects in the world of the living'. Mbembe elaborated:

> The moment was punctuated by innumerable slave revolts and the independence of Haiti in 1804, by the battle for abolition of the slave trade, by African decolonization, and by the struggle for civil rights in the United States. The second era culminated in the dismantling of apartheid during the last decades of the twentieth century.
>
> (Mbembe 2017: 3)

According to Mbembe:

> The third moment − the early twenty-first century − is one marked by the globalization of markets, the privatization of the world under the aegis of neoliberalism, and the increasing imbrications of the financial markets, the postimperial complex, and electronic and digital technologies.
>
> (Mbembe 2017: 3)

The significance of Mbembe's analysis is that it reinforces the idea of inter-connected histories within which 'black reason' emerged as a double sign of dehumanization and possibility (Mbembe 2017: 6). In Mbembe's (2017: 10) work the concept of 'black reason' is deployed to:

> [I]dentify several things at once: forms of knowledge; a model of extraction and depredation; a paradigm of subjection, including the modalities governing its eradication; and finally, a psycho-oneiric complex. Like a kind of a giant cage, Black reason is in truth a complicated network of doubling, uncertainty, and equivocation, built with race as its chassis.

Fundamentally, that which Nimako termed 'Africana intellectual tradition' is propelled by what Mbembe called 'black reason'. It is a challenging decolonial thought that is subversive and insurrectionary. It contests the long-standing ideas of Europe as the centre of the earth, the notion of Europe as the birthplace of reason, the myths of Europe as the spring of universal life and the site of all human inventions.

Thus, while it is inevitable for the anti-slavery, anti-racist and anti-colonial, anti-patriarchy, anti-capitalist, anti-Eurocentric hegemonic epistemology initiatives and movements not to use different nomenclatures, this does not rule out interconnections and transnational solidarities. For example, the drive to decolonize history in Asia assumed the name 'subaltern studies' partly because it entailed contesting elite and bourgeois-centric historiographies and partly due to its drive to construct what became known as writing 'history from below' that embraced the peasants and the workers (see Guha 1982; 1983; 1984; 1985; 1987). In the Middle East, Edward W. Said (1978) expressed his epistemic struggle against Western 'Othering' of Arabs and the entire Islamic world in terms of 'orientalism'. Orientalism is a naming of manifestations of coloniality in the Middle East and is deeply mediated by a particular epistemology and ontological differentiation.

Thinking about legacies of slavery, racism, colonialism, apartheid, imperialism and patriarchy from diverse geo-political sites has enriched the nomenclatures of decolonization and expanded the decolonial archive. The works of such decolonial thinkers from the Caribbean as Aime Cesaire (2000 [1955]), Frantz Fanon (1968a; 1968b) and Edouard Glissant (1989; 1997) have enormously enriched decolonial thought. For example, the current work of Glissant highlighted the difficulties of thinking about the human, identity, consciousness, freedom and the future from a geo-political space where history and memory lies buried deep into the sea.

This is why in his book entitled *Caribbean Discourse: Selected Essays* (1989: 6), Glissant posited: 'For history is not only absence for us. It is vertigo. This time that was never ours, we must now possess.' This reality led An Yountae (2017) to introduce the concept of 'the decolonial abyss' which speaks to what she termed 'groundlessness of being' with specific reference to the Caribbean. What emerges poignantly in the decolonial work from the Caribbean, particularly that of Glissant, is the challenges of making sense of the history of a people that emerged from an unprecedented violent rapture (commoditization and human trafficking species that became known as the Transatlantic Slave Trade) – a traumatic experience of dislocation, deportation, and mass deaths' (Yountae 2017: 88).

Glissant's concepts cascaded from engagement with the traumatic 'middle passage' and the floating 'ship/boat' as the birthplace of a people. This is why Cesaire (2001: 28) described the Caribbean people in this poetic yet traumatic expression: 'We, the vomit of slave ships.' But the best description of the dilemma of the Caribbean came from J. Michael Dash (1989: xxxii) (the translator of Glissant's *Caribbean Discourse*):

> The Caribbean in general suffers from the phenomenon of nonhistory. No collective memory, no sense of a chronology, the history of Martinique in particular is made up from a number of pseudo-events that have happened elsewhere. What is produced is a lack of any historical continuity or consciousness. Consequently, Martinique, as an example of an extreme case of historical dispossession in the Caribbean, is caught between the fallacy of the primitive paradise, the mirage of Africa, and the illusion of a metropolitan identity.

If the Caribbean thinkers are not thinking about the notorious 'middle passage' and the 'sea', they have to think about the equally notorious 'plantation' (Glissant 1997). It is in this Caribbean geo-political space and context where Rastafarianism emerged as a search for roots, where creolization appeared as a search for language, and where Antillanite as a search for identity called Caribbeanness ensued. The indigenous people of the Islands, known as the Arawaks and Caribs, were decimated by European invaders (see Glissant 1989; 1997). This has led Glissant to develop a useful way of understanding identity as taking two forms: 'root identity' and 'relation identity' (see Table 2.1).

Here, Glissant was seeking a way out the old idea of 'identity as root' and making a case for a new understanding of 'identity as a system of relation' in the Caribbean context of 'nonhistory'. The key point here is that decolonial initiatives and movements have produced a very rich vocabulary that speak to anti-slavery, anti-racist, anti-colonial, anti-apartheid, anti-women and anti-capitalist realities. The currents range from neo-colonialism, colonization of the mind, underdevelopment, subaltern, coloniality, colonization of a special type, creolization, Africanity, Afrocentricity, racial capitalism, pluriversity, transversity, black feminism, radical black tradition, presence Africaine, mestissage, black consciousness, black power, Africana existential philosophy, Rastafarianism, Ethiopianism, Negritude, Afrikology, dismemberment, re-membering, decoloniality, epistemologies of the South to decolonial turn.

These are concepts developed in struggle and are constitutive of the expansive decolonial archive and decolonial thought. While these concepts are related, they also reflect what Walter D. Mignolo (2000) articulated as the intersection of 'local histories/global designs' as well as the period during which they were emerged. Despite the emergence of these concepts and movements within particular

TABLE 2.1 Glissant's summary of varieties of identity

Root identity	Relation identity
Founded in the distant past in a vision, a myth of the creation of the world	Linked not to a creation of the world but to the conscious and contradictory experience of contacts among cultures
Sanctified by the hidden violence of a filiation that strictly follows from the founding episode	Produced in the chaotic network of Relation and not in the hidden violence of filiation
Ratified by a claim to legitimacy that allows a community to proclaim its entitlement to the possession of a land, which thus becomes a territory	Does not devise any legitimacy as its guarantee of entitlement, but circulates, newly extended
Preserved by being projected onto other territories, making their conquest legitimate – and through the project of a discursive knowledge	Does not think land as territory from which to project towards other territories but as a place where one gives-on-with rather than grasps

Source: Glissant, 1997, pp. 143–144.

geo-political sites and specific historical times, they also 'travelled' and they are mobilized and deployed in present decolonial struggles. Table 2.2 provides a summary of some of the key intellectual and cultural currents, the main proponents and the major political and epistemic concerns.

These diverse intellectual, cultural, philosophical, epistemological and political currents embody those important knowledges produced in the course of decolonial struggles, which are never complete and perfect. They highlight trials and tribulations of the struggle for life, identity, liberation and freedom in the face of colonial/imperial racial negations of black being (Mafeje 2011; Shillian 2015; Wilder 2015; Mbembe 2017). Isaac Kamola emphasized that in the face of inadequacy of existing concepts, ideas, and theories cascading mainly from the dominant Euro-North American-centric archive, the 'anti-colonial archive' has become very important:

> There are good reasons for this return. These voices are poetic yet strident, theoretical but immediately practical to the particularities of struggle. These writings on colonialism, race, class, violence, and governance avoid abstract musing – and the polish and perfection of argument that goes along with it. Instead, they are timely statements made with great urgency. The assumed audience of African anticolonial thought was often not scholars, but rather one's immediate and intimate comrades. The horizons of these texts and arguments often contain futures filled with possibility, even if the specific outlines are not entirely discernible in the present moment.
>
> (Kamola 2017: 2)

TABLE 2.2 Decolonial intellectual currents/movements/philosophies

Intellectual tradition	Theorists/Thinkers	Issues/Concerns
Ethiopianism/ Rastafarianism	Leonard Howell Robert Hinds Haile Selassie Mammo Muchie	Primacy of Ethiopia as the only African country that was never colonized Racial pride/black identity Diaspora memory of Africa Black independent churches Decolonization of popular culture Pan-Africanism Revolutionary music called reggae
Garveyism	Marcus Garvey Robert Mangaliso Sobukwe	Back-to-Africa Negro-self improvement Africa for Africans Black pride Black unity Black Republic Critique of racism Pan-Africanism
Negritude	Aime Cesaire Leopold Sedar Senghor Garry Wilder Souleymane Bachir Diagne Cheikh Thiam	Black/African arts/culture African identity African epistemology African ontology/black being African vitalism Critique of rationality African intuition Critique of racism
African personality	Edward Wilmot Blyden Kwame Nkrumah Ali A. Mazrui	African identity/black being African religion Concienscism Triple heritage African essence Critique of racism African unity African university African knowledge
African socialism and scientific socialism/Marxist socialism	Julius Nyerere Milton Obote Samora Machel Amilcar Cabral Leopold Sedar Senghor Kwame Nkrumah Thomas Sankara	African self-reliance No to class exploitation Egalitarianism Anti-capitalist Communalism/Ujamaa villages Distributive justice Eradication of racism and tribalism Reversing land dispossession

continued . . .

TABLE 2.2 Continued

Intellectual tradition	Theorists/Thinkers	Issues/Concerns
		Nationalization of economy
		Cooperatives
		National unity
		Eradication of poverty
African humanism	Kenneth Kaunda	Human equality/egalitarianism
	Nelson Mandela	Promotion of *ubuntu*
	Leopold Sedar Senghor	Classless societies
	Julius Nyerere	Moral and spiritual responsibilities
		Social peace
		Human rights
		Non-violence
		Anti-racism and tribalism
		Anti-individualism and pro-communalism
		Participatory governance/democracy
		Against exploitative capitalism
		Responsive state
Black consciousness/ Black radical tradition	William E. B. Dubois	Building black identity
	Steve Bantu Biko	Double-consciousness
	Marcus Garvey	Pan-Africanism
	Cedric Robinson	Racial capitalism
	Maya Angelou	Raising black consciousness
	Aime Cesaire	Liberation of black people from colonially imposed inferiority
	Kwame Nkrumah	Anti-white supremacy
	Julius Nyerere	Restoration of black dignity
	George Padmore	Building attitude of positive black affirmation
African renaissance	Cheikh Anta Diop	African unity
	Nnamdi Azikiwe	Rebirth of Africa
	Kwame Nkrumah	Recovery of African genius
	Julius Nyerere	Restoration of African dignity, memory and history
	Thabo Mbeki	Afro-modernity
	Dani Wadada Nabudere	Return to the source
	Shadrack Gutto	
Black feminism	Kimberle Crenshaw	Intersectionality of oppressions/matrix of domination/manifold, simultaneous, and interlocking oppressions
	Patricia Hill Collins	
	Angela Yvonne Davis	
	Ifi Amadiume	
		Critique of white feminism
		Queer theory/decentring heteronormativity
		Against white racism

continued . . .

TABLE 2.2 Continued

Intellectual tradition	Theorists/Thinkers	Issues/Concerns
Dependency theory/ Underdevelopment school/Centre- periphery	Walter Rodney Samir Amin Andre Gunder Frank Immanuel Wallerstein Bade Omimonde Enrique Dussel	How Europe underdeveloped Africa Uneven development Maldevelopment Economic dependence World systems analysis
Afrocentricity	Cheikh Anta Diop Molefi Kete Asante Maulana Karenga Mobutu Sese Seko	Classical African civilization African agency Authenticity Primacy of African history Primacy of Egyptian civilization Africa-centred knowledge
Postcolonial theory	Edward W. Said Achille Mbembe Gayatri Spivak Homi Bhabha Pal Ahluwalia Dipesh Chakrabarty Kwame Anthony Appiah Edouard Glissant	Travelling theory Orientalism Against meta-narrative Poststructuralism Anti-nativism Mimicry Creolization Hybridity Postcolony Co-invention Provincializing Europe Anti-historicism Literary approaches Cultural turn
Afrikology	Dani Wadada Nabudere	Africa-centred knowledge Africa-self understanding African civilizational achievements African Renaissance African liberation Africa as the cradle of humankind
Afro-Marxism	Cedric Robinson C. L. R James Moses Kotane Issa G. Shivji Sam Moyo Patrick Bond Ngugi wa Thiong'o Mahmood Mamdani Bernard Magubane Shadrack Gutto	Racial capitalism Indigenizing Marxism Class analysis Class formation Class struggles Revolutionary struggles Land reform and land redistribution

continued . . .

TABLE 2.2 Continued

Intellectual tradition	Theorists/Thinkers	Issues/Concerns
Nationalist historiography	Cheikh Anta Diop Jacob Ade Ajayi Theophilus Obenga Terence Osborne Ranger Toyin Falola Paul Tiyambe Zeleza Ngwabi Bhebhe Bethwell Ogot John D. Omer-Cooper	Restitution of African history Primacy of African factor in human history Domination and resistance Primacy of Egyptian civilization Countering imperialist/colonial historiography Positive evaluation of African nationalism and defence of African national projects Oral methodology African nationalist humanism African national projects Pan-Africanism Africanization
Decoloniality/ Decolonization	Aime Cesaire Valentin Y. Mudimbe Mahmood Mamdani Claude Ake Chinweizu Ngugi wa Thiong'o Enrique Dussel Sabelo J. Ndlovu-Gatsheni Kwame Nkrumah Yash Tandon Ali A. Mazrui Sylvia Wynter Cornel West Kuan-Hsing Chen Kwame Nimako Ramon Grosfoguel Albert Memmi Nelson Maldonado-Torres Bernard Magubane Paulin Hountondji Anibal Quijano Walter D. Mignolo Cathrine Odora Hoppers Kwesi Prah	Colonial library Decolonial turn Border gnosis Critique of modernity Transmodernity Decolonizing the African mind Moving the centre Neo-colonialism Coloniality Deimperialization African Diaspora Decoloniality Extroversion Dismemberment Colonial difference Epistemic disobedience Endogenous knowledge/Indigenous Knowledge System (IKS) Rethinking thinking Colonizer–colonized relations/ settler–native relations Africana intellectual tradition
African political economy	Samir Amin Ibbo Mandaza Issa G. Shivji Thandika Mkandawire Claude Ake	Disarticulation of African economies National question African development African postcolonial state Dispossession

continued . . .

TABLE 2.2 Continued

Intellectual tradition	Theorists / Thinkers	Issues / Concerns
	Adebayo Olukoshi	New world economic order
	Bernard Magubane	Class formation/class struggles
	Fantu Cheru	African economic development
	Peter Anyang Nyong'o	Structural adjustment programmes
Africana existential philosophy	Steve Biko	Black experience
	Frederick Douglas	Black prophetic tradition
	Cornel West	Being black/ontological questions
	Anton Wilhelm Amo	Africana cultures
	William E. B. Dubois	Decolonizing knowledge
	Frantz Fanon	Problems face by African Diaspora
	Alexander Crummell	Race and racism
	Antenor Firmin	Identity
	Martin Delany	
	Lewis R. Gordon	
	Mabogo Percy More	
Decolonial feminism	Ifi Amadiume	Decolonizing gender
	Oyeronke Oyewumi	Coloniality of gender
	Nkiru Uwechia Nzegwu	Invention of women
	Maria Lugones	Feminist border thinking
	Gloria Anzaldua	Understanding African social
	Linda Martin Alcoff	organization
		Critique of Eurocentric thought
Black Atlantic tradition	Paul Gilroy	Multiculturalism
	Stuart Hall	Black identity
	Henry Louis Gates, Jr	Black British Arts Movement
	Raymond Williams	Politics of representation
		Race and racism
		African Diaspora
		Culture
		Cultural studies
		Black studies

Source: This table was drawn by the author.

Taken together, the concepts, movements and archive, constitute what Meera Sabaratnam (2017: 7) depicted as 'other ways of thinking about and being in the world that can form alternative points of departure to the hegemonic knowledges of empire'. What hangs them together is what has come to be termed the 'decolonial turn' cascading from Cesaire's key question: 'what, fundamentally, is colonization?', which opened up key ontological and epistemological issues and inaugurated an epistemic paradigm shift in knowledge generation from Europe and North America to other epistemic sites (see Maldonado-Torres 2011; 2018). However, to develop an even deeper understanding of the terrain within which the decolonization of the twenty-first century is re-emerging, it is important to reflect of the role of empires in shaping modern architecture and configuration of power; conceptions of being human and forms of knowing.

'Empire' as a framing of coloniality

The leading South African economist Sampie Terreblanche in his groundbreaking work entitled *Western Empires, Christianity, and the Inequalities Between the West and the Rest, 1500–2010* (2014: 3) emphasized:

> We cannot understand the challenges of our time without understanding the ways in which 500 years of Western empire building, often with the complicit of the elites of the Restern world, have shaped our world into the deeply unequal and gratuitously unjust place that it is today. [. . .] We cannot hope to remedy the brokenness of our modern economic system without understanding the economic, social and political drivers that have brought us here, and that continue to dictate the narrative of institutionalised poverty and globalised inequality.

How empires contributed to the creation of the present is also a subject of Jane Burbank and Frederick Cooper in the award-winning book entitled *Empires in World History: Power and the Politics of Difference* (2010: 3) where they posited:

> Investigating the history of empires does not imply praising or condemning them. Instead, understanding possibilities as they appear to people in their times reveals the imperatives and actions that changed the past, created our present, and perhaps will shape the future.

Burbank and Cooper (2010: 9–12) emphasized that 'empire is a useful concept with which to think about world history' and added that 'empire-builders – explorers, missionaries, and scientists, as well as political and military leaders – strove to make "we/they", "self/other" distinctions between colonizing and colonized populations'. Today the world is haunted by the consequences of the inscription of the paradigm of difference, which according to Burbank and Copper (2010: 12) is traceable to the social engineering work of empires.

Reflecting on the African predicament in particular, Ngugi wa Thiong'o (1986: 2) warned us that 'imperialism is not a slogan. It is real; it is palpable in content and form and in its methods and effects'. He elaborated: 'Imperialism is total: it has economic, political, military, cultural and psychological consequences for the people of the world.' Regarding the current predicament of Africa specifically, Ngugi wa Thiong'o (1986: xii) boldly stated:

The present predicaments of Africa are often not a matter of personal choice: they arise from an historical situation. Their solutions are not so much a matter of personal decision as that of a fundamental social transformation of the structures of our societies starting with a real break with imperialism and its internal ruling allies. Imperialism and its comprador allies in Africa can never develop the continent.

This historical decolonial structural approach not only enabled a deeper understanding of concepts but also comprehension of challenges the modern world is facing today – particularly the systemic and epistemic crises. It was actually Immanuel Wallerstein in his book entitled *The Uncertainties of Knowledge* (2004: 58) who boldly stated:

> I believe that we live in a very exciting era in the world of knowledge, precisely because we are living in a systemic crisis that is forcing us to reopen the basic epistemological questions and look to structural reorganization of the world of knowledge. It is uncertain whether we shall rise adequately to the intellectual challenge, but it is there for us to address. We engage our responsibility as scientists/scholars in the way in which we address the multiple issues before us at this turning point of our structures of knowledge.

This crisis has thrown the modern world into the maelstrom of difficult epistemological debates that have produced new concepts and new interpretations of such terms as empire and decolonization that require clear understanding.

Three empires and three trajectories of decolonization

Empires have appeared in three main forms (physical, commercial–military–non-territorial, and metaphysical), in the process provoking three trajectories of decolonization (political, economic and epistemological). See Table 2.3 for diagrammatical representation.

The empire first appeared in a 'physical' form (physical empire). It was delivered through direct violent conquest, domination, exploitation, repression, and inferiorization of the colonized. This is what was targeted by political decolonization. Kwame Nkrumah's dictum 'seek ye the political kingdom and all else will be

TABLE 2.3 Empires and decolonial trajectories

Type of empire	Decolonial trajectory
Physical empire	Political decolonization
Commercial–military–non-territorial empire	Economic decolonization
Metaphysical empire	Epistemological decolonization

Source: This diagram was drawn by the author.

added unto you' was an elaboration of the primacy of political decolonization. At the centre of the physical empire emerged a struggle that pitted the entrenched white colonial administrative elite against the emergent black property-less native elite over state power. It was specifically with reference to political decolonization struggles that the Nigerian sociologist Peter Ekeh (1975) defined as constituted by contestations between colonizing elite and colonized elite both deploying 'interest-begotten' ideologies of legitimation. He elaborated:

> In many ways, the drama of colonization is the history of the clash between the European colonisers and African bourgeois class. Although native to Africa, the African bourgeois class depends on colonialism for its legitimacy. It accepts the principles implicit in colonialism but it rejects the foreign personnel that rule Africa. It claims to be competent enough to rule, but it has no traditional legitimacy. In order to replace the colonisers and rule its own people, it invented a number of interest-begotten theories to justify that rule.
>
> (Ekeh 1975: 96)

The 'physical empire' was successfully dismantled in the twentieth century. But it remained alive as a 'commercial–military–non-territorial' formation, which is consistently and constantly thirsty for oil and other strategic resources located in the Global South. David Nugent (2010) argued that this 'commercial–military–non-territorial' power structure and economic machine is in charge of production and division of labour on a world scale. It is underpinned by a particular epistemology predicated on 'area studies' that enables it to know its hunting grounds very well. It is this non-territorial empire that has established military bases in all the areas of its hunting for commercial resources. Nkrumah (1965) was referring to the technologies of the 'commercial–military–non-territorial empire' when he introduced the concept of 'neo-colonialism'. Nkrumah argued:

> In place of colonialism as the main instrument of imperialism we have today neo-colonialism. The essence of neo-colonialism is that the State which is subject to it is, in theory, independent and has all the outward trappings of international sovereignty. In reality its economic system and thus its political policy is directed from outside.
>
> (Nkrumah 1965: ix)

Nkrumah went on to explain the danger of neo-colonialism compared to the old form of colonialism that was symbolized by the 'physical empire':

> Neo-colonialism is also the worst form of imperialism. For those who practise it, it means power without responsibility and for those who suffer from it; it means exploitation without redress.
>
> (Nkrumah 1965: xi)

It is an irresponsible empire that used such slogans as 'the right to protect' to invade other countries. This empire speaks the rhetoric of democracy, human rights, and humanitarianism (Ndlovu-Gatsheni 2013a). It is this empire that Michael Hardt and Antonio Negri in their celebrated book simply entitled *Empire* (2000) tried to sell to the world as a benign, ethical and dedicated to maintaining world order. This is how they defined it:

> The concept of the Empire is characterised fundamentally by a lack of boundaries: Empire's rule has no limits. First and foremost, then, the concept of Empire posits a regime that effectively encompass the spatial totality, or reality that rules over the entire 'civilized' world. No territorial boundaries limit its reign. Second, the concept of the Empire presents itself not as a historical regime originating in conquest, but rather as an order that effectively suspends history and thereby fixes the existing state of affairs for eternity. [. . .] The Empire we are faced with wields enormous powers of oppression and destruction, but the fact should not make us nostalgic in any way for old forms of domination. The passage to Empire and its globalization offer new possibilities to forces of liberation.
>
> (Hardt and Negri 2000: xv)

The key problem with Hardt and Negri's analysis of the 'commercial–military–non-territorial' empire is that they fell for the rhetoric of this empire, particularly its discourse of maintaining order and stability and its claims to spread democracy and human rights across the world. So they 'misread not only the political constitution of the empire but also its global mission' (Ndlovu-Gatsheni 2013a: 21). Propelled by this misreading of the empire, Hardt and Negri argued:

> In the warning years and wake of the Cold War, the responsibility of exercising an international police 'fell' squarely on the shoulders of the United States. The Gulf War was the first time the United States could exercise this power in its full form. Really, the war was an operation of repression of very little interest from the point of view of the objectives, the regional interests, and the political ideologies involved. [. . .]. Iraq was accused of having broken international law, and it thus had to be judged and punished. The importance of the Gulf War derives rather from the fact that it presented the United States as the only power able to manage international justice, *not as a function of its own but in the name of global right.*
>
> (Hardt and Negri 2000: 180, emphasis is in the original)

Hardt and Negri left us with the idea of an empire that was decoupled from imperialism and conquest – an empire that offered possibilities for liberation. This is a distortion of the character of the empire. The Latin American scholar Atilio B. Boron (2005: 3) in his extended criticism of Hardt and Negri's conceptions of the empire argued:

Today's imperialism is not the same as the one that existed thirty years ago; it has changed, and in some ways the change has been important, but it has not changed into its opposite, as neo-liberal mystification suggests, giving rise to a 'global' economy in which we are all 'interdependent.' It still exists, and it still oppresses people and nations and creates pain, destruction and death. In spite of the changes, it still keeps its identity and structure, and it still plays the same historical role in the logic of the global accumulation of capital. Its mutations, its volatile and dangerous combinations of persistence and innovation, require the construction of a new framework that will allow us to capture its present nature.

The empire also assumed the character of a 'metaphysical' formation, which survived dismantlement of the 'physical empire' (Ngugi wa Thiong'o 1986). Ngugi wa Thiong'o explained that the 'metaphysical empire' is better understood in terms of how it worked on the minds of the colonized in the process adversely affecting the entire mental universe of the colonized through such technologies as epistemicides, linguicides, alienation and cultural imperialism. Ngugi wa Thiong'o enlightened us on how the 'metaphysical empire' operated through detonating a 'cultural bomb' at the centre of the universe of the colonized:

But the biggest weapon wielded and actually daily unleashed by imperialism against the collective defiance is the cultural bomb. The effect of the cultural bomb is to annihilate a people's belief in their names, in their language, in their environment, in their heritage of struggle, in their unity, in their capacities and ultimately in themselves. It makes them see their past as one wasteland of non-achievement and it makes them want to distance themselves from that wasteland. It makes them want to identify with that which is furthest removed from themselves; for instance, with other people's languages rather than their own. It makes them identify with that which is decadent and reactionary, all those forces which would stop their own springs of life. It even plants serious doubts about the moral rightness of struggle. Possibilities of triumph or victory are seen as remote, ridiculous dreams. The intended results are despair, despondency, and a collective death-wish. Amidst this wasteland which it has created, imperialism presents itself as the cure and demands that the dependent sing hymns of praise with the constant refrain: 'Theft is holy'.

(Ngugi wa Thiong'o 1986: 3)

The success of the 'metaphysical empire' has been in its submission of the colonized world to European memory. The consequence has been the remaking of the African people in the image of the colonial conqueror. Metaphysical empire even invented new political identities such as native. Mahmood Mamdani (2013: 2–3) explained the invention of 'natives' in these revealing words:

Unlike what is commonly thought, native does not designate a condition that is original and authentic. Rather, [. . .] the native is the creation of the colonial state: colonized, the native is pinned down, localized, thrown out of civilization as an outcast, confined to custom, and then defined as its product.

The 'metaphysical empire' targeted the minds of the colonized. When the Latin American decolonial theorists introduced the concept of 'coloniality' they were capturing the combination of the 'metaphysical' and 'commercial–military– non-territorial' empires in the creation of 'global coloniality' (Mignolo 2000; Quijano 2000; Grosfoguel 2007; Maldonado-Torres 2007).

Provoked by these three empires, it became logical for decolonization in Africa to take three inextricably intertwined trajectories. The first is political decolon- ization that is elaborated above. The Bandung Conference of 1955, that sought a decolonial pathway freed from Cold War global coloniality, spoke to both political and economic trajectories of decolonization. In his opening speech at the Bandung Conference, President Sukarno of Indonesia warned his colleagues to avoid a shallow understanding of colonialism:

> I beg of you do not think of colonialism only in the classical form which we of Indonesia, and our brothers in different parts of Asia and Africa, knew. Colonialism has its modern dress, in the form of economic control, intellectual control, actual physical control by a small but alien community within the nation. It is a skilful and determined enemy, and it appears in many disguises. It does not give up its loot easily.
>
> (Sukarno in *Asia-Africa Speaks* 1955: 23)

It was at the Bandung Conference that Asians and Africans posed soul-searching questions about a future defined by them as well as about their self-identity and rejection of being controlled and defined by others:

> Are we copies of Europeans or Americans or Russians? What are we? We are Asians or Africans. We are none else, and for anybody to tell us that we have to be camp-followers of Russia or America or any country of Europe, is, If I may say so, not very creditable to our dignity, our new independence, our new freedom and our new spirit and our new self-reliance.
>
> (Sukarno in *Asia-Africa Speaks* 1955: 186)

The Bandung Conference must be seen as launching of decolonization within a context of Cold War global coloniality and laying of the foundation for further political, cultural and economic decolonization.

Thus the second discernible trajectory of decolonization is that of economic decolonization. The demands for a New International Economic Order (NIEO) and the Lagos Plan of Action, among many other initiatives became the centrepiece of economic decolonization (Weber 2017). Political economy approaches dominated and inspired the struggles for economic decolonization. It was during the height of struggles for economic decolonization that Walter Rodney published his celebrated book entitled *How Europe Underdeveloped Africa* (1972) and Samir Amin published his *Delinking: Towards a Polycentric World* (1990a).

To Amin (1990b) one of the weaknesses of economic decolonization and African development plans it enabled has been the failure to think about the African economy outside classical economic thought. This means that there is indeed an epistemic trap at the very centre of economic decolonization. The necessity of economic decolonization is well articulated in Yash Tandon's book entitled *Trade Is War: The West's War Against the World* (2015) where he provided details of how Europe and North America have developed such institutions as the World Bank (WB), International Monetary Fund (IMF), General Agreement on Tariffs and Trade (GATT) and World Trade Organization (WTO) to underpin and drive the 'commercial–military empire'. On the WTO, Tandon argued:

> The WTO is a veritable battleground where the warring parties fight over real issues – as lethal in their impact on the lives of millions in the South as 'real wars'. Trade kills. The big and powerful employ sophisticated weapons – technical arguments, legalisms, and ideological and political weapons with deftness and chicanery – as lethal as drone attacks.
>
> (Tandon: 2015: 51)

The third is the current epistemological decolonization represented by the Rhodes Must Fall and Fees Must Fall movements in South Africa, and which demanded decommissioning of colonial/apartheid iconographies, changing of the very idea of the university, its curriculum, scholarship, institutional cultures and pedagogies (Mamdani 2016; Ndlovu-Gatsheni and Zondi 2016; Nyamnjoh 2016; Jansen 2017; Mbembe 2017). For details on Rhodes Must Fall and Fees Must Fall movements see Chapter 9 of this book).

Power, knowledge and being

The Latin American theorists have developed the concepts of coloniality and decoloniality as part of their efforts to name the current global state of affairs in which global power structure has remained asymmetrical, knowledge has remained Eurocentric and humanity has remained racially hierarchized (Mignolo 2000; Quijano 2000; Wynter 2003; Grosfoguel 2007; Maldonado-Torres 2007). The decolonization of the twenty-first century is intellectually very productive. It has produced useful units of analysis of the modern world system and its shifting modern global orders going as far back as the fifteenth century. There are three useful units of analysis/concepts that underpin decolonization of the twenty-first century. The first is the concept of power, which enables a deeper understanding of the invention, architecture, configuration and universalization of modern asymmetrical global power structures and its visible and invisible colonial matrices of dehumanization, exploitation, domination and control (Quijano 2000; Grosfoguel 2007; Ndlovu-Gatsheni 2013a; 2013b).

Decolonial analysis begins with the moment of 'modernity' as a 'dominant frame for social and political thought' (Bhambra 2007: 1). Decolonial theorists have revealed that 'coloniality' is constitutive of the underside of modernity (Mignolo 2011). Gurminder K. Bhambra (2007: 1) noted that modernity rests on 'two assumptions: rupture and difference – a temporal rapture that distinguishes a traditional, agrarian past from the modern, industrial present; and a fundamental difference that distinguishes Europe from the rest of the world'.

Deploying the concept of power, decolonial theorists have been able to understand that the dominant global power structure is constituted by 'hetararchies', that is, multiple, vertical, horizontal and criss-crossing strings of 'colonialities' that touch every aspect of human life (Grosfoguel 2007). Informed by a combination of Marxist and decolonial thought, Ngugi wa Thiong'o (1986) correctly depicted colonialism 'as a vast process' that affected even the consciousness of the colonized African people. Therefore, decolonization has to be an equally 'vast process' so as to expunged colonialism in every aspect of life ranging from ideology, language, aesthetics to sexual orientations (Ngugi wa Thiong'o 1986).

The complexity of modern asymmetrical power structures makes it hard to describe in one word or single phrase. This is why one finds such a long description as modern/colonial/capitalist/racial/hetero-normative/patriarchal/racist/sexist world system (Grosfoguel 2007; 2011). At the apex of this power structure is the United States of America with its Pentagon. The power structure is maintained above all other means by accumulation and monopolization of weapons of mass destruction (WMD).

The second important unit of analysis is that of being. Decolonial theorists have forcefully and convincingly argued that being human itself suffered a form of colonization known as 'coloniality of being' (Maldonado-Torres 2007). At the centre of 'coloniality of being' has been the consistent and systematic denial of humanity of those who became targets of enslavement and colonization. The denial of humanity of others was a major technology of domination that enabled pushing them out of the human family into a sub-human category and a zone of non-being (Fanon 1968a). Two techniques were deployed in the 'colonization of being'. The first was social classification of human species. The second was racial hierarchization of human species in accordance with invented differential ontological densities (Quijano 2000; Maldonado-Torres 2007; Dastile and Ndlovu-Gatsheni 2013).

During the first phase of the unfolding of Euro-North American–centric modernity, which was characterized by the so-called 'voyages of discovery' that resulted in the Portuguese and Spaniards colonizing the Americas, 'coloniality of being' entailed committing genocides – total elimination of those people whose being was denied. Later, the imperatives of capitalism indicated that these people whose being was denied were useful as sources and providers of cheap labour. This imperative led to a new colonial/imperial discourse of how forcing the colonized to labour in the mines, plantations and other sectors of colonial economy was justified as part of a civilization mission (labour civilizes the native) (Magubane 2010).

Ngugi wa Thiong'o (2009a; 2009b) introduced the concept of 'dismemberment' that speaks to both physical decapitation of those who were resisting colonialism and their heads being taken to decorate European museums. The example of King Hintsa of the Xhosa comes to the mind but there are many others like Waiyaki wa Hinga who had actively fought British colonization of Kenya who was buried alive (Ngugi wa Thiong'o 2009a: 3–4). Ngugi wa Thiong'o (2009a: 6) explains the colonial logic of cutting off heads of African leaders who resisted colonialism this way: 'The head that carries memory is cut off from the body and then either stored in the British Museum or buried upside down' so as to plant European memory. African memory had to be buried for European memory to flourish.

Dismemberment was defined by Ngugi wa Thiong'o (2009a: 5) as: 'An act of absolute social engineering, the continent's dismemberment was simultaneously the foundation, fuel, and consequence of Europe's capitalist modernity.' Beyond physical dismemberment, there was also the splitting of what Ngugi wa Thiong'o (2009a: 5) termed 'the African personhood' into 'two halves: the continental and its diaspora' during the enslavement of African people. This was followed by the Berlin Conference of 1884–1885 which 'literally fragmented and reconstituted Africa into British, French, Portuguese, German, Belgian, and Spanish Africa' (Ngugi wa Thiong'o 2009a: 5).

The decolonization of the twentieth century did not fully succeed in liberating Africans from the snares of social classification and racial hierarchization on a global scale. Today it is black people and Muslims who are finding it very difficult to travel freely within the modern world. They are interrogated at the borders and airports when they travel. Walls are being built to prevent the movement of people in a world that is said to be globalized (see Brown 2010). Figure 2.1 is a representation of a decolonial interpretation of the colonial cartography of power and the splitting of human species into two zones.

The third important unit of analysis is that of knowledge. The dehumanization of the colonized as part of the process of coloniality of being was accompanied by theft of history so as to sustain the myth of a people without history; appropriations of indigenous people's knowledges; outright epistemicides, linguicides and introduction of cultural imperialism. This constituted what is known as 'coloniality of knowledge' (Quijano 2007). Anibal Quijano (2007: 169) explained that coloniality of knowledge unfolded in terms of systematic repression of the specific beliefs, ideas, images and symbols constitutive of the colonized people's indigenous knowledge systems. Those aspects of African indigenous knowledges that were considered useful for global imperial designs and colonial process were looted and stolen.

Ngugi wa Thiong'o (2009a: 21) explained the modus operandi of the coloniality of knowledge in these very clear terms: 'Get a few of the natives, empty their hard

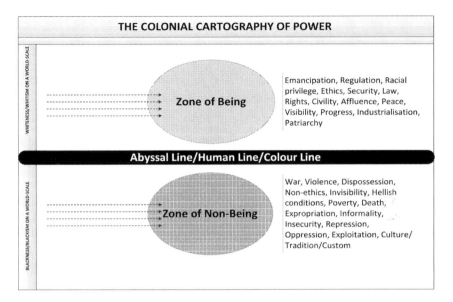

FIGURE 2.1 The colonial cartography of power

Source: This diagram draws on the work of: Dubois (1903); Fanon (1968a); Wynter (2003); Grosfoguel (2007); Maldonado-Torres (2007); Santos (2007).

TABLE 2.4 Basic analytics of coloniality

Analytics of coloniality	Basic dimensions
Power	Structure
	Culture
Knowledge	Object(ivity)
	Method(ology)
Being	Time
	Space
	Subject(ivity)

Source: Maldonado-Torres 2016, p. 20.

disk of previous memory, and download into them a software of European memory.' The long-term consequences of epistemicides, linguicides and cultural imperialism include 'annihilation' of a 'people's belief in their names, in their languages, in their environment', and 'in their heritage of struggle' (Ngugi wa Thiong'o 1986: 3). This is why today we find many Africans with European names and speaking those languages that were imposed by colonialism. Table 2.4 provides a diagrammatic summary of the analytics of coloniality.

TABLE 2.5 Analytics of decoloniality

Analytics of decoloniality	Dimensions
Power	An-other-structure
	An-other-culture
	Action: *Social activism*
Knowledge	More than Object(ivity)
	More than Method(ology)
	Action: *Questioning thinking and theorizing*
Being	Other time
	Other space
	Action: *Creating art, erotics, spirituality*

Source: Maldonado-Torres 2016, p. 30.

Alienation has re-emerged from the Rhodes Must Fall movements as one of those conditions that make it hard for black students to breathe within universities. Its genesis dates back to the unfolding of coloniality of knowledge and imposition of cultural imperialism. Alienation resulted in mental dislocation:

> The colonial process dislocates the traveller's mind from the place he or she already knows to a foreign starting point even with the body still remaining in his or her homeland. It is a process of continuous alienation from the base, a continuous process of looking at oneself from the outside of self or with the lenses of a stranger. One may end up identifying with the foreign base as the starting point towards self, that is from another self towards oneself, rather than the local being the starting point, from self to other selves.
>
> (Ngugi wa Thiong'o 2012: 39)

Imperialists and colonialists have used 'knowledge to obscure reality and force a certain perception of reality' (Ngugi wa Thiong'o 2012: 30). They were never satisfied with physical control only. They invaded the mental universe. The result has been well captured by Ngugi wa Thiong'o (2012: 38): 'Your past must give way to my past, your literature must give way to my literature, my way is the high way, in fact the only way'.

At the very centre of decoloniality is the aspiration to 'build the world of you' (Fanon 1968a: 206). This rebuilding of the world becomes necessary because of the continuing forces of dismemberment of the colonized. To gain a deeper understanding of colonialism it is important to know the epic school of colonialism because it reveals that it is not an event but a system.

The epic school of colonialism

Colonialism cannot be simplistically understood as an event of conquest and rule over Africa by Europeans. To gain a deeper meaning of colonialism, Peter Ekeh

(1983) distinguished it from 'colonization' even though they are connected. He emphasized that colonization is an event/episode, whereas colonialism is a process/movement and elaborated on this distinction this way:

> In addition to the disparate activities of the colonizers and the colonized, and in addition to the [. . .] colonial situation, colonialism may be considered as a *social movement* of epochal dimensions whose enduring significance, beyond the life-span of the colonial situation, lies in the *social formations* of supraindividual entities and constructs. These supraindividual formations developed from the volcano-sized social changes provoked into existence by the confrontations, contradictions, and incompatibilities in the colonial situation (emphasis in the original).
>
> (Ekeh 1983: 5)

The work of Ali A. Mazrui (1986) reinforced the epic school of colonialism just like Ekeh. This school underscored the fact that colonialism amounted to 'a revolution of epic propositions' (Mazrui 1986: 12). Mazrui identified six long-term consequences of colonialism. First, colonialism forcibly incorporated Africa into the world economy, beginning with the slave trade, 'which dragged African labour itself into the emerging international capitalist system' (Mazrui 1986: 12). African labour contributed immensely to the economic rise of a Euro-North American-centric transatlantic commerce. Second, Africa, which had been excluded from the post-1648 Westphalian sovereign state system and was physically partitioned after the Berlin Conference of 1884–1885, was later incorporated into the lowest echelons of the post-1945 United Nations' sovereign state system.

Third, Africa was incorporated into a Euro-North American-centric world culture and European languages. Four, Africa was incorporated into a heavily Euro-North American-centric world of international law. Five, as a consequence of colonialism, Africa was incorporated into the modern technological age, including being 'swallowed by the global system of dissemination of information' (Mazrui 1986: 12). Finally, Africa was dragged into a Euro-North American-centric moral order dominated by Christian thought. Mazrui's (1986: 13) conclusion was, therefore: 'what Africa knows about itself, what different parts of Africa know about each other, has been profoundly influenced by the West'. Below is a summary of seven phases and processes of dismemberment of Africa:

- *Foundational dismemberment*, which involved pushing black people out of human family.
- *Enslavement*, which not only commodified African people but also fragmented African personhood into two-halves: continental and Diaspora.
- *Berlin Conference of 1884–1885*, which literally fragmented and reconstituted Africa into British, French, Portuguese, German, Belgian and Spanish Africa.

- *Denial of African history*, which unfolded in terms of what I have described as the Hegelian-Conradian-Hugh Trevor-Ropian discourse that emphasized 'darkness' and 'emptiness' in Africa.
- *Colonial governmentality*, which reduced the colonized into rightless subjects who owned nothing beyond their labour that was sold cheaply to the colonizers.
- *'Postcolony'*, which assumed the form of reproduction of coloniality by African leaders who continue to reduce ordinary African people to 'subjects' rather than 'citizens'.
- *Patriarchy and sexism* that continues to dismember women from power, knowledge and being.

Conclusion

Decoloniality is against essentialism and fundamentalism. As eloquently presented by Grosfoguel (2007: 212) decoloniality is critical of both Eurocentric and Global South fundamentalisms. Decoloniality is essentially a repudiation of what Aime Cesaire (2000: 42) described as the 'European fundamental LIE: Colonization = Civilization'. Decoloniality provides ex-colonized peoples a space to judge and expose Euro-American deceit and hypocrisy (Cesaire, 2000). In this way, decoloniality enables a retelling of the history of humanity and knowledge from the vantage point of those epistemic sites that received the 'negatives' of modernity, highlighting appropriations, epistemicides, linguicides, and denials of the humanity of other people as part of the story of science. Decoloniality also accepts the fact of ontological pluralism as a reality that needs 'ecologies of knowledges' to understand (Santos, 2007). Decoloniality underscores the fact that human beings were/are born into a valid and legitimate knowledge system. This is an important decolonial attitude which enables one to be concerned about the marginalization if not absence of black people's knowledge in the modern academies. A decolonial attitude is meant to set Africa free from epistemic dependence. It acknowledges that the epic anti-colonial struggles of the twentieth century did not succeed in delivering a genuinely postcolonial world. Whereas the 'physical empire' which subsisted on direct territorial control and administration of colonies was dismantled, the 'metaphysical empire' that depended on invasion of the African mental universe remained intact as it was deeply etched in the colonized people's minds. Finally, the chapter demonstrated that coloniality is all over and as such is provoking various struggles in various sites of coloniality. These decolonial struggles have enriched the decolonial archive in terms of theory and concepts.

References

Adem, S. 2014. 'ASR on Ali A. Mazrui: Introduction'. *African Studies Review*, 57(1), pp.131–133.
Amin, S. 1990a. *Delinking: Towards a Polycentric World*. London: Zed Books.
Amin, S. 1990b. *Maldevelopment: Anatomy of a Global Failure*. London: Zed Books.

Asia-Africa Speaks from Bandung. 1955. Djakarta: The Ministry of Foreign Affairs, Republic of Indonesia.

Bhambra, G. K. 2007. *Rethinking Modernity: Postcolonialism and the Sociological Imagination*. London: Palgrave Macmillan.

Burbank, J. and Cooper, F. 2010. *Empires in World History: Power and the Politics of Difference*. Princeton, NJ and Oxford, UK: Princeton University Press.

Boron, A. B. 2005. *Empire and Imperialism: A Critical Reading of Michael Hardt and Antonio Negro*. London and New York: Zed Books.

Brown, W. 2010. *Walled States, Waning Sovereignty*. New York: Zone Books.

Cesaire, A. 2000. *Discourse on Colonialism*. Translated by Joan Pinkham. New York: Monthly Review Press.

Cesaire, A. 2001. *Notebook of a Return to the Native Land*. Translated by Clayton Eshlemann. Middletown, CT: Wesleyan University Press.

Chinweizu, I. 1987. *Decolonizing the African Mind*. Lagos: Pero Press.

Dash, J. M. 1989. 'Introduction'. In E. Glissant. *Caribbean Discourse: Selected Essays*. Charlottesville, VA: University Press of Virginia, pp. xi–xiv.

Dastile, N. P. and Ndlovu-Gatsheni, S. J. 2013. 'Power, Knowledge and Being: Decolonial Combative Discourse as a Survival Kit for Pan-Africanists in the 21st Century'. *Alternation: Interdisciplinary Journal for the Study of Arts and Humanities in Southern Africa*, 20(1), pp.105–134.

Dubois, W. E. B. 1903. *The Souls of Black Folk*. New York: Dover Publishers.

Ekeh, P. P. 1975. 'Colonialism and the Two Publics in Africa: A Theoretical Statement'. *Comparative Studies in Society and History*, 17(1), pp. 96–123.

Ekeh, P. 1983. *Colonialism and Social Structure: An Inaugural Lecture*. Ibadan: Ibadan University Press.

Fanon, F. 1968a. *The Wretched of the Earth*. New York: Grove Press.

Fanon, F. 1968b. *Black Skins, White Masks*. Translated by Charles Lam Markmann. New York: Grove Press.

Glissant, E. 1989. *Caribbean Discourse: Selected Essays*. Translated by Michael Dash. Charlottesville, NC: University Press of Virginia.

Glissant, E. 1997. *Poetics of Relation*. Translated by Besty Wing. Ann Arbor, MI: University of Michigan Press.

Goldberg, D. T. 2015. *Are We All Postracial Yet?* Cambridge, UK: Polity Press.

Grosfoguel, R. 2007. 'The Epistemic Decolonial Turn: Beyond Political-Economy Paradigms'. *Cultural Studies*, 21(2–3), (March/May), pp. 211–223.

Grosfoguel, R. 2011. 'Decolonizing Post-Colonial Studies and Paradigms of Political Economy: Transmodernity, Decolonial Thinking, and Global Coloniality'. *Transmodernity: Journal of Peripheral Cultural Production of the Luso-Hispanic World*, 1(1), pp. 1–35.

Guha, R. (ed.). 1982. *Subaltern Studies 1: Writings on South Asian History and Society*. Delhi: Oxford University Press.

Guha, R. (ed.). 1983. *Subaltern Studies 1I: Writings on South Asian History and Society*. Delhi: Oxford University Press.

Guha, R. (ed.). 1984. *Subaltern Studies 111: Writings on South Asian History and Society*. Delhi: Oxford University Press.

Guha, R. (ed.). 1985. *Subaltern Studies 1V: Writings on South Asian History and Society*. Delhi: Oxford University Press.

Guha, R. (ed.). 1987. *Subaltern Studies V: Writings on South Asian History and Society*. Delhi: Oxford University Press.

Hardt, M. and Negri, A. 2000. *Empire*. Cambridge, MA: Harvard University Press.

Jansen, J. 2017. *As By Fire: The End of the South African University*. Cape Town: Tafelberg.

Kamola, I. 2017. 'Review Essay: A Time for Anticolonial Theory'. *Contemporary Political Thought*, September, pp. 1–12.

Mafeje, A. 2011. 'Africanity: A Combative Ontology'. In R. Devisch and F. B. Nyamnjoh (eds), *The Postcolonial Turn: Re-Imagining Anthropology and Africa*. Bamenda and Leiden: Langaa and African Studies Centre, pp. 31–44.

Magubane, B. M. 2010. *Race and the Construction of the Dispensable Other*. Pretoria: UNISA Press.

Maldonado-Torres, N. 2007. 'On Coloniality of Being: Contributions to the Development of a Concept'. *Cultural Studies*, 21(2–3), (March/May), pp. 240–270.

Maldonado-Torres, N. 2011. 'Thinking Through the Decolonial Turn: Post-Continental Interventions in Theory, Philosophy, and Critique – An Introduction'. *Transmodernity: Journal of Peripheral Cultural Production of Luso-Hispanic World*, Fall, pp. 1–25.

Maldonado-Torres, N. 2016. *Outline of the Ten Theses on Coloniality and Decoloniality*. Paris: Frantz Fanon Foundation.

Maldonado-Torres, N. 2018. 'The Decolonial Turn'. In Juan Poblete (ed.), *New Approaches to Latin American Studies: Culture and Power*. New York and London: Routledge, pp. 111–127.

Mamdani, M. 2013. *Define and Rule: Native as Political Identity*. Johannesburg: Wits University Press.

Mamdani, M. 2016. 'Between the Public and the Scholar: Decolonization and Some Post-Independence Initiatives in Higher Education'. *Inter-Asia Studies*, 17(1), pp. 68–83.

Mazrui, A. A. 1986. *The Africans: A Triple Heritage*. London: BBC Publications.

Mbembe, A. 2016a. 'Future Knowledges' Unpublished Abiola Lecture Delivered at the Annual African Studies Association Annual Meeting, USA.

Mbembe, A. 2016b. 'The Society of Enmity'. *Radical Philosophy*, 200, (Nov/Dec), pp. 23–35.

Mbembe, A. 2017. *Critique of Black Reason*. Translated by Laurent Dubois. Durham, NC: Duke University Press.

Mignolo, W. D. 2000. *Local Histories/Global Designs: Coloniality, Subaltern Knowledges, and Border Thinking*. Princeton, NJ: Princeton University Press.

Mignolo, W. D. 2011. *The Darker Side of Western Modernity: Global Futures, Decolonial Options*. Durham, NC and London: Duke University Press.

Mignolo. W. D. 2014. 'Further Thoughts on (De)Coloniality'. In S. Broeck and C. Junker (eds), *Postcoloniality-Decoloniality-Black Critique: Joints and Fissures*. Frankfurt and New York: Campus Verlag, pp. 21–51.

Mignolo, W. D. 2016 'An Extended Conversation Between Aryan Kaganof and Walter Mignolo'. https://mail.google.com/mail/u/0/?ui=2&ik=8ebf44fbdf&jsver=W-O3ozL1KWY.en (accessed 12 June 2017).

Ndlovu-Gatsheni, S. J. 2013a. *Empire, Global Coloniality and African Subjectivity*. New York and Oxford, UK: Berghahn Books.

Ndlovu-Gatsheni, S. J. 2013b. *Coloniality of Power in Postcolonial Africa: Myths of Decolonization*. Dakar: CODESRIA Books.

Ndlovu-Gatsheni, S. J. and Zondi, S. (eds). 2016. *Decolonizing the University, Knowledge Systems and Disciplines in Africa*. Durham, NC: Carolina Academic Press.

Ngugi wa Thiong'o. 1986. *Decolonizing the Mind: The Politics of Language in African Literature*. Oxford, UK: James Currey.

Ngugi wa Thiong'o. 2009a. *Some Thing Torn and New: An African Renaissance*. New York: Basic Civitas Books.

Ngugi wa Thiong'o. 2009b. *Re-membering Africa*. Nairobi/Kampala/Dar es Salaam: East African Education Publishers.

Ngugi wa Thiong'o. 2012. *Globalectics: Theory and the Politics of Knowing*. New York: Columbia University Press.

Nimako, K. 2014. 'Location and Social Thought in the Black: A Testimony to Africana Intellectual Tradition'. In S. Broeck and C. Junker (eds), *Postcoloniality-Decoloniality-Black Critique: Joints and Fissures*. Frankfurt and New York: Campus Verlag, pp. 53–62.

Nkrumah, K. 1965. *Neo-Colonialism: The Last Stage of Imperialism*. London: PANAF.

Nugent, D. 2010. 'Knowledge and Empire: The Social Sciences and United States Imperial Expansion'. *Identities: Global Studies in Culture and Power*, 17(2), pp. 2–44.

Nyamnjoh, F. B. 2016. *RhodesMustFall: Nibbling at Resilient Colonialism in South Africa*. Bamenda: Langaa Research & Publishing CIG.

Quijano, A. 2000. 'Coloniality of Power, Eurocentrism, and Latin America'. *Nepantla: Views from the South*, 1(3), pp. 533–579.

Quijano, A. 2007. 'Coloniality and Modernity/Rationality'. *Cultural Studies*, 21(2–3), (March/May), pp. 168–178.

Rodney, W. 1972. *How Europe Underdeveloped Africa*. London and Dar es Salaam: Tanzania Publishing House and Bogle-L'Ouverture Publications.

Sabaratnam, M. 2017. *Decolonizing Intervention: International Statebuilding in Mozambique*. London and New York: Rowman & Littlefield International.

Said, E. W. 1978. *Orientalism: Western Conceptions of the Orient*. New York and London: Routledge & Kegan Paul.

Santos, B. de. S. 2007. 'Beyond Abyssal Thinking: From Global Lines to Ecologies of Knowledges'. *Review*, xxx(I), pp. 45–89.

Shillian, R. 2015. *The Black Pacific: Anti-Colonial Struggles and Oceanic Connections*. London: Bloomsbury.

Tandon, Y. 2015. *Trade Is War: The West's War Against the World*. New York and London: OR Books.

Terreblanche, S. 2014. *Western Empires, Christianity and the Inequalities Between the West and the Rest 1500–2010*. Johannesburg: Penguin Books.

Tesler, M. and Sears, D. 2010. *Obama's Race: The 2008 Elections and the Dream of a Post-Racial America*. Chicago, IL: University of Chicago Press.

Wallerstein, I. 2004. *The Uncertainties of Knowledge*. Philadelphia, PA: Temple University Press.

Weber, H. 2017. 'The Political Significance of Bandung for Development: Challenges, Contradictions and Struggles for Justice'. In Q. N. Pham and R. Shillian (eds), *Meanings of Bandung: Postcolonial Orders and Decolonial Visions*. New York and London: Rowman and Littlefield International, pp. 153–164.

Wilder, G. 2015. *Freedom Time: Negritude, Decolonization and the Future of the World*. Durham, NC: Duke University Press.

Wynter, S. 2003. 'Unsettling the Coloniality of Being/Power/Truth/Freedom: Towards the Human, After Man, Its Overrepresentation-An Argument'. *CR: The New Centennial Review*, 3(3), pp. 275–337.

Yountae, A. 2017. *The Decolonial Abyss: Mysticism and Cosmopolitics from the Ruins*. New York: Fordham University Press.

3

THE ONTO-DECOLONIAL TURN

Introduction

The present age of anthropocene is simultaneously driven by the 'ontological' and 'decolonial' turns constituting what can be named as 'onto-decolonial turn'. This 'onto-decolonial turn' emerged within a context and age of anger and hate. Pankaj Mishra's book entitled *Age of Anger: History of the Present* (2017) set out to make sense of the current state of paranoid hatreds that were reverberating at the very heart of a globalized world – signified by the rise of Trumpism with its racist, sexist, Islamophobic, patriarchal, nativist and xenophobic politics on the one hand, and on the other rise of Isis with its violent drive to build a 'Caliphate' as well as renewed crass racism and misogyny daily displayed on social media. Mishra's explanation is that as the world became 'modern', it did not succeed in fulfilling its promise of overcoming all human problems using science and rationality, rather it delivered a plethora of modern problems of racism, inequality, various forms of oppression and exploitation; which in turn provoked politics of hatred, invention of enemies as well as attempts to recreate imaginary golden ages (Mishra 2017).

However, Mishra did not spell out clearly the fact that the hatreds and anger haunting humanity today were mainly consequences of the 'colonial turn', which produced global coloniality as a 'death project' (see Suárez-Krabbe 2016). Under global coloniality, not only the 'human' was elevated above 'nature' but 'nature' was also reduced to a 'natural resource' available to the 'human' to exploit *ad infinitum*. Consequently, the relationship between the 'human' and others 'selves' became poisoned irreparably. At the centre of the 'unholy alliance' of modernity, racism, imperialism, colonialism and capitalism emerged new architecture and configuration of power as well as new Cartesian conceptions of the 'human' and knowledge (Dussel 2006). Human species were socially reorganized, classified and racially hierarchized. Here lie the roots of present-day anger and hatreds.

It is, therefore, not surprising that the 'onto-decolonial turn' calls for a radical rethinking if not mending of the damaged relationship of the 'human' with other 'selves' as well as other forms of 'matter' (both living and non-living), with which it shares the universe (Ngugi wa Thiong'o 1986; Cornell and Seely 2016). Historically speaking, this 'onto-decolonial turn' emerged within a context in which for over 500 years or so there was a strong belief in the abilities of 'Man' as the maker of the world as well as in 'his' power to change it into a better place to live (Cornell and Seely 2016). Alas, this confidence in 'Man' proved to be mistaken as it gave rise to phallocentrism, heteronormativity and the paradigm of racial difference that set afoot various forms of exclusions and discriminations and their naturalization and universalization (Wynter 2003; Maldonado-Torres 2007).

The modern world is today grappling with what Cornell and Seely (2016) have termed the 'dead ends of Man'. The 'human' has not emerged from the Eurocentric and ethnocentric conception of 'Man' as the 'sovereign subject of rationality' (Cornell and Seely 2016: 2). Thus, the 'onto-decolonial turn' has picked up both ontological and epistemological, and even pedagogical problems of today, particularly those to do with how to transcend race, patriarchy, sexism, capitalism, colonialism and epistemic hegemony of Europe and North America (Maldonado-Torres 2018). These issues are currently playing themselves actively and dramatically within the domain of knowledge and inside the institutions of higher education. The consequence has been the rise of difficult and complex but necessary questions and debates on such challenges as institutionalized racial hierarchies, epistemic violence, what counts as knowledge; potentiality of decolonization of academic institutions in such a way that they could become hospitable homes of everyone including the poor; possibilities of undercutting the reproduction of existing asymmetrical and alienating power relations by academic institutions, and changing the languages of instruction and research from colonially imposed one to indigenous African ones (Nyamnjoh 2016; Jansen 2017).

It is on the back of the 'onto-decolonial turn' that triple matrices of ontology, epistemology and pedagogy have come under the spotlight of epistemic struggles desirous of their decolonization. While the specific ontological concerns have produced three discourses of re-humanizing/re-membering, humaning and post-humanism, the epistemological issues have fuelled the calls for decolonization of the very idea of the university and its entire institutional frameworks and practices. This chapter explains the key contours of the 'onto-decolonial turn' as it lays out six dimensions of epistemological decolonization; articulates the necessary aspects of decolonial attitude and delineates the key contours of decolonial pedagogy. It ends, with an outline of a decolonial programme of re-education/re-socialization predicated on four key steps: (i) 'provincializing Europe' while 'deprovincializing Africa'; (ii) decolonizing the very normative foundations of dominant critical theory; (iii) 'rethinking thinking itself'; and (iv) the painstaking process of 'learning to unlearn in order to relearn'. These four steps enable a reasoned, practical and necessary response to colonial desocialization processes bequeathed on Africa by colonialism.

The onto-decolonial turn

The 'onto-decolonial turn' cannot be fully comprehended without an understanding of the 'colonial turn'. The troublesome spectre of Cartesian 'Man' haunting the modern world was invented by coloniality. It is, therefore, important to provide a summary of the invention of 'Man'. The Caribbean philosopher and decolonial theorist Sylvia Wynter (1984; 2001; 2003; 2007) provided a very cogent history of the invention of what she correctly termed the 'Euro-American white bourgeois ethnoclass genre' (Wynter 2003). Wynter's philosophical, historical and anthropological analysis of the rise of 'Man' concurrently reflects on the rise of modern science and philosophy as well as humanities as monopoly of 'white Man'. She also linked these developments with the unfolding of colonization of the non-European world in general. Wynter (2003) divided the rise of 'Man' into two historical phases: the first phase of emergence of 'Man' she coded it as 'Man1' and the second phase as 'Man2'.

'Man1' according to Wynter (2003), emerged during the era of the unfolding of European Renaissance – a period when the roots of diminishing hegemony of Christian theology 'over institutions and imagination of what is to be 'modern' Europe' are noticeable (see also Cornell and Seely 2016: 122). This was the first phase of the shifting of the order of things so as to set afoot 'Man1'. According to Wynter (1984), the invention of 'Man1' was part of 'heretical' act. But the best summary of what was taking place is given by Cornell and Seely:

> In conceptualizing God as a Caring Father who had created the universe for the sake of Man, the humanist philosophers and scientists broke with the order of divine causality unknowable to humans. If God created the world so than humans would appreciate it, then He would have bestowed on them the faculty of Reason, and the laws of Nature would be such that humans could rationalise them, thereby elevating the endeavour of human knowledge and enabling the break with the dominance of the clergy. Following this epistemological break, as well as the reorganization of the European political geography during the Renaissance, then, the descriptive statement of 'True Christian Self' as religious subject of the State (Man1, *homo politicus*).
> (Cornell and Seeley 2016: 123; see also Wynter 2003: 269)

Cornell and Seely (2016: 123) elaborated on the implications of this 'epistemo-ontological shift' in that it inaugurated the 'European Age of Discovery', which enabled 'the massive transformations in the physics and cosmology of the Copernican and Newtonian revolutions and the geographic voyages to the "New World"'. This paradigmatic shift took the form of the elimination of 'the physio-ontological principle of the non-homogeneity of substance between Earth (Fallen Flesh) and the Heavens (Redeemed Spirit)' in the process enabling 'geographers and scientists' to develop a new idea of 'a homogenous material universe in which the celestial bodies, the sea, and the earth are the same physical substance and could thus be observed, rationally comprehended, navigated, and manipulated' (Cornell and Seeley 2016: 123; see also Wynter 2003: 280). This birth of 'Man1' facilitated a shift in the way Europeans viewed non-Europeans. Prior to the invention of 'Man1', non-Europeans were viewed as a people who were 'pre-Christians' (who have not yet heard the Gospel/Untrue Christian Other'). Wynter explained the shift in these revealing words:

> In the wake of the West's reinvention of its True Christian Self in the transumed terms if the Rational Self of Man1 [. . .] it was to be the peoples of the militarily expropriated New World territories (i.e., Indians) as well as the enslaved peoples of Black Africa (i.e., Negroes), that were made to reoccupy the matrix slot of Otherness – to be made into the physical referent of the idea of the irrational/subrational Human Other, to first degodded (if still hybridly religio-secular) 'descriptive statement of the human in history, as the descriptive statement that would be foundational to modernity'.
>
> (Wynter 2003: 266)

The 'Other' category did not include only Africans and Native Americans; it included women, the poor and those considered to be mad. Here was born the colonial idea of only one human (the European Man) and only one 'truth-knowledge' (Reason) (Cornell and Seeley 2016: 125).

'Man2' emerged during the 'Age of Enlightenment' as a transmutation of 'Man1'. Wynter (2003: 282) explained the shift in these terms: from 'ratiocentric *homo politicus*' (Man1) to 'biocentric *homo economicus*' (Man2). Man2 is a creature and product of the changes that took place between the sixteenth to the eighteenth centuries. These are centuries that witnessed not only the unfolding of European bourgeois revolution but also the consolidation of capitalism as world economic system as well as the rise of social-evolutionary Darwinism and Eugenics.

In short, 'Man2' is the modern 'Euro-American white bourgeois ethnoclass'. The bourgeois of the non-European world are mere copycats of the 'Euro-American bourgeois ethnoclass' and they even mimic all its habits except those of respecting their own people and preserving their financial coffers. It was Wynter (2003) who called for a decolonial shift from 'Man' to the 'Human'. This is the core part of the 'onto-decolonial turn'. 'Onto-decolonial turn' is a planetary phenomenon ranged against the curse of coloniality. This is why Nelson Maldonado-Torres (2018: 123–124) posited:

> In order to escape from this curse/myth, it is necessary to rethink world history from the perspective of those who have been considered subjects without history proper, to critically review the entire arrangement of basic philosophical areas and concepts (ethics, politics, economics, rationality, consensus, critique, etc.), and to establish dialogical relations with colonial subjects everywhere, particularly those struggling against coloniality and for decolonization.

To understand the imperatives of the 'onto-decolonial turn' it is important to shift the geo-and bio-of knowledge to those people who suffered from being pushed out of the human family. These are the drivers and foot soldiers of the 'onto-decolonial turn'. Therefore, the ideal starting point in understanding the imperative of the 'onto-decolonial turn' is begin with Aime Cesaire's triple 'tormenting questions': Who am I? Who are we? What are we in this white world? (Cesaire cited in Thiam 2014: 2). These tormenting questions arose from the context of dehumanizing 'colonial abyss' to borrow a term from An Yountae (2017) and 'colonial death project' to use Julia Suárez-Krabbe (2016)'s terminology. Yountae (2017: 14) deployed the concept of the 'abyss' at three levels – theologically, philosophically and politically:

> The notion of the abyss interweaves three different disciplinary threads [. . .]: *theologically*, it denotes the blurring boundary between human finitude and divine potency; *philosophically*, it points to the incompleteness of the self (before 'the other'); *politically*, it bears a wider politico-historical meaning emerging from the history of suffering, the reality of coloniality, and a fragmented sense of collective identity. [. . .]. In other words, the commonality of the diverse abysses in my reading concerns the movement of the self who, dispossessed by its encounter with the abyss, emerges eventually as a reconstructed self. What does this process of remaking the self consist of? How is the newly emerging self different from the preabyssal? [. . .]. The self who is undone in the encounter with the abyss, that is, the pre-abyssal self, lives with a misguided consciousness. [. . .]. Conversely, the new self that emerges – if it does at all – from the abyss understands its nature not as an immutable substance but as multiple, fragmented, and always-in-becoming. In the abyss the old self is dissolved, emptied, abandoned, annihilated, lost, crushed, dismembered, shattered, and drowned [Emphasis is in the original text].

Yountae (2017:14) elaborated:

> That is, we observe in the three different abysses the self's passage from the old self to a new consciousness: from the self trapped in a dualistic illusion that valorises purity, completeness, and stasis over and against impurity, incompleteness, and change to a creolized self that finds its truth in the never-ending, pluri-singular acts of becoming in relation to the other; and from the self living with a teleological cosmology to a self who understands the end as a new beginning.

Yountae is indeed grappling with the difficult questions and processes of dehumanization and dismemberment on the one hand and the equally complex questions and processes of re-humanizing, re-membering and re-humaning on the other hand. Abyss is used as signifier of 'groundlessness of being' cascading from historico-socio-political colonial situation of dehumanization and trauma (Yountae 2017: 15–16). Reading decoloniality from this perspective, it becomes concerned with 'gathering of pieces', 'self-reconstruction' and 're-making of self' after centuries of dismemberment, dehumanization and negation as well as within the current age of global coloniality that Mbembe (2017: 7) articulated as 'the becoming black of the world'.

Thus the philosophical framing speaks to three related concepts with an ontological orientation. The first is *re-humanizing/re-membering*. The second is re-*humaning/humaning*. The third is *posthumanism*. The first is well expressed by Ngugi wa Thiong'o (2009a; 2009b) who defined colonialism as a grand dismembering/dehumanizing process that inscribed itself on the non-European world through a combination of physical decapitation of heads of resisting African leaders and metaphysical invasion of the mental universe of the colonized through such technologies genocides, epistemicides, and linguicides that enabled cultural imperialism and its alienating logics (see Ngugi wa Thiong'o 1986; Ngugi wa Thiong'o 2012). The long-term consequence has been mental dislocation.

Re-humanizing/re-membering for Ngugi wa Thiong'o (2009a; 2009b) is a struggle that is constituted by various initiatives. These initiatives date back to the mythical story of Osiris in Egypt who was killed by his evil brother who cut the body into 14 pieces and scattered them all over Egypt. This act provoked Isis ('in an act of love and devotion') to gather the fragments as part of re-membering (Ngugi wa Thiong'o 2009b: 24–25). To Ngugi wa Thiong'o (2009b: 25) re-humanizing entailed 're-membering' as a decolonial act underpinned by a 'quest for wholeness'. This quest 'has underlain African struggles since the Atlantic slave trade' (Ngugi wa Thiong'o 2009b: 25). The re-membering initiatives and struggles included Ethiopianism, Garveyism, Negritude, African Personality, Pan-Africanism, Harlem Renaissance, Afrocentricity, African Renaissance, and many others (Ngugi wa Thiong'o 2009b: 25–28).

Zimitri Erasmus (2017: xxii) introduced the concept of 're-humaning/humaning'. This constitutes the second philosophical framing. She posited:

> *Humaning* is a different activity from *humanizing*. To *human* is a lifelong process of life-in-the-making with others. To *humanize* is to impose upon the world a preconceived meaning of the human. [. . .]. There is no one way of humaning. There is no perfect way of going about it. Humaning is a social and cultural practice which we constantly hone. Humaning as praxis is historically and contextually specific (Emphasis is in the original text).

Erasmus, just like Frantz Fanon (1968) and Ngugi wa Thiong'o (2009a; 2009b) before her, is deeply committed to the struggles for setting afoot new humanism. Her book is actually subtitled 'Forging a New Humanism for South Africa'. Erasmus (2007: xxiii) makes two interrelated moves of acknowledging that we today live in a racialized world while at the same time refusing to be determined by race. She wrote:

All of us live in amongst racialised structures of social meaning. We cannot live outside, above, or beyond the past and the present. Nor can we be outside, above, or beyond the race. Because we are embedded in a racialised world, its ways of seeing and its injustices can be apparent to us, and we can be inspired to change it. [. . .]. In the ongoing process of our liberation we must create openings in the racial house. We must refuse to live by its rules of dominance and its significations.

(Erasmus 2007: xxiii)

The third philosophical framing is posthumanism. The posthumanism argument is well summarized by Drucilla Cornell and Stephen D. Seely (2016: 3):

For posthumanism, any focus on specifically human agency (such as that involved in the struggle against capitalism and colonialism) always risks a reinstatement of the old humanist subject, effectively smuggling in the Man who fucked everything up in the first place through the back door. Thus many posthumanist critics are engaged in a hypervigilant search for Man in every form of theory and politics, and any trace of him must be sussed out and rejected in the name of 'life itself' and the future of the planet.

Decoloniality is not for a posthuman world. It does not make sense for those people from the Global South who have not yet even enjoyed the status of being 'fully human' to join forces with those from the Global North who have been enjoying the monopoly of being human for over 500 years to push for 'posthumanism'. For decoloniality, another world underpinned by another knowledge that does not socially classify and racially hierarchize human species is possible. It is this decolonial struggle that pre-occupied such decolonial fighters as Steve Bantu Biko of South Africa who ended up losing his life during the course of the decolonial struggle. As detailed in Mabogo Percy More's book entitled *Biko: Philosophy, Identity and Liberation* (2017) the black consciousness struggle that Biko led was in reality ranged against dehumanization of black people and set out to re-humanize them beginning with changing their state of consciousness from that imposed by colonial apartheid, which generated inferiority complex to a new assertive and confident one of decolonization. Changing of attitude is a key component of changing consciousness, hence the importance of developing a decolonial attitude. This is why Maldonado-Torres (2018: 124–125) emphasized:

From a modern/colonial attitude of enchantment with modernity and either phobia or indifference towards the colonized, the decolonial turn generates a decolonial attitude that takes primacy over method, allowing subjects to uncover fundamental problems and join others in the effort to address them.

Decolonial attitude

To deal with dismemberment and dehumanization fundamentally requires a planetary change of attitude and cultivation of lost human love. The needed and necessary attitude is named decolonial attitude. It is founded on love of humanity. It is the opposite of colonial attitude, which is predicated on hatred of others, 'will to power' and 'paradigm of war' (Dussel 2008; Maldonado-Torres 2008; Ndlovu-Gatsheni 2016). Decolonial attitude is based on the 'will to live' and search for social peace (Dussel 2008; Maldonado-Torres 2008; Ndlovu-Gatsheni 2016). It begins from accepting that all human beings were/are born into valid and legitimate knowledge system. This decolonial attitude enables one to be concerned about epistemic dependence, which Paulin J. Hountondji (1997: 1) articulated as 'the logic of extroversion'. He posited:

> The fact bears repeating: in the fields of science and technology, Third World countries, especially those in Africa, are tied hand and foot to the apron strings of the West.
>
> (Hountondji 1997: 1)

Those who are today picking the fighting under the banner of decolonization are rational human beings and their decolonial agitation cascades from a deeply felt 'colonial wound' rather than their being stuck in the past or having in anyway surrendered to what Achille Mbembe (2002a; 2002b) termed 'the neurosis of victimhood'. There is a clear epistemic and systemic crisis. Students, teachers, administration and the broader society have been into a difficult and conflictual maelstrom, which Mahmood Mamdani (2007) depicted as 'the market place' – a direct consequence of neoliberalism and its market fundamentalism. Education has become a very expensive commodity. Inevitably, conflicts have broken out in the form of Rhodes Must Fall; Fees Must Fall and Outsourcing Must Fall movements (Booysen 2016; Ndlovu-Gatsheni and Zondi 2016; Nyamnjoh 2016; Ray 2016; Jansen 2017). The conflicts are not confined to South Africa – they are all over and they manifest what Immanuel Wallerstein highlighted as the 'uncertainties of knowledge' born out of a 'a systemic crisis that is forcing us to open the basic epistemological questions and look to structural reorganizations of the world of knowledge' (Wallerstein 2004: 58).

What is also needed is a decolonial shift from the Eurocentric 'vanguard scholarship/vanguard theorizing', which is characterized by dismissal of 'whatever does not fit the vanguardists' previsions or propositions' as non-existent or irrelevant' (Santos 2014: 11). It is 'vanguardist scholarship/vanguard theorizing' which breeds such arrogance as to even refuse to recognize other people's language of resistance. This behaviour amounts to the highest of form of arrogance. It is this arrogance that Nora Berenstain (2016: 569) depicted as constituted by 'epistemic exploitation' which occurs 'when privileged person compel marginalized persons to educate them about the nature of their oppression'. Toni Morrison (1975: 33) explained how this arrogance works:

> The function, the very serious function, of racism is distraction. It keeps you from doing your work. It keeps you explaining, over and over again, your reason for being. Someone says you have no language, so you spend twenty years proving that you do. [. . .] None of that is necessary. There will always be one more thing.

This questioning according to Berenstain (2016: 570): 'Rather, masquerades as a necessary and even epistemically virtuous form of intellectual engagement, and it is often treated as an indispensable method of attaining knowledge'. In the face of decolonial struggles, the beneficiaries of the status quo degenerate into epistemic deafness and continuously ask the same questions over and over about what decolonization means. Berenstain (2016: 570–571) correctly noted:

> Standard conversational norms allow epistemic exploitation to masquerade as any number of acceptable and normalized practices – 'exercising harmless curiosity', 'just asking a question', making a well-intentioned effort to learn', 'offering alternative explanation', and 'playing devil's advocate' are a few of the labels used to describe epistemically exploitative interactions. These innocuous euphemisms all help to mask the oppressive power dynamics at play in instances of epistemic exploitation.

Indeed, 'This creates a burden on the marginalized to educate and enlighten' in the face of doubting and disbelieving sceptics that are focused on erasing 'existing epistemic resources that undermine dominant narratives about the relationship of these experiences to larger structures of oppression' (Berenstain 2016: 571). These colonial attitudes led Manu Vimalassary, Juliana Hu Pegues and Alyosha Goldstein (2016: 1) to write about what they termed 'colonial unknowing' founded on 'colonial agnosia, agnotolgy, and epistemologies of ignorance' which enabled a refusal to engage with colonialism 'as an extensive and constitutive living formation by those situated in complicity with colonial occupation'. According to Vimalassary *et al.* (2016: 2), 'At stake in colonial agnosia is the profound investment in maintaining the failure to comprehend the realities of colonialism by those people who might most benefit from these conditions.'

What has compounded the decolonial struggles is the fact that racism has reached its most dangerous form where it is invisible and institutionalized. It, therefore, needs new tools of analysis to unmask it or else one falls into the neo-liberal trap and myth of a post-racial world and postcolonial world (Ndlovu-Gatsheni 2013). Taken together, all these decolonial attitudes are necessary in the decolonial struggle to implement epistemological decolonization and setting afoot new humanism.

Epistemological decolonization and circulation of knowledge

Denial of being automatically denies epistemic virtue. This is simply because non-humans do not produce knowledge. They might have instincts but not knowledge. Thus, the struggle for re-humanizing has to entail epistemological decolonization. Today the most important aspect of decoloniality is epistemological decoloniza-tion. We have not yet reached a stage where we can talk of 'global economy of knowledge' as a common human heritage. The work of Paulin J. Hountondji (1997; 2002) points to the continued asymmetry of power in knowledge production and circulation, which he understood as constituted by 'scientific extraversion' which necessitates the epistemic struggle to 'create, in Africa, of autonomous space for reflection and theoretical discussion that is indissolubly philosophical and scientific' (see Hountondji 2002: 103). Table 3.1 summarizes the complex dimensions of epistemological decolonization and the equally complex circulation of knowledge.

What is emerging is the importance of epistemic freedom as the foundation of other freedoms. Epistemic freedom has the potential to create new political consciousness and new economic thought necessary for creating African futures. Unless African people extricate themselves from epistemic coloniality first, even the 'political kingdom' would remain artificial presided over by leaders suffering from what Fanon termed 'pitfalls of consciousness' and what Steve Bantu Biko understood as imposed inferiority complexes (Fanon 1968; Biko 1978). Epistemic freedom is necessary for building decolonial consciousness and decolonial pedagogy as key aspect of epistemological decolonization.

TABLE 3.1 Dimensions of epistemic decolonization

Dimension of decolonization	Explanatory notes
1. Provincializing Europe while deprovincializing Africa/Moving the centre	This entails two moves: restoration of Africa as a legitimate epistemic site of knowledge and taking seriously African knowledge as a departure point without necessarily throwing away knowledge from Europe and North America. The purpose is to deal with the crisis of relevance and alienation. It is a restorative move that enable Africans to see themselves clearly. It entails shifting of a position from which Africans know and interpret the world (Ngugi wa Thiong'o 1986). Thus while others like Dipesh Chakrabarty (2000) emphasized the notion of 'provincializing Europe', the African decolonial theorists of the twenty-first century are pushing for 'deprovincializing Africa' making it a centre after centuries of peripherization (Mbembe 2017).

continued . . .

TABLE 3.1 Continued

Dimension of decolonization	Explanatory notes
2. Africanization of knowledge	This entails reassertion of African identity and refounding of knowledge on African cultures and values. It is a recovery process predicated on ideas of endogenous knowledge as 'an internal product drawn from a given cultural background, as opposed to another category of knowledge which would be imported from elsewhere' (Hountondji 1997: 17).
3. Adding/including African knowledge into existing canon of knowledge	This is a poor form of decolonization that takes the lazy format of just adding new items to the existing canon and existing curriculum. The pre-occupation here is with adding new content without reconfiguring the curriculum.
4. Decolonial critical engagement with existing knowledge	This approach entails deep questioning of 'received' knowledge and critical engagement with the politics of knowledge production and dissemination. This approach seeks to unmask the concealed problems such as racism and embedded asymmetrical power dynamics. Decolonial critical engagement with existing knowledge must also involve questioning even endogenous knowledge in the manner Hountondji did when he raised the problem of unanimity and collectivity in what became known as 'ethnophilosophy'.
5. Nativism and ghettoization of knowledge	This is a very poor understanding of epistemological decolonization as that of delinking and self-enclosure informed by racial essentialization of identity to the extent of reproducing that which colonialism imposed such as chauvinism, racism, sexism and xenophobia (Fanon 1968; Jansen 2017: 167–169). The unfortunate result is what one can term 'epistemic xenophobia' which impoverishes knowledge rather than enriching it.
6. Democratizing knowledge/ecologies of knowledge	This entails opening up of the academy to a plurality of knowledges including the subjugated ones as part of achievement of cognitive justice (Santos 2014). This opening up to ecologies of knowledge is meant to produce 'convivial scholarship' which 'confronts and humbles the challenge of over-prescription, over-standardization, over-routinization and over-prediction' (Nyamnjoh 2017: 5).

Sources: Ngugi wa Thiong'o 1986; Hountondji 1997; Santos 2014

Decolonial pedagogy

Epistemological decolonization cannot be fully realized without its partner, which is decolonial pedagogy. Decolonial pedagogy speak to the re-humanization in the domain of teaching and learning. Paulo Freire (1998: 89) posited 'I cannot be a teacher without exposing who I am.' Revealing one's epistemic positionality contributes towards building the necessary trust and confidence in the teacher-student relationship. Nothing has to be hidden. Epistemological decolonization demands a decolonial epistemic position that is consistently and systematically empathetic to those human species that Frantz Fanon (1968) depicted as the 'wretched of the earth', Paulo Freire (1970) simply termed 'the oppressed', Bernard Magubane (2010) described as the 'dispensable Other'; Madina V. Tlostanova and Walter D. Mignolo (2012) characterized as the 'anthropos of the planet' and Homi Bhabha understood as 'those who have suffered the sentence of history' (Bhabha cited in Sandoval 2000: 1).

The 'sentence of history' speaks to the systemic distancing of the colonized and (ex)-colonized people from their own knowledges and cultures so as to make them to enter the colonial path of imbibing and regurgitation of knowledges from Europe and North America. It also speaks to the process of deliberate 'stupidification' of African children, youth and even academics through consistent disciplining into abandonment of their mother tongues so as to use imperial and colonial languages of domination in their research, teaching, learning and even everyday conversations and communication. The fundamental challenge is, therefore, how to change the lives of 'those who have historically been hurt and silenced in the name of development or even internationalism' (De Lissovoy 2010: 280). This is where decolonial pedagogy emerges as a solution. Decolonial pedagogy seeks to radically transform hierarchical relations in the teaching-learning domain. It is a re-humanization pedagogy. Its key concern is to establish ethical university citizenship underpinned by ethics of living together. It is also a re-membering process that puts the student at the centre of the academic project of the university not as a customer but a co-producer of knowledge.

Decolonial pedagogy is 'a pedagogy of lovingness' committed to introduction of 'non-dominative principles of coexistence and kindredness' (De Lissovoy 2010: 279). Caring and love are central leitmotifs of decolonial pedagogy (De Lissovoy 2008). Thus decolonial pedagogy entails a paradigmatic shift from the long-standing hierarchical and dehumanizing 'lecturer-student' model that not only disempower the student but also fetishized the whole teaching-learning environment into a disciplinary site rather a space of co-creation of knowledge.

At the centre of decolonial pedagogy is the imperative of 'academic democracy'. Introducing this important concept, Ali A. Mazrui posited:

> Throughout the modern phase of history, the university as an institution in the world has rested on a basic contradiction. The contradiction lies in the tensions between academic freedom and academic democracy. Academic freedom includes within it the right to hold and to express opinions, the right to teach and to be taught without external interference, the right of access to academic knowledge, and the right to participate in expanding the frontiers of knowledge. Academic democracy, on the other hand, concerns

the process of decision making within the academic institution. How widely distributed is the right of participation in academic decision-making? How effectively are different interests within the institution represented within the structure of power? How powerful are heads of departments, deans, the vice-chancellor, and administrative committees of the university? What influences do junior staff and students exercise on policy making. We see here, then, that academic freedom is primarily a matter of freedom from interference, whilst academic democracy concerns the right to participate.

(Mazrui 1978: 235)

While academic freedom has many advocates, academic democracy remains an orphan because of acceptance of the hierarchical organization of university. This why Mazrui argued:

But academic democracy was less fortunate. The organization of universities continued to be hierarchical. [. . .] The rights to hold and express opinions were eloquently championed, and sometimes eloquently defended. But the right to participate in the decision-making process of the university was more restricted.

(Mazrui 1978: 237–238)

Academic democracy as opposed to academic freedom speaks to such rights as the student assessment of teachers, role in choice of courses/modules offered, influence in course/module development and even in the establishment of new disciplines and academic department. What is also privileged in decolonial pedagogy is attainment of 'epistemic freedom' – which entails the right to think and produce new knowledge from various epistemic sites including Africa.

Decolonization of teaching and learning entails anchoring pedagogy on African cultural foundation as part of dealing with the long-standing problems of epistemicides, linguicides and alienation. Decolonized education cannot continue to assume a civilizing mission paradigm aimed at producing Westernized African elites who are disconnected from Africa to the extent of looting its resources for individual enrichment (Ndlovu-Gatsheni 2017). Decolonial pedagogy is a necessity in the struggle to decolonize teaching and learning. However, any serious delving into the teaching and learning domain at any level of education in Africa encounters the realities of alienation, dislocated mentalities and resilient civilizing missing paradigm masquerading as teaching. This reality makes it necessary to focus attention on the teaching and learning domain as a theatre of dehumanization that needs to be urgently decolonized so as to make it a terrain of re-humanization.

Decolonizing teaching and learning

In a context where colonialism actively and deliberately desocialized Africans from their culture, values, languages, spiritualities and names, education has to be

a re-socialization activity. Ngugi wa Thiong'o (1986: 101–102) provided 11 questions that can guide us in our search for relevance in the domain of teaching and
learning. He emphasized seven important issues. The first is the 'base' on which
the education system is anchored. Is it Eurocentric or Africa-centred? The second
is the importance of the philosophy of the education system. The third is the
consciousness and identity of the teachers. The fourth is the reading material given
to students. The fifth is about the production of what kind of an African. The
sixth is the dominant economy and its requirements. The final is the government
policy. He concluded:

> Whether recommendations in the quest for relevance are successful or not
> ultimately depend on the entire government policy towards culture, educa-
> tion and language, and on where and how it stands in the anti-imperialist
> process in Africa today.
>
> (Ngugi wa Thiong'o 1986: 102)

The problem of consciousness of university teachers

In underscoring the importance of the consciousness of teachers in the delivery of
decolonized education, Ngugi wa Thiong'o (1986: 102) posed related but useful
questions:

> What then are the materials they should be exposed to: and in what order
> and perspective? Who should be interpreting that material to them: an
> African or non-African? If African, what kind of African? One who has
> internalized the colonial world outlook or one attempting to break free from
> the inherited slave consciousness?

What emerges from these questions is the importance of the material to which
students are exposed and the consciousness of the teachers in the delivery of the
material. Most often one gets the impression that it is the quality of students that
is discussed and very little is said about the quality of the teachers and their
consciousness. There is a lot that is wrong with the academics produced by
Western-style universities. The key problem is their mentalities and consciousness
cascading from what Carter G. Woodson (1933) termed 'miseducation'. The
result is that most of the academics and intellectuals continue to produce and
deliver what Claude Ake (1979) described as 'knowledges for equilibrium'.

If indeed the key problem with the African academics is that of consciousness
caused by miseducation, then the focus on changing the very idea of the university
as the factory that produced the academics and intellectuals should be accompanied by re-education of its products. The troubling aspect of miseducation is
that it promotes arrogance which is not consonant with the demands of decolonial pedagogy. It destroys the spirit of care and love that is core to the decolonial
pedagogy. The domain of assessment is where asymmetrical power relations and

open abuse of power manifest itself most. This reality led H. Giroux (1984: 84) to argue: 'The correlation between power and subordinancy in the classroom finds its most blatant expression in the grading process. Grades are used, in many cases, as soft cops to promote social conformity and to enforce institutional sanctions'.

When it comes to assessment that is where one can clearly see the fact that legacy and habit hangs on the minds of academics like a nightmare. They cannot change. Imagination, creativity and originality become very limited if not scarce. Those who try to deviate radically from this legacy and habit are punished severely (refer to the case of Professor Denis Rancourt of the University of Ottawa in Canada who lost his job in 2014 because he became convinced that grading undermines learning and is undemocratic and began to use other forms of assessment) (Tannock 2017: 1345–1346).

The second area of conservatism in academia is that of methodology, which is treated as a sacred cow despite the fact that Fanon (1968) not only critiqued it and advised us (those from humanities and social sciences) to leave it for 'botanists and mathematicians' and Linda Tuhiwai Smith (1999) revealed its dirty history. Students are still expected to reveal their methodology prior to even doing the actual research. Methodology is strictly assessed as though the student has already done the research. No compromises on methodology perhaps because it determines *a priori* the knowledge to be produced (Ndlovu-Gatsheni 2017a).

The challenge of re-education of the (ex-)colonized

The re-education process entails what Ngugi wa Thiong'o (1986) termed a 'return to the base' and what Ramon Grosfoguel (2007) articulated as the locus of enunciation. In his latest book entitled *Secure the Base: Making Africa Visible in the Globe* (2016: 50), Ngugi wa Thiong'o defined 'the base' as 'the people' and he elaborated:

> A return to the base, the people, must mean at the very least the use of a language and languages that the people speak. Any further linguistic additions should be for strengthening, deepening and widening this power of the languages spoken by the people.

South African universities in particular are currently engrossed in heated debates about 'intellectualization' of indigenous African languages, that is use of these as 'languages of learning and teaching' (Kaschula and Maseko 2017: 20). He urged the African academics and intellectuals not to remain 'outsiders in our own land' through reconnecting 'with the buried alluvium of African memory – that must become the base for planting African memory anew in the continent and the world' (Ngugi wa Thiong'o 2016: 76). The starting point is to be clear that Africa is the base from which we look at the world. This repositioning of our world-sensing entails taking African archive as the starting point in our research, teaching and learning.

Deprovincializing Africa

Knowledge continues to radiate from a hegemonic centre despite the existence of a globalized world. What masquerades as the 'global knowledge economy' has a hegemonic centre from which it circulates – that centre is Europe and North America. On this point Raewyn Connell (2016) posited: 'Modern universities and their staff and students exist in a global economy of knowledge, with a definite geography of production and circulation.'

Thus, one of the specific challenges we have to deal with as we engage in re-examination of teaching and learning is that of marginalization of African scholarship in the so-called 'global knowledge economy'. This marginalization of African scholarship is part of a deliberate division of labour rooted in imperialism and colonialism in which scholars of Africa and the rest of the Global South have been reduced to hunter-gatherers of raw data that is turned into theories in the Global North, 'native informants' as well as consumers of theories, concepts and method-ologies cascading from the Global North (Hountondji 1997).

Part of the practical solutions include the systematic shifting of the geography and biography of knowledge, partly because the knowledges that took us to this current phase of epistemic/systemic crisis cannot be the same knowledges that pull us out of this crisis and partly due to the fact that those considered to be giants in the modern academy still come from Europe and North America. Practically, we have to change the giants on whose shoulders we stand in terms of their geography of origin and their race, gender and generation, if we are to attain the desired 'ecologies of knowledges' (Santos 2014; Ndlovu-Gatsheni 2017b).

Decolonizing critical theory

Rethinking thinking itself also entails 'decolonizing the normative foundations of critical theory' itself and deployment of deep critical stance on the resilient ideas of progress, development, modernity and emancipation as scaffolds of dominant Western normative thought (Allen 2016). Delving into the necessary questioning of the very normative foundations of dominant critical theory, Edward Said (1993) criticized the Frankfurt School's critical theory for being 'stunningly silent on racist theory, anti-imperialist resistance, and oppositional practice in the empire' and for pursuing what he termed uncritical and false universalism predicated on 'inequality of races' and subordination of other parts of the world. What blinded the otherwise critical theorists of the Frankfurt School was the normative foundation of their thinking.

Amy Allen (2016: 3) noted that the Frankfurt scholars' fidelity to historical ideas of progress is 'the biggest obstacle to the project of decolonizing their approaches to critical theory'. What most Eurocentric theorists fail to accept is that the very processes of progress, modernity, development and even emancipation enabled de-humanization, enslavement, colonialism, imperialism, oppression, exploitation and domination of two-thirds of the world's population (Allen 2016: 3).

The second move is to always review the relevance of thinking itself. Immanuel Wallerstein (1999: 4) argued that it is a habit in scholarship to rethink issues in the context of new evidence that 'undermines old theories and predictions do not hold'. He went further to posit that 'we need to unthink nineteenth-century social science, because many of its presumption – which, in my view are misleading and constrictive – still have far too strong a hold on our mentalities' (Wallerstein 1999: 4). According to Wallerstein (1999: 4), the key 'presumptions' of the 'nineteenth-century social science', which were, once 'liberating of the spirit, serve today as central intellectual barrier to useful analysis of the social world'.

Wallerstein's concerns are shared by Patrick Chabal (2012: 335) who concluded 'The end of conceit is upon us. Western rationality must be rethought'. It is the same concerns that provoked Jean Comaroff and John L. Comaroff (2012: 1–2) to argue for a paradigm shift from Western Enlightenment 'epistemic scaffold' of knowledge to the Global South in general and Africa in particular as an epistemic site from which the world is understood and interpreted. This has been a long-standing argument of decolonial theorists. Thus, the imperative of rethinking and even unthinking 'thinking itself' is part of the necessary recognition of the limits and problems of the current knowledge and pedagogies. Cathrine Odora Hoppers and Howard Richards (2012; 8) defined 'rethinking thinking' as:

> The casting of light at last onto subjugated peoples, knowledges, histories and ways of living unsettles the toxic pond and transforms passive analysis into a generative force that valorises and recreates life for those previously museumised.

Learning to unlearn in order to relearn

Learning to unlearn in order to relearn speaks to the challenges of desocialization and re-socialization in the domain of knowledge as well as teaching and learning. This challenge arose from a context where missionary and colonial education taught Africans a lot of wrong things including negative perceptions of ourselves and our continent. This education taught us that white people were superior and black people were inferior. The forcible imposition of colonial languages like French and English as languages of teaching and learning created an impression that their mastery was a sign of being intelligent.

Consequently, many educated African people distanced themselves from their indigenous African languages and ancestors whom the Christian missionaries disparaged as 'demons'. This harm that was imposed on African people cannot be reversed unless African people deliberately embark on the painstaking process of 'learning to unlearn in order to re-learn'. Tlostanova and Mignolo (2012: 7) defined 'learning to unlearn' as 'to forget what we have been taught, to break free from the thinking programmes imposed on us by education, culture, and social environment, always marked by the Western imperial reason'. Decolonial pedagogy has to facilitate this unique pedagogy of unlearning as part of epistemological decolonization.

Conclusion

The reality of the existence of coloniality all over the world makes decoloniality a necessary and important planetary struggle. Decoloniality is not a backward-looking philosophy of liberation – it gestures towards a world that is better than both the pre-colonial and colonial worlds. The springs that water decoloniality is the anti-colonial archive – a rich and relevant human heritage and oasis of possibilities in world that is experiencing systemic and epistemic crisis (el-Malik and Kamola 2017). Issac Kamola (2017: 2) explained why this knowledge is key to human survival:

> The twentieth-century struggles against colonialism in Africa, the African Diaspora, and around the world, seem to once again speak in instructive and unexpected ways. There is good reason for this return. These voices are poetic yet strident, theoretical but immediately practical to the particularities of struggle. These writings on colonialism, race, class violence, and governance avoid abstract musing – and the polish and perfection of argument that goes along with it. Instead, they are timely statements made with great urgency. The assumed audience of African anticolonial thought was often not scholars, but rather one's immediate and intimate comrades. The horizons of these texts and arguments often contained futures filled with possibility, even if the specific outlines are not entirely discernible in the present moment.

Indeed, at the very centre of the anti-colonial archive is the very planetary horizon of human struggle for belonging to the world and consistent critique of exclusion of other human beings from the human family. It is, therefore, highly sensible to ground contemporary thought and imaginings of human freedom on the anti-colonial archive and the epistemologies of the South.

References

Ake, C. 1979. *Social Science as Imperialism: The Theory of Political Development*. Ibadan: University of Ibadan Press.

Allen, A. 2016. *The End of Progress: Decolonizing the Normative Foundations of Critical Theory*. New York: Columbia University Press.

Berenstain, N. 2016. 'Epistemic Exploitation'. *Ergo: An Open Access Journal of Philosophy*, 3(22), pp. 569–590.

Bhabha cited in Sandoval, C. 2000. *Methodology of the Oppressed*. Minneapolis, MT and London: University of Minnesota Press.

Biko, S. 1978. *I Write What I Want*. Harmondsworth, UK: Penguin Books.

Booysen, S. (ed.) 2016. *Fees Must Fall: Student Revolt, Decolonization and Governance in South Africa*. Johannesburg: Wits University Press.

Chabal, P. 2012. *The End of Conceit: Western Rationality after Postcolonialism*. London and New York: Zed Books.

Chakrabarty, D. 2000. *Provincializing Europe: Postcolonial Thought and Historical Difference*. Princeton, NJ: Princeton University Press.

Comaroff, J. and Comaroff, J. L. 2012. *Theory from the South or How Euro-America Is Evolving Towards Africa*. Boulder, CO and London: Paradigm.

Connell, R. 2016. 'Decolonizing Knowledge, Democratizing Curriculum'. Unpublished Paper Prepared for Presentation at the Decolonizing of Knowledge Discussion, University of Johannesburg, March.

Cornell, D. and Seely, S. D. 2016. *The Spirit of Revolution: Beyond the Dead Ends of Man*. Cambridge, UK: Polity Press.

De Lissovoy, N. 2008. *Power, Crisis, and Education for Liberation: Rethinking Critical Pedagogy*. New York: Palgrave Macmillan.

De Lissovoy, N. 2010. 'Decolonial Pedagogy and the Ethics of the Global'. *Discourse: Studies in the Cultural Politics of Education*, 31(3), pp. 279–293.

Dussel, E. 2006. 'The Anti-Cartesian Meditations'. Poligrafi, 41–42, 5–60. Available at: (accessed 5 January 2018).

Dussel, E. 2008. *Twenty Thesis on Politics*. Translated by George Ciccariello-Maher. Durham, NC: Duke University Press.

el-Malik, S. S. and Kamola, I. A. 2017. 'Introduction: Politics of African Anticolonial Archive'. In S. S. el-Malik and I A. Kamola (eds) *Politics of African Anticolonial Archive*. New York and London: Rowman and Littlefield International, pp. 1–15.

Erasmus, Z. 2017. *Race Otherwise: Forging New Humanism for South Africa*. Johannesburg: Wits University Press.

Fanon, F. 1968. *The Wretched of the Earth*. New York: Grove Press.

Freire, P. 1970. *Pedagogy of the Oppressed*. London: Penguin Books.

Freire, P. 1998. *Pedagogy of Freedom: Ethics, Democracy, and Civic Courage*. Lenham, MD: Rowman & Littlefield.

Giroux, H. 1984. *Ideology, Culture and the Process of Schooling*. London: Falmer.

Grosfoguel, R. 2007. 'The Epistemic Decolonial Turn: Beyond Political-Economy Paradigms'. *Cultural Studies*, 21(2–3), (March/May), pp. 211–223.

Hoppers, C. O. and Richards, H. 2012. *Rethinking Thinking: Modernity's 'Other' and the Transformation of the University*. Pretoria: UNISA Press.

Hountondji, P. J. 1997. 'Introduction: Recentring Africa' In P. Hountondji (ed.), *Endogenous Knowledge: Research Trails*. Dakar: CODESRIA Book Series, pp. 1–39.

Hountondji, P. J. 2002. *The Struggle for Meaning: Reflections on Philosophy, Culture and Democracy in Africa*. Translated by John Conteh-Morgan. Athens, OH: Ohio University Center for International Studies.

Jansen, J. 2017. *As By Fire: The End of the South African University*. Cape Town: Tafelberg.

Kamola, I. 2017. 'Review Essay: A Time for Anticolonial Theory'. *Contemporary Political Thought*, September, pp. 1–12.

Kaschula, R. H. and Maseko, P. 2017. 'Researching the Intellectualization of African Languages, Multilingualism and Education'. In R. H. Kaschula, P. Maseko and H. E. Wolff (eds), *Multilingualism and Intercultural Communication*. Johannesburg: Wits University Press, pp. 19–33.

Magubane, B. M. 2010. *Race and the Construction of the Dispensable Other*. Pretoria: UNISA Press.

Maldonado-Torres, N. 2007. 'On Coloniality of Being: Contributions to the Development of a Concept'. *Cultural Studies*, 21(2–3), (March/May), pp. 240–270.

Maldonado-Torres, N. 2008. *Against War: View from the Underside of Modernity*. Durham, NC: Duke University Press.

Maldonado-Torres, N. 2011. 'Thinking Through the Decolonial Turn: Post-Continental Interventions in Theory, Philosophy, and Critique – An Introduction'. *Transmodernity: Journal of Peripheral Cultural Production of Luso-Hispanic World*, Fall, pp. 1–25.

Maldonado-Torres, N. 2018. 'The Decolonial Turn'. In Juan Poblete (ed.), *New Approaches to Latin American Studies: Culture and Power*. New York and London: Routledge, pp. 111–127.

Mamdani, M. 2007. *Scholars in the Marketplace: The Dilemmas of Neo-Liberal Reform at Makerere University, 1989–2005*. Dakar: CODESRIA Books.

Mazrui, A. A. 1978. *Political Values and the Educated Class in Africa*. Berkeley and Los Angeles, CA: University of California Press.

Mbembe, A. 2002a. 'African Modes of Self-Writing'. *Public Culture*, 14(1), pp. 239–273.

Mbembe, A. 2002b. 'On the Power of the False'. *Public Culture*, 14(3), pp. 629–675.

Mbembe, A. 2017. *Critique of Black Reason*. Translated by Laurent Dubois. Durham, NC: Duke University Press.

Mishra, P. 2017. *Age of Anger: A History of the Present*. New York: Penguin Books.

More, M. P. 2017. *Biko: Philosophy, Identity and Liberation*. Cape Town: HSRC Press.

Morrison, T. 1975. 'A Humanistic View'. In *Public Dialogue on the American Dream Theme Part II*. Portland, OR: Portland State Black Studies Centre.

Mudimbe, V. Y. 1994. *The Idea of Africa*. Bloomington, IN: Indiana University Press.

Ndlovu-Gatsheni, S. J. 2013. *Coloniality of Power in Postcolonial Africa: Myths of Decolonization*. Dakar: CODESRIA Books.

Ndlovu-Gatsheni, S. J. 2016. *The Decolonial Mandela: Peace, Justice and the Politics of Life*. New York and Oxford, UK: Berghahn Books.

Ndlovu-Gatsheni, S. J. 2017a. 'Decolonizing Methodology Must Include Undoing Its Dirty History'. *The Conversation*, 28 September.

Ndlovu-Gatsheni, S. J. 2017b. 'The Changing Idea of the University and the Imperative of Decolonization in Higher Education Institutions of Technology in South Africa'. Unpublished Keynote Address Delivered at the 5th Annual Innovation in Learning and Teaching Conference: Re-Examining Teaching and Learning in the Context of University of Technology, Central University of Technology, Bloemfontein, 1–2 June.

Ndlovu-Gatsheni, S. J. and Zondi, S. (eds). 2016. *Decolonizing the University, Knowledge Systems and Disciplines in Africa*. Durham, NC: Carolina Academic Press.

Ngugi wa Thiong'o. 1986. *Decolonizing the Mind: The Politics of Language in African Literature*. Oxford, UK: James Currey.

Ngugi wa Thiong'o. 2009a. *Some Thing Torn and New: An African Renaissance*. New York: Basic Civitas Books.

Ngugi wa Thiong'o. 2009b. *Re-membering Africa*. Nairobi, Kampala and Dar es Salaam: East African Education Publishers.

Ngugi wa Thiong'o. 2012. *Globalectics: Theory and the Politics of Knowing*. New York: Columbia University Press.

Ngugi wa Thiong'o. 2016. *Secure the Base: Making Africa Visible in the Globe*. London, New York and Calcutta: Seagull Books.

Nyamnjoh, F. B. 2016. *Rhodes Must Fall: Nibbling at Resilient Colonialism in South Africa*. Bamenda: Langaa Research & Publishing CIG.

Nyamnjoh, F. B. 2017. *Drinking from the Cosmic Gourd: How Amos Tutuola Can Change Our Minds*. Bamenda: Langaa Research & Publishing CIG.

Ray, M. 2016. *Free Fall: Why South African Universities Are in a Race Against Time*. Johannesburg: Bookstorm.

Said, E. 1993. *Culture and Imperialism*. New York: Vintage.

Santos, B. de S. 2014. *Epistemologies of the South: Justice Against Epistemicide*. Boulder, CO and London: Paradigm.

Smith, L. T. 1999. *Decolonizing Methodologies*. Second Edition. London, New York and Dunedin: Zed Books and Otago University Press.

Suárez-Krabbe, J. 2016. *Race, Rights and Rebels: Alternatives to Human Rights and Development from the Global South*. London and New York: Rowman & Littlefield International.

Tannock, S. 2017. 'No Grades in Higher Education Now! Revisiting the Place of the Graded Assessment in the Reimagination of the Public University'. *Studies in Higher Education*, 42(8), pp. 1345–1357.

Thiam, C. 2014. *Return to the Kingdom of Childhood: Re-Envisioning the Legacy and Philosophical Relevance of Negritude*. Columbus, OH: The Ohio State University Press.

Tlostanova, M. V. and Mignolo, W. D. 2012. *Learning to Unlearn: Decolonial Reflections from Eurasia and the Americas*. Columbus, OH: The Ohio State University Press.

Vimalassery, M., Pegues, J. H. and Goldstein, A. 2016. 'On Colonial Unknowing'. *Theory and Event*, 19(4), (October), pp. 1–13.

Wallerstein, I. 1999. 'Introduction: Why Unthink?' In I. Wallerstein (ed.), *Unthinking Social Science: The Limits of Nineteenth-Century Paradigms*. Cambridge, UK: Polity Press, pp. 1–24.

Wallerstein, I. 2004. *The Uncertainties of Knowledge*. Philadelphia, PA: Temple University Press.

Wilder, G. 2015. *Freedom Time: Negritude, Decolonization and the Future of the World*. Durham, NC: Duke University Press.

Woodson, C. G. 1933. *The Miseducation of the Negro*. Virginia: Khalifa's Booksellers & Associates.

Wynter, S. 1984. 'The Economy Must be Found: After Humanism'. *Boundary*, 2(1), pp. 19–70.

Wynter, S. 2001. 'Towards the Sociogenetic Principle: Fanon, Identity, the Puzzle of Conscious Experience, and What It Is Like to Be 'Black'. In M. F. Duran-Cogan and A. Gomez-Moriana (eds), *National Identities and Sociopolitical Changes in Latin America*. New York: Routledge, pp. 30–66.

Wynter, S. 2003. 'Unsettling the Coloniality of Being/Power/Truth/Freedom: Towards the Human, After Man, Its Overrepresentation – An Argument'. *CR: The New Centennial Review*, 3(3), pp. 257–337.

Wynter, S. 2007. 'Human Being as Noun? Or Being Human as Praxis? Towards the Autopoietic Turn/Overturn: A Manifesto'. Available at: www.scribd.com/doc/23780 9437/Sylivia-Wynter-The-Autopoetic-Turn-scribd (accessed 5 January 2018).

Yountae, A. 2017. *The Decolonial Abyss: Mysticism and Cosmopolitics from the Ruins*. New York: Fordham University Press.

4

RECONSTITUTING THE POLITICAL

Introduction

Does the new testament 'Christian turn' offensive led by Jesus Christ of Nazareth targeting the old testament/Judaic/Abrahamic/Roman Christendom enclosed in rigidified Hebrew traditions and the ossified fundamentalist laws presided by an uncompromising and vengeful God (God of anger) not constitute, in a symbolic and ecclesiastical manner, what fundamentally is entailed in reconstitution of the political and setting afoot a new order of life? Jesus Christ's revolutionary humanistic politics predicated on a new gospel not only directly challenged the intellectuals of the old order known as the Sadducees and the Pharisees but consistently pushed the agenda of the poor into the centre of the new testament in the process, concretizing a clear 'Christian turn'. Jesus' sacrificial assassination on the cross at Calvary, partly in fulfillment of the scriptures and partly to enable the birth of a new order of life, which began with his resurrection after three days and the opening up of the 'Holy of Holies', not only enabled the excluded Gentiles into the direct love and favour of the new God (God of love) but also marked a very successful reconstituted of the old order. The line separating the Jews from the Gentiles was deleted. A new timescale emerged known as BC (Before Christ) and AD (After the Death of Christ). What emerges poignantly here is that a decolonial reconstitution of the political has to fundamentally redefine humanity in non-separatist terms and inaugurate a new dispensation of decolonial love (love thy neighbour in the same manner you love thy self). In this decolonized context, giving another chick to those still stuck in the paradigm of war and violence is symbolic of the banishment forever the 'eye-for-an-eye' barbaric warrior tradition.

It was perhaps this rather very successful ecclesiastical reconstitution of an old order of life that enchanted Karl Marx, a German Jew, who articulated a critical secular theory of conception of the political, which is today known Marxism. Most of the Marxist tenets such as the privileging of the poor workers as the key agents of history and the footsoldiers of planetary proletarian revolution and its horizon of socialism/communism appear to share a lot with Jesus' politics and gospel. For example, the promise of the poor inheriting the world is as Jesusian as it is Marxian. The horizon of the socialism/communism is akin to Jesusian Christian paradise. The neo-Marxist-Cabralian notion of 'class-suicide' is akin to the cruxification of Christ in the service of the poor. Carrying one's cross and abandoning all that which is material sounds like a revolutionary call to reject capitalism and its cultures of primitive accumulation, opulence and consumption predicated on exploitation of some human beings by others. But in a secular context, reconstituting the political takes the form of a decolonial move that entails a radical shift from the paradigm of war and the 'will to power' constitutive of coloniality to the 'will to live' and peace engrained in the decolonial politics (Dussel 2008).

Decolonial reconstitution of politics is founded on decolonial theory of life (Ndlovu-Gatsheni 2016). To gain a deeper understanding of the decolonial imperative of reconstituting the political it is necessary to begin with an evaluation of how the political has been constituted since the dawn of Euro-American modernity. The second intervention is to assess how African nationalists such as Patrice Lumumba, Amilcar Cabral, Kenneth Kaunda, Leopold Sedar Senghor and Nelson Rolihlahla Mandela deployed the philosophy of humanism in their contribution to the reconstitution of the political in the twentieth century. Such African leaders as Mandela and many others must also be understood as decolonial intellectuals because they not only dedicated their whole lives to the decolonial struggle aimed at setting afoot a new humanism but also developed decolonial concepts that help in reconstitution of the political.

In a broader sense, the reconstitution of the political is a decolonial struggle and process targeting coloniality. It seeks to dismantle its architecture and configuration. At the centre of the reconstituted political is a new ethics of living together that is not marked by what Boaventura de Sousa Santos (2007) described as 'abyssal thinking' and 'impossibility of copresence'. A reconstituted political also re-members and destroys the Manichean structure identified by Frantz Fanon (1968) where human species were divided into two zones of 'being' and 'non-being'. In a fundamental sense, the decolonial reconstitution of the political has to resolve what Nelson Maldonado-Torres (2007) termed 'coloniality of being' through facilitation of a shift from 'Man' to the 'Human' (see Wynter 2003). This chapter posits that the European conception of the political at the dawn of the Euromodernity corrupted the very noble vocation of the political through fetishism of power and naturalization of the paradigm of war and will to power that propelled them into enslavement of other human beings, conquest and colonization of other human beings, as well as denial of the very humanity of those who were considered non-European.

On the constitution of the political

In the European conception of the political there is its division into two related elements – the 'ontological' and the 'ontic' tenets. The former embraced such issues of norms, values, ideologies and notions of being human; and the latter is about political practices and institutions (see Mouffe 2005: 8). At the centre of the political as defined from the Euro-North-American-centric world is the paradigm of war. It was this centrality of war in the European constitution of the political which led the leading philosopher of liberation Enrique Dussel to posit:

> From Heraclitus to Karl von Clausewitz and Henry Kissinger, 'war is the origin of everything', if by 'everything' one understands the older or system that world dominators control by their power and armies. We are at war – a cold war for those who wage it, a hot war for those who suffer it, a peaceful coexistence for those who manufacture arms, a bloody existence for those obliged to buy and them.
>
> (Dussel 1985: 1)

This privileging of war bred *homo polemos* and the adversarial conception of the political. Here was also born the notion of 'ego conquiro' (I conquer, therefore I am), which preceded the Cartesian 'cogito ergo sum' (I think, therefore I am) (Dussel 1985: 3). This reality is well captured by Dussel (1985: 3): 'Before the *ego cogito* there is *ego conquiro*; "I conquer" is the practical foundation of "I think".' In other words, the unfolding of modernity became inextricable from the warrior and conqueror. To Nelson Maldonado-Torres (2008) the paradigm of war has existed as the naturalized underside of modernity.

One has to turn to the work of the European thinker Carl Schmitt (1976 [1932]) to gain a deeper understanding and veracity of Dussel's portrayal of the European constitution of the political. Schmitt posited that at the centre of the political is 'differentia specifica', that is friend/enemy discrimination, and he elaborated that the political 'can be understood only in the context of the friend/enemy grouping, regardless of the aspects which this possibility implies for morality, aesthetics and economic' (Schmitt 1976 [1932]: 35). Here was born the paradigm of difference, which is today haunting the modern world like a spectre. Chantal Mouffe (2005), in agreement with Schmitt, embraced his concept of 'constitutive outside' and stated:

> The aim is to highlight the fact that the creation of an identity implies the establishment of a difference, difference which is often constructed on the basis of a hierarchy, for example between form and matter, black and white, man and woman, etc. Once we have understood that every identity is relational and that the affirmation of a difference is a precondition for the existence of any identity, i.e. the perception of something 'other' which constitutes its 'exterior,' we are, I think, in a better position to understand Schmitt's point about the ever present possibility of antagonism and see how a social relation can become the breeding ground for antagonism.
>
> (Mouffe 2005: 15)

What Mouffe is doing here is reasserting the naturalization of paradigm of difference that set afoot what William E. B. Du Bois (1903) termed 'the colour line'. It is within this conception of the political that enslavement, imperialism, colonialism, apartheid and even genocides, epistemicides, culturecides and linguicides as constitutive elements of coloniality emerged. It is also in resistance to this Eurocentric conception of the political that the 'African anticolonial archive' emerged (e-Malik and Kamola 2017). Eurocentric conceptions of the political resulted in naturalization and routinization of the 'will to power' as the central leitmotif of pursuit of politics. Various European philosophers worked tirelessly to rationalize the paradigm of war and the will to power as legitimate drivers of politics.

However, philosophers and decolonial political activists from the Global South in general and those from Africa in particular; have mounted a robust critique of what Fanon (1968: 252) termed 'European technique and style'. At the scholarly level, Enrique Dussel (2008: xv) has worked towards reassertion of what he termed the 'noble vocation of politics'. This vocation has been patriotic and collective in essence. However, this vocation has been corrupted by the elites in charge of the modern global power architecture. The process of corrupting the political is known as 'fetishism of power' and it has taken the forms of rearticulation of politics in terms of the 'will to power' and the transformation of those entrusted to lead society turning out to be the centres and sources of power (Dussel 2008: 3). This is how Dussel explained the process of fetishism of power:

> This corruption, moreover, is double: it corrupts the governors who believe themselves to be sovereign centre of power, and it corrupts the political community that allows itself (consents) to become servile rather than be actor in the construction of the political [. . .] The Corrupted representative can use fetishized power for the pleasure of exercising his or her will as ostentatious vainglory, as despotic high-handedness, as sadism towards his or her enemies or toward the improper appropriation of goods and wealth.
>
> (Dussel 2008: 4)

Below is a rather telegraphic articulation of how African decolonial revolutionaries such as Patrice Lumumba, Kenneth Kaunda, Amilcar Cabral, Leopold Sedar Senghor and Nelson Mandela contributed to the reconstitution of the political.

Decolonial reconstitution of the political

While African decolonial nationalism has been heavily criticized in recent years for reproduction of colonial logics and failure to set afoot new humanism, it carried what Paul Tiyambe Zeleza (2003) termed 'nationalist humanism'. This African nationalist humanism was embodied by such leaders as Cabral, Mandela, Kwame Nkrumah, Julius Nyerere, Joshua Nkomo, Kaunda, Thomas Sankara,

Samoa Machel, Senghor, and Patrice Lumumba among many others. That they failed to implement it practically in most of the cases was due to the hovering colonial matrices of power always ready to punish those who demonstrated a radical commitment to abandon 'European game' and were prepared to something better. The list is long and made up of African leaders such as Nkrumah and Sankara who suffered sponsored military coup d'états and the likes of Cabral, Lumumba and Steve Biko who were assassinated. They suffered all these setbacks and direct eliminations because decolonial reconstitution of the political portended the end of Euro-American hegemony in all spheres of human life.

Patrice Lumumba

The case of Patrice Lumumba is a heroic and tragic one simultaneously. Lumumba was one of those earliest African leaders who embraced Pan-Africanism and was vehemently opposed to colonialism and imperialism. Coupled with the struggle for independence was the imperative for a unitary Congolese nation-state inhabited by citizens not subjects. This became the decolonial burden that Lumumba set himself as to achieve. Thus, out of all other anti-colonial movements, Lumumba's Mouvement National Congolais (MNC) stood for national unity whereas others succumbed to regional and ethnic politics and even neo-colonialist dirty politics (Nzongola-Ntalaja 2014: 66).

Ali Mazrui (1967)'s articulation of the context within which Lumumba of the Democratic Republic of Congo was assassinated revealed the challenges and dangers of facing those African leaders who were dedicated to the decolonial politics that entailed the very reconstitution of the political. Progressive decolonial nationalists like Lumumba dared to create something new and radically different from what was imposed by colonialism. But the structural and institutional terrain layout by colonialism was too inflexible to allow new politics and new humanism to emerge.

Lumumba died within a complicated political terrain of converging local and global power imperatives while he was trying to create Congolese for the first time out of a kaleidoscope of diverse ethnicities. Working within boundaries created by Belgian colonialism revealed the entrapment of African attempts to reconstitute the political in a politics shot through by the immanent logic of colonialism (Mazrui 1967: 6–7). Lumumba had the difficult task not only of defeating Belgian colonialism but also of making a people called Congolese. There were no Congolese in the pre-colonial period. Colonialism had never intended to invent Congolese. So the task to invent them for the first time fell on the shoulders of the African nationalists.

Thus, nationalist humanism was ranged against colonialism, tribalism, regionalism, global imperialism and the capitalism exploitative economic system – all evil inventions cascading from Euro-North American-centric modernity. Inevitably, these evil but powerful forces of tribalism and regionalism converged with the Cold War coloniality to enable the assassination of Lumumba on

17 January 1961. This is why Georges Nzongola-Ntalaja (2014: 117) concluded 'this assassination cannot be fully understood without reference to the world context, then dominated by the national liberation struggle in Africa and the Cold war internationally'. Ludo De Witte (2001: 53) depicted the death of Lumumba as 'one of the twentieth century's most important political assassinations'.

Lumumba was one of those African leaders who was working very hard against all odds of Belgian colonialists that were happy to offer only 'flag independence' and maintain control over the economy; the black people who were fragmented into different ethnic groups but were also impatient for radical change; the international community that was ideologically bifurcated into 'West' and 'East' blocs; and Africa that was not only on the cusp of fast-moving winds of change but was also engulfed by both the Bandung spirit and Pan-African spirit opposed to neo-colonialism. Nzongola-Ntalaja (2014: 117) captured well the imbroglio within which Lumumba found himself as he tried to reconstitute the political:

> It is in this regard that Lumumba's determination to achieve genuine independence and to have full control over Congo's resources in order to utilize them to improve the living conditions of its people was perceived as a threat to Western interests. To fight him, the United States and Belgium used all the tools and resources at their disposal, including the UN Secretariat under Hammarskjold and Bunche, Lumumba's Congolese political rivals, and hired killers.

The 30 June 1960 'Independence Speech' of Lumumba not only set him apart as an African leader committed to the decolonial agenda of reconstituting the political, but also exposed him as an enemy by those committed to the maintenance of coloniality. He put Belgian colonialism on public trial and exposed the falsity of colonial civilizing mission while at the same time openly claiming Congo natural resources for the Congolese.

Lumumba's decolonial thought is contained in four of his works: the 1959 poem entitled 'Weep O Beloved Black Brother'; his 'Independence Speech'; his last 'Prison Message' to the Congolese people; and his last 'Prison Letter' to his wife Pauline (Nzongola-Ntalaja 2014: 135). In the poem as well as in his speech, Lumumba pushed for economic and social justice for the colonized while also calling for cultural independence. But it was in his last letter to his wife that Lumumba displayed his radicalism and extraordinary commitment to liberation:

> Neither brutality, nor physical cruelty, nor torture has ever led me to beg for mercy, because I prefer dying with my head high, with unshakeable faith and deep confidence in the destiny of my country, rather than living in submission and contempt for sacred principles. History will one day have its say, but it will not be the history taught in Brussels, Washington, Paris, or at the United Nations, but the one taught in the countries emancipated

from colonialism and its puppet. Africa will write its own history, and it will be from north to south of the Sahara a history of glory and dignity.

(Lumumba cited in Nzongola-Ntalaja 2014: 140)

His commitment to Pan-Africanism spoke to the agenda of redrawing of African boundaries and the burial of the 'curse of Berlin' as Adebajo Adekeye (2010) named it. Between 25 and 31 August 1960, while already embroiled in a complex crisis, Lumumba organized and hosted a ministerial-level Pan-African conference in Kinshasa. In his opening address, he laid a Pan-African vision consisting of four points. The first point was total support for total liberation of Africa. The second point was non-alignment as the linchpin of international engagement and a sign of genuine independence. The third point was his commitment to the removal of all colonially inherited linguistic barriers to African integration. The fourth point was his vision of inter-African cooperation in the commercial, military, information, and scientific fields (Nzongola-Ntalaja 2014: 138). There is no doubt that the assassination of Lumumba robbed Africa of one of its most courageous and committed decolonial fighters.

Kenneth Kaunda

Kenneth Kaunda is one of those African leaders who understood that colonization did not operate as a political and economic system; it also intervened heavily on culture. Taking this reality into account, Kaunda posited that:

> This being the case, the act of political independence forms but the first part of the process of decolonization. This process is a very long one. Perhaps it is not possible to complete it in one generation, for it does not only require careful thought and planning, but also a lot of material, human and otherwise, to bring it about. In many ways it is even more difficult than attainment of political independence. All the same, time does come for leaders of any given revolution, if they know what they are doing, to think of starting to remould their society.

(Kaunda 1974: 3)

A clear drive to reconstitute the political was symbolized by Kaunda of Zambia's philosophy of humanism. In a pamphlet entitled *Humanism in Zambia and A Guide to Its Implementation* (1974), Kaunda outlined the content of his philosophy of humanism stating:

> I sincerely hope and pray that what follows will at least explain to him that I have long recognized the violent nature of the State today and that my colleagues and I have sought by working from inside the statecraft to make the world happier and less cruel than we found it.

(Kaunda 1974: ix)

Kaunda's philosophy of humanism was ranged against violence. He stated categorically clearly:

> Despite the fact that a humanist may be working within the power structure of the State, he must be a firm believer in non-violence; he must strive to create conditions – not only in one State but throughout the world – in which violence will cease to be the order of the day. One is thinking here about the violence that we witness in all walks of life, for example:
>
> – Self-violation of one's spiritual and moral being;
> – Physical violence against or between individuals;
> – Physical violence by the State against an individual and vice versa;
> – Physical violence between two States or indeed violence by one group of States against another group of States.
>
> (Kaunda 1974: x–xi)

Kaunda articulated and pitched his philosophy of humanism at the planetary level, stating:

> To begin with, the expectations of Man do not apply to Zambia alone insofar as Humanism is concerned. Humanism is looking at Man in global terms. Universally Man wants to love, to be loved, to seek truth and to create; he also wants peace, stability and progress, which translated into reality means, among other things, good food, good shelter, clean clothes and clean water, and he wants these things on the basis of freedom and justice.
>
> (Kaunda 1974: xii)

Zambia adopted humanism as its guiding liberatory philosophy in 1967. The aim was to build Zambia into an egalitarian society in which exploitation of one human being by another was not tolerated. Concretely, Kaunda tried to implement participatory democracy but within a framework of a one-party state and he also nationalized the commanding heights of the economy so as to make Zambia owners of the means of production. While Kaunda became increasingly criticized of being a dictator, this does not take away the fact that he is one of those African leaders who successfully built a stable 'nation-state' where ethnic difference was not a major problem.

What must be noted is that even the one-party state system of governance that was invented by such leaders as Kaunda and Julius Nyerere was part of the attempt to reconstitute the political. The logic was that competitive politics formed around multiple political parties tended to fragment society and threatened the young 'nation-states' that were being built in Africa. While the ideology of one-party-state ended up being a vehicle to nurture life-presidencies and monarchical forms of governance; it had emerged as part of political engineering by African leaders bent on inventing new forms of governance suited to their times and conditions.

What stands out about Kaunda is that he tried to govern in accordance with the philosophy of humanism where he was explicit on four key points:

- No person should starve in Zambia because there is no real land hunger as is the case in many other parts of the world.
- No person should really fail to have a decent two-or three-roomed Kimberly brick house.
- No person should really ever dress in rags in Zambia, nor, indeed go barefooted.
- No person should ever suffer from malnutrition in Zambia.

(Kaunda 1974: 39)

What is clear is that a humanistic national blueprint was clearly spelt out. Implementation depended on other factors. Kaunda's commitment to the total liberation of Africa, which entailed hosting such movements as Zimbabwe African People's Union (ZAPU), Zimbabwe African National Union (ZANU) and the African National Congress (ANC), contributed to the overstretching of national resources. Sabotage and open attacks by hostile white regimes bent on maintaining white settler colonial rule also contributed to the underdevelopment of Zambia. Of course, global coloniality was always against those African leaders like Kaunda who were committed to the reconstitution of the political and Pan-Africanism.

Amilcar Cabral

The other important decolonial theorist who contributed immensely to the rethinking and reconstitution of the political from a decolonial perspective was Amilcar Cabral of Cape Verde and Guinea-Bissau. His key concern was how to possibly invent a nation within a colonial structure that had produced racial, ethnic, class, and geographical differences (Kamola 2017: 83). The importance of Cabral lies in the production of an alternative language of politics that was anti-imperialist and decolonial. What distinguished Cabral as a decolonial theorist and humanist was the seriousness with which he took the local situation of Cape Verde and Guinea-Bissau in particular and Africa in general as his key locus of enunciation of decolonial revolutionary theory including indigenizing Marxism. He openly declared his locus of enunciation in these words: 'To start out from the reality of our land – to be realists' (Cabral 1979: 44).

Perhaps it was partly to do with his training as engineer that he had a profound ability to pay attention to factual detail of the society he was fighting to liberate in the same manner as an engineer concentrates on the components of a machine. He led an anti-colonial revolution that he also consistently studied in minute detail as he produced revolutionary theory. He declared:

Always bear in mind that the people are not fighting for ideas, for the things in anyone's head. They are fighting to win material benefits, to live better and in peace, to see their lives go forward, to guarantee the future of their children. [. . .]. We do not fall back on clichés or merely harp on the struggle against imperialism and colonialism in theoretical terms, but rather we point out concrete things [. . .]. Hide nothing from the masses of our people. Tell no lies. Expose lies whenever they are told. Mask no difficulties, mistakes, or failures. Claim no easy victories.

(Cabral 1970: 86)

Still emphasizing the importance of locus of enunciation in the development of alternative political and decolonial revolutionary theory which was realistic, Cabral (1979: 44) declared they had to start thinking 'with our feet planted on the ground'. Practically, this meant developing a very deep understanding of the reality on the ground and distilling positives and negatives as well as understanding weaknesses and strengths of the situation. To Cabral a national liberation struggle should be informed by reality not mere idealism and the strategy cannot be outsourced, hence he wrote that it would be a cardinal mistake 'to organize our Party on the lines of parties in France or any other country in Europe, or even Asia' (Cabral 1979: 45). Cabral was well aware of the fact that local reality was inextricably situated within a bigger reality that also needed to be fully understood:

Reality never exists in isolation. For example, our comrade Manuel Nandingma is a reality, is a real fact. But he cannot exist alone, he alone is nothing; a reality is never isolated from other realities.

(Cabral 1979: 47)

He understood that he was conducting a liberation war within a country, a region, a continent and the world. This is how Cabral reinterpreted the Marxist concept of dialectics to enlighten the African national liberation struggle's context of operation. This is why George Ciccariello-Maher, in his book entitled *Decolonizing Dialectics* (2017), emphasized the fact that anti–colonial/decolonial theorists and revolutionaries have long turned to dialectic thought as a central weapon in their fight against oppressive structures and conditions.

However, in their reconstitution of the political, the anti–colonial/decolonial theorists have resisted the historical determinism, economic determinism, teleology and Eurocentrism so as to rethink race, nation and popular identity. This way, African revolutionaries decolonize dialectics first in order to use them as weapon against coloniality. Thus, if indeed the Euro-dialectic of Hegel and Marx had limited its interventions to the problematics of master and slave and proletariat and bourgeoisie, the African decolonial revolutionaries like Cabral escalated it to challenge global coloniality.

Leopold Sedar Senghor

While Leopold Sedar Senghor's philosophy of Negritude was heavily criticized in the 1960s and 1970s, is today being rearticulated in positive terms by scholars such as Souleymane Bachir Diagne (2011); Cheikh Thiam (2014), and Gary Wilder (2015). Diagne is a leading Senegalese philosopher engaged in a new reading of Leopold Sedar Senghor's works. He sought to locate it historically and philosophically in what Henri Bergson termed 'the initial intuition' from which Senghor's work emerged and developed (Diagne 2011: 3). To Diagne, the 'initial intuition' for Senghor was 'African Art as philosophy' and 'the 1889 Revolution' that enabled him to understand 'vitalism' at the core of African religions and beliefs (Diagne 2011: 3–4). These religions and beliefs were also expressed in African arts. What Diagne uncovered was this:

> Negritude, as Senghor christened his philosophy, is a product of Africa and its diaspora; it is a product of the movement of the Harlem Renaissance; it is a product of Jean-Paul Satre, of Henri Bergson, of Lucien Levy-Bruhl, of Karl Marx and Friederich Engels, of Ferdinand Georg Frobenius, of Pablo Picasso, of Pierre Teihard de Chardin and of others. It is, in short, the theoretical use of all available means.
>
> (Diagne 2011: 5)

Building on all these resources, Senghor developed his own unique philosophy of Africanity. It is predicated on a deep appreciation of African art, an embodiment of African philosophy that is not reducible to Western rationalist thinking. It embodied feeling, intuition, thought, metaphysics, ontology, epistemology and humanism. This African philosophy emerged as Senghor delved deeper into the fundamental question: What do African masks mean? (Diagne 2011: 9–10). Senghor then posited that there are many ways of knowing. The scientific one is just another. This epistemic freedom enabled Senghor to construct an original philosophy of African cultures and was never shy to dialogue with the dominant thoughts of the time from his own African vantage point of African art. Negritude was never in the Senghorian sense an ideology of separated identities but that of diversity cascading from diverse cultures, civilizations and epistemologies (a tribute to mixture) (Diagne 2011: 200).

Thiam (2014) studied and affirmed Senghorian philosophy as an expression of 'an Afri-centred conception of the human' while remaining consistently critical of Western universalization of rationality as the only way of understanding the world. Afri-centred conception of the human is underpinned by an Afri-epistemology predicated on recognition of fluidity and plurality of states of being. While Diagne (2011) contextualized Senghor's philosophy in the initial intuition of African art, Thiam (2014) located a combination of youth experience (kingdom of childhood) in Senegal where he was exposed to African cultures and to the realities of racism in France. In Thiam's understanding of Senghor, he was consistently pre-occupied with three tormenting questions: 'Who am I? Who are we? What are we in this white world?' (Thiam 2014: 2), Hence to him Negritude was never a simplistic anti-rationality, a simplistic reverse-racism or a romantic culturalism. It was a form of 'decolonialitude': 'an anti-colonial discourse and a postcolonial reflection on otherness, an essentialist representation of Negroes and a Theory of Mestissage, a critique of Western rationality and an illustration of alternative modes of understanding the world' (Thiam 2014: 25).

Gary Wilder (2015) dug into the planetary dimension of Negritude, particularly its focus on restructuring the imperial world. He emphasized how Senghor and Cesaire deployed Negritude ideas to 'unthink France'. To Wilder (2015: 8), Negritude was not a simple 'affirmative theory of Africanity' but rather was also 'a critical theory of modernity'. Senghor (as cited in Wilder 2015: 51–52) had this to say about the struggle for inclusive civilization that transcended both 'abstract universalism' and 'concrete particularism':

> I believe that in the Civilization of the Universal into which we entered in the last quarter of century, Negritude will constitute, or already constitutes [. . .] an assembly of essential contributions [. . .] it will again play its essential role in the edification of a new humanism, more human because it will have reunited in their totality the contributions of all continents, of all races, of all nations.

Senghor articulated that Negritude began as a search for the 'return to [our] sources and the discovery of the black Grail' (ghetto-Negritude he termed it) tainted by racism before moving forward to 'open-Negritude' (planetary Negritude) (as cited in Wilder, 2015: 52). Building on 'open-Negritude', Senghor understood 'decolonization as a process of global restructuring wherein the fate of humanity and the future of the world were at stake' (as cited in Wilder 2015: 59). However painful the experiences of imperialism and colonialism were according to Senghor, they brought colonizers and colonized peoples together and the way forward was to create new inclusive transnational democratic arrangements as the colonized and the colonizers' worlds remain entangled forever (Wilder 2015).

Senghor remained critical of the Cartesian notion of being that privileged reason as a marker of being human. He said this notion reproduced the human as a 'reasonable animal' and he proceeded to spell out the gift of Negritude: 'to remake the unity of man and the World; to link flesh to spirit, man to his fellow man, the pebble to God' (Senghor cited in Wilder 2015: 61). Senghor envisaged a postcolonial world as 'a global mélange to which each civilization contributed its most distinctive and fully realized attributes' (Senghor cited in Wilder 2015: 61). Politically, Senghor favoured a democratic union of people irrespective of colour, rather than territorial political independence, and this made him the target of criticism as an apologist of colonialism in some quarters. Senghor, just like Fanon and Cesaire, emphasized human liberation over the sovereignty of states ('*Man* remains our ultimate concern, our *measure*') (Senghor cited in Wilder 2015: 224). He elaborated:

> *Man* must be the centre of our preoccupations. One does not construct a modern State for the pleasure of constructing it. The action is not an end

in itself. We must therefore protect ourselves from the will to power that defines the State, that crushes *Man* beneath the state. It is, in fact, about creating the black man within a humanity marching towards its total realization in time and space (emphasis in the original).

(Senghor cited in Wilder 2015: 230)

Senghor's idea was informed by four broad propositions: the first is that the world is composed of many distinct civilizations, each of which places the accent on a singular aspect of the human condition; the second is that every great civilization is a cultural crucible that accommodates contributions from other civilizations; the third is that imperialism created a situation of intense cultural interaction in which metropolitan and African peoples had an historic opportunity to fertilize each other; and, finally, that both colonizers and colonized will have to create a new civilization and a new humanism (Wilder, 2015).

It was Senghor who underscored the presence of Hitler in the bodies of modern women and men that needed to be exorcized for new humanism to emerge. To Senghor the essential pre-requisite for this was 'we must all kill the piece of [Hitler] that lives within us' (Senghor cited in Wilder 2015: 143). The second condition of possibility for the new humanism was a double decolonization involving colonizers abandoning their 'superiority complex' so as to recognize the colonized as equal human beings and the colonized rising up from an imposed 'inferiority complex' (Senghor cited in Wilder 2015: 162). These ideas led Senghor to present the idea of decolonization as 'a dialogical and dialectical gift between partners' (cited in Wilder 2015: 162). More profoundly, Senghor understood decolonization as a third revolution ranged against 'capitalist and communist materialisms' and aimed at bringing moral and religious concerns to the centre of the world while at the same time enabling 'peoples of colour' to play their role and 'contribute to the construction of the new planetary civilization' (cited in Wilder 2015: 228).

Senghor pushed for a combination of Negritude (old African collectivism) with Socialism (scientific socialism) as the building blocks in the creation of a better world (better than the colonially created one) and also 'better than our world before European conquest' (cited in Wilder 2015: 149). Consequently, Senghor also became a critic of both colonialism and territorial nationalism as he strongly believed that the unitary state was now historically outmoded. He pushed for a common French citizenship, not as an ethnicity or race, but as a political product of the empirical realities of encounters and interactions. His warning to fellow Africans was that even European nations were gravitating towards a larger pan-European community (the European Union) and that small colonies would never be 'truly independent', rather independence would be 'a poison gift' (Senghor cited in Wilder 2015: 152). He explained:

a mere nominal independence is a false independence. It can satisfy national pride, but it does not abolish the consciousness of alienation, the feeling of frustration, the inferiority complex, since it does not resolve the concrete problems facing the underdeveloped countries: to house, clothe, feed, cure, and educate the masses.

(Cited in Wilder 2015: 244)

Senghor envisaged a world that was not wholly African or European, but 'it will be a Métis world' (sort of Eurafrique) (cited in Wilder 2015: 161). Based on this understanding of Senghor's version of decolonization, Wilder (2015: 244) concluded:

An independent Senegal marked not the realization but the eclipse of his ultimate vision for decolonization. Rather than condemn Senghor as a failed national president, we should remember his warning that the form of freedom promised by territorial nationalism for African people was bound to fail.

The decolonial interventions of Senghor indicate that there was no singular understanding of decoloniality. They also highlight the planetary quality of decoloniality, whereby it was pitched at the level of human redemption and the remaking of the world. Mandela is another African thinker who contributed immensely to the reconstitution of the political.

Nelson Rolihlahla Mandela

Mandela's politics and philosophy of liberation manifested the desire for a world governed by what the Caribbean scholar Eduardo Mendieta (2008: vii) depicted as 'politics of life with others and for others'. In Mandela we witnessed a type of politics that was anchored on the 'will to live' rather than the 'will to power' (see Dussel 2008). He worked very hard towards the liberation of both the oppressed and the oppressor from the cul-de-sac of racial bitterness and hatred. Mandela's leadership during the transition from apartheid to democracy inaugurated a paradigm shift in understanding politics and political transition.

Mandela's approach subverted the long-standing Nuremberg paradigm of justice predominated since 1945. This paradigm focuses on prosecuting perpetrators of violence and other crimes. Mandela's new paradigm privileged political reform and social transformation of South Africa to end oppression and apartheid. However, the limit to Mandela's vision was that everything he envisioned depended on the total buy-in of both perpetrators and victims of apartheid. This is why, when he became the first black president of a democratic South Africa in May 1994, Mandela made important overtures to the erstwhile white racists; in doing so, he aimed to persuade them to abandon apartheid thinking and to travel with him to the new, inclusive, non-racial, democratic and 'pluriversal' society known as the 'rainbow nation'.

At the centre of Mandela's politics was a profound humanistic spirit of defending life itself. He opposed the paradigm of war even though the intransigency and brutality of apartheid forced him to embrace violence and war to protect those who were victims of the apartheid system. A paradigm of war defined as 'a way of conceiving humanity, knowledge, and social relations that privileges conflict or *polemos*' had no space in Mandela's politics. Mandela's predicated his politics on the philosophy of *ubuntu* (the African ethic of community, co-humanness, unity and harmony) and as he envisaged a non-racial, non-sexist, inclusive and democratic post-apartheid 'rainbow nation'. Mandela's life of struggle and his legacy embodied a consistent and active search for peace and harmony. In his autobiography, Mandela stated:

> I always know that deep down in every human heart, there was mercy and generosity. No one is born hating another person because of the colour of his skin, or his background, or his religion. People must learn to hate, and if they can learn to hate, they can be taught love, for love comes more naturally to the human heart than its opposite. Even the grimmest times in prison, when my comrades and I were pushed to our limits, I would see a glimmer of humanity in one of the guards, perhaps just for a second, but it was enough to assure me and keep me going. Man's goodness is a flame that can be hidden but never extinguished.
>
> (Mandela 1994: 609)

Mandela interpreted the anti-colonial/anti-apartheid struggle as a humanistic movement for restoration of human life. This is how he put it: 'This then is what the ANC (African National Congress) is fighting for. Their struggle is a truly national one. It is a struggle of the African people, inspired by their own suffering and their own experience. *It is a struggle for the right to live*' (Mandela 1994: 352 emphasis is mine).

Mandela's *Long Walk to Freedom* is a treatise in decolonial reconstitution of politics. In the face of apartheid's officially institutionalized racism, brutality and intolerance for dissent, Mandela emerged as the leading advocate of decolonization and the face of new non-racial inclusive humanism. Unlike cultural relativists and nativist nationalists, Mandela did not easily dismiss the Euro-North American modernist project of emancipation; instead, he fought for the realization of some of those positive aspects of it (human rights, democracy) that were denied to Africans but were enjoyed in Europe and North America. He was not obsessed with difference but fought to destroy it. This is why as a man from the 'zone of non-being', he was never shy of claiming entitlement to the fruits of human civilization that Europe and North America has stolen and were monopolizing as artefact of their particular history. Mandela used the basis of being a human being to claim human rights and democracy for African people.

Even intellectually flamboyant Eurocentric Slavoj Zizek (2013: 1) credited Mandela for providing a model of how to liberate a country from apartheid colonialism 'without succumbing to the temptation of dictatorial power and anti-capitalist posturing'. While during the course of the liberation struggle Mandela had imbibed Marxist ideas and the ANC had moved to the left at the time of the fall of juridical apartheid, he did not show any sign of being dogmatic and maintained South Africa as a multi-party-democracy, ensuring that the vibrancy of the national economy was insulated from hasty socialist experiments (Zizek 2013: 2). Mandela was worried more about denial of democracy rather than its Euro-North American genealogy and articulation. For example, Mandela expressed a deep appreciation of the British parliamentary democracy to the extent of depicting himself as 'an Anglophile' and stating openly:

> From the reading of Marxist literature and from conversations with Marxists, I have gained the impression that communists regard the parliamentary system of the West as undemocratic and reactionary. But, on the contrary, I am an admirer of such as system. The Magna Carta, the Petition of Rights and the Bill of Rights are documents which are held in veneration by democrats throughout the world. I have great respect for British political institutions, and for the country's system of justice. I regard the British Parliament as the most democratic institution in the world, and the independence and impartiality of its judiciary never fail to arouse my admiration. The American Congress, the country's doctrine of separation of powers, as well as the independence of its judiciary, arouse in me similar sentiments.
>
> (Mandela 1994: 351)

It would seem to Mandela that democracy and freedom were simple positive human values that should be enjoyed by every human being irrespective of race and location. This positive appraisal of the British political system must not be taken to mean that Mandela had no respect for his own African cultural and political background. Throughout his *Long Walk to Freedom*, Mandela frequently credited his own South African ethnic identity (the Xhosa people) and their traditional mode of governance, which he described as 'democracy in its purest form' because everyone involved, irrespective of societal rank, were allowed space to 'voice their opinions and were equal in their value as citizens' (Mandela 1994: 351).

Mandela on violence as a tool of liberation

It is best to understand Mandela a political pragmatist. He was instrumental in the formation of '*uMkhonto We Sizwe*' (Spear of the Nation) and became its commander-in-chief. But the humanist spirit had permeated the ANC to the extent that it subjected its fighting forces a strict ethical military conduct of only engaging in destabilization (attacking particular installations that represented the apartheid government such SASO Oil Refinery) and not in killing ordinary white people as military targets. Even when Mandela was being tried for treason, he continued to tower above the apartheid system's provocations, brutality and violence. He even invited the architects of apartheid to return to humanity in a moving speech delivered during the Rivonia Trials (1963–1964):

> During my lifetime, I have dedicated myself to this struggle of the African people. I have fought against white domination, and I have fought against black domination. I have cherished the ideal of a democratic and free society in which all persons live together in harmony with equal opportunities. It is an ideal which I hope to live for and to see realized. But if needs be, it is an ideal for which I am prepared to die.
>
> (Mandela 1994: 352)

Mandela (1994: 78) also articulated that the continued use of brutality and violence by the apartheid regime against unarmed anti-apartheid freedom fighters left them with no choice but 'to hit back by all means in our power in defense of our people, our future and our freedom'. Mandela committed his entire life to the liberation from the scourge of racial oppression of those who inhabited the 'zone of non-being'. Mandela developed a very deep concern about humanity as a whole and he wrote:

> It was during those long and lonely years that my hunger for the freedom of my people became a hunger for the freedom of all people, white and black. I knew as well as I know anything that the oppressor must be liberated just as surely as the oppressed. A man who takes away another man's freedom is a prisoner of hatred; he is locked behind the bars of prejudice and narrow-mindedness. I am not truly free if I am taking away someone else's freedom, just as surely as I am not free when my freedom is taken from me. The oppressed and the oppressor alike are robbed of their humanity.
>
> (Mandela 1994: 611)

Mandela's deep commitment to the liberation of humanity from the scourge of racism and coloniality informed his understanding of transitional justice.

Mandela on transitional justice

It was the Convention for a Democratic South Africa (CODESA) that Mandela pushed for political justice rather than the old-fashioned Nuremberg template of justice. The essential pre-requisite for CODESA's paradigm of justice was first, for warring South Africans to first of all find each other across the political divides, and second, for all South Africans to agree that apartheid was a crime against humanity. The third condition was to agree to build a better political society. Mahmood Mamdani (2013a: 33), a leading admirer of the CODESA paradigm of justice, argued that such a political justice must emerge from a particular understanding of mass violence as political rather than criminal. The expected outcome of such a political justice system is a reconstruction of political society through political reform as a lasting solution. In this context, both perpetrators and victims are redefined as 'survivors' in an attempt to find a way to transcend the paradigm of war and as part of the invention of new humanism (Mamdani 2013b: 12).

To achieve his goals, Mandela worked with other stalwarts of the anti-apartheid struggle like Joe Slovo (a leading South African communist who belonged to the South African Communist Party). Both men were fully committed to trying something new in the domain of transitional justice, and both identified that South Africa's political stalemate required political innovation and creativity to unblock. Mamdani (2013a: 36) captured this situation as follows: 'neither revolution (for liberation movements) nor military victory (for the apartheid regime) was on the cards'. Mandela (1994: 577) led the ANC into CODESA fully aware that it was another 'theatre of struggle, subject to advances and reverses as any other struggle'.

The anti-apartheid activist-cum scholar Frank B. Wilderson reinforced these points in 2010 when he argued that it took major tectonic shifts in the global paradigmatic arrangement of white power. Examples include the fall of the Soviet Union, which was the major backer of the ANC; the return of 40,000 exiles from Western capitals; and perhaps most notably, a crumbling global economy. According to Wilderson these factors played a crucial role 'for there to be synergistic meeting of Mandela's moral fiber and the aspirations of white economic power' (Wilderson 2010: 5). Indeed, imperatives and interests of white capitalists who were experiencing the biting effects of sanctions and popular unrest at home played an important role in influencing the negotiators. Apartheid South Africa was, by the late 1980s and early 1990s, essentially ungovernable – an anachronistic and dysfunctional system incompatible with capitalism. A way out of the crisis had to be found.

Clearly, what Mandela demanded from the apartheid regime was the dismantlement of apartheid and commitment to a non-racial, democratic and free society. He sought to achieve these goals through the following strategy: 'To make peace with an enemy, one must work with that enemy, and that enemy becomes your partner' (Mandela 1994: 598). From the ashes of juridical apartheid, the ANC and Mandela envisaged a new post-racial and 'pluriversal' political community founded on new humanism and inclusive citizenship. But the ghost of apartheid had to be exorcized. The Truth and Reconciliation Commission (TRC) was the chosen mechanism of 'laying ghosts of the dark past to rest with neither retributive justice nor promotion of a culture of impunity' (Ramphela 2008: 46). Mamdani (2013b: 13) credited the TRC for transcending the Nuremberg trap 'by displacing the logic of crime and punishment with that of crime and confession'.

Mamdani also distilled how the Nuremberg template of justice still influenced the TRC, particularly in its definition of a victim and a perpetrator. In the first place, victimhood was individualized as the responsibility of the perpetrator –

an assumption that had two immediate implications. The first was that a human rights violation could be narrowly defined 'as an action that violated the bodily integrity of an individual' (Mamdani 2013b: 13). The second implication was 'obscuring the fact that the violence of apartheid was mainly that of the state, not individual operatives' (Mamdani 2013b: 13).

ANC stalwart Joel Netshitenzhe (2012) explained the logic of the negotiations and the settlement from his organization's perspective:

> At the risk of oversimplification, it can be argued that a critical element of that settlement, from the point of view of the ANC, was the logic of capturing a bridgehead: to codify basic rights and use these as the basis for more thoroughgoing transformation of South African society.
>
> (Netshitenzhe 2012: 16)

Perhaps a strong confidence in the morality of decolonial humanism made the ANC, and Mandela even, naïve about how long the process of economic reconciliation could take. But Netshitenzhe reinforced the argument that decolonial humanism influenced Mandela's imagined post-apartheid South Africa. For him:

> The articulation of the ANC mission by some of its more visionary leaders suggests an approach that, in time, should transcend the detail of statistical bean counting and emphasis on race and explicitly incorporate *the desire to contribute to the evolution of human civilization. At the foundation of this should be democracy with a social content*, excellence in the acquisition of knowledge and the utilization of science and *a profound humanism*.
>
> (Netshitenzhe 2012: 27 emphasis is mine)

Mandela was a child of this ANC decolonial humanism, but concretely speaking, 1994 marked not only the end of administrative apartheid but more importantly the beginning of a difficult process of nation-building tempered by a delicate balance, one between allaying white fears and attending to black expectations and demands. This reality became a major test of the Mandela's political life.

Mandela as the first black president of South Africa

At a practical level Mandela's politics of life focused on ending the cycle of diminishing citizens' dignity. Thus, when he became the first black president of South Africa in 1994, Mandela practically implemented decolonial humanist vision of a post-racial pluriversal society. At the core of this vision was a rejection of racism and a deeper appreciation of difference. In this vision, difference is not interpreted in terms of superior and inferior races; instead, it is interpreted in terms of pluriversality and rainbow. Maldonado-Torres (2008: 45) has argued that the appreciation of human difference is informed by a humanistic 'interest in restoring authentic and critical sociality beyond the colour-line'. The leading philosopher of Africana existentialism Lewis R. Gordon (1995: 154) agreed, positing that 'the road out of misanthropy is a road that leads to the appreciation of the importance of difference'. Apartheid was a worse form of misanthropy founded on 'bad faith' and had to be transcended both symbolically and substantively.

This is why Mandela's presidency embraced a symbolic pedagogical nationalism towards the erstwhile racists in his forging of a new South Africa. Pedagogical nationalism is predicated on teaching and persuasion. Mandela's presidency practiced nation-building through the use of symbolic gestures such as sporting events or public appearances. For example, he visited the 94-year-old widow of Hendrik Verwoerd, an ideologue of apartheid and its architect. Mandela even agreed to the erection of a statue in remembrance of Verwoerd. He also visited Percy Yutar, a prosecutor during the Rivonia Trial that sentenced Mandela to life imprisonment. He even visited ex-apartheid President P. W. Botha. In response, he was criticized in some quarters of bending too much to placate whites, but his idea was to ensure that indeed the erstwhile 'settlers'/'citizens' and the erstwhile 'natives'/'subjects' were afforded enough room to be reborn politically into consenting citizens living in a new political society where racism was not tolerated (see Mamdani 1996).

Conclusion

Those African leaders such as Senghor, Nkrumah, Cabral, Kaunda, Lumumba and Mandela worked hard as committed fighters not only against colonialism but also for world peace in general. That the philosophy of humanism permeated their politics confirmed that they were committed ideologically to oppose the paradigm of war and its politics founded on 'the will to power' within which war was naturalized as a technique of pursuing politics by other means.

Perhaps partly because his country South Africa was the last to be freed from apartheid coloniality and partly due to the fact that he sacrificed almost the rest of his life in pursuit of a reconstituted political better than what imperialism and colonialism had bequeathed on modern society, Mandela's life of struggle and legacy embodied a new politics founded on 'the will to live', the politics of life and the paradigm of peace. Mandela provided an antidote to the paradigm of war. Mandela, unlike his colleagues such as Kaunda, who ended up accused of clinging to power and of being dictators, never became intoxicated by power.

However, today there is a young generation of political activists born after the end of juridical apartheid, and who are experiencing poverty and alienation, who are increasingly blaming Mandela for having sold them out. What is troubling about most of Mandela's critics is that they fail to appreciate the broader vision of reconstituting the political and because of that they are easily enchanted by politics stuck in the paradigm of war and its eye-for-an-eye traditions as the most revolutionary and progressive. They also easily forget the existential conditions, particularly the balance of forces that did not allow Mandela enough room to manoeuvre because he was dealing with an undefeated enemy. Mandela had to pursue a middle road through and through in the hopes that in the future white hegemony would be dismantled.

Mandela's vision of a post-racial pluriversal world remains powerful in a modern world that is trapped in a paradigm of war and a narrow Nuremberg paradigm of justice replicated by the International Criminal Court (ICC). The South African historian Paul Maylam (2009) rightfully argues that Mandela 'stands out among world leaders of the last century as a person not obsessed with power, not entangled in the politics of manipulation and spin, not enticed into conspicuous consumption, but forever humble, honest and human'. One wonders what Mandela would say about the rise of Donald Trump (Trumpism that is pivoted on the notion of 'America First') and such events as Brexit that seem to be fuelled by the resurgence of narrow territorial nationalism, nativism, xenophobia and myths of a world without others during the age of globalization.

References

Adekeye, A. 2010. *The Curse of Berlin: Africa After the Cold War*. Scottsville: University of KwaZulu-Natal Press.

Cabral, A. 1970. *Revolution in Guinea: Selected Texts*. New York and London: Monthly Review Press.

Cabral, A. 1979. *Unity and Struggle: Speeches and Writings of Amilcar Cabral*. New York and London: Monthly Review Press.

Ciccariello-Maher, G. 2017. *Decolonizing Dialectics*. Durham, NC and London: Duke University Press.

De Witte, L. 2001. *The Assassination of Lumumba*. Translated by Ann Wright and Renee Fenby. London: Verso.

Diagne, S. B. 2011. *African Art as Philosophy: Senghor, Bergeson and the Idea of Negritude*. Translated by Chike Jeffers. New York, London and Calcutta: Seagull Books.

Du Bois, W. E. B. 1903 [1994]. *The Souls of Black Folk*. New York: Dover Publications.

Dussel, E. 1985. *Philosophy of Liberation*. Translated from Spanish by Aquilina Martinez and Christine Morkovsky. Eugene, OR: Wipf & Stock.

Dussel, E. 2008. *Twenty Theses on Politics*. Translated by George Ciccariello-Maher. Durham, NC and London: Duke University Press.

e-Malik, S. S. and Kamola, I. A. 2017 (eds). *Politics of African Anticolonial Archive*. London and New York: Rowman & Littlefield International.

Fanon, F. 1968a. *The Wretched of the Earth*. New York: Grove Press.

Gordon, L. R. 1995. *Bad Faith and Antiblack Racism*. Atlantic Highlands. NJ: Humanities Press.

Kamola, I. A. 2017. 'Realism Without Abstraction: Amilcar Cabral and a Politics of the World'. In S. S. el-Malik and I. A. Kamola (eds), *Politics of African Anticolonial Archive*. London and New York: Rowman and Littlefield International, pp. 83–99.

Kaunda, K. K. 1974. *Humanism in Zambia and a Guide to Its Implementation Part II*. Lusaka: State House.

Maldonado-Torres, N. 2007. 'On the Coloniality of Being: Contr4ibutions to the Development of a Concept'. *Cultural Studies*, 21(2–3), (March/May), pp. 240–270.

Maldonado-Torres, N. 2008. *Against War: View from the Underside of Modernity*. Durham, NC and London: Duke University Press.

Mamdani, M. 1996. *Citizen and Subject: Contemporary Africa and the Legacy of Late* Princeton, NJ: Princeton University Press.

Mamdani, M. 2013a 'The Logic of Nuremberg'. *London Review of Books*, 7 November, pp. 33–34.

Mamdani, M. 2013b 'Beyond Nuremberg: The Historical Significance of the Post-Apartheid Transition in South Africa'. Unpublished Inaugural Lecture, Mapungubwe Institute for Strategic Reflection, University Witwatersrand, 18 March.

Mandela, N. 1994. *Long Walk to Freedom: The Autobiography of Nelson Mandela.* London: Little Brown.

Maylam, P. 2009. 'Archetypal Hero or Living Saint? The Veneration of Nelson Mandela'. *Historia*, 54(2), November, pp. 23–49.

Mazrui, A. A. 1967. *On Heroes and Uhuru-Worship: Essays on Independent Africa.* London: Longmans.

Mendieta, E. 2008. 'Foreword: The Liberation of Politics: Alterity, Solidarity, Liberation'. In E. Dussel, *Twenty Theses on Politics*, trans. George Ciccariello-Maher. Durham, NC and London: Duke University Press, pp. vii–xiii.

Mouffe, C. 2005. *On the Political.* London and New York: Routledge.

Ndlovu-Gatsheni, S. J. 2016. *The Decolonial Mandela: Peace, Justice and the Politics of Life.* New York: Berghahn Books.

Netshitenzhe, J. 2012, 'Second Keynote Address: A Continuing Search for Identity: Carrying The Burden of History'. In A. Lissoni, J. Soske, N. Erlank, N. Nieftagodien, and O. Badsha (eds), *One Hundred Years of the ANC: Debating Liberation Histories Today.* Johannesburg: Wits University Press. pp. 13–28.

Nzongola-Ntalaja, G. 2014. *Patrice Lumumba.* Athens, OH: Ohio University Press.

Ramphela, R. 2008. *Laying Ghosts to Rest: Dilemmas of the Transformation in South Africa.* Cape Town: Talfberg.

Thiam, C. 2014. *Return to the Kingdom of Childhood: Re-Envisioning the Legacy and Philosophical Relevance of Negritude.* Columbus, OH: The Ohio State University.

Santos, B. de S. 2007. 'Beyond Abyssal Thinking: From Global Lines to Ecologies of Knowledges'. *Review*, xxx(1), pp. 45–89.

Schmitt, C. 1976 [1932]. *The Concept of the Political.* New Brunswick, NJ: Rutgers University Press.

Wilder, G. 2015. *Freedom Time: Negritude, Decolonization and the Future of the World.* Durham, NC: Duke University Press.

Wilderson, F. B. 2010. 'Obama and Mandela: The Parallels and the Differences'. Unpublished Paper Presented at the Concerned Citizens of Laguna Woods Village, 2 February.

Wynter, S. 2003. 'Unsettling the Coloniality of Being/Power/Truth/Freedom: Towards then Human, After Man, Its Overrepresentation – An Argument'. *CR: The New Continental Review*, 3(3), pp. 257–337.

Zeleza, P. T. 2003. *Rethinking Africa's Globalization: Volume 1: The Intellectual Challenges.* Trenton, NJ: Africa World Press.

Zizek, S. 2013. 'Mandela's Socialist Failure'. *New York Times*, 6 December.

5

REINVENTING AFRICA

Introduction

The imperative of reinvention of Africa and creation of Africanity arises from a colonial historical context of a people who have experienced an existential quandary of being exiled from their ancestors, culture, language, history, knowledge, and even from themselves. Reinvention commences as a decolonial re-membering process in response to centuries of dismemberment and dehumanization. In this context, identity formation and intellectual formation become inextricably intertwined paradoxically just like power and knowledge in the Focauldian thinking. Thus the struggles for epistemic freedom are invariably a search for African identity.

This perspective came out clearly in Ngugi wa Thiong'o (1986: 87)'s definition of decolonization as the search for a liberating perspective, a quest for relevance and a secure base from which 'to see ourselves clearly in relationship to ourselves and to other selves in the universe'. By intellectual formations is meant a community of thinkers who share common epistemic, political, ideological, and pragmatic concerns as well as certain conceptions of knowledge and its role in society; cascading from common experiences which inform common consciousness (Muller 1997: 198). What linked intellectual formations with identity formations, are the constitutive conditions from which they emerged. Colonialism and global coloniality formed the constitutive conditions for both intellectual and identity formations in Africa.

Colonialism not only bequeathed on Africa a double crisis of identity and epistemology. As noted in Chapter 3, it also contributed to the current crisis of belonging and citizenship (see Mamdani 1996; Adebanwi 2009; Hunter 2016). In countries like South Africa, which were imagined as little Europe located at the Southern tip of the African continent and which exist today was as 'cultural fragments of Western world' (Mazrui 1990: 8), the white colonial invaders 'denationalized' the indigenous black people and created a problem of what Michael

Neocosmos (2010) aptly depicted as 'native foreigners' as they 'indigenized' themselves as 'foreign natives'. Here was born what Peter Geschiere (2009) termed 'perils of belonging'. This 'peril of belonging' is manifesting itself as a struggle between what Francis B. Nyamnjoh (2006) termed 'insiders and outsiders'.

It must be remembered (as highlighted in Chapter 3) that colonialism denied citizenship to the colonized and the 'postcolonial' regimes have continued to use citizenship instrumentally to exclude and punish political opponents. So sovereignty of the state has not automatically translated to the popular sovereignty of the people. This has led some scholars, particularly Neocosmos (2016), to be very critical of any emancipatory politics that still embraces the state as a site of liberation and any imaginations of liberation that sees freedom as realizable through the state. Neocosmos' intervention is a reinstatement of the potentiality of universal emancipation of humanity, which exceeds social place, particularistic interests and identities. What is worrying about Neocosmos' conception of emancipatory politics is his consistent attempt in decoupling of it from identity politics as though the category 'people' is not a form of identity itself.

What has continued to haunt Africa is what Valentin Y. Mudimbe (2013) correctly described as 'African fault lines' and 'politics of alterity'. Mudimbe directly situated African identity formations within intellectual and cultural configurations as well as structural disciplinary practices concerned with African difference. However, this chapter is not focused on the work of Mudimbe per se, but that of Ali A. Mazrui. But throughout the chapter, Mazrui's contribution to the pertinent subject of African subjectivity is historically situated within the wider context of the rich African archive, to which scholars like Mudimbe and many others have contributed. Mazrui is one of Africa's celebrated encyclopedic African scholars who contributed to almost every question pertaining to Africa and deepened the understanding of Africa immensely.

However, because of the sheer expansiveness of Mazrui's archive, it is not possible or even advisable to try and deal with it as whole. This chapter is focused on three carefully selected themes out of Mazrui's expansive archive. The first is that of African identity formation and the invention of Africa. Mazrui consistently contributed to the redefinition of Africa and the invention of 'Africanity' that cuts across geographical spaces, time and cultures. This way, Mazrui advanced the decolonial archive that rejected neo-imperialist paradigms and ontologies. What also made Mazrui's work attractive has been his boldness to question continental borders as well as confront the sensitive question of Arab identity in Africa. The second theme is what Mazrui termed the 'African condition' (see Mazrui 1980; Mazrui and Mutunga 2004). The third is Mazrui's contribution to the epistemic struggles to decolonize knowledge and the university.

What is beyond doubt about Mazrui's encyclopedic archive is that it touched on almost every aspect of human life – colonialism, education, nationalism, conflict, identities, cultures, power, ideology, economy, religion, politics, state, governance, gender, nuclear weapons, leadership, race, colonialism, intellectuals, Islamophobia and international relations. Mazrui's archive easily crossed academic disciplinary boundaries as well as geo-political frontiers. What can be posited with certainty is that Mazrui was many things at once: an African, a global citizen, a liberal nationalist, a Pan-Africanist, a Muslim, a leading and controversial political scientist, historian, international relations specialist, global cultural studies scholar, as well as a decolonial and postcolonial theorist among many descriptions.

Reinventing Africa and Africanity

Ali A. Mazrui's hybrid identity influenced his thinking on identity. He was living testimony of a triple heritage. He was a descendant of Arab-Muslims, an African and a respected intellectual product of 'Westernized' institutions of learning such as Manchester and Oxford universities in the United Kingdom. This is how Mazrui located his personal story in the discourse of reinvention of Africa and Africanity:

> I was born and brought up in Mombasa, one of the old Islamic city-states of East Africa. A historic landmark in the old town is Fort Jesus, from which the Mazrui family once ruled the city. Not far from the Fort is the old Supreme Court of Mombasa where Sheikh Ali-Amin bin Ali Mazrui used to hear appeal cases under the Shari'a. He was Kenya's chief judge of appeal under Islamic law. Sheikh Ali-Amin was my father. At the time of my birth and coming of age in Mombasa, Kenya was under British colonial rule. After the death of my father, I went to study at Manchester and Oxford rather than Al-Azhar (even though he would have preferred that I had studied at Al-Azhar) and that effectively widened my exposure to the Western branch of my own heritage. How much of a product of Africa's triple heritage am I? Am I a walking embodiment of that complex cultural mixture? Of course, it is not just my own identity that is affected by the Triple Heritage, but any identity in Africa as a whole. Who are the Africans? This heritage encompasses the full diversity of African identities and life-styles, including two commonly discussed and often romanticized types of African civilization: complex kingdoms and empires on the one side and decentralized 'tribes without rules' on the other.
>
> (Mazrui in Laremont *et al.* 2002: 99–100)

One can hazard that perhaps Mazrui's academic interest on the question of African identity arouse from his own personal complex identity. To Mazrui, Africanity is an idea rather than a point of origin just like the very idea of Africa (see Laremont *et al.* 2002). At its centre has been the search for an African past that was denied and silenced by imperial/colonial knowledge. The denial of the past amounted to deprivation of human dignity. This is why Mazrui emphasized the question of dignity as he engaged with the broader issues of reinvention of African and Africanity. He posited:

The African people may not be the most brutalized people in modern history, but they are almost certainly the most humiliated. The most brutalized people in modern history include indigenous people of the Americas and those of Australia, who were subjected to genocidal attacks by white invaders. Also among the most brutalized in modern times were the Jews and Gypsies in the Nazi Holocaust. On the other hand, no other groups were subjected to such large scale indignities of *enslavement* for several centuries in their millions as the Africans were. [After the legal abolition of slavery] No other group experienced to the same extent such indignities as *lynching*, systematic *segregation*, as well as well-planned *apartheid* as the Africans were.

It was against this background that Africa's dignitarian impulse was stimulated. A deep-seated African rebellion against humiliation was aroused. It has been a misnomer to call this rebellion 'nationalism'. This has not been an African quest for nationhood. At best nationhood has been the just means to an end. The deep-seated African struggle has been a quest for dignity – human and racial.

(Mazrui 2001: 107, emphasis is in the original text)

But at some level, enslavement of black people and the physical death toll that accompanied the capture and forced shipment across the Atlantic Ocean as well as the 'social death' within the plantations' amounted to another the earliest example of a Holocaust. What also emerged clearly from Mazrui's work is that the reinvention of Africa entailed the writing of African history by Africans themselves:

For me, as an African scholar, the process of writing the history of my own continent is a profound and sometimes agonizing experience. My first exposure to Western culture included a sense of shock at the West itself, but, as I got partially assimilated into the alien culture, the shock became directed at my own roots. In addition, two fears began to haunt me: one, the fear of my being part of a lost generation of Africans, culturally severed from their own societies; the other is the fear of a situation where all future generations of Africans would be culturally lost, like me.

(Mazrui in Laremont *et al.* 2002: 9–10)

Mazrui posited that 'only in true crisis of identity do we stand a chance of recognizing ourselves' and, it is when directly hit by this crisis that the journey to 'self-discovery' commenced (Mazrui in Laremont *et al.* 2002: 10). He made it clear that reinvention and self-definition cannot be anything other than recovery of history:

Partly because of the impact of Europe, Africa is currently in such a crisis of identity. It may well be on the edge of self-discovery. And what is self, after all, if not primarily the product of own past?

(Mazrui in Laremont *et al.* 2002: 10)

Since identity formation is interlinked inextricably with intellectual formation and knowledge production, it is not surprising that throughout his intellectual and scholarly writing, Mazrui became concerned about indigenous African knowledge. He identified three possible starting points of what became known as 'African Studies'. The first is ancient Egypt and the Nile Valley with its first grand African civilization. The second is to trace it to the 'observations about West and East Africa by the medieval North African traveller, Abu Abdallah Muhammad Ibn Battuta (1304–1368 CE)' (Mazrui in Laremont *et al.* 2002: 11). The third starting point is to 'trace to the time when Africa began to be truly identified as a continent in its own right' (Mazrui in Laremont *et al.* 2002: 11). But to untangle the knotty question of African Studies inevitably led Mazrui to engage with the question of what is 'African' and who is 'African'. These two questions emerged within a context of the existence of Islamic/Arabic intellectual tradition and identity that had permeated and intertwined with the African intellectual tradition and identity to the extent of inseparability. It was in an attempt to get around this reality that Mazrui began to introduce a flexible and generous conception of Africanity. This is how he thought about it:

> But what is an 'African'? There two main types – those who are 'African' in a continental sense (like Egyptians and Algerians) and those who are 'African' in a racial sense (like Nigerians, Ugandans and Senegalese). Egyptians and Algerians are Africa's children of the soil. Sub-Saharan Blacks are Africa's children of the blood. In reality all those who are natives of Africa are children of the soil (called *wana-nchi* in the Swahili language). But Sub-Saharan Blacks are in addition Africa's children by racial blood.
>
> (Mazrui in Leremont *et al.* 2002: 12)

Mazrui and the development of the triple heritage concept

Mazrui developed the concept of triple heritage concept while he was grappling with the difficult and complex African knowledge question and the Arab question. To him, the development of knowledge in Africa underwent a triple trajectory from oral, to written and to electronic whereas African identity also experienced a triple jump of indigenization, Islamification and Westernization (Mazrui in Laremont *et al.* 2002: 13). He elaborated on these complex historical trajectories beginning with indigenous knowledge:

> The more purely indigenous legacy of the study of Africa has on the whole been mainly of the oral tradition. It ranged from praise songs in honour of heroes to the wider gamut of oral history.
>
> (Mazrui in Laremont *et al.* 2002: 13)

African indigenous knowledge also intersected with the Islamic intellectual tradition that was both oral and written. This tradition produced Hausa and

Hausa-Fulani intellectual tradition that became both African and Arabic. Africanity and Islam as a culture, identity and intellectual tradition became inextricably intertwined paradoxically. Then the Western intellectual legacy and its interventionist tendencies came. It formed, in Mazrui's thinking the third layer of the triple heritage. Mazrui argued:

> The Western legacy leaned heavily toward the written tradition in the first half of the twentieth century. It subsequently also became part of the new electronic media (radio, television, and audiotape). As the twentieth century was coming to a close the Westernized legacy of African Studies was also venturing into cyberspace.
>
> (Mazrui in Laremont *et al.* 2002: 15–16)

Mazrui hastened to underscore a colonial reality, which haunted knowledge production in Africa as well as identity articulation:

> African studies was caught up in four intellectual denials to which the African people were subjected at the time: the denial of history, the denial of science, the denial of poetry, and the denial of philosophy, including religious philosophy. These four great intellectual denials affected areas of research, nature of syllabi and curricula both in Africa and abroad, what the next generation of African scholars was trained for, and which academic disciplines were regarded as relevant from an African perspective.
>
> (Mazrui in Laremont *et al.* 2002: 16)

According to Mazrui an important 'cultural paradigm' emerged out of the African epistemic struggles against the 'four great intellectual denials' – a paradigm that sought to understand Africa from the perspective of its own values, beliefs, symbols, modes of communication and lifestyles – as it countered Eurocentrism cascading from the Western legacy. The intellectual contributions of this cultural paradigm were noticeable in five domains of the African epistemic struggles: re-establishing that Africans were a historical people; linking Africans to the culture of science; re-establishing Africans as religious people prior to the rise of Christianity and Islam; demonstrating that African people have been philosophical all along; and linking African studies to multicultural movements (Mazrui in Laremont *et al.* 2002: 18).

The perennial question of African identity formation and African epistemology articulation pre-occupied many other African intellectuals who had a different genealogy from Mazrui. For example, the earliest advocate of 'African personality' if not the father of the 'triple heritage' idea was Edward Wilmot Blyden of Sierra Leone (1967). He grappled with the question of common African destiny, distinctiveness of African mentality; the role of religion in African life, the inherent socialist orientation of African society, and the notion of separation of races (see also Frenkel 1974: 277). It was Blyden who posited that 'African personality' would develop as an organic embracement of the best attributes from indigenous African, Arabic/Islamic and Euro-Christian-scientific traditions.

Some of Blyden's ideas re-emerged within the Negritude Movement as its advocates such as Aime Cesaire and Leopold Sedar Senghor engaged pertinent questions of universality, particularity, European rationality, reason, time, emotion, materiality, morality, and nature as resources that shaped humanity and the future of the world (Thiam 2014; Wilder 2015). In the 1970s the leading Pan-Africanist Kwame Nkrumah (1970) also contributed to the debate on African identity, its rootedness in African, Arabic–Islamic and Western–Christian traditions. He introduced the concept of 'concienscism' as he forged ahead in finding a formula of synthesizing cultural, historical and cognitive currents of Africa's communal and humanistic ethos with the Western capitalist, acquisitive, individualistic, scientific, Christian redemptive logic; and the secular, holistic and spiritual precepts of Arabic–Islamic heritage (Nkrumah 1970; Zeleza 2006). Nkrumah was optimistic that from this synthesis, there would emerge a 'postcolonial', liberated, modern and confident Africa subjectivity capable of creating African future.

In the 1980s and 1990s the Congolese scholar Valentin Y. Mudimbe published two of his most celebrated works, the first entitled *The Invention of Africa: Gnosis, Philosophy, and the Order of Knowledge* (1988) and the second being *The Idea of Africa* (1994), which also dealt extensively with the invention Africa and the idea of Africa as articulated mainly by Europeans beginning with the Greek stories about Africa, missionaries and the anthropologists right up to philosophers. Concerned with the workings of the discursive processes and the orders of knowledge, Mudimbe demonstrated how African intellectuals have consistently failed to liberate knowledge from the skein of colonialism/coloniality and the colonial library (Mudimbe 1988; 1994). Ngugi wa Thiong'o (2009: 72) had a different take from Mudimbe:

> V. Y. Mudimbe describes the idea of Africa as a product of the West's system of self-representation, which included creation of an otherness conceived and conveyed through conflicting systems of knowledge. But I prefer to think of the idea of Africa – or, more appropriately, the 'African idea', as African self-representation. To distinguish it from the Mudimbeist formula according to which Europe is finding itself through its invention of Africa, I see the African idea as that which was forged in the diaspora and travelled back to the continent.

Ngugi wa Thiong'o introduced the 'African idea' that spoke to how Africans invented themselves and how through ideas of Pan-Africanism they forged a common Pan-African identity. But the interventions of Kwame Anthony Appiah in his book entitled *In My Father's House: Africa in the Philosophy of Culture* (1992) challenged the use of 'race' to describe African people as a common 'black race', for instance. Appiah became very critical of what he viewed as essentialist ideas of Africa, arguing that African identity has never been a primordial racial fixture. To him, Africans were not common people as they were moulded from different racial and cultural 'clays' – to borrow a term from Paul Tiyambe Zeleza (2006: 16). Appiah's critique challenged narratives of nationalism and Pan-Africanism that were poised to be important resources in the formulation of an 'African idea' as opposed to the 'idea of Africa' *a la* Mudimbe.

Even former president of South Africa, Thabo Mbeki's widely quoted 'I am an African' speech of 1996 spoke to the complexity and contingent nature of African identity and articulated it as a hybrid and open identity born out of human encounters; some tragic and others heroic. The significance of the question emanated partly from the reality that such anthropologists as Melville Herskovits (1960) doubted the substance and essence of Africa arguing that it was a mere 'geographical fiction' which only existed as a product of 'the tyranny of the map maker'. Some African intellectuals challenged this denial of African existence and others sought to make sense of the impact of this existence of a geographical fiction.

As far back as 1963 Mazrui was engaging the complex question of African identity, making him part of the pioneers on this debate among the first generation of African scholars. In one of his earliest articles entitled 'On the Concept of "We Are All Africans"', Mazrui (1963) began to examine how African identity emerged as a complex product of 'double invention' by colonial imperatives and African imperatives. The colonial imperatives included map-making, partitioning of Africa, domination and promotion of a singular idea of an African people who were collectively thought of as inferior, backward and primitive beings. Mazrui ventured into making sense of the African ideas of Africa represented by such nationalists as Nkrumah and Julius Nyerere.

It was Nyerere who introduced the concept of 'African sentiment' as a form of consciousness born out of colonial racial humiliation of the black races. Mazrui also demonstrated empirically how African nationalist figures like Nkrumah, Gamal Abdul Nasser and Leopold Sedar Senghor actively played a role in the invention of African identity, using such means as the First All-Africa People's Conference held in Accra in December 1958 to 're-member' Africa after 'dismemberment' at the Berlin Conference of 1884–1885 (Mazrui, 1963; Ngugi wa Thiong'o 2009). African nationalism and Pan-Africanism provided the discursive framework for Africans on the continent and in the diaspora to invent themselves as one people.

To Seifudein Adem (2014a: 135), Mazrui's 'theory' of 'triple heritage' is 'his most innovative, and possibly, most enduring contribution to scholarship'. But as demonstrated above, the triple heritage thesis was not Mazrui's origination. He named a phenomenon that had already been distilled by others like Blyden and Nkrumah. This is why Zeleza (2006: 20) articulated the triple heritage thesis as the 'Blyden-Nkrumah-Mazrui cultural typologies'. The innovative part of the 'triple heritage' thesis is that it attempted to take into account the historical realities that have shaped ideas of Africanity – particularly how the indigenous African ethos intersected with the Arabic–Islamic and Western–Christian traditions. But Mazrui was heavily criticized by Wole Soyinka (1991) for subordination indigenous African religions and cultures to the Arabic–Islamic and Western ones. In the midst of what Zeleza (2006: 20) described as 'the clash of gigantic intellectual egos', Soyinka dismissed the triple heritage thesis as nothing other than a 'triple trope of trickery' (see Soyinka 1991).

What is important to note though in the complex themes of African identity and 'African condition' to which Mazrui actively contributed is that they were framed by two broad discursive strands, namely the post-Enlightenment Eurocentric-imperial/colonial view and the anti-colonial/decolonial perspective which is itself constituted by a diverse family of ideological and intellectual streams (Mazrui 1980; Mazrui 1986; Ndlovu-Gatsheni 2013a; 2013b). Mazrui emphasized the fragmentary nature of African identity in his pioneering article of 1963 and elaborated in Lecture 6 of *The African Condition*. The triple heritage that was emphasized by Mazrui in the 1980s embraced the 'double invention' of Africa that is highlighted by Lewis R. Gordon:

> It is in this sense that Africa is 'invented'. It is invented by systems of knowledge constituted by the processes of conquest and colonization, which always erupted with discovery, on the one hand, and it, is also constituted by the processes of resistance borne out of those events the consequence of which is an effect of both on each other.
>
> (Gordon 2008: 204)

Gordon (2008: 207) added that 'Africa is not, in other words, simply invented but continues to be invented and reinvented, both inside and outside the terms of African peoples'. Unlike Mazrui and Appiah, for instance, Soyinka (2012) highlighted primordiality of Africa as he launched a critique to the imperial/colonial 'discovery' paradigm, which privileged the agency of white colonial conquerors in the making of human history even outside Europe.

However, Mazrui's concept of 'triple heritage' problematized the ideas of a primordial and 'authentic' African identity without discarding the importance of an enduring pre-colonial African culture in the invention of Africa and shaping notions of Africanity. Soyinka (2012: 48) underscored the existence of 'the crisis of African emergence into modernity' that had profound effects on the development and fossilization Africanity as an identity. It was modernity that introduced the logic of imperial reason and the paradigm of difference. Taking into account this reality, Mudimbe (2013: 11) argued, 'As a conceptuality, Africa has been presumed a transparent concept in most politics of alterity and by almost everyone as a key to the assurance of a difference'.

Human species re-emerged as socially classified and racially hierarchized in accordance with assumed differential ontological densities at the dawn of modernity. At the apex of the invented pyramid is the white race and at the bottom is the black race. What Du Bois (1903) termed the 'colour line', what Nelson Maldonado-Torres (2007) named the 'imperial Manichean misanthropic skepticism' and what Boaventura de Sousa Santos described (2007) as the 'abyssal thinking' underscored the paradigm of difference in the modernist invention of human identities. Elaborating on the essence, meaning and implications of the colour line, the leading philosopher of Africana existentialism, Gordon, argued: 'Born from the divide of black and white, it serves as a blueprint of the ongoing division of humankind', adding:

> The colour line is also a metaphor that exceeds its own concrete formulation. It is the race line as well as the gender line, the class line, the sexual orientation line, the religious line – in short, the line between 'normal' and 'abnormal' identities.
>
> (Gordon 2000: 63)

This formed the basis for questioning of the very being/very humanity of black people. In summary, African subjectivity/Africanity emerged in the post-Enlightenment Eurocentric discourse of identity as a disabled, deficient and lacking essence/ontology: lacking souls/religion, history, civilization, development, democracy, human rights, and ethics (Ndlovu-Gatsheni 2013a; 2013b; 2014). The point is that the Cartesian subject monopolized complete being and sovereign subjectivity for itself and consigned others to a perpetual state of *becoming* if not totally denying humanity to others.

However, the Eurocentric discourse's presentation of Africa as a 'Dark Continent' inhabited by a deficient and lacking human subjects always locked horns with a decolonial perspective that was articulated in various ideological-intellectual terms ranging from Ethiopianism, Garveyism, Negritude, African Personality, Pan-Africanism, African Socialism, African humanism, Black Consciousness Movement (BCM) to African Renaissance (July 1968; Hensbroek 1999; Falola 2001; Creary 2012; Ngugi wa Thiong'o 2009). The logic informing the decolonial perspective is provided by Nigerian novelist Chinua Achebe:

> You have all heard of African personality; of African democracy; of the African way to socialism, of negritude, and so on. They are all props we have fashioned at different times to help us get on our feet again. Once we are up we shall not need any of them anymore. But for the moment it is in the nature of things that we may need to counter racism with what Jean-Paul Satre called an anti-racist racism, to announce not just that we are good as the next man but that we are better.
>
> (Achebe in Ahluwalia 2001: 68)

The decolonial perspective is informed by the spirit to assert African being (sovereign African subjectivity). It is largely a response to imperial and colonial discourse on African subjectivity. It was imposed on Africans as an agenda by history of domination, racial discrimination and exploitation. This reality is well captured by Archie Mafeje:

> We would not talk of freedom, if there was no prior condition in which this was denied; we would not be anti-racist if we had not been its victims; we would not proclaim Africanity, if it had not been denied or degraded; and we would not insist on Afrocentrism, if it had not been for Eurocentric negations [. . .] Of necessity, under the determinate global condition an African renaissance must entail a rebellion – a conscious rejection of past transgressions, a determined negation of negations.
>
> (Mafeje 2011: 31–32)

What complicates the triple heritage thesis is the reality of the inscription of Islamic and Western cultures, which were accompanied by epistemicides, that is, attempts to eradicate indigenous histories, cultures, religions and traditions. Generally speaking, the spread of Islam and Christianity was underpinned by violent *Jihads* and *Crusades*. Christian missionaries often worked closely with colonialists in their project of 'pacification of barbarous tribes'. We can, therefore, speak of colonially 'imposed heritages' with reference to Islamic and Western civilization. African culture pre-dated Islamic and Western cultures (Ndlovu-Gatsheni 2014). However, Mazrui deployed the concept of triple heritage in an endeavour to enable thinkability of the Arab identity as part of Africanity.

To further cement his strong belief in the reinvention of Africa in general and the possibilities of human social engineering of self, Mazrui (1990) expressed his strong belief in the power of culture not only in shaping African realities but even world politics. To elaborate on the importance of culture as the basis for politics and economics, Mazrui distilled and layout out seven functions of culture, which directly links it to the intellectual formations and identity formations. First, culture provided the 'lenses for perception and cognition' (Mazrui 1990: 7). This means that culture plays a fundamental role in conditioning a people's worldview and world sense. Second, culture provided the 'motives for human behaviour' (Mazrui 1990: 7).

The third function of culture is the provision of 'criteria of evaluation' of such issues as moral or immoral, ethical or unethical (Mazrui 1990: 7). The fourth function of culture is to form a 'basis of identity' (Mazrui 1990: 7). Fifth, culture is 'a mode of communication' with language as the 'most elaborate system of communication' but it can also embrace other forms such as 'music, the performing arts, and the wider world of ideas' (Mazrui 1990: 7). The sixth function of culture is as a 'basis of stratification' such as class, rank and status (Mazrui 1990: 7). The final function of culture 'lies in the system of production and consumption' and this challenges the Marxist thinking which privileged the economy (Mazrui 1990: 8). Culture rather than economy underpinned human behaviour and global politics. This approach reinforces the conception of identity as an idea rather than a fixated origin, which emboldened Mazrui to even question the continental boundaries of Africa.

Mazrui on the abolition of the Red Sea and invention of Afrabia

In deepening his conception of Africanity as an idea rather than origin, Mazrui made frantic intellectual efforts to bridge the gap between Africans of the soil and Africans of the blood. His call for the abolition of the Red Sea must be understood as key aspect of deprovincialization of both Africa and Asia as part of decolonial invention on identities. Regarding the Red Sea as border between Africa and Asia, Mazrui posited:

> What is not realized is that the toughest colonial border of them all is the border separating Africa from Asia. Is the Red Sea a rational line between Africa and Asia? Or was the Red Sea itself yet another irrational colonial border imposed by Europe, ignoring the cultural continuities and historical links across the strip of water?
>
> (Mazrui in Laremont *et al.* 2002: 79)

Mazrui boldly stated his thesis on the Red Sea: 'the Red Sea has no business defining the northeastern boundary of Africa – it has no right to divide Africa from Asia' (Mazrui in Laremont *et al.* 2002: 80). He elaborated: 'Why not refuse to recognize the Red Sea as a chasm, just as the Pan-Africanists have refused to concede such a role to the Sahara Desert?' (Mazrui in Laremont *et al.* 2002: 81). In Mazrui's decolonial thinking the abolition of the Red Sea as a boundary would resolve the perennial problem of North Africa, which is often understood as part of Arabia rather than Africa. To him, the Red Sea as a boundary emerged when three geological cracks emerged on the Eastern side of Africa resulting in Arabia breaking away producing the Gulf of Aden and the Red Sea. This natural geological process known as plate tectonics reduced the contact between Africa and Asia to the Isthmus of Suez (Mazrui in Laremont *et al.* 2002: 81). Before this crack Africa and Asia were not separate as there were flows of people, intellectual currents, religions and languages across.

This is why in Africa one found the Ahmara of Ethiopia with their Semitic language – a branch of the Afro-Asian family of languages. What this indicated is that before the geological secession of Arabia some 3 to 5 million years ago, there was cultural integration of Arabia, the Horn of Africa and the rest of Africa, Mazrui argued (Mazrui in Laremont *et al.* 2002: 82). Mazrui invented the concept of 'Afrabia' that signalled a reintegration of Arabia and Africa as a contribution to the resolution of what he depicted as 'agonizing problems of identity' (Mazrui in Laremont *et al.* 2002: 82). No scholar has been as brave and daring as Mazrui in questioning the continental boundaries and calling for their abolition as part of deprovincializing Africa. Listen to Mazrui's boldness:

> But if the Red Sea could be ignored in determining the northeastern limits of Africa, why cannot the Mediterranean also be ignored as an outer northern limit? There was indeed a time when North Africa was in fact regarded as

an extension of Europe. This goes back to the days of Carthage, of Hellenistic colonization, and later, of the Roman Empire.

(Mazrui in Laremont *et al.* 2002: 83)

The deprovincialization of Africa that Mazrui (in Laremont *et al.* 2202: 85) advocated is one that entailed 're-Africanization of the Arabian Peninsula'. To set afoot the revolutionary decolonial change Mazrui called for forgiveness and reconciliation between Arabs and Africans so as to transcend the memories of the Arab involvement in the slave trade in Africa. Mazrui's archive is also instructive on the long-term impact of colonialism on Africa.

Mazrui as the advocate of the epic school on colonialism

What is also enlightening about Mazrui's intellectual interventions on African identity is that he directly confronted the impact of colonialism and engaged with 'epic' and the 'episodic' schools. Mazrui belonged to the 'epic school', which emphasized the radical interventions of colonialism on African identity and mind-set. The school highlighted the violent incorporation of Africa into the world economy through 'the slave trade, which dragged African labour itself into the emerging international capitalist system' (Mazrui 1986: 13). This was followed by what Mazrui termed the 'territorial imperative', that is, conquest of African space as well as appropriation and physical occupation of territory. The third element was 'Africa's admission into the state system of the world emanating from European Peace of Westphalia of 1648' (Mazrui 1986: 13).

The fourth element was 'Africa's incorporation into world culture' that included imposition of colonial languages. The fifth element was 'Africa's incorporation into the world of international law, which is again heavily Eurocentric in origin' (Mazrui 1986: 13). Finally, Africa was 'incorporated into the modern technological age'. Colonialism even introduced a particular 'moral order' that was Western-centric (Mazrui 1986: 13). Thus if one takes into account all these interventions and their implications on the invention of Africa, the conclusion is that there was deliberate 'dis-Africanization' and 'Westernization' of Africa to the extent that: 'What Africa knows about itself, what different parts of Africa know about each other, have been profoundly influenced by the West' (Mazrui 1986: 13). Such colonially imposed identities as Anglophone, Francophone and Lusophone are good examples that indicate the influence of the enduring legacy of colonial encounters and colonialism.

Then the 'episodic history' as a counter to the 'epic school of history' became informed by nationalist historiography (Ajayi 2000). Nationalist historiography was ranged against imperial historiography that had denied the existence of African history prior to the colonial encounters (Temu and Swai 1981; Lovejoy 1986; Zeleza 1997). The important point of the 'episodic school' is that European impact on Africa was not profound; it was brief, shallow, transitional, and not long lasting. Capitalism as an economic system was shallow. Consequently, there was continuity of African history from pre-colonial period to the postcolonial period with colonialism having been a brief disruption to continuity. The implication of this interpretation of the impact of colonialism is that that Africans continued to make their own history and to invent themselves as a people with agency. To reconcile these two schools, Mazrui concluded:

> European colonial rule in Africa was more effective in destroying indigenous African *structures* than in destroying African *culture*. The tension between new imported structures and old resilient cultures is part of the post-colonial war of cultures in the African continent. The question has therefore arisen as to whether Africa is reclaiming its own.
>
> (Mazrui 1986: 20)

Mazrui has a point is that postcolonial Africa has been haunted by 'a war of cultures' but whether this cultural crisis is responsible for 'inefficiency, mismanagement, corruption and decay of the infrastructure' is debatable (Mazrui 1986: 12). Is postcolonial Africa suffering from 'failure of transplanted organs of the state and the economy'? Is the decay of infrastructure in postcolonial Africa to be celebrated as a form of African resistance to imposed Western civilization? Mazrui's take is contained in this statement:

> Before a seed germinates it must first decay. A mango tree grows out of a decaying mango seed. A new Africa may germinate in the decay of the present one – and the ancestors are presiding over the process.
>
> (Mazrui 1986: 21)

It was Mazrui who noted that what Africa knows about itself is informed by colonial thought and this has implications for understanding the 'African condition' which is an encapsulation of African postcolonial predicaments (Mazrui 1980). Before delving into Mazrui's perspective on the African condition, it is important to briefly engage with his idea on the role of education in identity formation and his views on decolonization of education.

Education, identity and decolonization of knowledge

In his book entitled *Political Values and the Educated Class in Africa* (1978), Mazrui engaged with various aspects of the impact of Western education on Africa. It is in this work that Mazrui critically reflected on the intersections of modern African identity formation and modern intellectual formations. The advent of Western missionary and colonial education fundamentally de-structured the pre-colonial social, political and economic order and restructured it for purposes of colonialism. Thus missionary and colonial education played a key role in the colonial reinvention of Africa. This is how Mazrui (1978: xiii) captured the profound impact of colonial education of the African social formation:

The colonial impact transformed the natural basis of stratification in Africa. Instead of status based on, say age, there emerged status based on literacy. Instead of classes emerging from the question 'who owned what?', class formation now responded to the question 'who knows what?'

This realization led Mazrui (1978: 23) to argue: 'Colonialism was not simply a political experience for Africa; it was even more fundamentally a cultural experience. The values of the African world were profoundly disturbed by what would otherwise have been a brief episode in African history'. He added:

> The modern school itself is an institution so borrowed. The style of instruction, the general ethos of the school, and the curriculum help to determine the values and techniques are transmitted within those walls.
>
> (Mazrui 1978: 23)

The mission boarding school, for example, played a key role in desocialization of African children and youth through separating them from their parents and society so as to enable them to imbibe foreign values. The 'home environment' was considered to be the site of inculcation of primitive values and African boys and girls had to be 'saved' from this institution (Mazrui 1978: 26). This is why Mazrui (1978: 27) concluded: 'The paradox of the missionary school has long-term consequences for Africa. It may even lie at the heart of widespread cultural schizophrenia in Africa as a whole.' The colonial desocialization process was deliberate as it was meant to extract the African boys and girls from their ancestral social structures into the colonial limbo.

Turning to the essence and role of higher education in Africa, Mazrui immediately raised the two perennial but fundamental questions of relevance of education and social mission of the university. This is how he posed the issues:

> The whole concept of modern education in Africa sometimes poses acute problems as to whether or not it really *belongs*. [. . .] It is too *foreign* and too *rationalist*. It is too foreign partly because it has emerged from foreign educational and academic traditions, and partly because a high proportion of the education innovators are still foreign. As for the African university itself, it is too rationalist for reasons connected with precisely its western ancestry. The ethos of western university system puts a special premium on a form of rationality which aspires to neutral universalism. To be 'scholarly' and to be 'scientific' are, in western terminology, sometimes interchangeable. And to be scientific includes a stance of disengagement. But scientific detachment could amount to social disengagement. The equation of detachment with disengagement has sometimes led to demands for rethinking about the role of academics in developing countries. Can Africa afford pure academics?
>
> (Mazrui 1978: 202, emphasis is in the original document)

This correct diagnosis of the crisis of education in Africa launched Mazrui into a search for how to decolonize economy, culture, knowledge, education and the university. The university is one of the important components of a chain of institutions that reproduce dependency on Europe and North America. Consequently, the so-called African universities have 'been the highest transmitters of Western culture in African societies' and 'The high priests of Western civilization in the continent are virtually all products of those cultural seminaries called universities' (Mazrui 2003: 147). This delving deeper into the crux of the African problem enabled Mazrui to reflect critically on the broader African liberatory project. This is how Mazrui understood it:

> Here we must distinguish three forms of liberation – political, economic and cultural. Political liberation in our context refers to the decolonization process which resulted in sovereign political independence for African states. Today each African country celebrates a day of independence. But independence in this context is purely political. The heavy weight of economic and cultural domination persists. Economic liberation will come when African economies acquire greater autonomy, and when they establish adequate economic leverage on the international economic system as a whole. The economic autonomy will be achieved partly through reorienting African economies away from excessive reliance on the export market and towards greater exploitation of the domestic market, away from excessive reliance on foreign capital and capital-intensive projects and towards more efficient use of surplus labour, and away from indiscriminate importation of foreign goods and towards developing the kind of import-substitution which has genuine developmental consequences. As for cultural liberation, this would come into two stages. One is the stage of some degree of cultural revivalism, involving readiness to pay renewed homage to local traditions and incorporate those traditions into educational system more systematically. The second state of cultural liberation would have to consist of cultural innovation, entailing a process of synthesizing the old with the new, and then moving on in independent intellectual directions.
>
> (Mazrui 1978: 297)

The current undecolonized education continue to produce 'deeply westernized' elites who are the 'most culturally dependent' (Mazrui 1978: 298). Mazrui also identified that the crisis of relevance is twofold: practical and cultural. The practical aspect referred to skills of the graduates. The cultural dimension is related to values (Mazrui 1978: 302). As a way forward Mazrui suggested various ways of decolonizing modernity itself as the discursive terrain within which all these problems of identity and knowledge emerged. His take is that modernity has to be decolonized in three ways: domestication of modernity in terms of firmly anchoring it on local cultural and economic needs and the second strategy is to diversify cultural content of modernity in terms of deprovincialization of Europe so as to open up to other non-European civilizations. It also entails diversification of production, sources of expertise, techniques of analysis, types of goods produced and markets for these products as a way of escaping dependence. With specific reference to the university, it has to be reorganized into 'a multicultural corporation' (Mazrui 1978: 307). The third strategy is that of counter-penetration of Western civilization itself. Mazrui posed the fundamental question: 'If African cultures have been penetrated so deeply by the West, how is western culture to be reciprocally penetrated by Africa?' (Mazrui 1978: 314) Counter-penetration as a strategy has two components. The first component is 'horizontal interpenetration' which means the working together of African and Global South countries. Mazrui elaborated on this strategy:

> In the field of trade this could mean promoting greater exchange among, say, African countries themselves. In the field of investment it could, for example, mean allowing Arab money to compete with western and Japanese money in establishing new industries or promoting new projects in Africa. In the field of aid it must also mean that oil-rich Third world countries should increase their contribution towards the economic and social development of their resource-poor sister-countries. In the field of technical assistance it would have to mean that Third World countries with apparent excess of skilled manpower in relation to their absorption capacity should not only be prepared but also be encouraged to facilitate temporary or permanent migration to other Third World countries. The last process is what might be called the horizontal brain drain – the transfer of skilled manpower from, say, Egypt to Abu Dhabi or from the Indian sub-continent to Nigeria.
>
> (Mazrui 1978: 337–338)

The second strand is called vertical counter-penetration. This is directed as entering 'the citadels of power in the north' – a process, which has already seen the rich oil-producing countries of the Middle East and China influencing even the money markets while also buying shares in Europe and opening banks in the United States (Mazrui 1978: 338). Mazrui also elaborated on the indigenization and domestication strategies in these words:

> The strategy of indigenization involves increasing the use of traditional local technology. But in applying this to the computer we have to relate it to the strategy of domestication as well. While indigenization means using local resources and making them more relevant to the modern age, domestication involves making imported versions of modernity more relevant to the local society. For example, the English language in East Africa is an alien medium. To domesticate it is to make it respond to local imagery, figures of speech, sound patterns and to the general cultural milieu of the region. On the other hand, the promotion of Swahili as against English in Tanzania is a process of indigenization.
>
> (Mazrui 1978: 335)

Mazrui on postcolonial African condition

To Mazrui, postcolonial predicaments and instabilities haunting postcolonial Africa were a 'symptom of cultures at war' with Africans fighting 'to avert the demise of Africanity' (Mazrui 1986: 21). At the centre of these 'culture wars' 'is Africa's triple heritage of indigenous, Islamic and Western forces – fusing and recoiling, at once competitive and complimentary' (Mazrui1986: 21). Therefore, liberation of Africa, according to Mazrui, lay in two options: 'the imperative of looking inwards towards Africa's ancestors' and 'the imperative of looking outward towards the wider world' (Mazrui 1986: 295). Indigenous African culture is the basis of the inward-looking option but 'is not identical with looking inwards at yesterday's Africa' but must gesture towards 'a special transition from the tribe to the human race, from the village to the world' (Mazrui 1986: 295).

But this option needs to take into account what Mazrui distilled as the 'six paradoxes' of the postcolonial African condition (Mazrui 1980). The first is the 'paradox of habitation', which speaks to how a continent that has been identified as the 'cradle of mankind' is at the same time the least hospitable today. The second is the 'paradox of humiliation', which highlights how Africa is a product of a humiliating history of enslavement, colonization and racial discrimination. The third is the 'paradox of acculturation' cascading from imposition of foreign cultural, political, economic and social forms that disturbed and reproduced Africanity as a nest of conflicting set of identities (Mazrui 1980: 34).

The fourth is the 'paradox of fragmentation' rooted in capitalist economic exploitation that reproduced Africa as a site of underdevelopment, maldistribution and economic disarticulation. The fifth is the 'paradox of retardation' manifesting itself in the form of Africa's failure to act as a unit due to internal weaknesses cascading from national, ethnic, ideological and religious cleavages. The last is the 'paradox of location' that speaks to how a continent which is centrally located geographically but is at the same time the most marginal in global power politics (Mazrui 1980: 34).

As noted in the previous section of this chapter, Mazrui offered seven solutions to the African postcolonial predicaments. The first is that Africa must indigenize its personnel and avoid relying on non-Africans for advice on governance issues. The second is that Africa must domesticate foreign resources making them relevant and appropriate to the African needs. The third is that Africa must diversify its products, trading partners, investors, sources of aid and foreign cultural relationships. The fourth is that Africa must pursue a strategy of 'horizontal interpenetration' in its economic relation. This strategy had to rely on pulling together of resources in an effort to subvert external domination. The fifth was that Africa must pursue 'vertical counter-penetration'. This is predicated on African self-assertion and projection of its identity in world affairs. The sixth is that Africa must work hard to narrow the gap between elites and ordinary people. The final is that that Africa should 'encourage northern extravagance, particularly in the form of oil consumption' so as to get resources in the short term to finance its own development (Wai 2013: 149).

To Mazrui, the postcolonial predicaments were compounded by a leadership crisis. This led him to try and categorize African leadership into four types: elder tradition whose symbol was Jomo Kenyatta of Kenya; warrior leadership represented by Idi Amin of Uganda; sage tradition typified by Julius Nyerere of Tanzania; and monarchical tradition that was portrayed by Kwame Nkrumah of Ghana. These types of leadership produced five problematic styles of leadership: intimidatory; patriarchal, reconciliatory, bureaucratic and mobilization leader (Makinda 2005). It would seem these types and styles of leadership had the following outcome:

> Almost every other African country which attained liberation from European colonial rule in the 20th century was unable to maintain its democratic order beyond its first decade of independence. Within the first decade either the military captured power, or the elected president became a dictator, or a civil war broke out, or the ruling party outlawed any rival political party and turned the country into a single-party state.
>
> (Mazrui 2011: 1)

Building on the work of Mazrui it becomes clear that the continuing struggle for democracy is intrinsically the struggle for a democratic tradition of leadership and democratic style of governance. South Africa, which Mazrui celebrated as 'truly democratized', as country that 'has not outlawed opposition parties', as a country that has not 'experienced a military coup', and as a country that has not 'permitted the head of state to govern' as a dictator, in his 2011 lecture delivered at the University of Free State, is facing its own challenges such as deepening inequalities, corruption and poor service delivery that speaks to the questionability of the quality of its democracy and prospects of its sustainability.

Conclusion

What emerges clearly from this chapter is the undisputable role of an African intellectual and academic in the diagnosis of the African problems, prognosis and prescription. Mazrui consistently maintained his Pan-Africanist orientation as he delved deeper into the complex subject and decolonial task of reinventing Africa and creating Africanity. The criticisms if not personal attacks on his Arabic genealogy did not deter Mazrui from boldly investigating what was ailing Africa and producing postcolonial African predicaments and dilemmas. He endeavoured to turn African nationalist sensibilities into a broader Pan-African sentiment capable of resolving long-standing challenges of dignity and identity. At the end of the day, like other Pan-African and decolonial scholars, Mazrui wished to see and worked towards reinvention of Africa, which was inhabited by Africans as masters of their own destiny. Without the realization of this decolonial task the ancestors of Africa would remain angry at Africans.

References

Adebanwi, W. 2009. 'Terror, Territoriality and the Struggle for Indigeneity and Citizenship in Northern Nigeria'. *Citizenship Studies*, 13(3), pp. 350–378.

Adem, S. 2014a. 'Ali A. Mazrui, the Postcolonial Theorist'. *African Studies Review*, 57(1), April, pp. 135–152.

Adem, S. 2014b. 'ASR Focus on Ali A Mazrui: Introduction'. *African Studies Review*, 57(1), pp. 131–133.

Ahluwalia, P. 2001. *Politics and Post-Colonial Theory: African Inflections*. London and New York: Routledge.

Ajayi, J. F. A. 2000. 'Colonialism: An Episode in African History'. In T. Falola (ed.), *Tradition and Change in Africa: The Essays of J. F. Ade Ajayi*, Trenton, NJ: Africa World Press, pp. 165–174.

Appiah, K. A. 1992. *In My Father's House: Africa in the Philosophy of Culture*. Cambridge, UK: Cambridge University Press.

Blyden, E. W. 1967. *Christianity, Islam and the Negro Race*. Third Edition. Edinburgh, UK: University of Edinburgh Press.

Creary, N. (ed.). 2012. *African Intellectuals and Decolonization*. Athens, OH: Ohio University Press, 2012.

Du Bois, W. E. B. [1903]. *The Souls of Black Folk*: Introduction by Nathan Hare and Alvin Poussaint. New York: New American Library, 1982.

Falola, T. 2001. *Nationalism and African Intellectuals*. Rochester, NY: The University of Rochester Press, 2001.

Frenkel, M. Y. 1974. 'Edward Blyden and the Concept of African Personality'. *African Affairs*, 73(292), 1974, pp. 277–289.

Geschiere, P. 2009. *The Perils of Belonging: Autochthony, Citizenship, and Exclusion in Africa and Europe*. Chicago, IL and London: The University of Chicago Press.

Gordon, L. R. 2000. *Existentia Africana: Understanding Africana Existential Thought*. New York and London: Routledge.

Gordon, L. R. 2008. *An Introduction to Africana Philosophy*. Cambridge, UK: Cambridge University Press.

Hensbroek, P B van. 1999. *Political Discourse in African Thought, 1860 to the Present*. Westport, CT: Praeger.

Herskovits, M. 1960. 'Does Africa Exist?' in *Symposium on Africa*. Wellesley, MA: Wellesley College.

Hunter, E (ed.). 2016. *Citizenship, Belonging, and Political Community in Africa: Dialogues Between Past and Present*. Athens, OH: Ohio University Press.

July, R. W. 1968. *The Origins of Modern African Thought: Its Development in West Africa During the Nineteenth and Twentieth Centuries*. London: Faber & Faber.

Laremont, R. E, Seghatolislami, T. L., Toler, M. A. and Kalouche, F. (eds). 2002. *Africanity Defined: Collected Essays of Ali A. Mazrui: Volume 1*. Trenton, NJ: Africa World Press.

Lovejoy, P. E. 1986. 'The Ibadan School and Its Critics'. In B. Jewsiewicki and D. Newbury (eds), *African Historiographies*. London: Sage Publications, pp. 197–205.

Mafeje, A. 2011. 'Africanity: A Combative Ontology'. In R. Devisch and Francis B. Nyamnjoh (eds), *The Postcolonial Turn: Re-Imagining Anthropology and Africa*. Bamenda and Leiden: Langaa and African Studies Centre, pp. 31–44.

Makinda, S. 2005. 'Leadership in Africa: A Contextual Essay'. In A. Mazrui and W. Mutunga (eds). *Governance and Leadership: Debating The African Condition: Mazrui and His Critics: Volume Two*. Trenton, NJ: Africa World Press, pp. 3–10.

Maldonado-Torres, N. 2007. 'On Coloniality of Being: Contributions to the Development of a Concept'. *Cultural Studies*, 21(2–3), pp. 240–270.

Mamdani, M. 1996. *Citizen and Subject: Contemporary Africa and the Legacy of Late Colonialism.* Princeton, NJ: Princeton University Press.

Mazrui, A. A. 1963. 'On the Concept of "We Are All Africans"'. *American Political Science Review*, 57(1), pp. 24–97.

Mazrui, A. A. 1978. *Political Values and the Educated Class in Africa.* Berkeley and Los Angeles, CA: University of California Press.

Mazrui, A. A. 1980. *The African Condition: A Diagnosis.* Cambridge, UK: Cambridge University Press.

Mazrui, A. A. 1986. *The Africans: A Triple Heritage.* London: BBC Publications.

Mazrui, A. A. 1990. *Cultural Forces in World Politics.* Nairobi: East African Educational Publishers.

Mazrui, A. A. 2001. 'Ideology and African Political Culture'. In T. Kiros (ed.), *Explorations in African Political Thought: Identity, Community, Ethic.* New York: Routledge, pp. 97–132.

Mazrui, A. A. 2003. 'Towards Re-Africanizing African Universities: Who Killed Intellectualism in the Post-Colonial Era?' *Alternatives: Turkish Journal of International Relations*, 2(3 and 4), Fall and Winter, pp. 135–163.

Mazrui, A. A. 2011. 'Pro-Democracy Uprisings in Africa's Experience: From Sharpeville to Benghazi'. Unpublished Paper Presented at the African Studies Centre at the University of Free State, Bloemfontein, South Africa.

Mazrui, A. and Mutunga, W. (eds). 2003. *Governance and Leadership: Debating the African Condition: Volume II.* Trenton, NJ: Africa World Press.

Mazrui, A. and Mutunga, W. (eds). 2004. *Race, Gender and Culture Conflict: Debating the African Condition: Mazrui and His Critics: Volume 1.* Trenton, NJ: Africa World Press.

Mudimbe, V. Y. 1988. *The Invention of Africa: Gnosis, Philosophy, and the Order of Knowledge.* Bloomington and Indianapolis, IN: Indiana University Press.

Mudimbe, V. Y. 1994. *The Idea of Africa.* Oxford, UK: James Currey.

Mudimbe, V Y. 2013. *On African Faultlines: Meditations on Alterity Politics.* Scottsville: University of KwaZulu-Natal Press.

Muller, J. 1997. 'Social Justice and Its Renewals: A Sociological Comment'. *International Studies in Sociology of Education*, 7(2), pp. 176–105.

Ndlovu-Gatsheni, S J. 2013a *Empire, Global Coloniality and African Subjectivity.* New York and Oxford, UK: Berghahn Books.

Ndlovu-Gatsheni, S, J. 2013b. *Coloniality of Power in Postcolonial Africa: Myths of Decolonization.* Dakar: CODESRIA Book Series.

Ndlovu-Gatsheni, S. J. 2014. 'Genealogies and Lineages of Coloniality in Africa: From Colonial Encounters to the Current Coloniality of Markets'. Paper Presented at the Council of Latin American Social Science (CLACSO) Congress, Buenos Aires, Argentina, 9–11 December.

Neocosmos, M. 2010. *From 'Foreign Natives' to 'Native Foreigners': Explaining Xenophobia in Post-Apartheid South Africa: Citizenship and Nationalism, Identity and Politics.* Dakar: CODESRIA Books.

Neocosmos, M. 2016. *Thinking Freedom in Africa: Towards a Theory of Emancipatory Politics.* Johannesburg: Wits University Press.

Ngugi wa Thiong'o. 1986. *Decolonizing the Mind: The Politics of Language in African Literature.* Oxford, UK: James Currey.

Ngugi wa Thiong'o. 2009. *Something Torn and New: An African Renaissance.* New York: Basic Civitas Books.

Nkrumah, K. 1970. *Concienscism: Philosophy and the Ideology for Decolonization.* New York: St. Martin's Press.

Nyamnjoh, F. B. 2006. *Insiders and Outsiders: Citizenship and Xenophobia in Contemporary Southern Africa*. Dakar and London: CODESRIA Books and Zed Books.

Said, E. 1994. *Culture and Imperialism*. New York: Vintage Books.

Santos, B. de S. 2007. 'Beyond Abyssal Thinking: From Global Lines to Ecologies of Knowledges'. *Review*, xxx(1), pp. 45–89.

Soyinka, W. 1991. 'Triple Tropes of Trickery'. *Transition*, 54, pp. 179–183.

Soyinka, W. 2012. *Of Africa*. New Haven and London: Yale University Press.

Temu, A. and Swai, B. 1981. *Historians and Africanist History: A Critique: Post-Colonial Historiography Examined*. London: Zed Books.

Thiam, C. 2014. *Return to the Kingdom of Childhood: Re-Envisioning the Legacy and Philosophical Relevance of Negritude*. Columbus, OH: The Ohio State University Press.

Wai, D. W. 2013. 'Mazruiphilia and Mazruiphobia'. In S. Adem, W. Mutunga and A. M. Mazrui (eds). *Black Orientalism and Pan-African Thought: Debating the African Condition: Ali A. Mazrui and His Critics: Volume III*. Trenton: Africa World Press, pp. 137–173.

Wilder, G. 2015. *Freedom Time: Negritude, Decolonization, and the Future of the World*. Durham, UK and London: Duke University Press.

Zeleza, P. T. 1997. *Manufacturing African Studies and Crises*. Dakar: CODESRIA Book Series.

Zeleza, P. T. 2006. 'The Invention of African Identities and Languages: The Discursive and Developmental Implications'. In O. F. Arasanyin and M. A. Pemberton (eds), *Selected Proceedings of the 36th Annual Conference on African Linguistics: Shifting the Centre of Africanism in Language Politics and Economic Globalization*. Somerville, MA: Cascadilla Proceeding Project, pp. 14–26.

6

EPISTEMIC LEGITIMACY OF AFRICA

Introduction

The domain of knowledge is a site of long-standing epistemic struggles. Epistemic struggles were and are inextricably intertwined with struggles over ontological issues. Racism spoiled ontology, epistemology and scholarship simultaneously. Racist dehumanization delineated not only the borders of being and power but also those of knowledge. In the process, epistemic racism deprived humanity of the chance to benefit from rich knowledge cascading from diverse geo-political sites of thought. This was possible because during the unfolding of imperialism and colonialism, colonial invaders did not only target the land and human resources, they also invaded the mental universe of those people they colonized. The mental universe of the colonized experienced the depth of epistemological violence. One of the long-term consequences of this invasion of the mental universe of the colonized world was the inscription of the debilitating Hegelian master-servant dialectic of Europe as the abode of knowers (teachers/civilizers of the world) and Africa as a dwelling of ignorant and primitive sub-human species; Europe as the originator of things and Africa as the imitator; as well as Europe as source of science and rationality and Africa as 'Dark Continent' engrossed in magic and superstition.

The climax of the Hegelian master-servant dialectic was the creation of resilient European colonizers and African colonized subjectivities that have proven difficult to transcend as they require, in the words of Mamdani (1998: 8), 'overall metamorphosis' and political rebirth. It must, therefore, not come as a surprise that the political, economic, social and intellectual history of Africa as well as African subjectivity, are still struggling for freedom from this Hegelian racist imperial/colonial dialectic. What was then lost was the epistemic legitimacy of Africa. Put in simpler terms, the loss of epistemic legitimacy fundamentally means denial of one's knowledge and imposition of someone else's knowledge. The intended impact of this epistemological colonization is well articulated by Ngugi wa

Thiong'o (Ngugi wa Thiong'o 1986) in terms of mental dislocation and alienation that created a very awkward form of subjectivity characterized by headless bodies and bodiless heads (see Ngugi wa Thiong'o 2012).

As a result of mental dislocation and alienation, Africans began to see themselves from outside themselves and to think about themselves not from the inside but from the outside using external lens. How this loss of epistemic legitimacy emerged in Africa is also well documented by Valentin Yves (Vumbi Yoka) Mudimbe (1988; 1994) who traced it back to the very invention of Africa and the making of the idea of Africa. Western travellers, missionaries and anthropologists actively worked to layout the invasion of the mental universe of Africa. It was this invasion of the mental universe of Africa that destroyed the authentic African genius, killed the spirit of invention and launched Africans into a long night of epistemic dependence. The key is how else we can explain the fact that Africa, in the fields of science and technology, is still 'tied hand and foot to the apron of the West' unless we understand 'the logic of extroversion' (Hountondji 1997: 1). Paulin J. Hountondji (1997: 2) explained that scientific dependence follows the same logic as economic dependence and its origins were traceable to the integration of Africa and the rest of the Global South 'into the world-wide process of intellectual production managed and controlled by the Northern countries'.

However, the pre-occupation of this chapter is not how Africa lost epistemic legitimacy but how African scholars have struggled to restore the epistemic legitimacy of the continent. It is focused on the reinvention of African gnosis by Africans themselves. The struggles to re-establish African gnosis as a way of restoration of the epistemic legitimacy of Africa began with such African scholars as Cheikh Anta Diop who directly challenged the dominance of Eurocentrism in the knowledge making on Africa. As he put it himself, his epistemic struggle was to 'reconquer the Promethean consciousnesses' of Africans of the ancient world (Diop 1974: xv). The significance of re-establishment of the epistemic legitimacy of Africa is that it formed a central part in the repositioning of African people in the modern world. Ngugi wa Thiong'o (2016) understood it as the strategy of securing the base and making Africa visible in the globe.

Thus the African struggles for epistemic freedom seek to restore historical and epistemic legitimacy of Africa as a site of knowledge. At the centre of this struggle is what Ngugi wa Thiong'o termed 'moving the centre', which means shifting the intellectual lens from an Africa that is defined from outside to an Africa that is interpreted from the inside so as to understand the world clearly and better. The case study here is the expansive work of the Ugandan political scientist Mahmood Mamdani who has consistently strove to decolonize knowledge and to restore the epistemic legitimacy of Africa. In his celebrated book entitled *Citizen and Subject: Contemporary Africa and the Legacy of Late Colonialism* (1996: 9), Mamdani explained that there was an urgent need to advance 'the historical legitimacy of Africa as a unit of analysis' if African scholars and Africanists were to transcend Euro-North American-centric and colonial historiographical practices of writing African history 'by analogy'.

Mahmood Mamdani's locus of enunciation

Lewis R. Gordon, a leading existential Africana philosopher, warned us about the tendency to reduce black intellectual work to the biographical and autobiographical (only informed and driven by the experiential). He underscored this warning in these words:

> The fallacy of intentionality in the history of ideas is well known: Do not confuse the intentions of an author with the object of his or her production, for it is often the case that the author has a problem of interpretation similar to that of the reader or other interpreter. Although at times intent may offer insight – for instance, into why the project 'failed' – the independence of the text has been a rule of thumb in the art of interpretation. This rule, however, has been violated in peculiar ways when it comes to the work of black theorists. For them, a different rule, an insidious rule, continues to reign: the fallacy of reductionistic 'experience'.
>
> (Gordon 2000: 22)

What is needed, therefore, is not to fall into 'reductionistic experience' as a mode of understanding the work of black scholars but to try and understand the scholars' locus of enunciation. Locus of enunciation is more than simple experience. It speaks to social location of the scholar on the side of the global racialized and hierarchized power spectrum. This is important because the biggest success of coloniality lies in how it bewitched and seduced African scholars to such an extent that they ended up thinking, speaking and writing as though they were located on the privileged side of the global racialized power spectrum. Not with Mamdani of course, his locus of enunciation has been very clear from the beginning. His epistemic interventions are part of what Isaac A. Kamola and Shiera S. el-Malik (2017) termed the 'African anti-colonial archive'/decolonial archive.

The African anti-colonial archive/decolonial archive is an embodiment of ideas, theories, manifestoes, slogans, concepts, critiques, hopes, utopic registers, trials and tribulations, prospects and possibilities, memories, texts, sounds and images; and is constitutive of an inheritance for the entire world (Kamola and el-Malik 2017: 3–4). Mamdani is part of what Kamola and el-Malik (2017: 4) depicted as 'a heterodox group of scholars, political leaders, peasants, teachers, journalists, and citizens engaged in the political struggles against colonial powers'. At the centre of the 'African anti-colonial archive' are pertinent questions of identity, history, epistemology, ideology, theory, and all those issues with the potential to either derail or advance national and human liberation.

What also characterized the 'African anti-colonial archive'/decolonial archive has been the tension 'between scholarship and politics, between the production of knowledge and the use of that knowledge within a particular conjuncture' (Kamola and el-Malik 2017: 9). Mamdani emerged as a scholar, public intellectual and activist within a context of decolonization and this is why his locus of enunciation fitted neatly within the 'African anti-colonial archive'/decolonial archive. In fact

Mamdani is one of the active producers of the anti-colonial archive/decolonial archive. At his intellectual formative stage, the Indian and African concerns pre-occupied Mamdani's mind mainly because he was born in India but grew up in Africa.

Ideologically, Mamdani, like his generation, was deeply influenced by a combination of many forces. The first influence was Marxist class analysis that he applied effectively in understanding African social formations. The second was African nationalism's anti-and decolonial orientation that dominated the twentieth century. The third was global struggles against racism and for civil and political rights that he experienced in the United States of America. The fourth was the direct personal experiences of expulsion and denial of citizenship in Uganda. The fifth was the life of exile in Britain and Tanzania. The sixth was the Pan-Africanist public intellectualism that dominated at the Council for Development of Social Science in Africa (CODESRIA). The seventh were the discourses of Thirdism and its anti-imperialism that enabled the hosting of the Bandung Conference, informed the demand for a New Economic World Order (NEO); produced the Non-Aligned Movement and offered ideological resources to resist neoliberal Washington Consensus in general and Structural Adjustment Programmes (SAPs) in particular. The final force was the direct experience of trying to decolonize curriculum at UCT in South Africa (see Sharawy 2010; Chen 2017).

Mamdani's intellectual interventions

Broadly speaking, Mamdani's intellectual and scholarly interventions are characterized by three commitments. The first is a commitment to understanding the local conditions as the basis of theory formulation. Thus, his theorization is always deeply sensitive to the local conditions even though gesturing to the wider world. The second is a fidelity to historicization of African issues. The third is his 'tenacious attempt to providing an alternative imagination for political alternatives' (Chen 2017: 581). Mamdani's work boldly confronted some of the most difficulty and controversial contemporary issues and questions. Kuan-Hsing Chen provided this concise summary of Mamdani's thematic interventions:

> Mahmood Mamdani has been a central figure engaging in explaining the most controversial issues such as refugees, popular versus state nationalism, mass killings (Rwanda), settler versus native, colonial citizenship and its governed subject, September 11, the Darfur movement (and its self-indulgence), Imperial Human Rights, decolonizing university and knowledge production, the USA as the first [settler colony] that is not yet decolonized, settler colonialism, etc.
>
> (Chen 2017: 580)

His selection and handling of the research themes that spoke directly to the key challenges facing humanity qualified Mamdani as a decolonial humanist. In his very first publication of 1972 entitled *The Myth of Population Control: Family, Class and Caste in an Indian Village*, Mamdani delved deeper into indigenous Indian knowledge of village life and directly challenged the then popular Malthusian theory that blamed the poor for lack of rational thought and education that led them to create the problem of high fertility (Mamdani 1972). This early work responded directly to the racist and imperial/colonial idea of a people without knowledge and rationality and he demonstrated empirically that the prevailing social and political order mediated by class and caste systems had to be understood if the challenges of high fertility among the poor were to be tackled. He recommended social reform of the family, class and caste systems of the Indian society as a way forward (Mamdani 1972).

Mamdani's next publication, entitled *From Citizen to Refugee: Uganda Asians Come to Britain* (1973), might not have been planned but emerged within a context of his own expulsion together with other Asians from Uganda by Idi Amin who claimed to be Africanizing commerce and industry in 1972. It might be from this personal experience that Mamdani developed interest in the intractable questions of racism, citizenship, belonging and power. In *From Citizen to Refugee* (1973), Mamdani critiqued the popular nationalism and populist politics of Amin's regime that produced a particularly narrow economic nationalism as well as politics of scapegoating of minorities. Here, signs of Mamdani's deep understanding of economic analysis, class struggles, and history of postcolonial Africa emerged.

By the time of the publication of his revised PhD thesis into a major work entitled *Politics and Class Formation in Uganda* (1976), Mamdani was deeply 'Marxist' in thinking and was effectively deploying class analysis to understand African social formations while at the same demonstrating a clear understanding of the limits of Marxist thought when applied to postcolonial situations of reproduction of racism. By this time, he was based at the University of Dar es Salaam (a seat of Marxist political economy approaches) and in a country where Mwalimu Julius Nyerere was busy experimenting and implementing what became known as 'African Socialism'. Mamdani launched a robust critique of what became known as the 'petty-bourgeoisie', who inherited the colonial state, and he traced economic and developmental challenges of Uganda to the role of colonialism and its exploitative practices. Even the 1972 expulsion of the Ugandan Asians was explained from a class analysis as an appeasement of the Ugandan black petty-bourgeoisie who were in competition with the Asian merchant class (Mamdani 1976, Sharawy 2010: 196).

While Mamdani did not abandon class analysis he gradually gravitated towards political and legal institutional analysis of power structures of colonialism and the subjectivities they produced as he focused on making sense of postcolonial African dilemmas of governance, nation-building and development. At the same time he began to deploy Kwame Nkrumah's concept of 'neo-colonialism' in his double critique of the local Ugandan bourgeoisie and global imperialism. For example his 1983 work entitled *Imperialism and Fascism in Uganda* became predicated on the concept of 'neo-colonialism' while at the same time drawing from his own political involvement in workers' struggles (Chen 1983: 585). This time Mamdani addressed the problem of connivance between local African bourgeoisie and the global transnational bourgeoisie in the exploitation of Africa and Africans. This analysis led him to engage the problem of imperialism and the drive towards monopolization of the African economies. This analysis, which implicated the local Ugandan leaders in the exploitation of their own people and resources, provoked Milton Obote (then president of Uganda) to suspend Mamdani's citizenship (Chen 2017: 585). It would seem the second expulsion from Uganda firmed up Mamdani's interest in researching the issues of citizenship in Africa. His major publication entitled *Citizen and Subject. Contemporary Africa and the Legacy of Late Colonialism* (1996) directly confronted two major questions:

> First, what was the historical/colonial process that produced the (bifurcated) power structure of contemporary Africa? And how did this bifurcation between 'race' (those who were identified as 'citizens') and 'ethnicity' (those who were identified as 'subjects') in turn fragment popular resistance and sustained (decentralised state despotism)? In other words, Mamdani was trying to historicise the postcolonial violence witnessed in Africa's recent history and traced their origin in colonial institutions and colonially crafted identities.
>
> (Chen 2017: 585)

As a person who had directly suffered two occasions of deprivation of citizenship, partly because of his Indian descent and partly because of his critical intellectual writings, Mamdani wanted to get into the depth of the question of settlers and natives in Africa and how that dilemma could be resolved. Below is a detailed engagement with the contents of *Citizen and Subject* (1996), a book that produced a framework that Mamdani applied to many other case studies including Rwanda and Sudan.

Mamdani's rethinking of thinking on Africa

At least five contributions of Mamdani to the rethinking thinking on Africa are discernible. The first is his decolonial approach to the study of Africa, which privileged internal historical dynamics. The second is his analysis of how colonial power worked and how it impinged on African resistance and generated postcolonial dilemmas. The third is his thesis on colonial manufacturing of political identities and how these continue to haunt contemporary Africa. The fourth is his concept of 'actually existing civil society' that is opposed to the abstract/programmatic conceptions of civil society in Africa. The fifth is his rearticulation of transitional justice beyond the traditional post-1945 Nuremberg template.

To Mamdani, rethinking thinking on Africa entailed changing the geography of reason and the casting of intellectual light directly on Africa as a legitimate unit of analysis. His approach was indeed an intellectual and academic rebellion against imperial and colonial historiographical tradition. This tradition privileged European and North American historical experience(s) as the 'touchstone, as the historical expression of the universal' (Mamdani 1996: 11–12). In this tradition, African historical realities had to be benchmarked or compared with Europe and North America. Mamdani's decolonial thinking dovetailed with that of Cathrine Odora Hoppers and Howard Richards (2012: 8) to whom rethinking thinking meant 'The casting of light at last onto subjugated peoples, knowledges, histories and ways of living unsettles the toxic pond and transforms passive analysis into a generative force that valorises and recreates life for those previously museumised'. Hoppers and Richards (2012: 8) elaborated that rethinking thinking 'is a process of engaging with colonialism in a manner that produces a program for its dislocation'.

Mamdani consistently emphasized the importance of a methodological approach that avoided lifting African historical experiences from their context. His departure point became the analysis of colonial power architecture and configuration. Thus, conceptually, Mamdani became increasingly concerned about what he termed 'a paralysis of perspective' as he endeavoured to unlock the 'impasse in Africa' that visibly manifested itself 'at the level of practical politics' (Mamdani 1996: 1). At the centre of this crisis of ideas were entrenched positions of 'modernists', 'communitarians', 'Eurocentrists', and 'Africanists' that Mamdani (1996: 1) briefly and neatly summarized as follows:

> Modernists take inspiration from East European uprisings of the late eighties; communitarians decry liberal or left Eurocentrism and call for a return to the source. For modernists, the problem is that civil society is embryonic and marginal construct in Africa; for communitarians, it is that real flesh-and-blood communities that comprise Africa are marginalised from public life as so many 'tribes'. The liberal solution is to locate politics in civil society, and the Africanist solution is to put Africa's old-age communities at the centre of African politics.
>
> (Mamdani 1996: 1)

Mamdani carefully avoided easy dismissal of these problematic positions. Instead he suggested that 'one needs to problematize each' so as 'to arrive at a creative synthesis transcending both positions' (Mamdani 1996: 1). But how do we move beyond this crisis of perspective? Mamdani (1996:1) suggested 'the way forward lies in sublating both, through a double move that simultaneously critiques and affirms'. Mamdani has also been critical of 'area studies' that to him were underpinned by two problematic methodological claims:

> The first sees state boundaries as boundaries of knowledge, thereby turning political into epistemological boundaries. [. . .] The second methodological claim is that knowledge is about the production of facts. This view translates into stubborn resistance to theory in the name of valorising the fact. From this point of view, the claim is that theory is deadening: instead of

illuminating, it manipulates the fact. The assumption is that facts speak for themselves. But facts needs to be put in context, and interpreted; neither is possible without a theoretical illumination.

(Mamdani 2001b: xii–xiii)

Having critiqued the methodological limits of area studies, Mamdani broke the 'rules of areas studies where every 'expert' must cultivate his or her own 'local' patch, where geography is forever fixed by contemporary political boundaries' (Mamdani 2001: xii). Mamdani termed this intellectual habit of conflating state boundaries with epistemological boundaries 'intellectual claustrophobia' involving linking 'local outcomes to colonialism historically, but not to broader regional developments' (Mamdani 2001: xiii). Mamdani broke with area studies tradition in two ways in his book entitled *When Victims Become Killers: Colonialism, Nativism, and the Genocide in Rwanda* (2001b) in which he sought to make the Rwanda Genocide of 1994 thinkable. At the first level, he historicized geography in the process challenging the processes of naturalizing political identities of the Hutu and Tutsi (Mamdani 2001a: xiii).

Through this approach Mamdani revealed the poverty of existing scholarship on the 1959 Revolution in Rwanda, which failed to problematize 'the ways in which the postcolonial state reproduced and reinforced colonially produced political identities in the name of justice' in the process 'treating these identities as if they were natural constructs' (Mamdani 2001b: xiii). At a second level, Mamdani broke with the 'antitheoretical thrust' through rethinking 'existing facts in light of rethought contexts, thereby to illuminate old facts and core realities in new light' (Mamdani 2001: xvi). This way, Mamdani managed to transcend clichés of horror and produced a scholarly work that took historical, regional, theoretical and moral perspective seriously in order to enable a deeper understanding of how social dynamics made the genocide possible.

Mamdani emphasized three important issues. The first is 'In pursuit of knowledge, we knew no boundaries' (Mamdani 2001b: xvi). The second is 'we looked at the world *from within Africa*' (Mamdani 2001b: xvi emphasis in original text). The third is that 'decolonization in one sphere of life does not necessarily and automatically lead to decolonization in other spheres' (Mamdani 2001b: xvi). In the case of Rwanda, politicized identities were never decolonized. The three concerns speak to the broader approach of Mamdani to the study of Africa that underscored the specificity of Africa and sought to transcend the colonial historiographical habit of writing African history by analogy (Mamdani 1996: 9–10). Broadly, Mamdani openly rebelled conceptually and methodologically from the traditional intellectual and academic habit of making European historical experience the template of all other historical experiences. In Mamdani we therefore read Africa that is not first of all lifted out of its context and process so as to write it by analogy.

In his interpretation of the subject of colonialism, Mamdani moved along with the epic rather than episodic school. The episodic school, as represented by the

Nigerian historian Jacob Ade Ajayi (1969) of the Ibadan Nationalist School, understood colonialism as a mere episode in African history as they frantically fought to counter colonial historiography that denied African agency in history. Mamdani's critique of those who laboured to restore historicity and agency to the subject is this: 'But if structuralism tended to straitjacket agency within iron laws of history, a strong tendency in poststructuralism is to diminish the significance of historical constraint in the name of salvaging agency' (Mamdani 1996: 10). Thus, if one closely reads Mamdani's seminal works, it became clear that his understanding of colonialism was closer to the epic school that captures the epic if not revolutionary impact of colonialism on Africa's conceptions of power and identity, for instance. The epic school embraced Aime Cesaire (1955) and his deep understanding of colonialism as a problematic civilizational process; Frantz Fanon (1968: 210) who posited that colonialism worked on the history of the oppressed people, distorting, disfiguring, and ultimately destroying it; Peter Ekeh (1983: 5) who defined colonialism as a 'social movement of epochal dimensions whose enduring significance' went 'beyond the life-span of the colonial situation', Ali A. Mazrui (1986: 12) who understood colonialism as a 'revolution of epic proportions'; and Ngugi wa Thiong'o (1986) who emphasized how colonialism amounted to an invasion of the mental universe of Africa.

Deploying sophisticated historicization and theorization of phenomena, Mamdani successfully explained, in a profound manner, the intricate linkages between how the 'regime of differentiation (institutional segregation) as fashioned in colonial Africa – and reformed after independence' bred a particularly poor form of resistance (Mamdani 1996: 7). Thus, from Mamdani's interventions one learnt that how Europe ruled Africa shaped the way Africans responded to it as well as impinging on how present structures of power in contemporary Africa worked.

In his latest book entitled *Define and Rule: Native as Political Identity* (2013), Mamdani made two profound interventions. The first was that 'colonial empires were the first political fundamentalists of the modern period' (Mamdani 2013: 50). The second was that 'the native is the creation of the colonial state: colonized, the native is pinned down, localized, thrown out of civilization as an outcast, confined to custom, and then defined as its product' (Mamdani 2013: 2–3). These two interventions spoke to what Valentin Y. Mudimbe (1994) termed the paradigm of difference, which produced what Boaventura de Sousa Santos (2007) described as 'abyssal thinking' and 'impossibility of co-presence'. For Africa and Africans, colonial fundamentalism, that was deployed in the invention of 'natives' as sub-human beings defined by geography rather than history and ruled by custom, resulted in their dismemberment from the human race (Ngugi wa Thiong'o 2009a; 2009b).

In another profound way, Mamdani revealed the dangers of importing theoretical frameworks and solutions from outside of Africa in the belief that they would work wonders on Africa. He boldly stated:

> For a curious feature of current African politics is to draw prescriptions from a context other than the one that gave rise to its problems. Whereas the

source of demands is the existing African context, the framework for solutions is generally a received theory of democracy which has little to do with contemporary realities in Africa.

(Mamdani 1992: 2228)

Building on this argument, Mamdani made a number of useful interventions. The first is that internal reform or even revolutionary movements from Africa were commonly read as influenced by external developments such as the infiltration of communists, the fall of the Soviet Union or influence of East European pro-democracy movements. Such an approach made it difficult for analysts to understand continuities in African history from armed liberation movements to social movements, from rural to urban protest movements, and from 'peasant society' ('the people') to civil society ('the citizens') (Mamdani 1992: 2228). His second intervention is captured below:

The framework of received theory is a set of assumptions which do not always reflect realities on the continent. The clash between assumptions and realities can either lead to sterile attempts to enforce textbook solutions or be a rich source of creative reflection.

(Mamdani 1992: 2223)

Mamdani traced the problems of narrow understanding of pluralism in post-colonial Africa to the post-World War II colonial reform that informed most of Africa's transition from colonialism to 'independence' in the 1960s. This is how he understood the problem:

It is an understanding which equated pluralism with only its political dimension; as a result, the same reform which recognised the existence of *political* movements undermined the autonomy of *social* movements. By cultivating the former but suffocating the latter, the reform drove a wedge between political and social movements, and created a post-independence environment for the emergence of state-parties, at first several, and then one. I shall argue that it is this highly restricted notion of pluralism which prepared the soil for single party dictatorships in a growing number of African countries.

(Mamdani 1992: 2228)

This analysis explained why democracy became reducible to multipatyism, a problem which continued to produce pseudo-democracies on the continent predicated on regular rituals of elections, which in substance largely reflect an ethnic census as those from majority ethnicities always win. Mamdani also critiqued the received liberal theory as it pertains to rights and citizenship in Africa. He posed the fundamental question: who are the legitimate bearers of rights in Africa? His response was:

I shall argue that notions received from Euro-American liberalism – that the bearer of the 'right to self-determination' is the nation, and that of 'human rights' is the citizen – are so restrictive that they have the unfortunate result of disenfranchising increasing number of groups and individuals under present conditions in Africa.

(Mamdani 1992: 2229)

Mamdani problematized the idea of the 'nation' as the bearer of 'right to self-determination' as influenced by European ideas and the notion of 'citizens' as the bearer of 'human rights' as informed by American constitutional thought (Mamdani 1992: 2230). Mamdani (1992: 2230–2231) posited 'one needs to begin with an understanding of what is unique about the African context to arrive at a notion of rights adequate to it'. He elaborated:

In Africa more than in any part of the world, there is little coincidence between the history of nation formation and that of state formation, between social history and political history. Many state boundaries date, not even from the Berlin Conference of the 1880s, but from the decade of inde-pendence of the 1960s. More than the outcome of internal social histories, they reflect the exigencies of external geopolitics.

(Mamdani 1992: 2231)

Mamdani noted that in Africa there were two main issues to consider in rethinking citizenship. The first is that of 'tribes' that aspired to form independent states and the second is the reality of migrant labour that ruptured the ideas of one's land of birth as the determinant of citizenship. Taking into account these realities, Mamdani concluded:

The African context is one where the liberal notion of rights as an attribute of citizenship, has increasingly anti-democratic consequences. To change this situation requires rescuing rights from the narrow shell of citizenship, and linking it to the more universal fact of labour (residence).

(Mamdani 1992: 2232)

However, to gain a deeper appreciation of the value of Mamdani's historicization and theorization as a form of rethinking thinking on Africa, one has to start with how he understood colonial governmentality and its long-term consequences for Africa.

Mamdani on colonialism and African responses

How power was organized and how it fragmented resistance in contemporary Africa is one of Mamdani's major departure points in understanding the colonial institutional legacy that continued to be reproduced through 'the dialectic of state reform and popular resistance' (Mamdani 1996: 1). He posed the question of how Europe ruled Africa, which concretely translated to the problematic of how alien rule was introduced and stabilized in Africa. This fundamental question led Mamdani to transcend the political economy perspective that privileged the labour question. Mamdani's enquiry was into how a minority of foreign invaders dealt with a majority of indigenous people and how 'the subject population' was 'incorporated into – and not excluded from – the arena of colonial power' (Mamdani 1996: 15). This approach led him to engage with the 'native question' rather than the 'labour question'. Mamdani (1996: 1) posited that the 'native question' 'was a dilemma that confronted every colonial power and a riddle that preoccupied the best of its minds'.

As a fundamental colonial challenge, the 'native question' pre-occupied such imperial/colonial ideologues as Sir Henry Maine in the colonization of India; Edmund Spencer in the colonization of the Irish; Cecil John Rhodes in Southern Africa; Lord Lugard in the colonization of Nigeria and Uganda; Lord Macaulay in India; and General Jan Smuts in his delivery of the prestigious Rhodes Memorial Lectures at Oxford University in 1929 as well as Verwoerd in his formulation of apartheid and its institutionalization in 1948 in South Africa. At the centre of the 'native question' has been a foundational paradigm of difference dated to the dawn of Euro-North American-centric modernity. Racial hierarchization and social classification of human species in accordance with invented and constructed differential ontological densities constituted the leitmotif of the paradigm of difference (Du Bois 1903; Quijano 2000; Ndlovu-Gatsheni 2013). This imperial reason amounted to what Nelson Maldonado-Torres (2007) termed 'coloniality of being' and Mamdani (2013) described as a process of defining and ruling of the 'natives'. In short, the 'native question', was informed by the questioning of the very humanity of the colonized people.

In response to the 'native question', colonial power evolved two forms of colonial governmentality: direct and indirect rule (Mamdani 1999). Under direct rule, 'native' institutions would be destroyed and replaced by a single Eurocentric legal order. As noted by Mamdani (1996: 16–17), this was the form of governmentality that Europeans experimented with in the eighteenth and nineteenth centuries. Direct rule was also predicated on a civilizing standard. This entailed a deliberate creation of 'a native elite' that would have assimilated colonial cultures to the extent of being eligible to be 'granted a modicum of civilized rights' by the colonial state (Mamdani 1999: 862).

The African native elite was expected to be carefully reproduced through education to be those people who would be African in blood and colour but colonial in opinions, morals and intellect so as to be able to effectively play the role of intermediaries between colonizers and the bulk of the 'uneducated' colonized peoples. But the experiences of resistance by the colonized in India and Africa provoked a shift from direct rule to indirect rule as a form of colonial reform of governance to rule indirectly through native authorities and recognition of native tradition and customs.

However, Mamdani (1999: 862) is quick to posit that 'indirect rule never entirely displaced direct rule' rather 'the two co-existed as two faces of power, direct rule a regime guaranteeing rights to racialized citizenry and indirect rule a regime enforcing culture on an ethnicized peasantry'. He went further to highlight that even under indirect rule, the colonial powers sought to shape the world of the conquered through inventing a particular form of native authority and reconstruction of tradition and cultures to suit colonial purposes (Mamdani 1999: 865). The thesis of 'invention of tradition' was initially posited by Terence Ranger (1983). The colonial logic was simply to 'recognise the historicity of the colony and the agency of the colonized' as well as confronting native 'custom analytically, rather than to dismiss it dogmatically' (Mamdani 1999: 865).

What emerged from this colonial exercise of power was a 'bifurcated state' mediated by race as reified identity that united the colons as citizens on the one hand, and on the other hand an equally reified ethnic identity that fragmented the colonized people into various unrelated tribes (Mamdani 1996; 1999). He elaborated:

> Unlike dependency theory whose focus was on the dependent economy created in the course of colonialism, I argue that the African colonial experience came to be crystallized in the nature of the state forged through that encounter. Organized differently in rural and urban areas, that state was Janus-faced, bifurcated. It contained a duality: two forms of power under singular authority. Urban power spoke the language of civil society and civil rights, rural power of community and culture. Civil power claimed to protect rights, customary power to enforce tradition.
>
> (Mamdani 1999: 866)

The consequences of this architecture of colonial power had far-reaching consequences for Africa. It led to invention of the identity of ethnicized tribes enveloped by an ossified shell of tradition and custom that had to be adhered to rather than questioned overseen by equally invented authoritarian, masculine and patriarchal 'administrative' rural authorities masquerading as embodiments of traditional African leadership. Mamdani (1999: 874) warned us not to be 'misled by the nomenclature to think of this as a handover from pre-colonial era' because these so-called chiefs were 'appointed, promoted and dismissed by the colonial power'.

The second consequence was that the form of colonial rule shaped the form of anti-colonial resistance in such a way that 'anti-colonial struggle was first and foremost a struggle against the hierarchy of the local state, the ethnically-organised Native Authority that claimed ethnic legitimacy' (Mamdani 1999: 875). At the same time, colonial racial exclusion shaped the development of a racial consciousness among those who fought against colonialism. The third was the creation of a rural-urban (town-country) dichotomy that continues to characterize contemporary Africa. As will be demonstrated later, these issues had implications for postcolonial reform, governance, citizenship, belonging and development.

Mamdani on political subjectivity in Africa

One of the major challenges in 'postcolonial' Africa has been how to move forward beyond 'settler' and 'native' political identities into a new humanity where race as an organizing principle was dead. Mamdani confronted this challenge directly in his AC Jordan Professorial Inaugural Lecture at UCT in 1998 posing the difficult question of when does a settler become a native. He posited:

> In the context of a former settler colony, a single citizenship for settlers and natives can only be the result of an overall metamorphosis whereby erstwhile colonizers and colonized are politically reborn as equal members of a single political community. The word reconciliation cannot capture this metamorphosis [. . .] This is about establishing for the first time, a political order based on consent and not conquest. It is about establishing a political community of equal and consenting citizens.
>
> (Mamdani 1998: 3)

Mamdani's robust interventions on the topical question of identities shifted the lens from class (market-determined identity) and ethnicity (culturally-determined identities) to political identities (products of state formation, crafted in law, determined by race and institutionalized by the state) within a colonial context. Within this colonial context, 'only the natives were said to belong to ethnic groups; nonnatives had no ethnicity. Nonnatives were identified racially, not ethnically' (Mamdani 2001a: 654). Among the races were Europeans (citizens) at the top and then subject races such as Asians, Coloured (mixed-races), Arabs and Hamites (Tutsi), and these in their different categories were considered to be civilized compared to natives as ethnicities that were said to be desperately in need of being civilized (Mamdani 2001a: 654). Mamdani summarized how political identities were constructed in this manner:

> The colonial state divided the population into two: races and ethnicities. Each lived in a different legal universe. Races were governed through civil law. They were considered as members, actually or potentially, of civil society. Civil society excluded ethnicities. [. . .] Ethnicities were governed through customary laws. While civil law spoke the language of rights, customary law spoke the language of tradition, of authenticity. [. . .] Colonial law made a fundamental distinction between two types of person: those indigenous and those not indigenous; in a word, natives and nonnatives. My first observation [. . .] is that rights belonged to nonnatives, not to natives. Natives had to live according to custom.
>
> (Mamdani 2001a: 654)

This politicization of identities had a direct implication for the formation of African national consciousness and nationalism itself. Mamdani (2001a: 654) correctly noted: 'Nationalism was a struggle of natives to be recognised as a transethnic identity, as a race, as "Africans," and thus – as a race – to gain admission to the world of rights, to civil society, which was a short form of civilized society.' How has postcolonial Africa attempted to dismantle what was created through indirect rule? Mamdani posited that postcolonial reform took two problematic forms: conservative and radical. The former simply inherited the local state apparatus (from chiefs to headmen) while trying to deracialize the central state. The latter tried to destroy the local state as imagined and constructed by colonialists and imposed a singular customary law transcending ethnic boundaries (chiefs were replaced with cadres and tradition/custom were replaced with ideas of revolution and development) (Mamdani 1996; 2001a). The consequences were the same: the peasants remained captured, rural-urban dichotomy was not broken and the rural sector was not democratized.

However, in *Define and Rule* (2013: 107), Mamdani provided the example of Mwalimu Julius Nyerere as one postcolonial African leader who 'successfully implemented an alternative form of statecraft' that dismantled 'the structures of indirect rule through sustained but peaceful reform'. Nyerere's success is attributed to correct diagnosis of where the legacy of colonial state lay, not in army and police but in 'its legal and administrative apparatus' (Mamdani 2013: 107). This correct identification of the problem enabled Nyerere to establish 'a singular and unified law-enforcing machinery' that 'meant that every citizen in mainland Tanzania was governed on the basis of the same set of rules, enforced by a single court system' (Mamdani 2013: 108). Nyerere's achievement was therefore in the creation of an inclusive citizenship and a cohesive nation-state. This success was owed to Nyerere's commitment since 1962 to build a united nation under-pinned by human equality and dignity that transcended race and ethnicity. The first move that was taken by Nyerere was to abolish all race-based distinctions in civil law as well as ethnic-based distinctions enshrined in customary law (Mamdani 2013: 109).

What must be emphasized is that Mamdani's historicization and theorization of politicized identities emanated from his concern with postcolonial challenges. This is how he posed his concern: 'how does this institutional inheritance, with its legacy enforced distinctions between races and ethnicities, civil law and customary law, rights and custom, subject races and subject ethnicities, play out after colonialism?' (Mamdani 2001a: 657). We will deal with these implications in the concluding section of this chapter. For now let's turn to how colonial power architecture shaped the formation of 'indigenous' civil society.

Mamdani on indigenous civil society in Africa

Mamdani's work is insightful on how 'actually existing civil society in Africa' as opposed to the programmatic, ideological, abstract and sponsored civil society described by Karl Marx, Antonio Gramsci, Talcott Parsons, Jurgen Habermas, and others drawing from European and North American experiences, emerged

(Mamdani 1996: 13–21). Again, Mamdani (1996: 15) underscored how a historical understanding of 'how the subject population was incorporated into – and not excluded from – the arena of colonial power' enabled a better comprehension of the formation and character of 'indigenous civil' society.

Mamdani (1996: 15)'s first point is that the 'exclusion that defined the specificity of civil society under colonial rule was that of race'. The second is that citizenship was 'a privilege of the civilized; the uncivilized would be subject to an all-round tutelage' (Mamdani 1996: 17). The third is that 'a propertied franchise separated the civilized from the uncivilized' making it impossible for those considered uncivilized to enjoy and civil and political rights (Mamdani 1996: 17). As noted above, the consequence of all this was the construction of a bifurcated colonial state characterized by 'two forms of power under a single hegemonic authority' with 'urban power' speaking 'the language of civil society and civil rights' (direct rule through use of civil protected rights) and 'rural power' speaking that of 'community and culture' (indirect rule enforced tradition) (Mamdani 1996: 18).

What is interesting is how Mamdani historically established the connections between civil society and nationalism that is often missing in 'postcolonial' situations where nationalism has mutated into state ideology opposed to civil society. The colonial practice of racially sanitizing civil society as a sole preserve of the colons (citizens), and closing out the colonized (subjects) from civil society including even the educated and urban-based 'natives' 'who were exempt from the lash of customary law' who 'languished in a juridical limbo', inevitably shaped the anti-colonial national consciousness formation process into a struggle for access to civil society (Mamdani 1996: 19). This reality has deep implications for the character of the anti-colonial nationalist liberation struggles. Inevitably, the struggles of the colonized subjects became ranged against both 'customary authorities in the local state and against racial barriers in civil society' (Mamdani 1996: 19).

Mamdani identified four moments in the production of 'actually existing civil society'. The first is the moment of racially sanitized civil society that excluded all those considered to be uncivilized. The second moment of development of civil society is that of the anti-colonial struggle, 'for the anti-colonial struggle was at the same time a struggle for embryonic middle class and working classes, the native strata in limbo, for entry into civil society' (Mamdani 1996: 19). The anti-colonial struggle was in a way a struggle of those deemed to be uncivilized for inclusion into civil society that was ring-fenced by race and privilege. One can argue that 'an indigenous civil society' emerged within the context of anti-colonial and anti-racial struggles. These struggles could not be achieved without decolonization, deracialization and democratization of the state. The third moment of development of civil society is that of political independence that produced a deracialized state without a deracialized civil society that continued to protect colonially accumulated privileges. In the struggle to deracialized state and civil society 'state-civil society antagonism diminished' (Mamdani 1996: 20).

The state pushed the agenda of deracialization of civil society through such initiatives as Africanization, affirmative action and indigenization projects.

This agenda united 'the victims of colonial racism' (Mamdani 1996: 20). As Mamdani put it (1996: 20–21): 'To the victims of racism the vocabulary of rights rang hollow, a lullaby for perpetuating racial privilege.' The rapture between state and civil society came during the fourth moment of redistribution of resources which became imbricated in regional, partisan, class, ethnic, gender and even familial cleavages. Mamdani argued that the fourth moment of actually existing civil society became 'the moment of the collapse of an embryonic indigenous society, of trade unions and autonomous civil organizations, and its absorption into political society' and he elaborated:

> It is the moment of the marriage between technism and nationalism, of the proliferation of state nationalism in a context where the claims of the state – both developmentalist and equalizing – had a powerful resonance, particularly for the fast-expanding educated strata. It is the time when civil society-based social movements became demobilized and political movements statized.
>
> (Mamdani 1996: 21)

The fourth moment also witnessed activities of those who had benefitted from the colonial order fighting to defend racial privileges within a postcolonial context. Thus while Mamdani's analysis of the four moments of the development of actually existing civil society were useful in deepening an understanding of contemporary African realities, he tended to ignore the debilitating hegemonic character of African nationalism even during the course of the anti-colonial nationalist-led liberation struggle even before it assumed the status of state ideology. This nationalism unfolded through subordination of all social movements, be it labour or church, to its imperative, as it did not tolerate any form of dissent from its own ranks.

But what is important about Mamdani analysis is that it underscored how colonial power configurations created 'postcolonial' difficulties concerning reforming the state and civil society. As he puts it: 'To understand the limits of deracialization of civil society, one needs to grasp the specificity of the local state, which was organized not as a racial power denying rights to urbanized subjects, but as an ethnic power enforcing custom on tribespeople' (Mamdani 1996: 21). Besides deracialization as a reform process there is need for detribalization. To his insightful analysis of decolonization, deracialization, detribalization and democratization, Mamdani has recently turned his attention to the equally important challenges of transitional justice in Africa.

Mamdani on transition justice in Africa

In his recent interventions on transitional justice, Mamdani (2015: 63) posed two fundamental questions: 'How shall we think of extreme violence, of mass violence – as criminal or political?' and 'How shall we define responsibility for large scale violence – as criminal or political?' His response to these two questions is that we need to move beyond confusing political with criminal violence at one level, and at another level, beyond a focus on perpetrators at the expense of the complex issues that drive violence. According to Mamdani (2015), it would seem that initiatives aimed at achieving transitional justice were hostage to the post-1945 Nuremberg paradigm that continued to define justice as criminal justice and this 'ideologized' paradigm is also informing the work of the ICC. To Mamdani (2015: 63), the best way to move beyond Nuremberg is to consider lessons from CODESA, which privileged political justice, replaced punishment with forgiveness – producing what he specifically termed 'survivor's justice' as opposed to 'victor's justice'.

Mamdani (2015: 63) is very critical of the use of courtroom solutions to violence and conflict as advocated by human rights activists and advocates because they were informed by a narrow understanding of conflict and violence. He posits that it was easy to apply the Nuremberg solution to the crimes committed by Nazis against the Jews because the perpetrators and the victims were to be separated: 'Perpetrators would remain in Germany and victims would depart for another homeland; Yesterday's perpetrators and victims would not have to live together, for there would be separate state – Israel – for survivors' (Mamdani 2015: 66). What about in 'postcolonial' Africa where perpetrators and victims have to live together? This is where CODESA came in as an innovative transitional justice mechanism albeit a problematic one too because it privileged forgiveness and reconciliation at the expense of justice itself. Mamdani (2015: 66) argues that what was important in the South Africa transition was that amnesty was not exchanged for truth but for willingness to reform and he elaborated:

> Rather than put justice in the back seat, CODESA presents a radically new way of thinking about justice. It presents a double breakthrough. To begin with, CODESA distinguished between different forms of justice – criminal, political and social. It prioritized political justice, the reform of the political system, over the other two. The difference between political and criminal justice is twofold. One, political justice affects groups, whereas criminal justice targets individuals. Two, the object of criminal justice is punishment; that of political justice is political reform. A shift of logic from the criminal to political led to decriminalizing and legitimizing both sides to the conflict.
>
> (Mamdani 2015: 67)

For Mamdani (2015: 81), the way forward entailed moving beyond the naming and shaming to focus on the context within which conflict and violence emerged; and locating the motivation for violence not in individual psychology or a culture of a group. He suggested: 'To break out of the cycle of violence we need to displace the victim narrative with that of the survivor. A survivor narrative is less perpetrator-driven, more issue-driven' (Mamdani 2015: 81). For Mamdani, there is a need 'to look for solution within the problem and not outside it'. The purpose of transitional justice for Mamdani is: 'The point of it all was not to avenge the dead, but to give the living a second chance' (Mamdani 2015: 82).

These interventions have provoked some criticism, particularly from those scholars who still believed in the Nuremberg forms of trials for perpetrators of violence and still have confidence in the global human rights and democracy discourses as potential solutions to political crimes committed during situations of mass violence. The critics argued that to privilege survivor's justice that embraced both victims and perpetrators of violence is unfair to the victims. For example, Michael Neocosmos, in his recent award-winning book entitled *Thinking Freedom in Africa: Towards a Theory of Emancipation* (2016: 13), agrees with Mamdani's critique of the human rights discourse and the concomitant interventionist Western humanitarianism as solutions to the African crisis as 'providing a neo-colonial response to Africa's problems which hides the agenda of recolonization', though that he is stuck in providing 'statist solutions'. Neocosmos (2016: 13) is advocating non-statist solutions that seriously take into account the ideas of the ordinary people. Despite these important criticisms, what cannot be taken from Mamdani is his original thinking and innovative suggestions for alternative interventions even on sensitive subjects like mass violence and genocides.

Conclusion

There is no doubt that the original and innovative analytical framework that Mamdani developed in *Citizen and Subject* (1996) became useful for his understanding other sites of conflict related to citizenship as well as theatres of violence even beyond Africa. It also enabled Mamdani to delve deeper into the sensitive subject of transitional justice and to influence a paradigm shift from the post-1945 thinking to a new one crafted from CODESA. His analysis on transitional justice highlighted the need rethink the relationship between law and politics so as to break out of the old Nuremberg template of justice.

His overarching interventions on the architecture and configuration of the colonial power enabled a historically informed and theoretically enriching understanding of postcolonial conditions and dilemmas of reforming institutions, practices and power itself. Throughout Mamdani's contributions there are clear methodological suggestions, ranging from taking Africa as a legitimate epistemic unit of analysis; avoiding the pitfalls of simply importing of theories from elsewhere that tend to run roughshod over internal realities of the continent; seeking 'actually existing civil society' rather than programmatic civil society drawing from external thinkers; and emphasis on seeking solution to the African conflicts and violence through looking inside rather than outside the problem.

Mamdani's writing has revolutionized studies and approaches to the subjects of national belonging, citizenship, entitlements and rights. Colonial legacy emerged in Mamdani's analysis as that structure of power that made it difficult for the postcolonial state to do genuine decolonization, detribalization, deracialization and democratization. Mamdani captured the citizenship dilemmas of postcolonial Africa in these revealing words:

> If we look at the definition of citizenship in most African states, we realize that the colonial state lives on, albeit with some reforms. My point is that in privileging the indigenous over the nonindigenous, we turned the colonial world upside down, but we did not change it. As a result, the native sat on top of the political world designed by the settler. Indigeneity remained the test for rights.
>
> (Mamdani 2001a: 658)

His insistence that Africa must formulate its own conceptions of belonging and citizenship that take into account its particular trajectories of state formation, colonial experience and political economy that provoked migration makes a lot of sense in a continent where struggles over resources have assumed ethnic and communal forms. Mamdani's (2015: 659) warning is that the time has passed when those who were branded foreigners 'would leave, their belongings on their heads, and run in the direction of home. Now, the tendency is for them to fight it out'. Today, those who are excluded from citizenship, belonging, entitlements and rights 'arm themselves in self-defence' hence 'the proliferation of armed militias in the context of ethnically driven clashes around land and other rights' (Mamdani 2001a: 659).

Mamdani (1996; 2001a) has also enabled African scholarship on human identities to move beyond traditional Marxist and liberal understanding of identities as 'either market-based or cultural' and introduced 'political identities as distinct from economic or cultural identities'. He correctly identified that one of the legacies of colonialism is that it bequeathed on Africa a problematic state in which the 'economy dynamises, and the state disenfranchises the most dynamic' (Mamdani 2001a: 663). Mamdani has contributed immensely to what his student Suren Pillay (2013: 1) termed 'the contemporary predicament of decolonizing citizenship'.

Even his *Good Muslim, Bad Muslim: America, the Cold War and the Roots of Terror* (2004), which addressed a non-African problem of 'global terrorism', conceptually falls neatly within his intellectual trademark of historicizing and theorizing issues closely. He highlighted how the end of the Cold War resulted in politicization of culture and the invention of 'good' and 'bad' Muslim. Building on his critique of imperialism, Mamdani was also able to provide an original analysis of the problems haunting Sudan, emphasizing throughout the need to understand the local origins and dynamics of violence in the Darfur region. Chen is correct to note:

> Based on the theoretical framework developed in *Citizen and Subject*, *When Victims Become Killers* was Mamdani's show case of his capability to go against popular opinion even if they were supported by the state and nearly one million people. And his insistence on intellectual analysis undertaken by historicizing the source of postcolonial violence that took into account the

local, national and global conditions. He ultimately illustrated the power of historical analysis. And, in the end, he proposed an alternative solution to US and UN military 'humanitarian intervention' (which, from the history of colonialism, was always justified as a 'civilizing mission' by the big powers). Instead, Mamdani advocated for a consociation mechanism that included the Sudanese population as well as the regional governments in order to truly achieve a peaceful resolution for all parties. From *Good Muslim, Bad Muslim* to *Saviours and Survivors*, Mamdani has extended the scope of his internal comparative analysis of postcolonial African countries to address issues of global powers.

(Chen 2017: 589–590)

Mamdani is currently engaged in advancing thinking in relation to the topical issue of decolonizing the universities. His intervention is once more informed by historicizing both the idea of the university and its social mission as well as the institutional history of the university going back to its post-Renaissance European and pre-colonial genealogies. He also linked the epistemological questions with the long-standing ontological issues as he contributed to the reorganization of knowledge and disciplines as part of decolonization. For details on decolonization of the university and the Rhodes Must Fall and Fees Must Fall movements refer to Chapter 7 and Chapter 9 in this book.

Finally, in a new preface to the edition of *Citizen and Subject* (2017) published by Wits University Press and Makerere Institute of Social Research, Mamdani has responded to his critics and in the process underscored the canonical place this work occupies in his entire academic career and as a classic of African political science. He posited: 'Citizen and Subject was the result of ten years of reflection, study, writing and rewriting. Its prehistory began in 1974, when I completed my PhD dissertation' (Mamdani 2017). While Mamdani's earlier work emphasized the workings of the market, particularly its role in class formation, in *Citizen and Subject* he delved deeper into the dynamics driving non-market relations actively, mainly in rural Africa where the bulk of the population resides.

Thus, in *Citizen and Subject*, Mamdani critiqued the political economy approach as he sought to understand how colonialism impinged on the development of subjectivity in modern Africa. One noticed intellectual value in Mamdani's paradigm shift from the labour question to the 'native question', which necessarily meant shifting also from race to the 'tribal' issue, without necessarily decoupling the two. What Mamdani delivered was a work that spoke to the pertinent issues of structure and agency, as well as colonial power and response of the colonized – a framework that has helped to understand the postcolony as an invention of colonialism and nationalism. On a global scale, Mamdani's work successfully countered the colonially created reasoning by analogy whereby Africa has been approached as a poor copy of Europe or prehistory of Europe. What has been restored is the epistemic legitimacy of Africa.

References

Cesaire, A. 1955 [2000]. *Discourse on Colonialism*. Translated by J. Pinkham. New York: Monthly Review Press.

Chen, K-H. 2017. 'Review Essay: On Mamdani's Mode of Thought'. *Cultural Studies*, 31(4), pp. 580–601

Diop, C. A. 1974. *Precolonial Black Africa*. New York: Lawrence Hills Books.

Du Bois, W. E. B. 1903. *The Souls of Black Folk*. New York: Dover Publications.

Ekeh, P. 1983. *Colonialism and Social Structure: University of Ibadan Inaugural Lecture, 1980*. Ibadan: Ibadan University Press.

Fanon, F. 1968. *The Wretched of the Earth*. New York: Grove Press.

Gordon, L. R. 2000. *Existentia Africana: Understanding Africana Existential Thought*. New York and London: Routledge.

Hoppers, C. O. and Richards, H. 2012. *Rethinking Thinking: Modernity's 'Other' and the Transformation of the University*. Pretoria: UNISA Press.

Hountondji, P. J. 1997. 'Introduction: Recentring Africa'. In P. Hountondji (ed.), *Endogenous Knowledge: Research Trails*. Dakar: CODESRIA Books, pp. 1–39.

Kamola, I. A. and el-Malik, S. S. 2017. 'Introduction: Politics of African Anti-Colonial Archive'. In S. S. el-Malik and I. A. Kamola (eds). *Politics of African Anticolonial Archive*. London and New York: Rowman & Littlefield International, pp. 1–15.

Maldonado-Torres, N. 2007. 'On Coloniality of Being: Contributions to the Development of a Concept'. *Cultural Studies*, 21(2–3), (March/May), pp. 240–270.

Mamdani, M. 1972. *The Myth of Population Control: Family, Class and Caste in an Indian Village*. New York: Monthly Review Press.

Mamdani, M. 1973. *From Citizen to Refugee: Uganda Asians Come to Britain*. London: Francis Pinter.

Mamdani, M. 1976. *Politics and Class Formation in Uganda*. London: Heinemann.

Mamdani, M. 1992. 'Africa: Democratic Theory and Democratic Struggles'. *Economic and Political Weekly*, 27(41), October, pp. 2228–2232.

Mamdani, M. 1996. *Citizen and Subject: Contemporary Africa and the Legacy of Late Colonialism*. Princeton, NJ: Princeton University Press,

Mamdani, Ma. 1998. 'When Does a Settler Become a Native? Reflections on the Roots of Citizenship in Equatorial and South Africa'. Text of Inaugural Lecture Delivered as AC Jordan Professor of African Studies, University of Cape Town, Wednesday, 13 May 1998.

Mamdani, M. 1999. Historicizing Power and Responses to Power: Indirect rule and Its Reform'. *Social Research*, 66(3), Fall, pp. 859–886.

Mamdani, M. 2001a. 'Beyond Settler and Native as Political Identities: Overcoming the Political Legacy of Colonialism'. *Comparative Studies in Society and History*, 43(4), October, pp. 651–664.

Mamdani, M. 2001b. *When Victims Become Killers: Colonialism, Nativism, and the Genocide in Rwanda*. Oxford, UK: James Currey.

Mamdani, M. 2004. *Good Muslim, Bad Muslim: America, the Cold War and the Roots of Terror*. New York: Pantheon.

Mamdani, M. 2013. *Define and Rule: Native as Political Identity*. Johannesburg: Wits University Press.

Mamdani, M. 2015. 'Beyond Nuremberg: The Historical Significance of the Post-Apartheid Transition in South Africa'. *Politics and Society*, 43(1), pp. 61–88.

Mamdani, M. 2017. 'Preface'. In M. Mamdani. *Citizen and Subject: Contemporary Africa and the Legacy of Late Colonialism*. Johannesburg and Kampala: Wits University Press and Makerere Institute of Social Research.

Mazrui, A. A. 1986. *The Africans: A Triple Heritage*. London: BBC Publications.

Mudimbe, V. Y. 1988. *The Invention of Africa: Gnosis, Philosophy, and the Order of Knowledge*. Bloomington and Indianapolis, IN: Indiana University Press.

Mudimbe, V. Y. 1994. *The Idea of Africa*. Bloomington and Indianapolis, IN: Indian University Press.

Ndlovu-Gatsheni, S. J. 2013. *Empire, Global Coloniality and African Subjectivity*. Oxford, UK and New York: Berghahn Books.

Neocosmos, M. 2016. *Thinking Freedom in Africa: Towards a Theory of Emancipatory Politics*. Johannesburg: Wits University Press.

Ngugi wa Thiong'o. 1986. *Decolonizing the Mind: The Politics of Language in African Literature*. Oxford, UK: James Currey.

Ngugi wa Thiong'o. 2009a. *Something Torn and New: An African Renaissance*. New York: Basic Civitas Books.

Ngugi wa Thiong'o. 2009b. *Re-membering Africa*. Nairobi: East African Educational Publishers.

Ngugi wa Thiong'o. 2012. *Globalectics: Theory and the Politics of Knowing*. New York: Columbia University Press.

Ngugi wa Thiong'o. 2016. *Secure the Base: Making Africa Visible in the Globe*. London and New York: Seagull Books.

Pillay, S. 2013. 'Anxious Urbanity: Xenophobia, the Native Subject and the Refugee Camp'. *Social Dynamics*, 39(1), pp. 1–17

Quijano, A. 2000. 'The Coloniality of Power and Social Classification'. *Journal of World Systems Analysis*, 6(2), (Summer–Fall), pp. 342–386.

Ranger, T. 1983. 'The Invention of Tradition in Colonial Africa'. In E. Hobsbawn and T. O. Ranger (eds). *The Invention of Tradition*. Cambridge, UK: Cambridge University Press.

Santos, B. de S. 2007. 'Beyond Abyssal Thinking: From Global Lines to Ecologies of Knowledge. *Review*, xxx(1), pp. 45–89.

Sharawy, H. 2010. *Political and Social Thought in Africa*. Cairo: Supreme Council of Culture.

Suárez-Krabbe, J. 2016. *Race, Rights and Rebels: Alternatives to Human Rights and Development from the Global South*. London and New York: Rowman & Littlefield International.

7

EDUCATION/UNIVERSITY IN AFRICA

Introduction

The modern 'Westernized' university played a central role in the invention and universalization of what James Blaut (1993) termed the 'colonizer's model of the world'. The university inevitably became intimately imbricated in spread and naturalization of 'imperial reason' as well as institutionalization of 'Eurocentrism' (Amin 2009). Thus, the genocides, ontolocides, epistemicides, culturecides and linguicides committed by the imperial/colonial footsoldiers on the ground became rationalized within the modern Westernized university intellectually. Ironically, it was also at the university that the subject of the 'human' was researched and debated endlessly, going as far back as the School of Salamanca and the time of the Valladolid Debates (1550–1551) (Castro 2007; Suárez-Krabbe 2016). It was perhaps this irony, if not outright hypocrisy, of Eurocentric modernity and the modern institutions it laid out on earth that provoked Frantz Fanon (1968: 251) to urge his comrades to 'Leave this Europe where they are never done talking of Man, yet murder men everywhere they find them, at the corner of every one of their streets, in all the corners of the globe'. Decolonization of the university is part of the broader struggles to escape from the 'European game'.

At another level, the historical record indicates that universities were never an exclusive heritage and gift of Europe to the world. The Arabic/Muslim civilization as well as pre-colonial African civilization enabled universities to emerge from indigenous cultural soil and the sociopolitical and economic climate. But these non-European universities, just like African religion, were not hegemonic and imperial in character. This partly explains why they were easily overtaken by the modern Westernized model of the university. At another level, a combination of the negative impact of the Transatlantic Slave Trade (trafficking of black human beings like commodities) and violent European colonial conquest eroded and destroyed pre-colonial institutions including those of learning and teaching. After the demise of its indigenous universities, Africa then became vulnerable to the spread of Western ideas and institutions. What exists up to today is best understood as universities in Africa rather than African universities because they did not germinate from the African cultural soil and ideological climate. It is this modern Westernized university that is today facing its worse systemic, epistemic and institutional crisis.

What this chapter offers is an overview of the indigenous education systems that were underpinned by indigenous African knowledges that did not survive the colonial onslaught, while at the same time highlighting African epistemic struggles for an 'African university' and capturing its trajectories across time up to the present. It posits that even those universities that appear like a gift of African nationalist decolonization struggles were systemically, institutionally and epistemically Western in orientation. To borrow concepts from the decolonial freedom fighter and decolonial theorist Amilcar Cabral (1979), the chapter warns against claiming 'easy victories' and telling 'lies' about defeating epistemological colonization, which had invaded the mental universe of Africa. Indigenization initiatives that resulted in the re-naming of universities in the vernacular languages and the Africanization processes that changed the management of the universities from white colonizers to black African leaders, the proliferation of black African professors in the universities as well as increasing access to the university by black African students, did not amount to the decolonization of universities. This is why Adebayo Olukoshi and Paul Tiyambe Zeleza (2004: 2) could still write that 'The need for redefining the role and defending the importance of universities has never been greater than it is now'. They proceeded to summarize the key challenges facing the modern university in Africa in these words:

> How to balance autonomy and viability, expansion and excellence, representation and responsibility, diversification and differentiation, internationalization and indigenization, global presence/visibility and local anchorage, academic freedom and professional ethics, privatization and the public purpose, teaching and research, community service/social responsibility and consultancy, diversity and uniformity, the preservation of local knowledge systems and the adoption of global knowledge systems, knowledge production and knowledge dissemination, the knowledge economy and the knowledge society?
>
> (Olukoshi and Zeleza 2004: 3)

It is not surprising that, as an institution, the Westernized university in Africa is today the key site of struggles for decolonization. In the first place, it is the universities that promised freedom of thought only to stifle it through religiously adhering to a Eurocentric epistemology and Western-centric cultures and practices. In the second place, the university has the highest concentration of young people who are eager to understand why the institution is still maintaining alienating

Eurocentric cultures and is not resolving the question of cultural and practical relevance of what it delivers. In the third place, despite the institutional constraints, the university is still the space where ideas are explored endlessly. Finally, it is within the confines of the Westernized university located in Africa that the youth encounter face-to-face epistemic and pedagogical brutalities that provoke them to rebel. But let's begin with understanding the genealogies of education in Africa in general and the university in Africa in particular before delving deeper into the long-standing struggles for the decolonization of the university.

Pre-colonial genealogies of education in Africa

If we seriously take into account Valentin Y. Mudimbe's (1988) decolonial intervention that every human being was and is born into a valid knowledge system, then education has always been indigenous to every human society. What may differ is the form in which knowledge was and is kept and the ways in which it was and is organized and disseminated. With reference to Africa, prior to colonial rule, knowledge was transmitted orally, though they were early African civilizations like the Egyptian one that had developed writing (see the work of Cheikh Anta Diop 1974; 1981). It is, therefore, logical that pre-colonial Africa developed its own indigenous education systems and universities even prior to the colonial encounters.

The 'primary' teacher in the African indigenous education system was the mother (Ajayi 1985: 11). Primary here is used to mean important not the elementary phase in a hierarchized education system. The teaching of the mother was not limited to 'primary' education only. Building on the work of the Nigerian sociologist and feminist Oyeronke Oyewumi (2016: 3), what is emphasized is 'maternal ideology' in African indigenous education, which compelled 'obedience from everyone who gestated in a womb' (see also Nzegwu 2006: 53). Grandmothers were also important teachers within the African indigenous education system. They actively participated in primary education and their most common pedagogical mode was folktales delivered in the evening mainly to children (Ndlovu-Gatsheni 2009).

What also manifested and reinforced the 'maternal ideology' within African indigenous education was the primacy of what is known as the 'mother tongue' as the language of instruction in pre-colonial Africa (see Ngugi wa Thiong'o 2013). In her most recent work Oyewumi (2016), on the subject of the gender of motherhood, highlighted the 'supremacy of motherhood' in the Yoruba pre-colonial epistemology. She coined and introduced the concept of 'matripotency' to highlight the centrality of motherhood in *Ifa* – 'the most important endogenous system of knowledge' (Oyewumi 2016: 2). Oyewumi explained Yoruba endogenous system of knowledge like this:

> *Ifa* is a system of knowledge that was transmitted orally originally. Structured into the institution are sets of procedures that facilitate the retrieval of

information on all aspects of Yoruba life past, present, and future. The knowledge is made accessible through a system of divination, a process that generates stories, myths, and narratives that profess to be God send, and which make assertions about anything and everything in Yoruba life.

(Oyewumi 2016: 12)

Ifa is a clear example of one of the constitutive elements of African indigenous knowledge systems. To some extent the identity of who propagated African indigenous education depended on the nature of the African pre-colonial society, that is, whether it was a patriarchal society where men constituted the household heads or a matriarchal one where women led in society (see Amadiume 1987). But even in matriarchal societies men were not excluded from teaching. While in the African indigenous education system education was not formally organized hierarchically into 'primary', 'secondary' and 'higher education', one can argue, without necessarily falling into what Mahmood Mamdani (1996) termed writing African history 'by analogy', that the 'primary' institution of learning was the extended family.

Beyond the mothers as primary teachers in the African indigenous education system, there were many other specialized teachers in pre-colonial Africa, including priests, diviners, kings, chiefs, poets, griots, rainmakers and merchants who constituted what the distinguished historian Toyin Falola (2001: 3) termed 'traditional intellectuals'. As a result of the knowledge they embodied, generated and disseminated, these 'traditional intellectuals' exercised considerable power and authority. Besides the family as the 'primary' school, there were other important schools in pre-colonial Africa, such as the famous initiation schools and age-set institutions where knowledges of masculinity, femininity, entry into adulthood, collective identity, working together and patriotism were inculcated (see Ndlovu-Gatsheni 2009). Individualism was not promoted in African indigenous education. Harmony between humans and nature was emphasized. Perhaps a detailed example of Ethiopian indigenous knowledge and indigenous education system, the only African country that never experienced direct colonial conquest and direct colonial administration, will add more light on the understanding of African pre-colonial indigenous knowledge systems and dissemination of this knowledge.

Kebra Nagast and indigenous schooling in Ethiopia

The Ethiopian case study is important in two major ways. The first is that it is one African country that survived colonial conquest and direct colonial administration. As such it was expected to have kept and maintained its indigenous knowledge system and African education system compared to the rest of Africa that suffered conquest and direct colonial administration. The second reason is that despite having survived colonial conquest and direct colonial administration, Ethiopia could not successfully escape the impact of the Western metaphysical empire. Consequently, Ethiopia is one of those countries that deliberately 'colonized itself' with foreign Western institutions and Eurocentric ideas (see Woldeyes 2017). This amounts to a paradoxical situation in the African struggles for decolonization and deprovincialization, worthy detailed exploration before one turns to reflect on the rise of the modern Westernized education in Africa.

The Ethiopian scholar Yirga Gelaw Woldeyes's recent groundbreaking book entitled *Native Colonialism: Education and the Economy of Violence Against Traditions in Ethiopia* (2017) grappled with the paradoxical case of a country that was never colonized but 'voluntarily' rebelled against its indigenous knowledge, indigenous education system, indigenous languages, indigenous philosophy as well as its indigenous institutions so as to adopt Western epistemology, models of education and a European language. The book also delves deeper into Ethiopia's little-known wealth of traditional knowledge and functioning indigenous education system. Ethiopian indigenous education has a long history going back to the time of the translation of the Bible into the Ge'ez language in the fifth century. The indigenous Ethiopian education system is an amalgamation of a wide range of indigenous Ethiopian, ancient Hebrew, Aramaic, Greek, Syriac, Muslim and other works (Isaac 2013; Woldeyes 2017).

At the centre of Ethiopian indigenous knowledge is the importance of wisdom. To the Ethiopians knowledge is wisdom not power. So they consistently and systematically sought wisdom whereever it existed. *Kebra Nagast* is one of the most revered indigenous Ethiopian books, which contains all the tenets of Ethiopian philosophy and life including that nation's myth of foundation as a chosen place by God. It occupied the same status that Plato's *Republic* enjoyed in Western tradition of political thought (Woldeyes 2017: 23). Relating to the myth of foundation of Ethiopia as contained in Kebra Nagast, Woldeyes provided a good summary:

> The common narrative about Kebra Nagast focuses on the story of the Queen of Sheba meeting King Solomon of Israel and the coming of the Ark of the Covenant. The Ethiopian Queen of Sheba heard of the wisdom of King Solomon and travelled to Jerusalem to visit him. During her stay she was tricked into sleeping with King Solomon. On her way back to Ethiopia, she gave birth to a boy, Menelik I. Later, the young Menelik travelled to Israel to visit his father in Jerusalem. King Solomon rejoiced and wanted Menelik to succeed his throne in Israel after him. However, Menelik refused the offer out of his love for Ethiopia, and wanted to return home. Solomon then ordered the noble men of Israel to send their firstborn sons to serve Menelik in Ethiopia. The sons of the noble men abducted the Ark of the Covenant from the Temple of Solomon and brought it with them to Ethiopia. It is believed that the true Ark of the Covenant is still in the Axum Church of Zion Maryam. From that time onwards, Ethiopia became the chosen nation of God, and Menelik I became the founder of the Solomonic dynasty in the country.

(Woldeyes 2017: 24)

Kebra Nagast plays a number of important roles in Ethiopian indigenous knowledge and self-definition. At the political level, it conferred a divine power to the Ethiopian emperors. The divinity did not translate to absolute monarchs but those leaders who had to rule in the likeness of God with commitment, compassion, humility, love, justice, mercy, glory, blessings and wisdom as well as in fear of God (Woldeyes 2017: 42). At the social level, it defined the national identity of Ethiopia as a chosen place. Israel is the chosen nation not place. It plays the role of a national epic (Kebede 2008).

The Ark of the Covenant became the centre of social and spiritual life as well as political legitimacy. When Ethiopians were resisting Italian colonial invasion in 1896, the Ark of the Covenant was carried to the theatre of war and it galvanized Ethiopians to fight to preserve the chosen place of God (a covenant land) (Woldeyes 2017: 27). The sacredness of Ethiopia even informed struggles in the Black Diaspora where Ethiopia stood for Africa. Back-to-Africa movements were predicated on Ethiopianism, which became 'the precursor of pan-Africanism, and Rastafarianism' all of which 'looked to Ethiopia as a source of spiritual meaning and a place to be' (Woldeyes 2017: 28).

Turning to Ethiopian traditional conceptions of knowledge, it is clear that wisdom is privileged above all else. While God is the fountain of all wisdom, Ethiopians strongly believed that human beings played an important role in seeking to obtain wisdom. Thus before her journey in search of wisdom in Jerusalem, the Queen of Sheba addressed her nobles and stated:

> Hearken, O ye who are my people, and give ye ear to my words. For I desire wisdom and my heart seekth to find understanding. I am smitten with love of wisdom. [. . .] wisdom is far better than treasure of gold and silver, and wisdom is the best of everything that hath been created on earth [. . .]. It maketh the ears to hear and hearts to understand, it is a source of joy for the heart, and a bright and shining lamb for the eyes; it is a teacher of those who learned [. . .]. As for a kingdom, it cannot stand without wisdom.
>
> (*Kebra Nagast* 1932: 20–24)

According to Woldeyes (2017: 57) *Kebra Nagast* provided the framework within which Ethiopian traditional schooling and indigenous knowledge production ensured. Ethiopian indigenous schooling and indigenous knowledge were predicated on seeking wisdom, interpreting knowledge from the rest of the world and not imitation. Woldeyes (2017: 58) argued 'The traditional schools became centres of learning for sixteen centuries until they were progressively supplanted by Westernized government schools since the middle of the 20th century'. Below is a summary of Ethiopian traditional schools, fields of study and duration of study.

The church played a major role in the Ethiopian indigenous education system. The teachers ranged from spiritual fathers and mothers, exorcists, preachers, hymnists, healers, mediators, counsellors to judges (Woldeyes 2017: 58). Woldeyes

TABLE 7.1 Ethiopian Indigenous school system and fields of study

School and field of study	Average time of completion
Nibab Bet (House of Reading)	2 years
Zema Bet (House of Hymn)	4 years
Kidassie (House of Holy Mass)	6 months
Zema Bet: zimare and mewasit zema	1 year
Zema Bet: akwakwam	3 years
Qine Bet (House of Poetry)	5 years
Metsehaf Bet (House of Books)	4 years
Liqawunit (Interpretation of the books of scholars and monasticism)	3 years
Merha Ewur ((Mathematical computation of time)	6 months
Yetarik Tinat (Study of history)	1 year
Yetegibare'ed Timhirt (Art and handcraft)	4 years
Masmesker (Certification)	2 years
Total Years of Study in Traditional Education School	30 years

Source: Woldeyes, *Native Colonialism*, p. 59.

(2017: 61) posited: 'Because traditional scholars understand the philosophy, language, literature, history, and tradition of the people better than those educated based on the European model of education in Ethiopia, until now the former have influenced the lives of the people more deeply and directly than the latter.' At the centre of the Ethiopian indigenous school system was the desire to socialize the students and that is making them understand their Ethiopian world deeply rather than desocialization akin to the colonial education. Even imported knowledge was incorporated into 'Ethiopian realities as perceived and understood by the scholars and scribes of the time' (Wagaw 1990: 47–48).

The Ethiopian indigenous education system produced such philosophers as Zara Yacob, a contemporary of Rene Descartes of Europe (Woldeyes 2017: 89). His prominent student was Walda Hiwot. Yacob became well known for his critical inquiry tradition and he taught at the House of Books in Axum in the seventeenth century. Three issues distinguished Yacob's philosophy. The first was fidelity to critical examination of all faith and customs. The second was his idea of reason as a light that leads to truth. The third was his strong belief in the goodness of nature (Sumner 2004: 176).

What is very ironic and even tragic about the Ethiopian situation is that that very noble spirit of seeking wisdom led such leaders as Towodros II to seek knowledge in Europe and this desire eventually produced Western-educated Ethiopians who became the 'missionaries' for the replacement of everything Ethiopian with Western ideas and institutions. This irony is well captured by Woldeyes:

> The Ethiopian experience of modernization differs from the rest of Africa, given that it was the only African country never to be colonized but

remarkably it is still heavily influenced by western epistemology. Ethiopia was initially defiant of the powerful colonial master, both epistemologically and militarily. Its indigenous worldview helped mobilize its people from the vast and rugged plateau land of Abyssinia to stand in unison and defeat the Italian colonial attempt at the Battle of Adwa in 1896. However, like many other African countries, eventually Ethiopia fell victim of Eurocentrism that presents modernization as synonymous with Westernization. The process of this transition involves two types of violence: epistemic violence against traditions and physical violence to quell dissent.

(Woldeyes 2017: 96)

Woldeyes is one of those modern Ethiopian scholars who are dismayed by the fact that the elite leadership of his country and other Western-educated Ethiopians colluded to dismiss the rich Ethiopian indigenous knowledge and excluded it from the curriculum and even abandoned use of indigenous languages for foreign European languages under the pretext o0f modernizing Ethiopia. In his call for Ethiopia to build its knowledge from its indigenous knowledge, Woldeyes (2017: 2010) concluded:

The only way to defend the people is to support their tradition, which includes their beliefs, experiences, customs, rituals and aspirations. Traditions are rooted, not imprisoned, in history; they are not closed but open to the future. Embracing tradition is not to travel to the past. It is to live in the present of those dispossessed of their right to exist now.

It seems the Ethiopian indigenous education system was not organized into a vertical hierarchical order of primary, secondary, high school and tertiary introduced by colonial modernity in Africa. How then did the university emerge in pre-colonial Africa?

Alexandria and Timbuktu models of the university

It was only when the African indigenous education system intersected with the Islamic/Arabic system of education that it embraced the alphabet and a writing system in addition to its primary oral transmission. The oldest known writing system in Africa is hieroglyphics, found in Egypt – an African/Arabic site of knowledge generation including arithmetic, geometry and algebra (Diop 1987). Highlighting the intersection of Islamic and African indigenous education systems is not intended to downplay the Arab colonization of Africa, but rather to highlight how the two systems of education influenced each other in terms of cultures, values and philosophies (Ajayi 1985).

The intersections of the African indigenous education system and the Islamic education system are reflected in the cross-cutting recognition of ancestors, 'the cult of saints, some aspects of the mysticism of Sufi orders and maraboutism' in Islamic thought and education (Ajayi 1985: 12–13). The intersections also reflect in Semitic languages such as Amharic. It was this intersectionality of languages, knowledges and religions that provoked Ali A. Mazrui to coin the concept of 'Afrabia' and to push for the 'abolition' of the Red Sea as a boundary separating Africa and Arabia (Mazrui 1984: 98). It is this perspective of the intersection of cultures that gave birth to the concept of 'triple heritage' that is traceable to Edward Wilmot Blyden (1888), Kwame Nkrumah (1970) and Mazrui (1986). The concept of 'triple heritage' acknowledges that three civilizations shaped contemporary Africa: Africa's own rich cultures/traditions, Islamic cultures/traditions and Western cultures/traditions.

This is why it is important to clearly understand the genealogies of education in Africa. With specific reference to the 'university in Africa' three genealogies if not 'triple heritages' are discernible (see Mazrui 1986). The first is the pre-colonial African/Bantu/Nilotic/Arabic/Muslim genealogy. This pre-colonial genealogy speaks to the intellectual tradition of the Nile Valley Egyptian–Nubian–Ethiopian civilization, the Afro-Arabic/Muslim intellectual tradition as well as the pre-colonial Mali–Songhai–Ghana Timbuktu intellectual tradition. Taken together, these traditions produced the earliest universities on the African soil (Assié-Lumumba 2006; Ajayi *et al.* 1996).

The University of Qarawiyyin in Fes in Morocco, founded in AD 859; the University of Al-Azhar in Cairo in Egypt, founded in AD 972; and Sankoré University in Timbuktu in Mali, traceable to the twelfth century, constitute some of the oldest universities in the world (Wandira 1977: 38).These institutions, just like their modern counterparts, were pre-occupied with understanding the world, the nature of the human, dynamics of society, and the promotion of agriculture, health, literature and philosophy (Ajayi *et al.* 1996; Lulat 2003).The foundational base for the pre-colonial genealogy of the university has been a combination of the African indigenous education system and the Islamic system of education.

The pre-colonial Mali–Songhai–Ghana Timbuktu and the pre-colonial African/Nilotic/Arabic/Muslim intellectual traditions that produced the first African universities are a collective pride of Africans, African Muslims and Arab–Muslim Africans. What is disappointing though is the weak link between the pre-colonial African universities and the modern 'university in Africa'.

Even those that have survived, like the Al-Azhar University in Cairo and the University of Qarawiyyin in Fes, seem not to have managed to escape Westernization. Factors that help to explain the discontinuity rather than continuity include 'the breakup of the Sudanic Empires and the coming of the slave trade', which resulted in Africa suffering 'a period of relative intellectual isolation and stagnation' (Wandira 1977: 38). The scramble for Africa, the partition of Africa and the conquest of Africa; 'did not assist the intellectual recovery of the continent' (Wandira 1997: 38). However, the continuing existence of the Al-Azhar University in Cairo enables us to talk of the 'Alexandria model' of the university.

The rise of modern Western education system and university in Africa

The demise of the pre-colonial African/Islamic University opened the way for the second and third genealogies of the idea of the university in Africa. The Western imperial/colonial tradition constitutes the second and the anti-colonial African nationalist liberatory developmental heritage delivered the third layer of a university but without liberating it from the Western tradition. Thus, the former has had the most enduring impact and even the anti-colonial African nationalist liberatory developmental genealogy could not fully decentre it (Nwauwa 1996).

Perhaps what must be made clear is that the modern university in Africa was both fought for by Africans and a colonial imposition. Early African educated elites like Blyden and James Africanus Beale Horton of Sierra Leone, and J.E. Casely Hayford of Ghana, agitated and fought for the establishment of universities in Africa from as early as 1868 (Ashby 1964). While these early African educated elites fought for a very particular type of university – the 'African university' (rooted in African cultural and intellectual soil and climate) – the reluctant colonial regimes imposed the 'university in Africa' (transplanted from Europe).

The contestation over the model of the university is as old as the initial agitation for the 'African university'. For example, Horton, who in his will gave his own house in Freetown in Sierra Leone to become the nucleus of a university, saw no problem in universities coming to Africa as raw transplants from Europe. He was in favour of 'undiluted Western education' (Ashby 1964: 12).One can argue that Horton represented a particular constituency of African people who had undergone deep Westernization processes to the extent that they became fully converted to the idea of the superiority of Western education and its values for the rest of humanity. The attitudes and psyches of these Africans revealed the ambivalence born out of their encounters with Western civilization and the direct impact of Western education on African consciousness.

Horton's contemporaries Blyden and Hayford represented another constituency of Western-educated elite that had a radically different take on the nature and character of the higher education they wanted for Africa. Blyden and Hayford exhibited the earliest ideas of a decolonized higher education. According to Eric Ashby, Blyden advocated for an African university that was free from the grip of the 'despotic Europeanizing influences which had warped and crushed the Negro mind' (Ashby 1964: 12–23; see also Blyden 1882).

Blyden became the leading advocate, if not the pioneer, of the philosophy of 'African personality', which he did not want Western education to destroy. Rather, he wanted it to be nurtured as part of the restoration of African cultural self-respect. The philosophy of 'African personality' was predicated on five key issues: the separate and unique destiny of black people from Europeans; the development of a distinctive African mentality; religion's place of pride in African thought and life; the inherent socialist/communal nature of Africa society; and the strong idea of 'Africa for Africans' (Frankel 1974). Blyden was opposed to modern Western civilization as he saw it as a carrier of 'race poison', and harked back to the Greek and Latin civilizations as classics that could nourish Africa intellectually without racism (Ashby 1964: 13). Blyden is also the earliest advocate to promote African languages, African songs and African oral traditions as part of higher education. His decolonial ideas were echoed by Reverend James Johnson of Sierra Leone who wanted a higher education institution that would 'Leave undisturbed our particularities' (Wandira 1977: 40).

Hayford was another early African decolonial thinker who advocated for a decolonized higher education for Africa. His ideas about an indigenous university were captured in his book *Ethiopia Unbound* (1911). Hayford, a pioneer African nationalist and advocate of Ethiopianism, was very critical of an African university that was a mere replica of European institutions and that mimicked and reproduced foreign influences. He went further to propose the use of African indigenous languages in teaching and learning. Like Blyden, Hayford was a proponent of an African university that 'would preserve in the students a sense of African Nationality' (Hayford 2011).

If these struggles are taken seriously, they indicate that decolonization struggles/decoloniality is traceable to as far back as the time of colonial encounters themselves. Decolonization/decoloniality is one of the most resilient languages of liberation ranged against colonialism/coloniality. It has today re-emerged in a far more radical form in Latin America, where concepts such as coloniality and decoloniality have been coined and where the 'decolonial turn' has been emphasized and is traceable to the Haitian Revolution. The decolonial struggles in the Americas, Asia and Africa which delivered the new flags and anthems are today being carried over to the realm of epistemic freedom (Ndlovu-Gatsheni 2013a; Ndlovu-Gatsheni 2013b).

What happened to these early struggles and demands for an African university is analogous to what happened to the person who cried for a fish and was given a snake instead. In the first place, the colonial regimes argued for a sound African secondary education as an essential pre-requisite and foundation for African university education. Second, the early educational institutions established in Africa, such as Fourah Bay College in Sierra Leone (1876), emerged as 'colleges' of overseas universities (Ashby 1964). Third, the colonial regimes continued to turn a blind eye to the expansion of higher education for Africans, leaving the missionaries to concentrate on primary and secondary sectors. As argued by Mazrui, mission education inaugurated the first form of African intellectual dependency and acculturation/'cultural schizophrenia' through separating young Africans from their parents and enclosing them in mission boarding schools (Mazrui 1978: 27).

The church and the mission school performed the colonial purpose of the 'desocialization of African education' (Mazrui 1978: 29). The introduction of colonial languages such as English and French completed the desocialization process. Even more profoundly, Mazrui posited that by the time the European missionaries came to Africa to introduce Christian education and theology, Europe and North America were undergoing secularization and religion was on the retreat since the time of Enlightenment (Mazrui 1978: 29). Thus, it is in the unfolding of mission education in Africa that the origins of the crisis of relevance lay of the (mis)education of the African.

Colonial delaying strategies

Colonial delaying strategies in the provision of higher education took the form of setting up commissions of enquiry in the 1920s, 1930s and 1940s. In 1920/1921, the Phelps Stokes Fund in the USA sent a commission led by Jesse Jones to enquire into education in Africa. The commission confirmed the hunger for higher education in West, South and Equatorial Africa. The Jones commission's findings culminated in the White Paper of 1925 (Wandira 1977). The core message of the White Paper was that 'Education should be adapted to the mentality, aptitudes, occupations and traditions of the various peoples, conserving as far as possible all sound and healthy elements in the fabric of their social life' (Ashby 1964: 16–17).

However, it was only in 1933 that James Currie, who was part of an Advisory Committee on Education in the Colonies under the terms of the White Paper of 1925, produced a brief report making 'an eloquent and urgent plea for the founding of universities in tropical Africa' (Ashby 1964: 17). The combined results of these initiatives were a few colleges ('Jones Colleges') that emerged between 1922 and 1934: Makerere College in Uganda (1922); Gordon Memorial College and the Kitchener School of Medicine in Khartoum in Sudan (1924); the Princess of Wales School and College in Achimota in Ghana (1927); and Higher College in Yaka in Nigeria (1934) (Wandira 1977).

According to Asavia Wandira, the Jones Colleges faced two 'conceptual problems'. The first he described as the 'problem of apex', which spoke to the necessity of synchronizing the need for a university with the level reached by the secondary education system. The second problem spoke to comparable standards – should the Jones Colleges be allowed to depart from recognized international standards and establish an identity of their own? (Wandira 1977) These two problems were reflected in the recommendations of the British Advisory Committee on Education in the Colonies of 1933, but the 1937 De La Warr Commission nonetheless recommended developing Makerere College in Uganda into the University College for East Africa:

> We are aware of the present very flimsy foundations of primary and secondary education upon which such institutions will need to be based, and realize the possible risks of too rapid advance and of a top heavy structure. Nevertheless, we are convinced that the material needs of the country and the intellectual needs of its people require that such risks as there may, should be taken.
>
> (Wandira 1977: 12)

Another factor that informed the colonial reluctance to establish universities in Africa was monetary in nature: who was going to pay for them? It was not until the adoption of the Colonial Development and Welfare Paper of 1940, which became the basis for the Colonial Development and Welfare Act, that the British government committed itself to funding universities in Africa. However, another Commission on Higher Education in the Colonies was launched in 1943, under the chairmanship of Justice Asquith, and its 1945 report became the basis for developing university colleges after the end of the Second World War.

Ashby (1964: 19) argues 'The Asquith Report was Britain's blueprint for the export of universities to her people overseas'. This is why such 'university colleges' as the Ibadan in Nigeria, Legon in Ghana, Khartoum in Sudan, Mona in the West Indies and Makerere in Uganda became known as 'Asquith Colleges'. As noted by Ashby, the basic assumption of the 'Asquith Doctrine' 'was that a university system appropriate for Europeans brought up in London and Manchester and Hull was also appropriate for Africans brought up in Lagos and Kumasi and Kampala' (Ashby 1964). The university colleges in Salisbury (University College of Rhodesia/University of Zimbabwe), Nairobi (University of Nairobi) and Dar es Salaam (University of Dar es Salaam) emerged later but as part of the existing Asquith Colleges imperial/colonial tradition. These university colleges became sites of the coloniality of knowledge, cultural imperialism and purveyors of Eurocentric knowledge. In francophone Africa, institutions of higher learning such as the University of Dakar unproblematically took the model of the university system in France as well as standards from Paris and Bordeaux. The same is true of the University of Kinshasa, which closely embraced the model and curriculum of the University of Louvain in Brussels, Belgium (Wandira 1977).

South African universities emerged as part of the imperial/colonial/apartheid tradition. Their earlier emergence than those in the rest of Africa was due to the fact that, from the beginning of the unfolding of colonial modernity, South Africa was imagined as a 'little Europe' at the Southern tip of the African continent (see Magubane 2007). There was a long-standing white presence, since 1652, and over the years a white South Africa emerged through the process of a 'moving frontier' and 'great treks' from the coast, conquering, dispossessing, displacing and occupying what used to be black indigenous people's land (Etherington 2001).

Because of its European character, South Africa's first university, known as the South African College, was established in 1829 – in 1918 it officially became the University of Cape Town (UCT). This was an English university that catered for and prepared white students for degree examinations of the University of London. Africans were not admitted into the university. It was not until 1916 that the first university for Africans was established, known as the South African Native College of Fort Hare (Bitzer 2009). Although South Africa had many colleges and universities before 1948 – such as South African College/UCT (1829); Grey College/the University College of the Orange Free State/University of the Orange Free State (1855); St. Andrews College/Rhodes University College/Rhodes University (1855); Stellenbosch Gymnasium/Stellenbosch College/Victoria

College/University of Stellenbosch (1866); Theological School of the Reformed Church/Potchefstroom University College/Potchefstroom University for Christian Higher Education (1869) – they did not admit black people (Bitzer 2009).

To understand the South African situation one has to delve deeper into the broader early white colonial thought and later apartheid thought about Africans. Suffice to say that the London Missionary Society under Superintendent John Philip, and other denominational missionaries, provided African education (known as 'native education') through mission schools (Majeke 1986). Native education was a particular form of education which, under the apartheid regime, became known as 'Bantu Education'. This provoked South African anti-colonial leader Isaac Bongani Tabata of the Non-European Unity Movement to declare:

> The apostles of Apartheid have fathered a new monstrosity, called Bantu Education, by means of which they aim to arrest the development of the African people, who comprise more than nine million, or nearly three-quarters of the total population. It has its counter-part in 'Coloured Education' for the Coloured people of South Africa, comprising, with Indians, about one and a half million. They want to re-create for the subject races a social order belonging to the pre-industrial age.
>
> (Tabata 1959: 15)

Tabata described 'Bantu Education' as 'education for barbarism' because it was not meant to be 'intellectual' but was deliberately invented as 'industrial'. Through this type of education, African people were being prepared to be providers of the desperately needed cheap labour (Ray 2016). For its genesis, one has to go back to Philip's 1828 paper 'Researches in South Africa'. There he laid down the role of the Christian missionary as being to spread British imperial/colonial interests in South Africa and the purpose of 'native education' as being to eradicate 'native indolence' in order for Africans to be useful servants and labourers of the colony (Ray 2016: 24). What was distinctive about South African higher education was that from the beginning it was shot through with a strong racial and ethnic paradigm of difference, producing 'English universities', 'Afrikaans universities', 'universities for coloureds and Indians' and 'universities for Natives', which were from 1959 further bifurcated into 'black ethnic universities' (White 1997: 69). About this segregated higher education, Tabata concluded that:

> This Apartheid university education is not simply a matter of separating the races at the universities. It is an end result, the logical completion of a systematic process not only of robbing Non-Whites of education but turning a whole population back to barbarism. To put it another way: if Bantu Education is the bricks of that immense edifice, the retribalization of a whole people, the Apartheid university is its capping stone.
>
> (Tabata 1959: 16–17)

The time of reckoning for South African higher education institutions came in 2015, with students – most of them born after the dismantlement of juridical apartheid – spearheading the struggle for decolonization of the universities. What has come to be known as the Rhodes Must Fall movement (discussed later) must be understood as part of the long trajectory in the struggle for the decolonization of education, which began with the likes of Blyden and Hayford. What compounded the predicament of South African higher education institutions is the fact that while the rest of the African continent began to decolonize after 1945, South Africa entered the difficult journey of institutionalized apartheid in 1948. This resulted in the invention of 'Bantustans' at a time when other parts of Africa were gaining political independence. Bantustans were fake 'independent ethnic republics' invented by the apartheid regime but were politically unsustainable as they were in fact mere reservoirs of black cheap labour for the white-owned economy.

Apartheid, which endured as a colonial racist monstrosity until 1994, consistently struggled not only to keep the people of South Africa in separate race and ethnic groups, but also to keep institutions of higher learning racially and ethnically separated. This history partly explains why Malcolm Ray (2016) depicted South African universities as currently engaged 'in a race against time'. Other universities in Africa underwent 'Africanization' in the 1960s and 1970s. Because of the long shadow of apartheid, South African universities are currently engulfed by the spirit of both Africanization and decolonization. What must not be forgotten though, is that the Africanization and decolonization of the universities in the 1960s and 1970s was largely superficial, entailing changing the names of universities, taking over the administration of universities by installing black chancellors and vice-chancellors, increasing the number of black academics and black students as well as including work by African academics in the curriculum. This type of Africanization and decolonization did not touch the structural Eurocentric epistemological scaffolding on which the university in Africa is built and did not constitute the genuine 'epistemic disobedience' called for by advocates of decoloniality (Mignolo 2008).

What was achieved was inclusion of Africans into a long-existing 'European game' without changing the rules of the game (see Fanon 1968). This is why the struggle for an African university continues. The 'decolonization' struggle which is upon us is not simply for inclusion but to change the very rules of the game. Its logic is well captured by Catherine Odora Hoppers and Howard Richards in terms of 'rethinking thinking' itself, involving the radical move of 'casting [. . .] light at last onto subjugated peoples, knowledges, histories and ways of living', which fundamentally 'unsettles the toxic pond and transforms passive analysis into a generative force that valorizes and recreates life for those previously museumised' (Hoppers and Richards 2012: 8). But let us carefully track the trajectories of the African struggle for an African university since 1960 – the year of African political liberation.

Africanization and African developmental university

The dawn of African political independence in the 1960s was accompanied by intensified struggles to transform/Africanize/decolonize the university in Africa into an African university. At its deepest level, this struggle entailed formulating a new philosophy of higher education informed by African histories, cultures, ideas and aspirations as well as a fundamental redefinition of the role of the university. But to achieve this decolonial objective, there was a need to navigate carefully not only the imperatives of 'standards' set in Europe and the African local imperatives of the 'social function' of the university, but also the dangers of looking 'inward' at the expense of the universal aspect of knowledge. Mobutu Sese Seko of Zaire expressed the 'inward'-looking imperative when he said:

> We need to emancipate the educational system in the Congo from the Western model by going back to the Authenticity while paying due attention to scientific knowledge. I have always thought it inappropriate for us to train our youth as if they were Westerners. It would be more desirable to have an educational system which shapes the youth according to our requirements. That would make them authentically Congolese. Their ideas, reasoning and actions would be Congolese, and they would see the future in Congolese terms.
>
> (Mobutu cited in Mkandawire 2005a: 22–23)

Mobutu Sese Seko was an advocate of what became known as 'Authenticite', which entailed even abandoning the use of European names as part of the national project of Africanization. In a speech delivered at Léopold Sédar Senghor's seventieth birthday celebrations, Mobutu Sese Seko made a distinction between his own idea of authenticity and Senghor's Negritude. He said while Negritude was a rebellion against the arrogance of the French colonizers, 'authenticity was a rebellion against one's own dependency and imitativeness' (Mobutu cited in Mazrui 1978: 13–14). While this was an unexpected and brilliant intervention from Mobutu Sese Seko, what fundamentally discredited his Africanization project was his anti-human political behaviour, which turned him into the archetypal notorious 'postcolonial' African dictator. He abused the ideologies of decolonization and African symbolism to invent himself as an 'absolute modern monarch' who single-handedly captured the state of Zaire and successfully turned it into a personal fiefdom, using the country's expansive resources for his personal benefit. Mobutu Sese Seko is a leading example of what Michael G. Schatzberg (2001: 8) described as 'Presidential-Father-Chief' of 'middle Africa'.

Other African nationalists like Julius Nyerere of Tanzania, who became the first black chancellor of the University of East Africa (consisting of the University of Makerere in Uganda, the University of Nairobi in Kenya and the University of Dar es Salaam in Tanzania) on 28 June 1963, were attentive to the dilemma facing the processes of Africanizing the university in Africa:

There are two possible dangers facing a university in a developing nation: the danger of blindly adoring mythical 'international standards' which may cast a shadow on national development objectives, and the danger of forcing our university to look inwards and isolate itself from the world.

(Nyerere 1966: 218–219)

While Nyerere emphasized the dangers of failing to maintain a balance between the national and international character of the university in Africa, Mazrui highlighted three important relationships that the university in Africa has to navigate and negotiate:

A university has to be politically distant from the state; secondly, a university has also to be culturally close to society; and thirdly, a university has to be intellectually linked to wider scholarly and scientific values of the world of learning.

(Mazrui 2003: 141)

At the same time, while Nyerere was cognisant of the dilemma of indigenization/Africanization versus internationalization, like other African nationalists he was forthright about the role that the African university had to play in an independent African state and continent. He demanded that the university 'takes an active part in the social revolution we are engineering' and that social revolution was predicated on nation-building, economic development and promoting African consciousness (Nyerere 1966: 219). Nyerere elaborated:

For twentieth century nationalism is part of a social revolution; an essential part of the development of man as a human being whose freedom depends on his equal membership of the world. Modern nationalism is necessarily humanitarian and international; it is therefore incompatible with racialism. One of the basic tasks of this University is to make this truth an instinctive part of our nationalist expression.

(Nyerere 1966: 219)

Because colonialism had dispossessed Africans, reduced them to 'subjects' rather than 'citizens' and plunged them into poverty and misery, the immediate task of the new black governments was to deliver economic and social development (Mamdani 1996). It was within this context that the university in Africa was reimagined and redefined as an engine of development – a 'developmental university' (Mkandawire 2005). The universities were expected to carry the burden of African nationalism, which claimed to express African aspirations. But Thandika Mkandawire argues:

What African governments wanted was not critical support but subservience and sycophancy. With their ears finely tuned to the voices of foreign experts and deaf to local voices, African states simply didn't care about local debates, except when they threatened state authority.

(Mkandawire 2005b: 2)

Indeed, while African nationalists were pushing for the Africanization of universities and urging African intellectuals to be actively engaged in state-led development projects, they also displayed disdain for African intellectuals by inviting foreigners as close advisers. Mkandawire reveals that Nyerere surrounded himself with foreign 'Fabian socialists' in contrast to Tanzanian intellectuals; Kenneth Kaunda of Zambia's closest intellectual associate was John Hatch, who even became the first director of the Institute for Humanism; and Nkrumah surrounded himself with foreign Pan-Africanists like George Padmore and William E.B. Dubois (Mkandawire 2005a).

However, while African nationalist leaders like Nkrumah were guilty of surrounding themselves with foreign advisers and ignored local intellectuals, they continued to argue for the Africanization of the university as well as active participation of the university in state development projects. Thus, when Nkrumah officially opened the Akuafo Hall of Residence at the University College of Ghana in 1958, he stated: 'We must in the development of our University bear in mind that once it has been planted in African soil it must take root amidst African traditions and culture' (Ashby 1964: 61). The demand by founding leaders of independent African states for the universities to embrace the national projects spearheaded by the state set the institutions of higher learning into a new relationship with the state. Notions of academic freedom and university autonomy immediately locked horns with state imperatives, to the extent that by as early as 1963, Nkrumah critiqued a particular notion of academic freedom:

> There is, however, sometimes a tendency to use the words 'academic freedom' in another sense and to assert the claim that a university is more or less an institution of learning having no respect or allegiance to the community or to the country in which it exists [. . .] This assertion is unsound in principle and objectionable in practice.
>
> (Nkrumah cited in Ashby 1964: 78)

Nkrumah became notorious for interfering with the universities' autonomy and academic freedom in Ghana. During this period, there was an emerging nationalist belief that universities occupied an important position and could not be left alone to determine their own priorities without the influence of the state and government (Yesufu 1973a). Nkrumah expressed the mood of the time well when he declared that, as the government of Ghana:

> We do not intend to sit idly by and see these institutions which are supported by millions of pounds produced out of the sweat and toil of common people

continue to be centres of anti-government activities. We want the university college to cease being an alien institution and to take on the character of a Ghanaian University, loyally serving the interests of the nation and the well-being of our people. If reforms do not come from within, we intend to impose them from outside, and no resort to the cry of academic freedom (for academic freedom does not mean irresponsibility) is going to restrain us from seeing that our university is a healthy university devoted to Ghanaian interest.

(Nkrumah cited in Mkandawire 2005a: 22)

What is poignant about these utterances of African nationalist leaders is that even the Africanization initiatives of the 1960s did not take place within a context of social and political harmony and consensus between those in charge of the state and the African intellectuals, most of whom were foreign trained. It would also seem that the nationalist leaders often used the argument of Africanization as a strategy to interfere and impose their views on the universities. Some African nationalists, like Nnamdi Azikiwe of Nigeria, pushed for the adoption of the 'American model' (Yankee-style) of the university within a context where there was a pre-occupation with 'Nigerianization' as a major component of the national project (Okeke 1946). Azikiwe had studied in America and was enchanted by the American model of the university, to the extent of dedicating efforts to creating one in Nigeria. His efforts resulted in the establishment of the University of Nigeria at Nsukka in Eastern Nigeria as a replica of the American model of the university (Ashby 1964). What this indicated was that the agenda of Africanizing the university in Africa unfolded within the context of a nationalist ideology of 'one country, one university', as part of increasing access to higher education for an African people who had been deliberately starved of higher education by colonial regimes. A major achievement of African nationalism was opening the gates of learning and education to African people.

Thus, on another level, the 1960s constituted the 'golden age' of the African higher education sector. Not only did the institutions of higher learning multiply, but the Africanization agenda was embraced by leading scholars such as Cheikh Anta Diop, a nationalist scholar based at the University of Dakar, who dedicated his entire career to producing Africa-centred knowledge and exploding the myths created by imperial colonial historiography (Diop 1974; Diop 1981). Diop ranks among the founding fathers of 'Afrocentricity' and African nationalist historiography as he consistently worked to claim the Egyptian civilization as an African invention. A vibrant and respected African Nationalist School emerged at the University of Ibadan in Nigeria, led by historians such as Kenneth Onwuka Dike, Jacob Ade Ajayi, John Omer-Cooper and many others who contributed immensely to the Africanization of history as a discipline, as well as to the African nation-building project (Ifemesia 1988). Falola provides the most comprehensive and exhaustive definition of nationalist historiography:

[T]he use of history in the service of the nation – a way of writing that makes history valuable in defining the nation and shaping its future. Nationalist historiography is the representation of elite interests in the nation, as the elite uses its knowledge to define its leadership role. It is a counter-discourse used for attacking European representation of Africa. It is a deliberate attempt to provide credible evidence for the achievements of Africa and the glories of the past in order to indicate possibilities for the future and combat racist views that Africans are incapable of managing themselves [. . .] Nationalist historiography is about power: the ability of an intelligentsia to assert itself, to generate knowledge about its own people and continent, to show where others are either wrong or right in what they say of its people and continent, to attack views and people who are perceived as hostile or racist, to defend people who are patriotic in their representation of Africa, to justify or explain all aspects of African history and institutions that outsiders condemn, and to create a response to the consequences of European domination of the continent.

(Falola 2001: 224)

In terms of key features, nationalist historiography was 'passionate, combative, and revisionist' as it consistently and persistently dethroned the 'Eurocentric perceptions of Africa' and Africans (Falola 2001: 224). It was the historians of the Ibadan, Dakar, Maputo and Dar-se-Salaam nationalist history schools that introduced the oral tradition methodology in their writing of African history; they successfully countered the negatives imparted by imperial/colonial historiography; and they shifted the African historical focus from 'conquest' to 'resistance' as part of their recovery of African agency in history (Falola 2001). The nationalist historians also actively and tirelessly worked to change history curricula and to put at the centre of history courses what they termed 'the African factor' (Falola 1993: 72).

The Dar es Salaam School of History, while nationalist in orientation, also increasingly became a home for Marxist thought and political economy approaches. Walter Rodney's celebrated *How Europe Underdeveloped Africa* (1972) proudly represented the ideological orientation and perspective of the Dar es Salaam School in the 1970s. What the Dar es Salaam School brought to the fore was the importance of class analysis to understand the questions of capitalist exploitation, and the dynamics of African indigenous producers. It also revealed the existence of various African social formations and processes of accumulation as well as dispossession (Temu and Swai 1981).

While the Ibadan School was criticized for overconcentration on political history, to the extent of creating an impression that only kings and queens (Great Man Theory) made African history; for ignoring questions of class, gender, labour and economy; as well as underestimating the epic impact of colonialism on Africa, the Dar es Salaam School's Marxist orientation exposed it to criticism of being stuck in economic determinism (Wrigley 1971: Ekeh 1980). Mazrui criticized the

Dar es Salaam School for its Marxist approach, arguing that Marxism was a foreign ideology that was stifling the emergence of genuine African thought (Mazrui 1974). It would seem that what the nationalist historians succeeded in doing was to Africanize history but they failed to decolonize it. This point becomes even more poignant if one takes into account Jacques Depelchin's (2005) view that African history has remained colonized in terms of its themes, perspectives, periodization and problems to be investigated.

The formation of the Association of African Universities (AAU) in Rabat in Morocco in 1967 revealed the continued commitment by African leaders to decolonize and Africanize universities in Africa and make them truly African universities. But unlike the nationalist political leaders, African intellectuals never tired of defending so-called 'international standards' while Africanizing and decolonizing the university in Africa. The AAU expressed adherence to world academic standards and development of a higher education in the service of Africa, and was in favour of linking the African spirit of the university with the Pan-African spirit embodied by the Organisation of African Unity (Yesufu 1973b: 5). At its first general conference held in Kinshasa, Zaire, in September 1969, the AAU's chosen theme – 'The University and Development' – was revealing of the envisaged role of the university.

Creating the African developmental university

A 1972 AAU workshop, themed 'Creating the African University: Emerging Issues in the 1970s', which ran from 10–15 July in Accra, Ghana, demonstrated that the struggle for an African university was continuing even within a context where African economies were beginning to collapse. The Workshop's purpose was to formulate a new philosophy of higher education and develop institutions of higher education that were truly African, drawing 'inspiration from Africa, and intelligently dedicated to her ideas and aspirations' (Yesufu 1973b: 5). The workshop delegates concluded that an African university must not be an ivory-tower institution occupied by an elite minority 'indifferent to the prevailing poverty and squalor that surround them'. They elaborated:

> The African university must in the 1970s not only wear a different cloak, but must also be differently motivated. It must be made of a different and distinctive substance from the traditions of Western universities, and must evolve a different attitude and a different approach to its task. The truly African university must be one that draws its inspiration from its environment, not a transplanted tree, but growing from a seed that is planted and nurtured in the African soil.
>
> (Yesufu 1973a: 40)

Importantly, the workshop delegates agreed that tinkering with imported ideas was not enough and that what was needed was a fundamental reconceptualization

TABLE 7.2 Summary of core functions of an African university in the 1970s

Function	Explanation
Pursuit, promotion and dissemination of knowledge	Practical, immediately useful to the ordinary people and locally-oriented
Research	Research priority given to local problems and improvement of rural life and that of ordinary people
Provision of intellectual leadership	Cutting-edge leadership capable of leading government, society and commerce in devising and implementing meaningful economic and social development
Manpower development	Relevant skilled graduates capable of playing a leading role in the social revolution and production
Promotion of social and economic modernization	Breaking the chains of tradition that inhibit the African genius capable of advancing social and economic development
Promotion of intercontinental unity and international understanding	Responsibility to emancipate the African continent from isolation, marginality and pursuit of Pan-Africanism

Source: Yesufu 1973a, 42–43.

of the very idea of the university in Africa. In line with this decolonial thinking, six functions of the African university were delineated (Table 7.2).

There was a clear agreement among the members of the AAU that the African university must be a developmental one. However, Wandira raised critical concerns about what he termed the 'Yesufu University Model' which emerged from the 1972 AAU workshop. The actual role of the university in development and its relationship with the state remained open to conflicts. The questions of academic freedom and autonomy versus the role of the state were not clearly defined. Attempts to create an African university in the 1970s coincided with the realities of collapsing African economies. The existing African universities inevitably began to succumb to the debilitating economic crisis. Inevitably, the 1970s became characterized by rising student protests. Colin Legum (1972) termed 1971 'the year of the students' as 11 universities had to close down and dissolve their student unions. This means that the 1972 AAU workshop took place within a context of crisis and was bound to fail, however well meaning its resolutions were to invent relevant universities reflecting African identity and African soul. Despite the difficulties of the time, African intellectuals and academics continued to fight for intellectual spaces, this time outside the declining universities. The formation of the Council for the Development of Social Science Research in Africa (CODESRIA) in 1973 is a case in point.

Council for the Development of Social Science in Africa

With the support of donor funding, CODESRIA emerged as a research council that became a comfortable home for exiled academics like Thandika Mkandawire from Malawi and Archie Mafeje from South Africa. It also became a home for radical left-leaning intellectuals like Samir Amin from Egypt, Mahmood Mamdani from Uganda, Sam Moyo from Zimbabwe, Issa Shivji from Tanzania and many others. In the words of Mamdani (2016: 78), CODESRIA 'was a ready-made forum for public intellectuals'.

What distinguished CODESRIA was the intense public debates it generated on topical issues affecting Africa, such as African politics and the problem of political authoritarianism; African political economy; dependency; democracy; gender and emancipation of women; the agrarian question and land reform; neoliberalism and SAPS; higher education; economic and social development; and the national question and constitutionalism. What also distinguished CODESRIA was its 'non-disciplinary' orientation. According to Mamdani:

> CODESRIA developed as a non-disciplinary space where all shed our disciplinary specialization and took on non-disciplinary perspective; on the downside, all took on the mantle of political economy. The political economy emerged as the master discipline in the academy, the more it came to be marked by different tendencies; whether on the left or the right, each heralded the human as an 'economic man' [. . .] CODESRIA was the home of radical scholars who swore by political economy, as if it were an oath of loyalty.
>
> (Mamdani 2016: 78–79)

Mamdani laments how CODESRIA's intellectual programmes did not directly prioritize and pursue the agenda of epistemic decolonization systematically and purposeful. One wonders whether the political economy approach did not free CODESRIA to directly engage in any systemic manner with the ontological question that is always linked to the epistemological question. One may also argue that if the decolonization trajectory in Africa moved from the political question to the economic question to the epistemological question, CODESRIA became overly pre-occupied by the economic decolonization question typical of all those epistemic communities informed by left-wing thought. In his lament, Mamdani (2016) even argued that CODESRIA missed an opportunity when Achille Mbembe joined in the 1990s and tried to shift its orientation from the public debate tradition informed by political economy to that of a scholarly community that took up other important themes, such as the discourse and representation that pre-occupied the global scholarly community. The truth though is that Mbembe has maintained a very controversial intellectual position with regards to the decolonization of knowledge and has mounted some of the most brutal criticism of what he has termed 'Afro-Marxism', 'nativism', 'African modes of self-writing', and most recently 'black reason' (Mbembe 2002a; Mbembe 2002b; Mbembe 2017).

At another level, it would seem that Mamdani's criticism of CODESRIA somehow ignored some of the groundbreaking researches and animated debates that were initiated by key members of CODESRIA such as Samir Amin (2009) that directly confronted Eurocentrism (the mother and father of epistemological colonization) as well as the work of Archie Mafeje that directly and consistently challenged anthropology as a handmaiden of colonial knowledge. It was actually CODESRIA which published two of the most influential volumes on the university in Africa: *African Universities in the Twenty-First Century: Volume 1: Liberalization and Internationalization* (2004) and *African Universities in the Twenty-First Century: Volume 2: Knowledge and Society* (2004). To its credit, CODESRIA has maintained a clear oppositional position to imperialism, colonialism and neo-colonialism.

The distinguished Kenyan historian Bethwell A. Ogot has critiqued those who embraced the Marxist political economy of adhering to Western science and Western theoretical tools in order to understand Africa, charging that, 'This was a sad episode of intellectual capitulation' (Ogot 2009: 18). Does this critique not apply to CODESRIA too? Mamdani (2016: 79) admitted:

> The epistemological dimension of decolonization has focused on the categories with which we make, unmake and remake, and thereby apprehend, the world. It is intimately tied to our notions of what is human, what is particular and what is universal. *This debate has not found room in CODESRIA.*

CODESRIA is still a vibrant intellectual space and one can only hope that it builds on its unparalleled intellectual work to directly address the topical issue of the decolonization of the universities and the epistemological question. At a general level, the decline of African intellectualism in the mid-1970s provoked two important but broad questions. The first is why African intellectualism declined in the early 1970s. Why did the early decolonization/Africanization initiatives fail? These issues led Mazrui (2003: 137) to pose the question: 'Who has killed intellectualism in East Africa?' The first killer of intellectualism was the rise of brutal dictatorship, symbolized in East Africa by the coming to power of Idi Amin Dada in Uganda through a military coup in January 1971. He unleashed a reign of terror that had an immense impact on intellectualism (Mazrui 2003).

The second killer was the advent of the Cold War between Western powers and the Soviet bloc. The Cold War not only polarized Africans into pro-West and pro-East ideological dichotomies, but within states like Kenya that became pro-West, '[b]eing socialist or left-wing as an intellectual became a political hazard' (Mazrui 2003: 138). In the same manner, in a country like Tanzania, led by respected intellectual Mwalimu Julius Nyerere, who chose the path of socialism, the local excessive enthusiasm for socialism bred ideological 'intimidation in the name of socialism' and respect for Nyerere that Mazrui critiqued as 'Tanzaphilia' (Mazrui 1967). What suffered severely in both cases was academic freedom.

To Mbembe (2002a), as mentioned above, the combination of African nationalism and Marxism produced a powerful but false Afro–Marxist radicalism that subsisted on the narcissism of minor difference and victimhood. This thinking, according to Mbembe, has imprisoned the expression of 'black reason' (Mbembe 2017). To Mbembe, two narratives of African identity (nativism and Afro-radicalism) are premised on a false claim 'that their [the African] race, traditions, and customs confer to them [Africans] a peculiar self irreducible to that of any other human group'(Mbembe 2006: 8). If Mbembe is this critical of a pre-occupation with identity and authenticity as well as of initiatives aimed at breaking away from imperialism, neo-colonialism, dependence and neoliberalism, one wonders how he was going to steer CODESRIA to the epistemological decolon-ization. Ontology and epistemology are inextricably intertwined. But to Mbembe, besides these pre-occupations being fed by a 'neurosis of victimhood' linked to the triple events of slavery, colonialism and apartheid, they also promoted the 'ghettoization' of Africa (Mbembe 2002b). Cascading from this analysis, Mbembe (2002a: 242) would not support the African struggle for the decolonization of universities as this would amount to what he has caricatured as Africans' desire 'to know themselves (*identity*), to recapture their destiny (*sovereignty*), and to belong to themselves in the world (*autonomy*)'. To him this is a result of a pre-occupation with African history as nothing but a catalogue and a 'series of subjugations, narrativized in a seamless continuity'(Mbembe 2002a: 243).

While Mbembe's the warnings about the limits of both Marxism and African nationalism as philosophies of liberation are well taken, there is a danger of his analysis inadvertently falling into unintended apologia for the slave trade, colonialism and apartheid. Epistemological decolonization is not about 'navel-gazing', 'nativism' and 'ghettoization'. It is about cognitive/epistemic justice as an essential pre-requisite for social justice (Santos 2014). Epistemological decolonization is about opening rather than closing the academy to a plurality of knowledges. Mbembe's analysis is also not critical of globalization and the notions of global knowledge that continue to circulate from the hegemonic centres of Europe and North America.

Epistemological decolonization is important in dealing with the asymmetrical global intellectual division of labour in which Europe and North America not only masquerade as teachers of the rest of the world, but also as sites of theory and concept production, which are then consumed by Africa and the rest of the world. This point is brought home clearly by Raewyn Connell (2016:1): 'Modern universities and their staff and students exist in a global economy of knowledge, with a definite geography of production and circulation.' Of course, since the outbreak of the Rhodes Must Fall and the Fees Must Fall movements in 2015 and 2016, Mbembe slightly rethought his earlier position, accepting to some extent the need for decolonization, and enthusiastically joined the voices that were consistently critical of the Eurocentric canon and the corporate university. But he has again take a de tour and is very critical of the student movements and the decolonial struggles; arguing that pre-occupation with decolonization might be a focus on and shooting a target that has long moved. We leave Mbembe's controversial positionality here and we proceed with our analysis of the crisis undercutting the struggles to create genuine African universities.

Taking into account the preceding analysis, it is not surprising that the 1980s and 1990s became crisis years for the university in Africa, and attempts to create an African university collapsed. New factors intervened to deepen the crisis. For example, the WB introduced a negative attitude towards universities, discrediting them as agencies of development and public institutions worthy of government and international support. Instead, the WB (1986) prioritized secondary education. The idea of creating African universities died as the powerful international forces of neoliberalism and global finance posited that Africa had no need for universities, and that what was taught at them was irrelevant to the needs of the global market and national development (Olukoshi and Zeleza 2004). It was during this period that the humanities and social sciences were challenged to demonstrate their relevance and value to the technically and narrowly defined programme of development that was now driven by the Bretton Woods institutions under the so-called SAPs (Mazrui 1975). The example of history departments mutating overnight into departments of development studies and departments of international studies to avoid closure and to demonstrate relevance to the demands of a world captured by market forces is instructive of the power of neoliberal interventions into higher education.

Falola (2001) identifies four major factors that led to the decline of universities in Africa in the 1980s. The first factor was the decline in African economies, which made it impossible for African governments to continue financing higher education. The second was the migration of academics to Europe and North America. The third was the rising tide of political authoritarianism, noted above, and the fourth was the marginalization of Africa in global affairs and the renewal of dependency through the SAPs. The consequences of these developments have been far reaching for the university in Africa. According to Falola (2001), the role of academics in society was diminished, leading to a crisis of self-production as it became difficult to attract gifted young people into the academic profession.

Those academics that remained behind literally abandoned academic work and concentrated on survival. In addition, scholarship itself suffered debasement as academics pursued wealth, fame and power, to the extent of reducing themselves to being sycophants to those in state power. Lastly, university education underwent instrumentalization as more and more people wanted it not for knowledge's sake but for certificates, diplomas, degrees and occupational mobility. The focus became 'on how to pass examinations, then throw away the books and seek remunerative occupations' (Falola 2001: 216–217). The neoliberal project spearheaded by the WB and the IMF constituted 'one of the most significant changes and challenges to face higher educational systems in Africa since independence' (Olukoshi and Zeleza 2004: 6). The forced mutation of the university in Africa into a 'corporate university' in the 1980s and 1990s was a major blow to the struggles for a decolonized university. Markets became the major agents of coloniality.

The corporate university and commodification of knowledge

The African struggle for an African university failed in the 1960s and 1970s. The late 1980s and the 1990s witnessed the rise of the 'corporate university', characterized not only by the invasion of the university by business models but also by 'great antipathy to thinking' (Gordon 2006: 5). The corporate university is a product of the triumph of the Washington Consensus, which routinized the neoliberal dispensation.

Besides well-known features of neoliberalism such as deregulation, privatization and withdrawal of the state from provision of social services, Paul Tiyambe Zeleza (2004) has identified what he terms the 'six Cs' that speak directly to how higher education has been shaped by neoliberal thinking. First is the *corporatization* of management through adopting business models for organizing and administering the university. Second is the process of *collectivizing* access through the massification of higher education, continuing learning and accountability to outside stakeholders. Third is the *commercialization* of learning through expansion of private universities, private programmes in public universities and vocational training. Fourth is the *commodification* of knowledge through increased production, sponsorship and dissemination of research by commercial enterprises, applied research and intellectual property norms. Fifth is the *computerization* of education through incorporating new information technologies into the knowledge activities of teaching, research and publication. Sixth is the *connectivity* of institutions of higher learning through institutional cooperation and coordination within and across countries (Zeleza 2004: 56).

Within the corporate university arose what Lewis R. Gordon (2006: 9–10) terms the 'academic managerial class' using 'corporate analogs' as its basis of governing the institutions. Gordon (2006: 10) elaborates that the rise of this 'academic managerial class has been, perhaps the most catastrophic development in the modern university'. The catastrophic aspect of this phenomenon is multi-dimensional. First, this academic managerial class, according to Gordon (2006: 10), is 'unlike past scholars who so happened also to administrate' because it 'no longer has knowledge as part of its telos'. Worse still, this academic managerial class 'has folded onto itself as the object of its own preservation, and the result is its proliferation' (Gordon 2006: 10). Gordon further characterizes the composition of this academic managerial class as 'consisting of failed academics and scholars whose credentials do not extend beyond their doctorates' and who practise the 'sociology of revenge and entrenched resentment toward productive and influential scholars' (Gordon 2006: 10). It is this academic managerial class that 'seeks inspiration from the corporate world primarily because of a form of decadence of the imagination in which corporate management is equated with management itself' (Gordon 2006: 10–11).

It is within this context of a decadent corporate university presided over by an equally decadent academic managerial class that many scholars found themselves in the midst of what Mamdani (2007) termed the 'market place'. Within this 'market place', evaluation of scholarship is through the principles of quantification and annual reports. It is also within this context that research is measured in accordance with 'the immediate demands of a consumer society'; anything which looks into the long term is discredited as irrelevant (Gordon 2006: 11). Thus, instead of deploying a pedagogy that really develops informed African citizenry, education is reduced to the skilling of students. What has compounded the crisis in a corporate university is what Gordon terms 'disciplinary decadence':

> *Disciplinary decadence* is the ontologizing or reification of a discipline. In such an attitude, we treat our discipline as though it was never born and has always existed and will never change or, in some cases, die. More than immortal, it is eternal. Yet as something that came into being, it lives, in such an attitude, as monstrosity, as an instance of a human creation that can never die.
>
> (Gordon 2006: 4–5)

For the decolonization of knowledge to take place, it is important for this 'disciplinary decadence' to die. This death must take the form of a discipline suspending 'its own centering because of a commitment to questions greater than the discipline itself' (Gordon 2006: 34). But what has really plunged the corporate university into violent crisis is its commodification of education, which has reduced students to customers and the professoriate to an academic proletariat. Within the corporate university, higher education has been turned into a seductive 'marketable product, rated, bought and sold by standard units, measured, counted and reduced to staple equivalence by impersonal, mechanical tests and therefore readily subject to statistical consistency, with numerical standards and units' (Mbembe 2016: 30).

The pegging of higher education at a commercial value has not only closed out of the university students from poor family backgrounds, it has also burdened those who went through the corporate university with a huge debt. This reality has provoked student protests across the world. A good example of the most recent student protest is the Rhodes Must Fall movement that broke out in 2015 in South Africa and that inspired protests in other parts of the world. The Rhodes Must Fall movement is analysed below as a typical example of the resurgent call for decolonization of the university in the twenty-first century, at a time when the wider social role of the institution is, in the words of Bill Readings (1996: 2), 'now up for grabs' and '[i]t is no longer clear what the place of the University is within society nor what exactly [the] nature of that society is'.

Resurgent struggles for a decolonized university

By 2015 the idea of the university prescribed by the colonial and apartheid past was targeted by radical student movements in South Africa. While on the surface the 2015/2016 Rhodes Must Fall movement was sparked by the existence of the offensive statue of leading British imperialist Cecil John Rhodes at UCT, there were deeper challenges behind this movement (Ndlovu-Gatsheni 2016). These included the deepening and widening socio-economic inequalities that breed poverty; the legitimate demand for expansion of access to higher education, which speaks directly to social justice issues connected to the skewed demographic and unequal economic wealth distribution; low throughput and retention of students; the irrelevance of what is taught in universities and its misalignment with labour market demands; and the connection between student demands and workers' demands, which manifested in the call for the outsourcing of workers to end. A combination of these factors forced the students to begin the struggle of 'nibbling at resilient colonialism in South Africa' (Nyamnjoh 2016).

The South African students who spearhead the Rhodes Must Fall and the Fees Must Fall movements must be understood broadly as heirs to the long-standing struggles for an African university and the wider decolonization of Africa. What the South African students put to the fore is Oginga Odinga's (1968) 'Not Yet Uhuru' clarion call to continue the struggle for decolonization even after the dismantlement of direct colonial administrations and juridical apartheid (see also Ndlovu-Gatsheni 2017). It is not surprising that South Africa, hailed by neoliberals as a democratic society with one of the most liberal, progressive constitutions in the world, has become the site of resurgent decolonial struggles, because what was gained in 1994 was democracy without decolonization. The celebrated constitution 'constitutionalized injustices' (Ramose 2003: 470). 'Neo-apartheid' rather than 'post-apartheid' best describes present-day South Africa, where racism, inequalities and exclusions signify a problematic democracy; where a dispossessed black majority refuses to accept the constitutionalized apartheid theft of resources and their continued concentration in the hands of the minority white population; and where a few black people use control of the state to engage in bureaucratic petit-bourgeois looting.

While Susan Booysen (2016)'s definition and analysis of the South African student movement is limited by her neoliberal concerns with the governance failures of the ANC as a former liberation movement, she is correct in locating the student struggles within the broader revolts against the sociopolitical dispensation resulting from the 1994 social compact between big business, the white ruling elite and the black-dominated liberation movements. What the Rhodes Must Fall and Fees Must Fall movements have successfully brought to the fore are the long-standing but unresolved issues of opening the doors of learning and education to everyone, as promised by the ANC in the Freedom Charter of 1955; rescuing the university from capture by neoliberal market forces and repositioning it as a public good; rethinking and redefining the university as a truly African public institution serving African communities; rethinking and rearticulating the broader philosophical foundations of higher education in Africa to enhance relevance; financing and funding higher education to enable access; decolonizing the epistemology, curricula and alienating institutional cultures of the universities; democratizing student–staff relations to enhance teaching and learning; using indigenous languages for learning and teaching; ending the dehumanizing outsourcing of black workers; as well as the depatriarchalization, deracialization and dewesternization of universities (Ndlovu-Gatsheni 2017).

Like all struggles of decolonization, the Rhodes Must Fall and Fees Must Fall movements were inevitably riddled with internal ructions, contradictions, ambiguities and struggles within the struggle. This has given ammunition to its opponents like Jonathan Jansen who in his book entitled *As By Fire* (2017) to mount some of the criticism which borders on dismissal and discrediting of the movements. The outbreaks of violence in particular have armed the opponents of the Rhodes Must Fall and Fees Must Fall movements including justifications of employing and deploying private security companies, resulting in the militarization of campuses. Rather than diminishing it, this contributed to an escalation in the violence. But the opponents of the student movements as well as the broader struggle for epistemic freedom have not missed the opportunity to instrumentalize the inevitable ambiguities, ambivalences, and even contradictions to support the status quo.

To the credit of the movements, there has always been a robust internal critique if not auto-critique that raised such issues as the patriarchal tendencies; intolerance of divergent views; the sometimes careless use of the discourse of racism, which affected the initial multiracial quality of the student movements; weak responses to the realities of the intersectionality of student struggles, which caused struggles within the struggle as the lesbian, gay, bisexual and trans-gender community complained of being sidelined; and the challenge of avoiding being used by external political forces (see Chinguno *et al.* 2017). However, the fact remains that South African students have taken the torch of epistemic decolonization and successfully put decolonization squarely on the public agenda. In the process, they have forced universities to revive their mission to be torch-bearers of equality, democracy, justice and human rights. Whether they will genuinely rise adequately to these noble demands is yet to be seen.

Conclusion

By engaging in historicizing and problematizing the genealogy of education systems and the role of indigenous knowledge, tracking the very idea of the university and unpacking the institutional history of the university in Africa, this chapter was able to highlight the intersecting traditions that coalesced to produce it in the first place and its mutating models. It revealed how the European model of the university displaced pre-existing universities and demonstrated how the imposition of the modern Westernized university resulted in radical transformation of existing intellectual traditions if not their destruction. The case study of Ethiopia highlighted one of the ironic if not tragic African situations of an important country that survived colonial conquest and direct colonialism but failed to defend its indigenous knowledge and education system in the twentieth century. Ethiopia today, just like other African countries that were conquered and colonized, has discarded its indigenous government, legal system and educational institutions, and replaced them with foreign European imitations. Even more disappointing is the fact that Ethiopia has also discarded its indigenous languages and adopted a European language as its medium of higher education.

The Ethiopian situation underscores the dangerous operations of the metaphysical empire and its long-term consequence of the imposition of the modern Westernized university. What also emerged clearly from this chapter are the paradoxes and limits of the long struggles for an African university. The paradoxical structural situation bequeathed on Africa by colonialism is that a modern education which produced a people who were deeply alienated from themselves, their cultures, languages, ancestors and knowledges but were at the same time eager to end colonial rule. It is, therefore, not surprising that these very Africans whose minds have been deeply invaded by epistemological colonialism have continued to reproduce cultural colonialism. Consequently, the struggle to decolonize the 'university in Africa' so as to create an 'African university' is still on course in the twenty-first century.

References

Ajayi, F. F A. 1985. 'The Education Process and Historiography in Contemporary Africa: Background Paper'. In Unesco, *The Education Process and Historiography in Africa*. Paris: Unesco, pp. 11–20.

Ajayi, J. E. A., Lameck, K. H. and Goma, G. 1996. *The African Experience with Higher Education*. Accra: Association of African Universities.

Amadiume, I. 1987. *Male Daughters, Female Husbands: Gender and Sex in an African Society*. London: Zed Books.

Amin, S. 2009. *Eurocentrism: Modernity, Religion, and Democracy: A Critique of Eurocentrism and Culturalism*. Second Edition. New York: Monthly Review Press,

Ashby, E. 1964. *African Universities and Western Tradition*. Cambridge, MA: Harvard University Press.

Assié-Lumumba, N. T. 2006. *Higher Education in Africa: Crises, Reforms and Transformation*. Dakar: CODESRIA Books.

Bitzer, E. (ed.). 2009. *Higher Education in South Africa: A Scholarly Look behind the Scenes*. Stellenbosch: SUN MeDIA Stellenbosch.

Blaut, J. M. 1993. *The Colonizer's Model of the World: Geographical Diffusionism and Eurocentric History*. New York and London: The Gilford Press.

Blyden, E. W. 1882. *The Aims and Methods of a Liberal Education for Africans: Inaugural Address Delivered by Edward Wilmot Blyden, LLD., President of Liberia College, January 5, 1881.* Cambridge, MA: Harvard University Press.

Blyden, E. W. 1888 [1967]. *Christianity, Islam and the Negro Race*. London: Edinburgh University Press.

Booysen, S. 2016. 'Two Weeks in October: Changing Governance in South Africa'. In S. Booysen (ed.), *Fees Must Fall: Student Revolt, Decolonization and Governance in South Africa*. Johannesburg: Wits University Press, pp. 22–52.

Cabral, A. 1979. *Unity and Struggle: Speeches and Writings of Amilcar Cabral*. New York and London: Monthly Review Press.

Castro, D. 2007. *Another Face of Empire: Bartolome de Las Casas, Indigenous Rights, and Ecclesiastical Imperialism*. Durham, NC: Duke University Press.

Chinguno, C., Kgoroba, M., Mashibini, S., Masilela, B. N., Maubane, B., Mthombeni, A. and Ndlovu, H., 2017. *Rioting and Writing: Diaries of Wits Fallists.* Johannesburg: Society, Work and Development Institute.

Connell, R. 2016. 'Decolonizing Knowledge, Democratizing Curriculum'. Unpublished Paper Prepared for University of Johannesburg Discussions on Decolonization of Knowledge, March.

Depelchin, J. 2005. *Silences in African History: Between Syndromes of Discovery and Abolition.* Dar es Salaam: Mkuki Na Nyota Publishers.

Diop, C. A. 1974. *The African Origin of Civilization: Myth or Reality.* Chicago, IL: Lawrence Hill.

Diop, C. A. 1981. *Civilization or Barbarism: An Authentic Anthropology.* Chicago, IL: Lawrence Hill.

Diop, C. A. 1987. *Precolonial Black Africa: A Comparative Study of the Political and Social Systems of Europe and Black Africa, from Antiquity to the Formation of Modern States.* Trenton, NJ: Africa World Press.

Ekeh, P. 1980. 'Colonialism and Social Structure'. Inaugural Lecture delivered at the University of Ibadan, 5 June.

Etherington, N. 2001. *The Great Treks: The Transformation of Southern Africa 1815–1854.* London: Longman/Pearson Education.

Falola, T. (ed.). 1993. *African Historiography: Essays in Honour of J. F. Ade Ajayi.* London: Longman.

Falola, T. 2001. *Nationalism and African Intellectuals.* Rochester, NY: University of Rochester Press.

Fanon, F. 1968. *The Wretched of the Earth.* New York: Grove Press.

Frankel, M. Y. 1974. 'Edward Blyden and the Concept of African Personality'. *African Affairs*, 73(292), pp. 277–289.

Gordon, L. R. 2006. *Disciplinary Decadence: Living Thought in Trying Times.* Boulder, CO, and London: Paradigm.

Hayford, J. E C. 1911. *Ethiopia Unbound: Studies in Race Emancipation.* London: C.M. Phillips.

Hayford, J. E. C. 2011. *Memorandum of the Case of the National Congress of British West Africa for a Memorial Based Upon the Resolution to be Presented to His Majesty the King Emperor in Council through the Right Honourable the Secretary of State for the Colonies.* London.

Ifemesia, C. (ed.). 1988. *Issues in African Studies and National Education: Selected Work of Kenneth Onwuka Dike.* Awka: K.O. Dike Centre.

Isaac, E. 2013. *The Ethiopian Orthodox Tawahido Church.* Trenton, NJ: The Red Sea Press.

Jansen, J. 2017. *As By Fire: The End of the South African University.* Cape Town: Tafelberg.

Joseph, G. G. 2011. *The Crest of the Peacock: Non-European Roots of Mathematics.* Princeton, NJ and Oxford, UK: Princeton University Press.

Kebede, M. 2008. *Radicalism and Cultural Dislocation in Ethiopia, 1960–1974.* New York: University Rochester Press.

Kebra Nagast. 1932. *The Queen of Sheba and Her Only Son Menelik I.* Translated by W. Budge. London: Oxford University Press.

Legum, C. 1972. *Africa: The Year of the Students.* London: Rex Collins.

Lulat, Y. G. M. 2003. 'Confronting the Burden of the Past: The Historical Antecedents of the Present Predicament of African Universities'. In J.C. Smart (ed.), *Higher Education: Handbook of Theory and Research: Volume XVIII.* London: Kluwer Academic Publishers, pp. 595–667.

Magubane, B. M. 2007. *Race and the Construction of the Dispensable Other.* Pretoria: UNISA Press.

Majeke, N. 1986. *The Role of the Missionaries in Conquest.* Cape Town: Apdusa.

Mamdani, M. 1996. *Citizen and Subject: Contemporary Africa and the Legacy of Late Colonialism.* Princeton, NJ: Princeton University Press.

Mamdani, M. 2007. *Scholars in the Market Place: The Dilemmas of Neo-Liberal Reform at Makerere University, 1989–2005.* Dakar: CODESRIA Books.

Mamdani, M. 2016. 'Between the Public Intellectual and the Scholar: Decolonization and Some Post-Independence Initiatives in Higher Education'. *Inter-Asia Studies*, 17(1), pp. 56–98.

Mazrui, A. A. 1967. 'Tanzaphilia: A Diagnosis'. *Transition*, 27, pp. 13–23.

Mazrui, A. A. 1974. 'Africa, My Conscience and I'. *Transition*, 46(4), pp. 67–71.

Mazrui, A. A. 1975. 'The African University as a Multinational Corporation: Problems of Penetration and Dependency'. *Harvard Educational Review*, 45(2), pp. 191–210.

Mazrui, A. A. 1978. *Political Values and the Educated Class in Africa.* Berkeley, MA, and Los Angeles, CA: University of California Press.

Mazrui, A. A. 1984. 'Towards Abolishing the Red Sea and Re-Africanizing the Arabian Peninsula'. In J. C. Stone (ed.), *Africa and the Sea: Proceedings of a Colloquium at the University of Aberdeen, March 1984.* Aberdeen, UK: Aberdeen University, pp. 98–104.

Mazrui, A. A. 1986. *The Africans: A Triple Heritage.* London: BBC Publications.

Mazrui, A. A. 2003. 'Towards Re-Africanizing African Universities: Who Killed Intellectualism in the Post-Colonial Era?' *Alternatives: Turkish Journal of International Relations*, 2(3 and 4) (Fall and Winter), pp. 135–163.

Mbembe, A. 2006. 'The Cultural Politics of South Africa's Foreign Policy: Between Black (Inter)-Nationalism and Afropolitanism'. Unpublished Paper Presented at Wits Institute of Economic and Social Research, University of the Witwatersrand.

Mbembe, A. 2002a. 'African Modes of Self-Writing', *Public Culture*, 14(1), pp. 239–273.

Mbembe, A. 2002b. 'On the Power of False', *Public Culture*, 14(3), pp. 619–643.

Mbembe, A. J. 2016. 'Decolonizing the University: New Directions'. *Arts and Humanities in Higher Education*, 15(1), pp. 26–46.

Mbembe, A. 2017. *Critique of Black Reason.* Translated and with an Introduction by Laurent Dubois. Durham, NC and London: Duke University Press.

Mignolo, W. D. 2008. 'Epistemic Disobedience, Independent Thought and De-Colonial Freedom', *Theory, Culture and Society*, 26(7–8), pp. 1–23.

Mkandawire, M. 2005a. 'African Intellectuals and Nationalism' in T. Mkandawire (ed.), *African Intellectuals: Rethinking Politics, Language, Gender and Development.* Dakar and London: CODESRIA and Zed Books, pp. 9–39.

Mkandawire, T. 2005b. 'Introduction' in T. Mkandawire (ed.), *African Intellectuals: Rethinking Politics, Language, Gender and Development.* Dakar and London: CODESRIA and Zed Books, pp. 1–15.

Mudimbe, V. Y. 1998. *Gnosis, Philosophy, and the Order of Knowledge.* Bloomington and Indianapolis, IN: Indiana University Press.

Ndlovu-Gatsheni, S. J. 2009. *The Ndebele Nation: Reflections on Historiography, Hegemony and Memory.* Amsterdam and Pretoria: Rozenberg Publishers and UNISA Press.

Ndlovu-Gatsheni, S. J. 2013a. *Empire, Global Coloniality and African Subjectivity.* New York and Oxford: Berghahn Books.

Ndlovu-Gatsheni, S. J. 2013b. *Coloniality of Power in Postcolonial Africa: Myths of Decolonization.* Dakar: CODESRIA.

Ndlovu-Gatsheni, S. J. 2016. 'Why Are South Africa Universities Sites of Struggle Today?' *The Thinker: A Pan-African Quarterly for Thought Leaders*, 4(70), pp. 52–61.

Ndlovu-Gatsheni, S. J. 2017. 'Sites of Struggle: South African Universities and Student Protests'. Public Lecture delivered at the Conference on Middle Classes, Protests and Social Change in Africa and Beyond, University of Stellenbosch, 17–21 March.

Ngugi wa Thiong'o. 2013 *In the Name of the Mother: Reflections on Writers and Empire.* Nairobi: East African Educational Publishers.

Nkrumah, K. 1970. *Consciencism: Philosophy and Ideology for De-Colonization and Development with Particular Reference to the African Revolution.* New York: Monthly Review Press.

Nwauwa, A. O. 1996. *Imperialism, Academe and Nationalism: Britain and University Education for Africans 1860–1960.* London: Frank Cass.

Nyamnjoh, F. B. 2016. *Rhodes Must Fall: Nibbling at Resilient Colonialism in South Africa.* Bamenda: Langaa Research and Publishing Common Initiative Group.

Nyerere, J. K. 1966. *Freedom and Unity: Uhuru na Umoja. A Selection from Writings and Speeches 1952–65.* Dar es Salaam: Oxford University Press

Nzegwu, N. U. 2006. *Family Matters: Feminist Concepts in African Philosophy of Culture.* New York: State University of New York Press.

Odora Hoppers, C. O. and Richards, H. 2012. *Rethinking Thinking: Modernity's 'Other' and the Transformation of the University.* Pretoria: Unisa Press.

Oginga Odinga, A. 1968. *Not Yet Uhuru.* London: Heinemann.

Ogot, B. A. 2009. 'Rereading the History and Historiography of Epistemic Domination and Resistance in Africa', *African Studies Review*, 52(1), pp 1–30

Okeke, U. 1946. 'Educational Reconstruction in an Independent Nigeria'. PhD thesis, School of Education, New York University.

Olukoshi, A. And Zeleza, P. T. 2004. 'Introduction: The Struggle for African Universities and Knowledges'. In P. T. Zeleza and A. Olukoshi (eds), *African Universities in the Twenty-First Century: Volume 1: Liberalization and Internationalization.* Dakar: CODESRIA Books, pp. 1–41.

Oyewumi, O. 2016. *What Gender Is Motherhood? Changing Yoruba Ideas of Power, Procreation, and Identity in the Age of Modernity.* London: Palgrave Macmillan.

Ramose, M. B. 2003. 'I Conquer, Therefore I am the Sovereign: Reflections upon Sovereignty, Constitutionalism, and Democracy in Zimbabwe and South Africa'. In P. H. Coetzee and A. P. J. Roux (eds), *The African Philosophy Reader: Second Edition,* London: Routledge, pp. 467–498.

Ray, M. 2016. *Free Fall: Why South African Universities Are in a Race against Time.* Johannesburg: Bookstorm.

Readings, B. 1996. *The University in Ruins.* Cambridge, MA: Harvard University Press.

Rodney, W. 1972. *How Europe Underdeveloped Africa.* London: Bogle-L'Ouverture Publications.

Santos, B. de. S. 2014. *Epistemologies of the South: Justice against Epistemicide.* London and Boulder, CO: Paradigm Publishers.

Schatzberg, M. G. 2001. *Political Legitimacy in Middle Africa: Father, Family, Food.* Bloomington, IN: Indiana University Press.

Sumner, C. 2004. 'The Light and the Shadow: Sera Yacob and Walda Heywat: Two Ethiopian Philosophers of the Seventeenth Century'. In K. Wiredu (ed.), *A Companion to African Philosophy.* Oxford, UK: Wiley, pp. 156–189.

Tabata, I. B. 1959. *Education for Barbarism: Bantu (Apartheid) Education in South Africa.* London: Prometheus.

Temu, A. J. and Swai, B. 1981. *Historians and Africanist Historiography: A Critique.* London: Zed Books.

Wagaw, T. G. 1990. *The Development of Higher Education in Africa: An Ethiopian Experience.* Ann Arbor, MI: Michigan University Press.

Wandira, A. 1977. *The African University in Development.* Johannesburg: Ravan Press.

White, C. 1997. *From Despair to Hope: The Turfloop Experience.* Sovenga: University of the North Press.

Woldeyes, Y. G. 2017. *Native Colonialism: Education and the Economy of Violence Against Traditions in Ethiopia*. Trenton, NJ: The Red Sea Press.

World Bank. 1986. *Financing Education in Developing Societies: An Exploration of Policy Options*. Washington, DC: World Bank.

Wrigley, C. 1971'Historicism in Africa: Slavery and State Formation'. *African Affairs*, 70(279) pp. 113–124.

Yesufu, T. M. 1973a. 'Emerging Issues of the 1970s'. In T.M. Yesufu (ed.), *Creating the African University: Emerging Issues in the 1970s*. Ibadan: Oxford University Press, pp. 37–81.

Yesufu, T. M. 1973b. 'Introduction'. In T.M. Yesufu, (ed.), 1973. *Creating the African University: Emerging Issues in the 1970s*. Ibadan: Oxford University Press.

Zeleza, P. T. 2003. *Rethinking Africa's Globalization: Volume 1: The Intellectual Challenges*. Trenton, NJ: Africa World Press.

Zeleza, P. T. 2004. 'Neo-Liberalism and Academic Freedom'. In P. T. Zeleza and A. Olukoshi (eds), *African Universities in the Twenty-First Century: Volume 1: Liberalisation and Internationalisation*. Dakar: CODESRIA, pp. 42–68.

Zeleza, P. T. and Olukoshi, A. 2004. (eds). *African Universities in the Twenty-First Century: Volume 1: Liberalization and Internationalization*. Dakar: CODESRIA Books.

8
NATIONAL QUESTION

Introduction

The national question in Africa became a contested site of diverse intellectual currents if not pedagogical nationalisms partly because colonialists worked tirelessly to suppress the coalescence of the colonized people into broader national identities and partly due to the fact that freedom from colonialism became understood in terms of attainment of national sovereignty. Colonialists insisted that Africans were 'tribal' subjects rather than 'national' citizens. At the same time, it was colonialism that introduced the idea of modern nation-state as social organization of human life where there was a tight correspondence between the 'nation' and the 'state' albeit with modifications in the service of the colonial project. As a European phenomenon, the modern nation-state was born out of conflict and violence. No wonder the notion assumed a concrete form at Westphalia in 1648 after the Thirty Years War. It formed part of what Frantz Fanon (1968: 252) depicted as 'the technique and style of Europe' that produced a catalogue of 'negations' of the human and actual physical annihilation of all those whose identity did not easily fit into the drawn boundaries and imagined political communities. Fanon elaborated:

> When I search for Man in the technique and style of Europe, I see only succession of negations of man and an avalanche of murders. The human condition, plans for mankind and collaboration between men in those tasks which increase the sum total of humanity are now problems, which demand true inventions. Let us decide not to imitate Europe; let us combine our muscles and our brains in a new direction. Let us try to create the whole man, whom Europe has been incapable of bringing to triumphant birth. Two centuries ago, a former European colony decided to catch up with Europe. It succeeded so well that the United States of America became a monster, in which the taints, the sickness and inhumanity of Europe have

grown to appalling dimensions. Comrades, have we not other work to do
than to create a third Europe?

(Fanon 1968: 252)

After the creation of the United States as the second Europe, other 'Europes'
emerged in the form of Australia, New Zealand, Canada and South Africa (known
as the dominions). Genocides, enslavement, violent conquest, material dispossession,
epistemicides, linguicides and culturecides became the major imperial technologies
and styles of inventing Europe outside Europe. But what is ironic is how the drive
to imitate Europe in terms of borrowing its institutional frameworks has so
animated African nationalists to the extent that Basil Davidson (1992) depicted
the adoption of the Westphalian template as the 'Black Man's Burden' and the
'curse of the nation-state in Africa'. It became a curse mainly because the template was being imposed everywhere, including in geo-political spaces like Africa,
characterized by a kaleidoscope of multiple-cultures, multiple-languages, multiple-
ethnicities and multiple-religions (Laakso and Olukoshi 1996). It also became a
curse because the modern nation-state in Africa had to be built within the iron-
cages of the randomly crafted colonial boundaries.

This chapter turns to the work of Neville Alexander, one of South Africa's
leading intellectuals, who consistently studied the national question – a question
another South African scholar, Colin Bundy (2007: 79), depicted as the central
leitmotif of the political catechism of the new South Africa. After Australia, New
Zealand and Canada, South Africa emerged as the fourth 'little Europe' located at
the Southern tip of the African continent. The chapter opens the canvas to reflect
critically on colonialism, imperialism, capitalism and apartheid as constitutive of
'global coloniality', which formed the most important discursive context within
which the national question emerged as a key challenge in (ex)-colonized societies
(Quijano 2000a; 2000b; Ndlovu-Gatsheni 2013a; 2013b; Suárez-Krabbe 2016:
16). Thus, the chapter situates the national question historically within the context
of modernity, colonialism, decolonization and postcolonialism, and highlights
the fact that decolonization has taken three pathways (political, economic and
epistemological) and maps out five discursive contexts within which the national
question can be understood. In the second place, it briefly summarizes Alexander's
interventions on the national question in South Africa. In the third place, it
grapples with the contested idea of South Africa as a national question, in the
process defining it, historicizing it including its pre-colonial lineage, which is often
ignored, and highlighting the areas of divergence and conflict in the various
imaginations of post-apartheid South Africa. Finally, it concludes with a reflection
on idea of South Africa as a difficult liberal experiment.

The national question is a perennial challenge in Africa in general and South
Africa in particular. It haunted colonialism (as the native question), African
nationalism and decolonization (as a racial and colonial question) and 'postcolonialism' (as nation-building and state-making). It has re-emerged today as
a constitutive element of epistemological decolonization. The national question

speaks to the difficult aspects of political, economic, social, ideological and epistemic change. Five interrelated discursive and historical contexts frame it. The first is the colonial terrain where it emerged as the 'native question', that is, the concern among white colonialists about how to establish colonial minority rule over a majority of black people. It also entailed the challenge of how to invent 'citizens' and 'subjects' as well as how to 'define' and 'rule' the conquered African people (Mamdani 1996; 2013).

The second context is the anti-colonial nationalist struggle where the national question not only became constitutive of a people's struggle for national self-determination and sovereignty but also as a nationalist task of raising common consciousness across different ethnic, linguistic and cultural groups that were 'defined' and 'invented' by colonialism as various 'tribes'. The third context is the 'postcolonial' dispensation where the national question assumed the form of how to translate anti-colonial nationalism into postcolonial pan-ethnic patriotism. This challenge became known as 'nation-building' as well as 'state-making' (Laakso and Olukoshi 1996).

The fourth context is the 'post-nationalist' demand, mainly spearheaded by those born after colonialism and apartheid ('born-frees'), for social justice, accountable and transparent governance, employment opportunities, economic empowerment, democracy, human rights, and free, quality and relevant education. This context is inextricably intertwined with what became known as the 'third wave of democracy' in the 1990s and has graduated into what is today termed the 'decolonial turn' (Maldonado-Torres, 2011; Ndlovu-Gatsheni 2013a; 2013b; Maldonado-Torres, 2018). Thandika Mkandawire (2009) understood this aspect as the 'social question'.

The fifth context is that of resurgent identitarian politics which foregrounds struggles of indigenous, feminist, queer, trans-gender, disabilities and migrant movements – contesting resilient patriarchal, racial, capitalist, colonial and imperialist hierarchies of power and exclusion (Lugones 2003). These five contextualizations of the national question enable a broader understanding of the national question and capture its various metamorphosis, shifts and mutations across time and space, right up to the current age of epistemological decolonization.

In terms of definition of the national question, the celebrated Nigerian historian Jacob F. Ade Ajayi (2000: 218) defined the national question as a 'perennial debate' about 'how to order the relations between the different ethnic, linguistic, and cultural groupings so that they have the same rights and privileges, access to power and equitable share of natural resources'; 'the debate as to whether or not we are on the right course towards the goal of nationhood'; the 'debate as to whether our constitutions facilitate or inhibit our march to nationhood'; and the debate whether 'we should seek other political arrangements to facilitate our search for legitimacy and development'. Even though Ajayi was specifically reflecting on the national question in Nigeria, his articulation of the constituent elements of the national question speaks to other African situations including South Africa.

Neville Alexander on the national question

Neville Alexander was a political activist against apartheid and a leading intellectual. The national question pre-occupied him a lot to the extent of writing the book *One Azania, One Nation: The National Question in South Africa* (1979). Just like other South African leaders such as Steve Biko, Alexander (1979: ii) was inspired by the 'desire to facilitate the unification of the national liberation movement'. His research explored the history of South Africa with a view to understand ideologies of domination and racial exclusion on the one hand which resulted in the institutionalization of apartheid and invention of Bantustans on the one hand and on the other the key contours of liberal ideas of the nation that recognized the plurality South African social groups. Alexander's mind was troubled by the how divergent imaginations of the post-apartheid nation and the diverse ideologies it produced ended up not only reverberating within the liberation movements but also divided it into various fragments (Alexander 1979: viii; Motala and Vally 2017: 130–131). At the sociological level, Alexander set out to explain the complex concepts of race, class, nation, nationality and ethnicity that not only constituted the debates on the national question but contributed to the different understanding of its possible resolutions. Alexander was worried about what he considered to be 'reactionary' and 'bogus nationalisms' (Alexander 1979: 4). He was sympathetic to a liberation struggle that put the interests of the working class at its centre, and was ranged against 'capitalist exploitation and racist oppression' (Alexander 1979: 178).

The expansive archive of Alexander on the national question revealed that his ideas were not static. He reflected on the ideas of nation and language and concluded that nation-states could exist without necessarily being underpinned by common language (Alexander 1986: 73). But he was consistent in his rejection of racial and ethnic ideas of nation, arguing that the post-apartheid government has to deal with systemic and structural issues of inequality and poverty that breed such issues as ethnicity and xenophobia (Alexander 2002). As to the failures of post-apartheid South Africa, Alexander posited that the 1994 transition did not produced a 'social revolution' that shook the economic power, rather what took place was a mere 'regime change' (Alexander 2010: 2). Alexander played a major role in the invention of South Africa though he was not satisfied by the product. He posited:

> To begin with, the demise of apartheid as a political-ideological system, with all its attendant rigmarole of Bantustans, 'bush colleges', separate schools for separate 'races' and 'nations', among all its other tragic absurdities, did not lead to the kind of society that many of us, including many in the present government, had imagined a post-apartheid South Africa would be.
> (Alexander 2013: 41)

It was Alexander (2002) who depicted South Africa as an 'ordinary country'. He meant that it would be haunted by all those problems that troubled the rest of 'postcolonial' Africa. Before his death in 2012, Alexander was pre-occupied with the crisis of education and the problems of languages in South Africa without abandoning the perennial issue of racism. His point on language was clear:

> We have to change radically the inherited linguistic *habitus* in terms of which English is the only feasible candidate for language of high status – a view which, among other things, implies that it is the language especially of science, mathematics, technology and business.
>
> (Alexander 2013: 77)

All the issues that pre-occupied the mind of Alexander were constitutive of the very idea of South Africa as a national question.

The idea of South Africa as the national question

Shula Marks and Stanley Trapido noted that by the 1870s South Africa was a mere geographical expression:

> In the 1870s at the beginning of the mineral revolution, South Africa was a geographical expression. Pre-capitalist and capitalist modes of production existed side by side, as did state forms of varying size with their own ruling groups and systems of exploitation. There were two British colonies, two ostensibly politically independent republics and numerous still autonomous African polities. All these were multi-ethnic and multilingual, although not all languages and ethnicities were equal. Colonists of British and European descent lived side by side in the colonies with large numbers of indigenous peoples, and in Natal with indentured labourers from the Indian sub-continent; African kingdoms were equally heterogeneous entities, composed of peoples of different origins.
>
> (Marks and Trapido 1987: 3)

The question that arises is how did a mere geographical expression become a name of a country and a people? How did the 'translation' take place? Who was involved? What forms did the 'translation' take? What struggles and contestations were provoked? What solutions were developed? What is the current state of the idea of South Africa? Is it still a terrain of struggles and contestations after 1994? These are the key questions at the centre of this chapter and the response to them takes the form of historiographical and conceptual definition of the idea of South Africa that takes into account epochal shifts, struggles and contestations.

The pre-colonial lineage

In existing literature, the idea of South Africa is often traced to the imperial/colonial period. The pre-colonial genealogy is often ignored. But the idea of South Africa, which Chief Albert Luthuli in his autobiography entitled *Let My People Go* (2006), rendered as a fundamental question of 'whose is South Africa' is also imbricated in complicated questions of human migrations and struggles over space dating back to the pre-colonial times, and which have often been used to sustain colonial myths of empty lands (Blaut 1993). Are present-day South Africans immigrants genealogically speaking, hailing from somewhere, except the Khoisan?

This question arises because there is a stubborn colonial discourse rooted in white settler historiography that claims that white and black people of South Africa arrived as migrants from somewhere in the seventeenth century (see Theal 1877; Saunders 1988; Bank 1997 on South African historiography). It is a question that is meant to complicate the notions of 'natives' and 'settlers' as political identities. In this colonial discourse of empty lands, the idea of the *Mfecane* as a period of unprecedented 'black-on-black violence' that resulted in depopulation of large areas of South Africa to the extent that white settlers found empty lands and occupied those lands without dispossessing anyone of land is brought in.

Consequently, these two issues cannot be ignored in our endeavours to unpack and understand the idea of South Africa. In the first place, it seems the ideas of Bantu migration and the notions of the *Mfecane* have been used to construct and orchestrate a colonial discourse of empty lands in South Africa. What needs to be understood is the logic behind the colonial discourse of empty lands. James M. Blaut (1993) captured the colonial/imperial logic, which is resisting both archaeo-logical and historical evidence and continues to raise its ugly head in the twenty-first century. This is how Blaut distilled the colonial logic of empty lands:

> This proposition makes a series of claims, each layered upon the others: (i) A non-European region is empty or nearly empty of people (hence settlement by Europeans does not displace any native peoples). (ii) The region is empty of settled population: the inhabitants are mobile, nomadic, wanderers (hence European settlement violates no political sovereignty, since wanderers make no claim to territory). (iii) The cultures of this region do not possess an understanding of private property – that is, the region is empty of property rights and claims (hence colonial occupiers can freely give land to settlers since no one owns it). The final layer, applied to all of the Outside sector, is an emptiness of intellectual creativity and spiritual values, sometimes described by Europeans [. . .] as an absence of 'rationality'.
>
> (Blaut 1993:15)

For South Africa, archaeologists have demonstrated that such places as Transvaal, Eastern Cape and Natal-Swazi border were homes to early hominids who are the known ancestors of modern Homo sapiens (Klein 1984; Phillipson 1985; Hall 1987; Parkington and Hall 1987). Rich archaeological evidence disputes the idea of Europeans and Bantu (Africans) arriving in South Africa at the same time in the seventeenth century.

C. W. Kiewiet (1966: 58) also explained that the areas beyond the Cape Colony were 'an area of settlement, of settlement by great Bantu population.

Much of the energy and determination of the Boers was used more against the natives than against Nature'. But despite the fact that even modern historians Shula Marks (1980) has demonstrated the falsity of the notion of 'empty lands', such politicians as Pieter Mulder of the Freedom Front Plus (FPP) could still respond to President Jacob Zuma's 2012 State of the Nation Address through invoking the idea of empty lands stating that 'The Bantu-speaking people moved from the Equator down South while white people moved from the Cape to meet each other at the Kei River' (Mulder 2012).

Julian Cobbing convincingly challenged the accepted version of the *Mfecane*, noting that what was described as the time of troubles in Southern Africa were not a consequence of the rise of the Zulu kingdom under King Shaka KaSenzanga-khona; that a number of writers who were seeking to justify white settlement blamed the Zulu people and their King Shaka kaSenzangakhona for devastating and depopulating vast territories; and finally, that the causes of the so-called *Mfecane* were labour raiding and slaving expeditions emanating from the Cape Colony and Delagoa Bay in Portuguese Mozambique (Cobbing 1988).

Inevitably Cobbing's interventions were contested heavily to the extent that an *International Colloquium: The Mfecane Aftermath: Towards a New Paradigm* was held at the University of the Witwatersrand (Wits) in September 1991 that was attended by Cobbing who maintained his position that the *Mfecane* was an *alibi* (Hamilton 1995). All these issues had to be raised because the questions of Bantu migration and the *Mfecane* are imbricated in the idea of South Africa.

At another level, it must be noted that pre-colonial Africans did not use the name South Africa. Those who used South Africa as a name of a place were sometimes not clear even of the boundaries of what they had named. This is why to some it became a reference to the region extending Northwards from the Cape to the Zambezi River. For instance, P. A. Molteno had this to say about what South Africa means:

> When we speak of South Africa, we speak of the country bounded by the sea on all sides except the north, where the boundaries may roughly be said to be the Cunene towards the west and the Zambezi towards the east.
>
> (Molteno 1896: 39)

To the early white settler historian George McCall Theal (1873), South Africa was a collective term for the Cape Colony, Natal, Orange Free State, South African Republic and all other territories South of the Zambezi.

Paul S. Landau (2010) raises another important aspect of pre-colonial Southern African societies that has a lesson for those concerned with the idea of South Africa. He argued that pre-colonial societies of Southern Africa had a long history of encountering, embracing and absorbing strangers into their ranks in the making of chiefdoms, kingdoms, nations and states. He elaborates that the 'Nineteenth-century European new comers were different and attempted to repudiate mixing, politically and otherwise, albeit with only partial success' (Landau 2010: xi).

What Landau is alerting us to is that the colonial encounters introduced what the Portuguese sociologist Boaventura de Sousa Santos (2007) described as 'abyssal thinking' that produced 'impossibility of co-presence' between black and white races. This paradigm of difference complicated the idea of South Africa and eventually produced apartheid. Thiven Reddy (2000) effectively mobilized conceptual ideas from Antonio Gramsci (hegemony), Michel Foucault (discourse) and Edward Said (Othering) to articulate how the trope of the 'frontier' was used to reproduce black people as the 'subaltern other' in the process of construction of segregation and apartheid.

Conceptually speaking, the idea of South Africa speaks to the fundamental questions of what Valentin Y. Mudimbe termed 'a paradigm of difference'. The idea of South Africa can therefore be rendered as a big question mark that entails trying to understand the triumphs and tragedies dominating and shaping the contested, complex and shifting meanings of *being South African* across time and space. It is a point that was also articulated by the historian Saul Dubow (2007: 72) when he argued that 'we should remember that the struggle for South Africa has long been, and continues to be, a struggle to become South African'.

As a geo-social construct, the idea of South Africa can be traceable to the unfolding modern world system. One can trace its genealogy back to 1488 when Bartholomew Diaz circumnavigated the Cape. If we trace it back, the idea of South Africa emerges concurrently with idea of the Americas, which is traceable to the arrival of Christopher Columbus in the so-called 'New World' in 1492. Figuratively speaking, 1492 is identified as a date when Euro-North American-centric modernity began. Understood from this vantage point, the idea of South Africa becomes a question of genealogy of South African modernity – that is a tale of its insertion into the modern world capitalist system and the inscription of what Timothy Keegan understood as 'the origins of the racial order' (Keegan 1996; Tafira 2014).

However, the idea of South Africa is more than a mere question of South African modernity. It exists as a perennial identitarian question that speaks to how the past, the present and the future are entangled paradoxically. Thus, reverberating at the centre of the idea of South Africa is a complex past that has been identified as an obstacle that has to be transcended and a burden that has to be off-loaded, but without South Africans falling into amnesia. As such, the idea of South Africa is inherently a multifaceted phenomenon.

It is a question which, politically speaking, encapsulates various searches for particular configurations of power and particular ideological frameworks that are sensitive to the realities of a society characterized by a kaleidoscope of ethnic, racial, class and gender cleavages. What is emphasized here is that while at the centre of the idea of South Africa have been various initiatives seeking to inscribe particular forms of domination, these have from the beginning locked horns with counter-initiatives aimed at crafting new social and political systems that would respond more effectively and with greater legitimacy and durability to the needs and exigencies of the majority of South African people. This is why the idea of

South Africa speaks to the limits of imperial/colonial/apartheid civilizational project on the one hand and the struggle for liberation and freedom on the other.

At the centre of the idea of South Africa emerged and subsisted various forms of identities. These ranged from historical and culture-based identities commonly referred to as ethnic identities that were reinvented and reified under apartheid colonialism; market-based identities commonly known as classes born out of processes of dispossession, primitive accumulation, peasantization, proleterianization, embourgeoisement and compradorialization; gendered-identities born out of various patriarchal forms of socialization that were reinforced by colonial/apartheid ideologies of female domesticity; colonially-invented political identities such as black vs. white, citizens vs. subjects, natives vs. non-natives and civilized vs. primitive people.

Dubow (2006) argued that 'South Africanism' as a form of imagination of a unitary nation 'took many forms and resists easy definition', adding that 'South Africanism' developed as a 'version of the patriotic or dominion nationalisms'. To him, South Africanism began as 'the expression of a developing settler society, and as such marginalized or denied the rights of indigenous African peoples' (Dubow 2006: vi).

The complex imperial and colonial encounters involving the Afrikaners, the British, and the wars of conquest and resistance of the late nineteenth and early twentieth centuries, also formed the broader discursive terrain within which the idea of South Africa developed as a contested concept this time with a racial tinge. The idea of South Africa also emerged between and betwixt clashes and syntheses of imperial and colonial imperatives, annexations, negotiations, reconciliations and unions that were invariably shaped by diverging and converging nationalisms of the English, Afrikaners and Africans.

The idea of South Africa on the one hand reveals an inclusionary-exclusionary motif which haunted the making of South Africa throughout various historical epochs and continues to reverberate even within the present 'rainbow nation' and, on the other hand, the idea of South Africa can be interpreted as a theory of South African society and its mutations across time and space – a social theory of the subject (black and white), subjection and subjectivity. The idea of South Africa as a theory of South African society encapsulated a number of societal trajectories if not imaginations of society. The first was an imperial and colonial trajectory that was constituted by an antinomy that split the Briton and the Afrikaner.

The second was a long-standing liberal trajectory that projected the economic logic of free market exchange as the life-blood of a successful capitalist civilizational project. Anything outside the logic of the market was considered to be irrational as long as it impinged on improving productivity and impeded free competition. The advocates of this liberal imaginary saw a contradiction between capitalism and racial domination hence they supported the anti-apartheid struggle (Hutt, 1964; Lipton 1986).

The third was a complex African nationalist trajectory that was shot through by various antinomies, and which branched into such political–cultural–nativist formations as Inkatha Freedom Party (IFP), Africanist formations such as the ANC Youth League in the 1940s, the Pan-Africanist Congress (PAC), Azania People's Organization (AZAPO) and Charterist formation in the mould of the ANC as well as psychological-oriented formations such as the Black Consciousness Movement (BCM). The South African Community Party (SACP) projected a class-oriented trajectory that gestured towards a socialist post-apartheid South Africa (Ndlovu-Gatsheni 2007; 2008; Ramphalile 2011; Padayachee 2012).

Chief Albert Luthuli (2006) castigated apartheid as a product of a tragic failure of imagination in the face of human diversity resulting in an unsustainable trajectory of depersonalization/dehumanization of black people. Luthuli is one of the earliest African nationalist humanists who understood the idea of South Africa from a decolonial humanist perspective as involving recovery of human dignity. His imagination was clear:

> The task is not finished. South Africa is not yet a home for all her sons and daughters. Such a home we wish to ensure. From the beginning our history has been one of ascending unities, the breaking of tribal, racial and creedal barriers. [. . .]. There remains before us the building of a new land, a home for men [and women] who are black, white, brown, from the ruins of the old narrow groups, a synthesis of rich cultural strains we have inherited.
>
> (Luthuli 2006: 229)

Liberal genealogy of the idea of South Africa

Inevitably, the idea of South Africa pre-occupied such early liberal minds as Olive Cronwright Schreiner as far back as 1923, who reflected deeply on the complexity of the idea of South Africa in these revealing words:

> If a crude and homely illustration may be allowed, the peoples of South Africa resemble the constituents of a plum-pudding when in the process of being mixed; the plums, the peel, the currants; the flour, the eggs, and the water are mingled together. Here plums may predominate, there the peel; one part may be slightly thinner than another, but it is useless to try to resort them; they have permeated each other's substance: they cannot be reseparated; to cut off a part would not be to resort them; it would be dividing a complex but homogenous substance into parts which would repeat its complexity. What then shall be said of the South African problem as a whole? Is it impossible for the South African peoples to attain to any form of unity, organization, and national life? Must we forever remain a vast, inchoate, invertebrate mass of humans, divided horizontally into layers of race, mutually antagonistic, and vertically severed by lines of political state division, which cut up our races without simplifying our problems, and which add to the bitterness of race conflict the irritation of political divisions? Is national life and organization unattainable by us? [. . .] We believe that

no one can impartially study the condition of South Africa and feel that it is so. Impossible as it is that our isolated states should consolidate, and attain to a complete national life, there is a form of organic union which is possible to us. For there is a sense in which all South Africans are one [. . .] there is a subtle but a very real bond, which unites all South Africans, and differentiates us from all other people in the world. This bond is our mixture of races itself. It is this which divides South Africa from all other peoples in the world, and makes us one.

(Schreiner 1923: 60–61)

It would seem Schreiner was already imagining a rainbow nation during the early twentieth century. She was described by her contemporaries as the spiritual progenitor of the South African nation. She posed the challenge of nation-building in this way: 'How, of our divided peoples, can a great healthy, harmonious and desirable nation be formed? This is the final problem of South Africa. If we cannot solve it, our fate is sealed' (Schreiner 1923: 62). Schreiner clearly identified the core problem of South Africa:

If our view be right, the problem which South Africa has before it today is this: How from our political states and our discordant races, can a great, healthy, united, organized nation be formed? [. . .] Our race question is complicated by a question of colour, which presents itself to us in a form more virulent and intense than that in which it has met any modern people.

(Schreiner 1923: 62–64)

Sounding rather prophetic, Schreiner had this say about the future of South Africa:

Our South African national structure in the future will not and cannot be identical with that of any other people, our national origin being so wholly unlike that of any other; our social polity must be developed by ourselves through the interaction of our parts with one another and in harmony with our complex needs. For good or evil, the South African nation will be an absolutely new thing under the sun, perhaps, owing to its mixture of races, possessing that strange vitality and originality which appears to rise so often from the mixture of human varieties: perhaps, in general human advance, ranking higher than other societies more simply constructed; perhaps lower – according as we shall shape it: but this, certainly – will be a new social entity, with new problems, new gifts, new failings, new accomplishments.

(Schreiner 1923: 370)

However, as late as 1941, G. H. Calpin could still write a book entitled *There Are No South Africans* and could still posit 'The worst of South Africa is that you never come across a South African' (Calpin 1941: 9). This intervention spoke to the daunting task of translating a geographical expression into an identity of a people. By then, however, three broad identities were being projected in colonial discourse: Bantu, Britons and Afrikaners (Macmillan 1963).

The modern historian Saul Dubow understood the idea of South Africa as 'an ideology of compromise' that 'developed out of a prior sense of colonial identity, namely, that which developed in the Cape from the early years of British occupation at the turn of the nineteenth century' (Dubow 2006: viii). While to imperialists and colonialists the idea was about subjugation, occupation, annexation, dispossession and subordination of weaker groups to the will of the powerful, to those on the receiving end of imperial/colonial/apartheid modernity, the idea was a consistent search for a criterion of living together – about how to turn a society that has embraced race as an organizing principle to another one in which race could be transcended. Inevitably, to those people who were being written out of the nation, the idea of South Africa developed into a form of resistance. But within imperial and colonial discourses of domination and exploitation, the idea of South Africa was also articulated as the 'native question', that is the burden of how to turn Africans into providers of cheap labour, how to govern them and how to relate to them (Smuts 1929; Mamdani 1996).

It was during the heydays of African nationalism and ant apartheid struggles that debates over the idea of South Africa became intense. The SACP introduced the theory of Colonialism of a Special Type (CSP) as it grappled with the national question (Alexander 1979). This rendition of the idea of South Africa culminated in the ideas of a NDR that is the nodal point on which the Tripartite Alliance was constituted (Alexander 1986, SACP 1962).

The power of articulating the idea of South Africa in terms of CST is in capturing three interrelated problems of colonialism, racism and class (Magubane 1979). This interpretation of the idea of South Africa meant that the liberation struggle should be two-pronged: against colonial national domination that was consummated in 1910 and against capitalist domination. It was from this analysis that the SACP built the idea of two-staged revolutions: NDR and the socialist revolution (SACP 1962; Wolpe 1972; 1973; 1988; Posel 1983).

The continuing complexities of the idea of South Africa led Ivor Chipkin to pose the question *Do South Africans Exist?* (2007). His analysis focused on how an 'African people' as a collectivity organized in pursuit of a political agenda came into being. He confined his analysis of the genealogy of a national identity called South African to the period of the African nationalist struggle and the post-apartheid period as though the idea of the nation started in the 1960s (Chipkin 2007). Chipkin's main concern was to correct a false idea common within existing narratives of resistance, oppression, exploitation and popular nationalist discourses whereby 'the people' were viewed as 'existing' prior to the period of the nationalist struggle (Chipkin 2007: 2). The central thesis of Chipkin's study is that the African people that are today called South Africans emerged primarily in and through the process of nationalist resistance to colonialism.

Chipkin made a clear distinction between 'the people as datum and the people as political subjects' (Chipkin 2007: 2). He made it clear that he was not interested in studying people as mere datum or as 'an empirical collectivity of individuals in a given geography', rather he was approaching the concept of 'the people' from a political angle as 'a collectivity organized in pursuit of a political end' (Chipkin 2007: 1–2). To Chipkin, once the concept of the people was clarified as a political one, then it was possible to step up the argument to engage with the meaning of 'nation'. He defined a nation as 'not simply a cultural artifact' but as a political phenomenon. His definition of a nation is: 'a political community whose form is given in relation to the pursuit of democracy and freedom' (Chipkin 2007: 2–3). Chipkin concluded:

> In this sense, the nation precedes the state, not because it has always already existed, but because it emerges in and through the nationalist struggle for state power. The history of the postcolony is, in this sense, the history of 'the people' qua production.
>
> (Chipkin 2007: 2)

While Chipkin's robust intellectual interventions on the subject of identity and nation-building were useful in understanding the making of people and nations in postcolonial Africa in general and post-apartheid South Africa in particular, the key problem is that he confined his study to the period of the African nationalist struggle. He missed the point that the African nationalist struggle was just another layer and one version of nationalist imaginations of the nation that emerged on top of earlier ones such as the 'Bantucization', 'Anglicization' and 'Afrikanerization' processes that also contributed to the construction of 'South Africanism' (Dubow 2006: v–vii).

Historical framings of the idea of South Africa

Five historical-discursive-ideological framings of the idea of South Africa are discernible running from pre-colonial periods to the present. These can be articulated as Bantucization, Anglicization, Afrikanerization, Africanization, Rainbowism and Rhodes Must Fall. The term Bantucization is used to depict the pre-colonial genealogy of the South Africa idea encapsulating processes of state formation and nation-building that left an imprint on present-day identities. The second process that is entangled with the third process is that of Anglicization as an identitarian process. What must be noted is that by the late nineteenth century 'all the peoples of southern Africa existed to a greater or lesser extent under the hegemony of a mainly British merchant capitalism and a British imperialism' (Marks and Trapido 1987: 4). Anglicization witnessed some tensions and clashes between imperialism and Afrikaner colonial nationalism, leading Dubow to argue:

Yet, from a late nineteenth century perspective the colonial-imperial antinomy was all too apparent. Colonialism could well exist within a wider sense of imperial belonging, and it shared many common features with imperialism – most obviously a shared agreement that white political ascendancy should not be threatened. But those who considered themselves colonists took pride in their independence and achievements, and were resentful of unwanted external intervention. Jingo imperialists were scornful of pretensions to independence where these might challenge metropolitan interests, and were increasingly intolerant of local nationalisms.

(Dubow 2006: 153)

The template for Anglicization as an identitarian process was the Cape Colony where the English language and other paraphernalia of British culture and ideology were in place. British colonial nationalism and British Crown imperialism tended to complement each other with some few areas of misunderstandings (Dubow 1997). The Cape Colony was a key launching pad for British imaginations of South Africa as an 'anglicized nation'. In the Anglicization mind-map, the South African nation was to be nothing other than a 'greater Cape Colony' together with its institutions replicated across South Africa. The Afrikaners had already rebelled against the anglicized Cape Colony and embarked on the Great Trek in the 1830s that carried them into the interior.

The confrontation between forces of imperialism/Anglicization and Afrikaner-ization/Boer colonial nationalism/republicanism resulted in the Anglo-Boer/South African War of 1899–1902 that became a decider of the future trajectory of imaginations and reconstructions of the idea of white South Africa. Dubow had this to say about the place of this war in the construction of South Africanism:

A war that was at once fought over possession of the country's riches, by what were to become South Africans, in what was to become South Africa, has surely to be understood as war for South Africa, not only in the immediate sense of acquisition and control, but also in the forward-looking sense of making a new nation-state – in effect, a 'white man's country'.

(Dubow 2006: 158–159)

As articulated by Lord Milner, the core thinking within Anglicization was to construct a white self-governing polity comprising both British and Afrikaners but subsisting under the British Union Jack as a national symbol (Dubow 2006: 159). Within this compromise between British imperialism and Afrikaner national colonialism, Africans were to feature as labourers in the farms, mines and industries.

The problem with what was achieved by the Treaty of Vereeniging of May 1902 was a peace born out of conquest of the Afrikaners and the exclusion of Africans from the nation. Both Afrikaners and Africans were resentful of British triumphalism. Anglicization did not succeed in constructing a stable white South African nation. Afrikaners were mainly in agreement with the British on exclusion of blacks from citizenship but still resented being dominated politically and economically by a minority (British people). Afrikaner colonial nationalism was not eradicated as an aspiration.

Just like the English, the Afrikaners were developing a particular vision of a South African nation informed partly by their tradition of ethnic republicanism engendered by the experiences of the 'Great Trek' and partly by challenges they met after the momentous events of the South Africa (1899–1902) and the Act of Union of 1910. The Great Trek provided the myth of foundation of Afrikaner nationhood and the Calvinist religion provided the ideology (Norval 1996).

Under Afrikaner colonial nationalism the idea of South Africa was deliberately 'Afrikanerized', that is, Afrikaner identity became the central leitmotif of the imagined nation. Afrikanerization triumphed over other competing nationalisms in 1948 resulting in the institutionalization of apartheid. Institutionalized racism was introduced as solution to the contested idea of South Africa. This solution was contested from a number of angles as unsustainable as it denied citizenship to the majority of African people. The solution was based on a deliberate misunderstanding of African identities. Under apartheid, African people were understood as contending 'tribes' (Mamdani 1996). This is why African people were pushed into 'Bantustans'.

Africanism and imaginations of South Africa

Afrikanerization, which unfolded as a form of internal colonialism and nationalism predicated on racial separation of people and reduction of black people into sources of cheap labour, provoked various forms of African nationalisms (various forms of Africanization). These African imaginations of a South African nation were born within the context of resisting imperial, colonial and apartheid imaginations that excluded Africans from the imagined nation and citizenship. As noted by C. R. D. Halisi:

> Forged in the crucible of racial oppression, black political thought fluctuates incessantly between the values of racial autonomy and interracial social incorporation. Consequently, the paring of black republican identity and multiracial union has become a core antinomy of political thought for black South Africans.
>
> (Halisi 1999: 1)

Halisi further argues:

> In a very fundamental sense, the struggle for liberation required black activists to confront nascent questions of citizenship and national identity – how the 'people' are to be defined, who belongs to the political community, and what are the criteria of inclusion and exclusion.
>
> (Halisi 1999: 4)

Consequently, the African nationalist struggle became shaped in various ways by what Halisi (1999: 4) terms 'a prime polarity in black political thought', taking the form of black republicanism (Africanism/race-conscious) and black liberal (multi-racialist) thought. Throughout the liberation struggle, intense debates took place over the meanings of liberation, democracy and citizenship, as constitutive elements of a new idea of South Africa. The rise and entry of Marxist thought further complicated the debates over race and class producing what Halisi (1999: 12) termed 'the conceptual purgatory of race and class interpretation of liberation politics'.

Historically speaking, the first semi-political African political formation was the Native Educational Association (NEA) formed in 1882 as a vehicle to promote African interests in modern education, social morality and general welfare of the 'natives' (Ondendaal 1984). This was followed in September 1882 by the earliest political organization that captured African imagination of a nation known as *Imbumba Yaba Mnyama* formed in response to the growth of the Afrikaner Bond that was viewed as threat to African people's interests. *Imbumba*'s key aim was to unite Africans so as to enable them 'in fighting for national rights' (Ondendaal 1984: 8). A construction of national African identity by Africans themselves was beginning. This construction of African identity had a clear political goal of fighting for national rights.

By 1912 the South African Native National Congress (SANNC), a black national political movement, was formed in response to the promulgation of the Union of South Africa that excluded black people. Beginning with the SANNC, the African political organizations simultaneously contested racial discrimination while working to create national unity among Africans. For instance, Pixley Ka Isaka Seme's speech at the formation of SANNC emphasized that the white people had formed the Union of South Africa that excluded black people and that this action called for an African counter-union 'for the purpose of creating national unity and defending our rights and privileges' (Ondendaal 1984: 273).

The idea of South Africa found different interpretations and expressions under African nationalisms. These ranged from radical Africanism of the ANC Youth League of the 1940s credited to Anton Lembede who advocated for the liberation of South Africa as a black republic; Pan-Africanism of the PAC that articulated the idea of South Africa in terms of a white nation dominating a black nation; ANC that adopted the Freedom Charter in 1956 and interpreted the idea of South Africa in inclusivist terms of a struggle for non-racial, non-sexist and democratic society; to the SACP that interpreted the idea of South Africa from a Marxist perspective which emphasized its class character as the problem to be solved through achievement of socialism (Halisi 1999; Ndlovu-Gatsheni 2008; 2013a).

There was also the BCM under Stephen Bantu Biko that interpreted the idea of South Africa from a cultural and psychological perspective gesturing towards decolonization of the mind as an essential pre-requisite for political liberation of black people. To them, the construction of a new idea of South Africa entailed struggling for 'a new consciousness, a reawakening of a self-consciousness, re-appropriation of Black self-consciousness from the clutches of an appropriative and dominating white consciousness, a rediscovery of a black self which lay buried beneath white consciousness on blacks by cultural, political, economic, linguistic, and religious domination' (More 2012: 28).

The Freedom Charter of 1955 became a major 'multiracial manifesto' as it opened up with declaration that 'South Africa belongs to all who live in it, black and white' (Halisi 1999). The ANC idea of South Africa that emphasized inclusivity and democracy gained support ahead of others. The popularity and success of the Charterist trajectory might be due to the fact it chose to avoid reverse-racism and articulated a different logic from that of apartheid, logic of non-racial, non-sexist, inclusive and democratic South Africa as the horizon of the idea of South Africa. The ANC refused to fall into another system of exclusion and difference that had haunted the idea of South Africa since the time of colonial encounters.

The idea of South Africa today: a difficult liberal experiment

If the South African idea that emerged was a brutal imperial and colonial experiment in human domination over other human beings and the consequent experimentation with the dehumanizing colonial philosophy of separate development of races that became known as apartheid; then the current South African idea cascading from the anti-apartheid liberation movements is an equally difficult nationalist-liberal experiment. We are, therefore, dealing with a highly politicized and contested national question that emerged with the colonial/imperial experimentation with translation of a geographical expression into an identity of a people. What was fundamentally problematic about the imperial/colonial experimentation in nation-building was obsession with difference born out of what Alexander (1979) termed 'bogus sociology'. The colonial/imperial logic of 'de-nationalization' of the indigenous people and the material dispossessions has come to haunt post-apartheid South Africa.

What emerges clearly is that the national question stands at the centre of two equally problematic experiments. The first was the dehumanizing colonial/imperial approach that culminated in institutionalized racism known as apartheid. The second is re-humanizing anti-apartheid movements that grappled with how to destroy a racial order and build a non-racial democratic South Africa. What emerged were experiments within experiments such as the Africanists who imagined a 'native' black and Pan-Africanist republic of Azania; Steve Biko and the BCM who imagined a broader black identity that embraced Africans, Indians and Coloureds freed from imposed inferiority complexes; the Charterists who imagined an inclusive and non-racial liberal republic where everyone belonged irrespective of race; the communists who experimented with the ideas of Marx, Lenin, Stalin and Trotsky as they imagined a socialist republic born out of a proletarian revolution; and the cultural nationalists who harked back to pre-colonial history and advocated for separate ethnic republics.

Thus at CODESA, the central issue was to try and find common ground among the various experiments and across the fundamentalist paradigm of difference introduced by the imperial/colonial idea of South Africa that rejected any possibility of co-presence of races and even ethnicities. The gift of CODESA was the notion of political justice as opposed to criminal justice (Nuremberg) deployed in the resolution of the Holocaust, which involved not only naming and shaming but also legal punishment of those identified as perpetrators as well as the physically separation of perpetrators (the Germans) and the victims (the Jews). The Germans remained in Germany and the Jews were taken out and the new state of Israel was established in 1948 in the Palestinian land in the Middle East.

The next experiment was the TRC. At its centre was Nelson Mandela's peda-gogical liberal/humanist nationalism in combination with Archbishop Desmond Tutu's ecclesiastical humanist interventions that was meant to symbolically deal with accumulated racial anger and laid a foundation for new ethics of living together for a country where the victim and the perpetrator had no option but to live together. The result was what became known as the 'New South Africa' predicated on the ideology of 'rainbowism' and liberal democratic constitutionalism.

The experimentation did not come to an end. Setting afoot new humanism on the ashes of colonizer–colonized, subject–citizen and victim–perpetrator dichot-omies was a major challenge. Proclamation of reconciliation was not enough. The challenge is well captured by Mahmood Mamdani:

> In the context of a former settler colony, a single citizenship for settlers and natives can only be the result of an overall metamorphosis whereby erstwhile colonizers and colonized are politically reborn as equal members of a single political community. The world reconciliation cannot capture this meta-morphosis. [. . .] This is about establishing, for the first time, a political order based on consent and not conquest. It is about establishing a political com-munity of equal and consenting citizens.
>
> (Mamdani 1998: 3)

We therefore see Mandela as the first black president of South Africa hard at work to breathe new life into the 'rainbow nation' where freedom had to be exercised without justice. We see the crafting of one of the most liberal constitutions as part of re-nationalizing the de-nationalized as well as constituting new subjectivity in 1996. Did the 1996 South African Constitution just like the Lancaster House Constitution in Zimbabwe not result in 'constitutionalization' of some injustices? In Zimbabwe, non-delivery of land became a major grievance that set in motion the *Third Chimurenga* and the Fast-Track Land Reform Programme (FTLRP).

However, in his exploration of possible tensions between NDR and liberal constitutional democracy in South Africa, Daryl Glaser (2017: 294) concluded that 'South Africa's specific variant of constitutionalism allows – even mandates – substantive pro-poor social and economic change'. He added that 'there is no reason to think that failure to address poverty and inequality more effectively in South Africa has less to do with the Constitution than with absent political will' (Glaser 2017: 294). He gives the examples of 'implementation of some of the largest housing and social grant programmes in the developing world' to justify his defence of what the constitution can enable and allow (Glaser 2017: 294). However, he admits that 'Doubtless, constitutionalism will hamper decision-making in certain instances, sometimes in ways that frustrate needed redistributions' (Glaser 2017: 294). One wonders whether the land redistribution might be one of those 'redistributions' frustrated by constitutionalism in South Africa!

It would seem such new political formations such as the Economic Freedom Fighters (EFF), Rhodes Must Fall, Fees Must Fall and Black First, Land First (BFLF) are embodying a new 'South African idea' as opposed to the 'idea of South Africa'. It is now the descendants of those who had been enslaved, racialized, dispossessed and dehumanized born after the end of juridical apartheid who are fighting to define the country they want to live in – where black lives matter. While the EFF emphasizes the nationalization of the commanding heights of the South African economy, the BFLF focuses on compulsory land reclamation, and the Rhodes Must Fall and Fees Must Fall have escalated the struggles to the institutions of higher learning where they are demanding their decolonization and free education. South Africa is poised for other experiments with decolonized universities and free education at a time when the world has been captured by market fundamentalism and its commodification of everything including life itself.

As Mandela put it in the last page of his *Long Walk to Freedom: The Autobiography of Nelson Mandela* (1994: 611): 'The true test of our devotion to freedom is just beginning.' The settlement of 1994 was the beginning and not the end. South Africa has now travelled 24 years of this 'test of our devotion to freedom'. We are back to what Halisi warned us about:

> Rival populisms, nourished by competing visions of liberation are bound to have an impact on the evolution of South African citizenship. In addition, to popular democratic traditions, of which populism is one manifestation, are among the most durable sources of inspiration for democratic thinkers. After centuries of racial domination, it would be unrealistic to expect an ethos of nonracial citizenship to prevail unchallenged by older political perceptions. Eventually, black liberation struggle may come to be viewed by all South Africans as a national achievement and, therefore, a cornerstone of nonracial citizenship identity. For the immediate future, however, successive governments will have to cope with the implications of both nonracial and race-conscious political sensibilities.
>
> (Halisi 1999: 133)

To Halisi, it was going to take time for the 'test of our devotion to freedom' to work. Continuing economic inequalities has been a major test. This is why to the South Africa economist Sampie Terreblanche (2002), the idea of South Africa has been always shot through by a fundamental problem that he termed (2002) 'a history of inequality' running through from the time of colonial encounters to the present. It is 'a history of inequality' whose resolution since 1994 is currently 'lost in transition' according to Terreblanche (2012).

This loss in transition is articulated as predication of the South African socio-economic system on what Terreblanche (2012) termed 'Americanization' of South Africa resulting in a convoluted post-1994 transformation initiative based on wrong ideological frameworks, wrong power structures, wrong developmental path, and integrated into the nexus of wrong and criminalized global structures. But to Adam Habib (2013), a South African political scientist, the resolution of complexities of idea of South Africa is currently lost in a 'suspended revolution' and this notion is used to explain 'why our present is not what we had hoped it would be' (Habib 2013: ix).

Conclusion

Today, South Africa is still struggling to transcend the racial categories and identities constructed by apartheid. The ANC as a former liberation movement is facing various questions as the liberation myth is eroding and is being replaced by increasing demands for service delivery. The failure to deliver economic freedom by the ANC has been put on the centre of political contestation by the EFF. The question of ownership of property has always been at the centre of the South African idea. Luthuli in his autobiography had defined the struggles over the idea of South Africa as constituted by the 'question of ownership' of resources. Today, the rise of the EFF has been interpreted as 'a metaphor for the structural incompleteness of South Africa's democracy' (Mbembe 2014a: 10).

As noted by Achille Mbembe (2014a), South Africa has delivered a democracy of a property-less people and such a democracy is unsustainable. We have witnessed a South Africa where those who are experiencing various forms of hardships particularly the unemployed and the working poor have to engage in riots or demonstrations so as to be heard (Mbembe 2014a). Thus to Mbembe (2014b: 39), the idea of South Africa is today caught up in a 'confusion between the rule of the people, the rule of law and the rule of property'.

One is therefore left hard pressed whether to conclude that the idea of an inclusive South Africa is still in the making, or is it incomplete, or it proving very hard to resolve. What is clear though is that indeed South Africa seems to be 'lost in transition' to the extent of provoking struggles from below for life as well as intra-elite/class struggles from above for power and consumption.

It would seem that South Africa needs to free its politics from being considered a bureaucratic profession in which those in office use their tenure to accumulate resources to one in which politics becomes a vocation – a calling to serve others (Dussel 2008). Liberatory politics is driven by the logic of politics as a vocation rather than profession. A politics of liberation is basically a politics of life with others and for others (Mendieta 2008). Only if politics is understood this way can service delivery be achieved and *ubuntu* be restored.

References

Ajayi, F. J. Ade. 2000. 'The National Question in Nigeria in Historical Perspective'. In T. Falola (ed.), *Tradition and Change in Africa: The Essays of J. F. Ade Ajayi*. Trenton, NJ: Africa World Press, pp. 217–241.

Alexander, N. (writing as No Sizwe). 1979. *One Azania, One Nation: The National Question in South Africa*. London: Zed Books.

Alexander, N. 1986. 'Approaches to the National Question in South Africa'. *Transformation*, 1, pp. 63–95.

Alexander, N. 2002. *An Ordinary Country: Issues in the Transition from Apartheid to Democracy in South Africa*. Pietermaritzburg: University of Kwazulu-Natal Press.

Alexander, N. 2010. 'South Africa: An Unfinished Revolution'. (Unpublished 4th Strini Moodley Annual Memorial Lecture), University of KwaZulu-Natal, 13 May.

Alexander, N. 2013. *Thoughts on the New South Africa*. Johannesburg: Jacana Media.

Bank, A. 1997. 'The Great Debate and the Origins of South African Historiography'. *Journal of African History*, 38, pp. 261–281.

Blaut, J. M. 1993. *The Colonizer's Model of the World: Geographical Diffusion and Eurocentric History*. New York and London: The Guilford Press.

Bundy, C. 2007. 'New Nation, New History? Constructing the Past in Post-Apartheid South Africa'. in S. Stolten (ed.), *History Making and Present Day Politics: The Meaning of Collective Memory in South Africa*. Uppsala: Nordic Africa Institute, pp. 73–97.

Caplin, G. H. 1941. *There Are No South Africans*. London: Thomas Nelson & Sons.

Chipkin, I. 2007. *Do South Africans Exist? Nationalism, Democracy and the Identity of 'the People'*. Johannesburg: Wits University Press.

Cobbing, 1988. 'The Mfecane as Alibi: Thoughts on Dithakong amend Mbolopo'. *Journal of African History*, 29, pp. 487–519.

Davidson, B. 1992. *The Black Man's Burden*. Oxford, UK: James Currey.

Dubow, S. 1997. 'Colonial Nationalism, the Milner Kindergarten and the Rise of South Africanism, 1902–10'. *History Workshop Journal*, 43, pp. 45–67.

Dubow, S. 2006. *A Commonwealth of Knowledge: Science, Sensibility, and White South Africa, 1820–2000*. Oxford, UK: Oxford University Press.

Dubow, S. 2007. 'Thoughts on South Africa: Some Preliminary Ideas'. In H. E. Stolten (ed.), *History Making and Present Day Politics: The Meaning of Collective Memory in South Africa*. Uppsala: Nordic Africa Institute, pp. 51–72.

Dussel, E. 2008. *Twenty Theses on Politics*. Translated by George Ciccariello-Maher. Durham, NC and London: Duke University Press.

Fanon, F. 1968. *The Wretched of the Earth*. New York: Grove Press.

Glaser, D. 2017. 'National Democratic Revolution Meets Constitutional Democracy'. In E. Webster and K. Pampallis (eds), *The Unresolved National Question: Left Thought Under Apartheid*. Johannesburg: Wits University Press, pp. 274–296.

Habib, A. 2013. *South Africa's Suspended Revolution: Hopes and Prospects*. Johannesburg: Wits University Press.

Halisi, C. R. D. 1999. *Black Political Thought in the Making of South African Democracy*. Bloomington and Indianapolis, IN: Indiana University Press.

Hall, M. 1987. *The Changing Past: Farmers, Kings and Traders in Southern Africa, 200–1860*. Cape Town: David Philip.

Hamilton, C. 1995 (ed.). *The Mfecane Aftermath: Reconstructive Debates in Southern African History*. Johannesburg and Pietermaritzburg: Witwatersrand University Press and University of Natal Press.

Hutt, W. H. 1964. *The Economics of the Colour Bar: A Study of the Economic Origins and Consequences of Racial Segregation in South Africa*. London: Institute of Economic Affairs.

Keegan, T. 1996. *Colonial South Africa and the Origins of the Racial Order.* Cape Town and Johannesburg: David Philip.

Kiewiet, C. W. 1966. *A History of South Africa, Social and Economic.* Oxford, UK: Oxford University Press.

Klein. R. 1984. (ed.). *Southern African Prehistory and Paleoenvironments.* Rotterdam and Boston.

Laakso, L. and Olukoshi, A. 1996. 'The Crisis of the Post-Colonial Nation-State Project in Africa'. In A. O. Olukoshi and L. Laakso (eds), *Challenges to the Nation-State in Africa.* Uppsala: Nordic Africa Institute, pp. 7–39.

Landau, P. S. 2010. *Popular Politics in the History of South Africa, 1400–1948.* Cambridge, UK: Cambridge University Press.

Lipton, M. 1986. *Capitalism and Apartheid: South Africa, 1910–84.* Cape Town: David Philip.

Lugones, M. 2003. *Pilgrimages/Peregrinajes: Theorising Coalition Against Multiple Oppressions.* Lenham, MD, Boulder, CO, New York and Oxford, UK: Rownman & Littlefield Publishers.

Luthuli, A. 2006. *Let My People Go: The Autobiography of Albert Luthuli Nobel Peace Prize Winner.* Tafelberg and Mafube: Tafelberg Publishers and Mafube Publishing.

MacMillan, W. M. 1963. *Bantu, Boer, and Briton: The Making of South African Native Problem.* London: Clarendon Press.

Magubane, BM. 1979. *The Political Economy of Race and Class in South Africa.* New York and London: Monthly Review Press.

Maldonado-Torres, N. 2011. 'Thinking Through the Decolonial Turn: Post-Continental Interventions in Theory, Philosophy, and Critique – An Introduction'. *Transmodernity: Journal of Peripheral Cultural Production of the Luso-Hispanic World,* Fall, pp. 1–25.

Maldonado-Torres, N. 2018. 'The Decolonial Turn'. In Juan Poblete (ed.), *New Approaches to Latin American Studies: Culture and Power.* New York: Routledge.

Mamdani, M. 1996. *Citizen and Subject: Contemporary Africa and the Legacy of Late Colonialism.* Princeton, NJ: Princeton University Press.

Mamdani, M. 1998. 'When Does a Settler become a Native? Reflections on the Roots of Citizenship in Equatorial and South Africa'. Unpublished Professorial Inaugural Lecture Delivered as A. C. Jordan Professor of African Studies, University of Cape Town, 13 May.

Mamdani, M. 2013. *Define and Rule: Native as Political Identity.* Johannesburg: Wits University Press.

Mandela, N. 1994. *Long Walk to Freedom: The Autobiography of Nelson Mandela.* London: Little, Brown and Company.

Marks, S. 1980. 'The Vacant Land: The Mythology of British Expansion in the Eastern Cape, South Africa'. *Journal of Social History,* 25(2), pp. 255–275.

Marks, S. and Trapido, S. 1987. 'The Politics of Race, Class and Nationalism'. In S. Marks and S. Trapido (eds), *The Politics of Race, Class and Nationalism in Twentieth-Century South Africa.* London and New York: Longman, pp. 1–24.

Mbembe, A. 2014a. 'Difference and Repetition: Reflections on South Africa Now'. (Presentation Delivered at the Research and Innovation Week, University of South Africa, 4 March).

Mbembe, A. 2014b. 'Class, Rave and the New Native'. *Mail* and *Guardian,* 26 September–2 October.

Mendieta, E. 2008. 'Foreword: The Liberation of Politics: Alterity, Solidarity, Liberation'. In E. Dussel (ed.) *Twenty Theses on Politics.* Translated by George Ciccariello-Maher. Durham, NC and London: Duke University Press, pp. vii–xiii.

Mkandawire, T. 2009. 'From the National Question to the Social Question'. *Transformation: Critical Perspectives on Southern Africa*, 69, pp. 130–160.

Molteno. P. A. 1896. *A Federal South Africa*. Cape of Good Hope: Marton & Company.

More, M. P. 2012. 'Black Consciousness Movement's Ontology: The Politics of Being'. *Philosophia Africana*, 14(1), Spring, pp. 23

Motala, E. and Vally, S. 2017. 'Neville Alexander and the National Question'. In E. Webster and K. Pampallis (eds), *The Unresolved National Question: Left Thought Under Apartheid*. Johannesburg: Wits University Press, pp. 130–148.

Mudimbe, V. Y. 1994. *The Idea of Africa*. Bloomington, IN and Oxford, UK: Indiana University Press and James Currey.

Mulder, P. 2012. 'Are Sexwale and Ramaphosa Really White Land Owners?' Available at: www.politicsweb.co.za/politicsweb/view/politicsweb/en/page71654?oid=280327&sn= Detail&pid=71654 (accessed 5 October 2017).

Ndlovu-Gatsheni, S. J. 2007. 'Tracking the Historical Roots of Post-Apartheid Citizenship Problems: The Native Club, Restless Natives, Panicking Settlers and the Politics of Nativism in South Africa'. *African Studies Centre Working Paper 72*, pp. 1–70.

Ndlovu-Gatsheni, S. J. 2008. 'Black Republicanism, Nativism and Populist Politics in South Africa'. *Transformation*, 68, pp. 53–86.

Ndlovu-Gatsheni, S. J. 2013a. *Empire, Global Coloniality and African Subjectivity*. New York and Oxford, UK: Berghahn Books.

Ndlovu-Gatsheni, S. J. 2013b. *Coloniality of Power in Postcolonial Africa: Myths of Decolonization*. Dakar: CODESRIA Books.

Norval, A. J. 1996. *Deconstruction Apartheid Discourse*. London and New York: Verso.

Ondendaal, A. 1984. *Vukani Bantu! The Beginnings of Black Protest Politics in South Africa to 1912*. Cape Town and Johannesburg: David Philip.

Padayachee, A. 2012. 'Structure, Subject and Colonialism: Tracing Black and White Subjectivity in South Africa'. MA Thesis, University of the Witwatersrand.

Parkington, J. and Martin, H. 1987. 'Patterning Recent Radiocarbon Dates from Southern Africa as a Reflection of Prehistoric Settlement and Interaction'. *Journal of African History*, 28, pp. 1–25.

Phillipson, D. *African Archaeology*. Cambridge, UK: Cambridge University Press.

Posel, D. 1983. 'Rethinking the "Race-Class Debate" in South African Historiography'. *Social Dynamics*, 9(1), pp. 50–66.

Quijano, A. 2000a. 'The Coloniality of Power and Social Classification'. *Journal of World Systems*, 6(2), (Summer–Fall), pp. 342–386.

Quijano, A. 2000b. 'Coloniality of Power, Eurocentrism, and Latin America'. *Nepantla: View from the South*, 1(3), pp. 533–579.

Ramphalile, M. 2011. 'Patriotic Blackness' and 'Liberal/Anti-Patriotic' Whiteness: Charting the Emergence and Character of An Articulation of Black/White Racial Subjectivity Peculiar to Post-Apartheid South Africa'. MA Thesis, University of the Witwatersrand.

Reddy, T. 2000. *Hegemony and Resistance: Contesting Identities in South Africa*. Aldershot, UK: Ashgate.

Santos, B. de. S. 2007. 'Beyond Abyssal Thinking: From Global Lines to Ecologies of Knowledges'. *Review*, xxx(1), pp. 45–89.

Saunders, 1988. *The Making of the South African Past: Major Historians on Race and Class*. Cape Town: David Philip.

Schreiner, O. C. [1923]. 1976. *Thoughts on South Africa: Africana Reprint Library Volume 10*. Johannesburg: Africana Book Society.

Smuts, J. C. 1929. *Africa and Some World Problems, Including the Rhodes Memorial Lectures Delivered in Michaelmas Term, 1929*. Oxford, UK: Clarendon Press.

South African Communist Party (SACP). 1962. *The Road to South African Freedom: Programmes of the South African Communist Party*. London: Inkululeko Press.

South African Communist Party (SACP). 2002. 'Socialism Is the Future, Build it Now: Strategy and Tactics of the SACP in the National Democratic Revolution'. *Bua Komanisi*, June.

Suárez-Krabbe, J. 2016. *Race, Rights and Rebels: Alternatives to Human Rights and Development from the Global South*. London and New York: Rowman and Littlefield International.

Tafira, C. K. 2014. 'The Foundations of South African Modernity and Coloniality: 1488 Onwards'. (Unpublished Presented at the Celebrations of African Day: South African Democracy @20' Kgorong Building, University of South Africa, 30 May).

Terreblanche, S. 2002. *A History of Inequality in South Africa, 1652–2002*. Scottsville and Sandton: University of KwaZulu-Natal Press and KMM Review Publishing Company.

Terreblanche, S. 2012. *Lost in Transformation: South Africa's Search for a New Future Since 1986*. Sandton: KMM Review Publishing Company.

Theal, G. M. 1873. *Compendium of South African History and Geography*. Cape Town: Lovedale Press.

Theal, G. M. 1877. *Compendium of South African History and Geography*. Lovedale: Lovedale Press.

Wolpe, H. 1972. 'Capitalism and Cheap Labour-Power in South Africa: From Segregation to Apartheid'. *Economy and Society*, 1(4), pp. 425–456.

Wolpe, 1973. 'The Theory of Internal Colonialism-The South African Case'. In Oxaal, I. (ed.), *Beyond the Sociology of Development*. London: Routledge and Kegan Paul.

Wolpe, H. 1988. *Race, Class and the Apartheid State*. London: James Currey.

9

RHODES MUST FALL

Introduction

Cecil John Rhodes was a leading British imperialist whose imperial ambition was to colonize the whole of Africa and turning it into a colony of Britain. After more than 100 years, Rhodes continues to live in the form of memorials and statues, a university that is named after him (Rhodes University in Grahamstown), a prestigious scholarship known as the Rhodes Scholarship, a Rhodes Professorial Chair of Race Relations at Oxford University and a Foundation known as Mandela-Rhodes Foundation that conjoined the name of a leading African decolonial fighter to that of the notorious imperialist (see Maylam 2005; Ndlovu-Gatsheni 2016b). One wonders why such a racist who openly declared that he valued land over the lives of African people received such recognition and symbolization that transcends the colonial/apartheid period.

One strand of explanation is that there is no doubt that Rhodes was a major historical figure and that his memorials and statues are recognition of history not celebration of his violent colonial deeds. Is keeping the memorials and statues of Rhodes, who committed genocides, dispossessed Africans of their lands, colonized them, exploited them and looted their resources, under the pretext of preservation of history not tantamount to asking a raped woman to keep a big picture of a rapist in her bedroom as a sign of an event which took place and that cannot be erased? Is keeping Rhodes' statue at the centre of UCT too different from keeping Adolf Hitler's statue in Israel? Even Germans have been too ashamed to erect statues of Hitler, even in Germany itself. It is these questions that led to the second strand of argument, which is decolonial in orientation and views the continued existence of Rhodes' memorials and statues in South Africa as a sign of colonial/apartheid arrogance and refusal by those who benefitted from his colonial plunder to express repentance and tolerance of the feelings of those who Rhodes abused.

It is the decolonial perspective that sparked the Rhodes Must Fall movements in South Africa in 2015. In decolonial thought Rhodes is a symbol of genocide, enslavement, conquest, colonization, apartheid, material dispossession and author of inequalities haunting South Africa today. Thus, the attacking of the statue was a decolonial symbolic gesture of confronting a system of coloniality. It is therefore not surprising that what emerged as Rhodes Must Fall quickly mutated into sub-nomenclatures and hashtags such as Fees Must Fall, Open Stellenbosch, Transform Wits, Patriarchy Must Fall and many others. This is how decoloniality announced itself in South Africa, drawing inspiration from such earlier decolonial movements as the Black Consciousness as well as Fanonian decolonial thought.

However, to gain a deeper understanding of this movement, it is vital to open the canvas and contextualize it within the evolving and contested idea of South Africa at the national level.

At the continental level, Rhodes Must Fall is part of the three phases of African protest movement (anti-colonial protests of the 1950s and 1960s; the 1980s and 1990s waves of anti-austerity protests that dragged into the Arab Spring/Arab Awakening that engulfed North Africa). At the planetary level, it is part of those political and epistemological decolonial formations that are targeting global coloniality as it is currently represented by neoliberal capitalism. Only through such an approach that simultaneously historicizes, contextualizes and theorizes, will we develop the correct vocabulary of naming the student protests that broke out in South Africa in 2015 and 2016. They were part of a resurgent decolonial struggles of the twenty-first century. They demonstrate that decolonization is a true liberatory idea, which has defied many attempts to bury it.

At the centre of the Rhodes Must Fall is an ideological amalgamation of radical black feminism, black consciousness, Fanonianism and Pan-Africanism as constitutive parts of decolonial thought. Decolonial thought has never been a singular closed system of knowledge feeding into decolonial struggles. The demands of the Rhodes Must Fall movements were clearly framed by a broader demand for decolonization of the university in South Africa. More specifically, the demands can be categorized into free, quality, decolonized education; end to sexism, patriarchy and racism; decommissioning of all offensive colonial/apartheid iconographies; restoration of use of indigenous African languages in teaching, learning and research in universities; and re-humanizing those outsourced workers through insourcing of their services. This is why the student activist Athabile Nonxuba defined Rhodes Must Fall movements as propelled by 'an oath of allegiance that everything to do with oppression and conquest of black people by white power must fall and be destroyed' (cited in Booysen 2016: 4).

Theorizing and contextualizing protests in Africa

The leading South African sociologist Bernard Makhosezwe Magubane (1977) posed five arguments about the importance of theory and history in the analysis of contemporary developments. First, he emphasized the importance deployment of 'comprehensive theory of social change, for an understanding of the laws of motion that define the epoch and the social formation under examination' (Magubane 1977: 148). Second, he noted that 'Fragmentary descriptions, however voluminous and detailed, provide no substitute whatsoever for sustained reasoned theoretical argument' (Magubane 1977: 48). Third, he criticized academics involved in Southern Africa studies of 'participating in the tacit intellectual consensus to avoid seeing the present problems as historical problems' (Magubane 1977: 148). Fourth, he reiterated that 'Once again, the detailed examination of tress eliminates the forest from sight' (Magubane 1977: 148). Finally, he criticized liberal scholars for contributing 'little or nothing to our understanding of the current era in Southern Africa' and only succeeding in obfuscation of 'the complexities of the social movement in Southern Africa' as they avoided genuine and rigorous historicization of issues (Magubane 1977: 148).

Indeed, the current 'uprisings' rocking 'postcolonial' Africa in particular and the world at large have revealed the core inadequacies of existing social theories, particularly the Marxist and liberal analyses. For example, from both a Marxist and liberal understanding, the contemporary world is facing a 'middle class revolt' (Branch and Mamphilly 2015: 201). The thinking is that a disgruntled professional class that is globalized is pushing for deeper liberal democratization. If it is not the middle class that is identified as the drivers of protests, then it is the 'precariat' class/new proletariat/multitudes of precarious working classes of unemployed, underemployed and indebted experiencing the harsh effects of global capitalism (Harvey 2012; Branch and Mamphilly 2015: 203).

This analysis is inadequate at many levels. While it tries to provide a universalist interpretation of contemporary complex politics of protest, it remained locked in narrow class analysis that obscures the complexities and multifaceted issues at play in the contemporary protest movements. What it then missed are the varying historical contexts within which contemporary African protests have emerged. The reality is that Rhodes Must Fall movements defy easy class analysis because they are an amalgam of many class and non-class issues of gender, culture, language, symbols, curriculum, finance and epistemology. The very category of 'middle class', which is increasingly being used today, tends to encompass a bulk of property-less people who were highly indebted whereas the category 'working class' embraced millions of what can be correctly termed 'working poor' like security guards and cleaners who were paid R2000 per month in South Africa. This is why Adam Branch and Zachariah Mampilly argued 'A realistically defined middle class would comprise only a narrow silver of Africa's population, set against a backdrop in which nearly half of all Africans live in extreme poverty, with numbers growing' (Branch and Mamphilly 2015: 1).

Race rather than class is still an invisible but active organizing principle of informing unchanging patterns of inequality, poverty, Eurocentric curriculum, alienating university cultures, use of 'foreign'/colonial languages of instruction and standing colonial/apartheid symbols. Like all other protests, Rhodes Must Fall movements were riddled by tensions, contradictions, ambivalences and violence, making them difficult to interpret from a singular class perspective. But it is not only Marxist and liberal theories that were limited, existing social theories coming from Europe and North America in their market (materialist/class analysis), sociological (race theory), psychoanalytical, culturalist, poststructuralist, postmodernist and postcolonial versions have reached an 'epistemic break'/crisis/exhaustion (Ndlovu-Gatsheni 2015).

It was Immanuel Wallerstein (1991) who revealed that nineteenth-century social science's presumptions were previously considered to possess a 'liberating of the spirit' served 'today as the central intellectual barrier to useful analysis of the social world'. This delving into the epistemological questions and crisis is important because the Rhodes Must Fall movements were loudly calling for what Brenda Cooper and Robert Morrell (2014) termed 'Africa-centred knowledges' as a form of cognitive justice.

What is fuelling contemporary African protest movements in general and South African student movements in particular cannot be simply reduced to a crisis of capitalism as an economic system. In the Rhodes Must Fall movements particularly, there is a clear revolt against epistemological domination and cultural extroversion. A modern civilizational crisis better encapsulates what is generating protests. Aime Cesaire (1972: 31) described European civilization predicated on imperialism and colonialism as a 'decadent civilization' and 'dying civilization' as far back as 1955. A crisis of civilization is also highlighted by Cornel West (1987) who wrote of 'a pervasive and profound crisis of North Atlantic civilization' as he tried to understand the specific problems of black Americans. Slavoj Zizek (2011: x) also underscored the enormity of a civilizational crisis when he posited that the global capitalist system was approaching 'an apocalyptic zero-point' in the process, producing ecological crises, inequalities and poverty, struggles over raw materials, food and water as well as 'the explosive growth of social divisions and exclusions'.

Adam Branch and Zachariah Mampilly (2015) provided a good contextualization of contemporary African protests in recent African history. They correctly emphasized 'the need to look inward to Africa's own past and its own history of protest before looking outward to events in the rest of the world in order to explain today's continental protest wave' (Branch and Mamphilly 2015, p. 2). This approach is very important as it addresses the problem that Mahmood Mamdani (1996) described as writing 'history by analogy'. Mamdani specifically revealed the problem of 'received democratic theory' in these revealing ways:

> For a curious feature of current African politics is to draw prescription from a context other than the one that gave rise to its problems. Whereas the source of demands is the existing African context, the framework for solutions is generally a received theory of democracy which has little to do with contemporary realities in Africa.
>
> (Mamdani 1992: 2228)

He went further to state:

> The framework of received theory is a set of assumptions which do not always reflect realities on the continent. The clash between assumptions and realities can either lead to sterile attempts to enforce textbook solution or be rich source of creative reflection.
>
> (Mamdani 1992: 2228)

What emerges poignantly from this analysis is that any comprehensive and correct understanding of protest politics in Africa must focus on actually existing protest politics and in its complex dynamics. Branch and Mampilly (2015) categorized the actually existing protest politics into three broad waves while concentrating on the identification of the active motive forces/social bases of each of the protests. The first wave was that of anti-colonial protests that culminated in 'political independence' of Africa. The second emerged in the 1980s and 1990s ranged against single-party, military dictatorships and austerity measures imposed by Bretton Woods institutions. Today, we are facing a 'third wave' of protests of which we are engage in understanding 'what political transformations it may foretell' (Branch and Mamphilly 2015: 3). What is clear is that the ideology of 'fallism' that involved removal of colonial statues is framed by a broad resurgence of decolonial demands and decolonial politics.

The anti-colonial protests of the 1950s and 1960s were spearheaded by a 'detribalized' (see Mamdani 1996) urban 'underclass' of Africans who constituted a 'political society' (Chatterjee 2011) of those who had nothing to lose and everything to win in the dismantlement of colonialism. These Africans had a very conflictual relationship with the colonial state – 'a relation defined by an alternation between neglect and direct violence, between extra-legality and illegality' (Branch and Mamphilly 2015: 20). This social category of Africans faced urban controls, night searches, forced removals and overt violence of the state. The category 'worker' does not include these people's identity within a colonial political economy and governmentality: they were dispossessed and unemployed. They were uprooted from rural areas, separated from their kinsmen and women, they lived in 'the shanty town' and constantly faced the full force of colonial power.

This 'political identity' made them to constitute in Frantz Fanon's (1968: 129) analysis 'one of most spontaneous and the most radical revolutionary forces of a colonized people'. What emerges from this analysis is: 'Different political identities, based on different relations to state power, produce different forms of political action' (Branch and Mamphilly 2015: 21). Unlike workers in a colonial environment who tend to protest for higher wages or improved working conditions while conscious of preserving their jobs, what Fanon termed the 'lumpenproletariat' do not fight for reforms – they are propelled 'by a more radical need to transform the very conditions of life, which are enforced by an arbitrary and violent state power' (Branch and Mamphilly 2015: 21). It was this social base that provided the foot soldiers of the anti-colonial forces. But the anti-colonial struggles did not succeed in delivering a genuinely 'postcolonial' dispensation. As eloquently articulated by Grosfoguel:

The heterogeneous and multiple global structures put in place over a period of 450 years did not evaporate with the juridical-political decolonization of the periphery over the past 50 years. We continue to live under the same 'colonial power matrix'. With juridical-political decolonization we moved from a period of 'global colonialism' to the current period of 'global coloniality'.

(Grosfoguel 2007: 219)

Inevitably, the second wave of protests of the 1980s and 1990s were sparked by a combination of realization of the 'myths of decolonization' (see Ndlovu-Gatsheni 2013b), failure of the 'postcolonial' redistributive developmental state, dictatorship, austerity measures and repression that was encouraged by Bretton Woods institutions (Onimode 1992). The activists included nascent civil society, students, workers and intellectuals. The struggles were multifaceted to the extent that the concept of 'third wave of democratization' occludes the complexities, ambivalences, ambiguities, diversities and other alternative readings of protests and the concomitant diverse imagined horizons (Branch and Mamphilly 2015: 65–66).

The 'third wave of African protest' is what we are seeing today, of which Rhodes Must Fall movements are part. At the forefront seems to be a category called 'the youth', tired on being put in a permanent state of what Alcinda Honwana (2013) termed 'waithood'. Branch and Mampilly (2015) have distilled broad causes of the current wave of protests. First: 'The multiparty regimes and neoliberal economies that emerged from the upheavals of the late 1980s and early 1990s have proven unable to meet popular aspirations for fundamental change' (Branch and Mamphilly 2015: 67). In short, the changes of the 1990s left the 'precarious livelihoods of urban political society' unresolved, hence today's vehement 'rejection of the neoliberal economy by Africa's poor' (Branch and Mamphilly 2015: 70). The second condition precipitating current protests is the continuing lack of accountability, poor delivery of service and use of violence by the state even under multiparty democracy (Branch and Mamphilly 2015: 72). In all this, the Arab Spring/Arab Awakening that emerged in North Africa seem to fall within the second wave of democratic transition that took place in the rest of Africa in the late 1980s and 1990s (Juma 2011).

Having framed the core issues of protest from the continental perspective, a turn to South Africa is in order. Julian Brown (2015) argues that 'a consensus politics' of 1994 and the post-apartheid dream of a rainbow nation has collapsed and in the cracks and fractures of South Africa's political order has emerged an 'insurgent citizen', new forms of activity, new leaders and new movements. Brown posited that 'our existing society has inequality at its core. The formal political order seems to separate from the social and political worlds of ordinary citizens, and the poor' (Brown 2015: 148).

The spectre of the paradigm of difference in South Africa

A problematic paradigm of difference produced a conflict-ridden and contested idea of South Africa. Economic and social inequality haunting South Africa is a consequence of the colonial/apartheid implementation the paradigm of difference. The root of all political, economic, social and epistemological problems haunting South Africa today and provoking current citizen uprisings are genealogically and historically traceable to the implementation of the paradigm of difference.

Valentin Y. Mudimbe (1988: 4) explained that the paradigm of difference enacted 'the colonizing structure responsible for producing marginal societies, cultures, and human beings'. As articulated in the previous chapters, the other name for the 'paradigm of difference' is the 'colour line' (Du Bois 1903). It is a very troublesome line because it gave birth to other lines such as the gender line, the class line, the sexual orientation line and many others (Gordon 2000: 63). The paradigm of difference is the mother and father of all forms fundamentalisms and politics of alterity.

In South Africa the paradigm of difference produced apartheid, which was institutionalized in 1948. Its short-sighted ideologues celebrated and sold it to their white constituencies as 'separate development' (a colonial euphemism for legalized racial inequality and oppression). Chief Albert Luthuli (2006: 148) correctly characterized the institutionalization of apartheid as 'a tragic failure of imagination' in which 'We Africans are depersonalized by whites, our humanity and dignity reduced in their imagination to a minimum'. What was 'tragic' was its inscription of what Boaventura de Sousa Santos (2007) termed 'impossibility of co-presence' through such legislation as the Native Land Act of 1913, Urban Areas Act of 1923, Extension of University of Education Act of 1959, among many others that not only demarcated land but segregated people as well as students into black and white spaces and white, black, Indian and coloured universities (Davies 1996, pp. 319–332).

What was even more 'tragic' was apartheid government's official attempts to 'de-nationalize' the majority black indigenous population through forced removals from urban areas and pushing all black people into invented 'Bantustans' as well as fragmenting black people into rigid tribal identities (Neocosmos 2010: 20). This created a misnomer that Michael Neocosmos (2010) rendered as a shift from 'foreign natives' to 'native foreigners'. Since then, South Africa has been haunted by complex struggles not only for simple inclusion and equality by those who were excluded, peripherized and pauperized but for humanity itself.

The very idea of South Africa became spoiled from its birth by this paradigm of difference and its practice of 'impossibility of co-presence' and 'de-national-ization' of indigenous people. Inevitably it unfolded and fossilized as a highly contested and conflict-generating identitarian phenomenon. Here was born the core problem of South Africa, which is that of 'a struggle to become South African' and human by those who were excluded (Dubow 2007: 72). This problem can be rendered as an idea, a national question, and a liberation challenge. As an idea, it was well captured by Kader Asmal (2001: 1) in these words:

> Here was born an idea, a South African idea, of moulding a people from diverse origins, cultural practices, languages, into one, within a framework

democratic in character, that can absorb, accommodate and mediate conflicts and adversarial interests without oppression and injustice.

At the centre of this idea were such national questions as 'What is the post-apartheid nation?' 'Who belongs or is excluded, and on what basis?' 'How does a "national identity gain its salience and power to transcend the particularities of ethnicity and race?"' (Bundy 2007: 79). Inevitably, the contested idea of South Africa imposed itself on the liberatory discourse and agenda as a challenge of how to resolve the related questions of being human, nationality and citizenship. This liberatory challenge was well expressed by C. R. D. Halisi (1999: 4):

> In a very fundamental sense, the struggle for liberation required black activists to confront nascent questions of citizenship and national identity – how the 'people' are to be defined, who belongs to the political community, and what are the criteria of inclusion and exclusion.

In short, the still unresolved idea of South Africa has a long history beginning with Dutch settlement at the Cape and their inauguration of a violent colonial politics of a moving 'frontier' of genocide, enslavement, conquest, dispossession, displacement, colonization and exploitation. This was followed by Anglicization as an imperial phenomenon accompanied by conquest, racism, dispossession, exploitation and segregation. British liberal pretensions that made them to claim to be more civilized than the Dutch (Afrikaners) was only used as a colonial weapon rather than a genuine desire to restore humanity as well as civil and political rights to the dispossessed and dehumanized black indigenous people. Anglicization as an imperial and colonial project directly locked horns with Afrikanerization as a colonial process of institutionalization of racism and de-nationalization of black people. The competing Dutch/Afrikaner and British imperial and colonial projects resulted in open conflicts that became known as the Anglo-Boer Wars that only ended in 1902 with the signing of the Treaty of Vereening (Dubow 2007). What emerged from the treaty of 1902 was an agreement to construct South Africa into a white state with the British and Afrikaners in charge. This was concretized through promulgation of the South Africa Act of Union of 1910 (Dubow 2007).

As the British and the Afrikaners accommodated each other into an invented white South Africa they behaved as though indigenous African people were non-existent. They all featured in the discussions as providers of cheap labour. Inevitably, such exclusion and total neglect provoked various forms of African resistance that branched into black republicanism, cultural nationalism, Pan-Africanism, black consciousness formations, socialist-class-based imaginations, liberal nationalism and non-racialism (Ndlovu-Gatsheni 2008; Ndlovu-Gatsheni 2013a). The consequence of the African struggles against apartheid, which are document in previous chapters of this book, culminated in what Julian Brown (2015: 1) termed the 'social consensus' of a 'New South Africa' founded on rainbowism (inclusive and democratic society).

Alexander Johnston (2014) termed it an 'improvised nation'. But Brown (2015: 1) depicted the discourses of a successful transition, miracle and 'new South Africa' as 'a dated' stories because 'South Africa is once again in flux – caught in a moment in which the boundaries of politics and society are unstable'. As far back 1999, R. C. D. Halisi correctly predicted the current ructions and convulsions rocking post-apartheid South Africa, arguing that there were resilient rival populisms cascading from 'competing visions of liberation' that were bound to have an 'impact on the evolution of South African citizenship' (Halisi 1999: 133). Indeed, it is not only the popular democratic traditions that are durable, but also there are deep-seated 'race-conscious political sensibilities' that are equally powerful (Halisi 1999: 133).

Thus, the rise of such political and social formations as the EFF, BFLF and Rhodes Must Fall cannot be divorced from the long-standing contestations over the idea of South Africa. These movements are challenging what Johnston (2014) has described as an 'identity of convenience' as they continue to fight for a 'South African idea' based on the imaginations, knowledges, experiences and aspirations of the formerly enslaved, colonized, racialized, dispossessed and dehumanized. The current struggles, which have produced what Brown (2015) termed 'insurgent citizens', are deeply etched within the painful reality of living an illusion of an insider, a citizen and a human rights-bearing human being, while the reality is still keeping black people outside through economic and epistemological exclusion that produce a property-less people. At the forefront of this struggle are students, many of whom were born after the dismantlement of juridical apartheid but were experiencing cultural alienation, exclusion from higher education due to high fees and exposure to ideas of dead white men as a form of education inside universities. In reaction, they have turned the university into a site of struggles.

The university as a site of struggle

As noted in previous chapters, the existing universities in Africa did not grow from the African seed. They were never a product of deliberate and slow growth from the African socio-cultural and politico-economic developments (Pratt 1965). They are transplants from Europe and North America. It was this transplantation of universities into Africa that provoked resistance from early African elites like Edward Wilmot Blyden and J. E. Casley Hayford (Ashby 1964; Blyden 1967). The point here is that the struggle for access to higher education and an African university goes as far back as the 1860s and 1870s.

While the colonial regimes increasingly opened new universities in Africa after 1945, they were all transplantations from Europe. This is why Robert R. July (1987) emphasized 'The first universities in black Africa were imports, their purpose the indoctrination of a foreign culture'. The previous chapter documented how colonial education negatively impacted on Africa. The first casualty was the 'mother tongue' of African people that were replaced with colonial languages. The second was African cultures and knowledge that were never taken seriously.

The result of colonial education was the production of deeply alienated colonial subjects. Ngugi wa Thiong'o (1986: 28) eloquently described the crisis of alienation in these revealing words:

> It starts with a deliberate disassociation of the language of conceptualization, of thinking, of formal education, of mental development, from the language of daily interaction in the home and in the community. It is like separating the mind from the body so that they occupy two unrelated linguistic spheres in the same person. On a large social scale it is like producing a society of bodiless heads and headless bodies.

If one takes into account desocializing implications of colonial education then it is not surprising that decolonization entailed revival of indigenous cultures, reaffirmation of African identities, rise of nationalist historiography and other initiatives aimed at reversing alienation imposed by colonialism. Initiatives such as the 'African personality', 'Ethiopianism', 'Negritude' and many others were part of the decolonial drive to epistemic and cultural liberation (Owomonyela 1996). The challenge was that the African elites spearheading these initiatives were 'men of two worlds, true cultural hybrids' which created a lot of contradictions, ambivalences and ambiguities in the way they spearheaded decolonization (July 1987:13). Those who were highly conscious like Kwame Nkrumah pushed for both political liberation and epistemic freedom. They made commendable efforts in turning inherited 'universities in Africa' into 'African universities' that reflected African traditions and cultures. This drive to transform 'universities in Africa' into 'African universities', became known as 'Africanization' and was part and parcel of the African national project (Falola 2001).

Turning to the genealogy of South African universities, it is clear that some of them pre-dated 1945. However, they were all born into a toxic environment marked by a rigid paradigm of difference and practices of impossibility of co-presence. Racial categorization of universities in accordance with race and ethnicity became the norm. South African universities became a detestable reflection and macrocosm of a society bifurcated by an indelible human-invented paradigm of difference and racial fundamentalist impossibility of co-presence. These racially and ethnically bifurcated universities became consumers and sites of reproduction of Eurocentric ideas, including even those that were designated for African people. Those that were designated for blacks deliberately taught a poor version of Western epistemology that Isaac Bongani Tabata (1959) described as 'education for barbarism'.

Bantu Education according to Tabata (1959: 13) became a 'monstrosity' that existed to 'arrest the development of the African people'. Its counterpart was 'Coloured Education' for the Coloured people and the overarching objective was to 're-create for the subject races a social order belonging to the pre-industrial age' (Tabata 1959:13). As a colonial instrument of control Bantu Education produced a people whose purpose was 'minister the whites' through provision of cheap labour. It deliberately incapacitated 'the African student from reaching the required standard for entering a university' (Tabata 1959: 46).

Tabata was very correct in concluding:

> This Apartheid in university education is not simply a matter of separating the races at the universities. It is an end result, the logical completion of a systematic process not only of robbing Non-Whites of education but turning a whole population back to barbarism. To put it another way: if Bantu Education is the bricks of that immense edifice, the retribalization of a whole people, the Apartheid university is its coping stone.
>
> (Tabata 1959: 48)

Tabata (1959) concluded his book with a chapter entitled 'Bantu Education Must Fail', that is, it must 'fall'.

What is important to note is that the bifurcation of universities along racial and ethnic lines impinged on the formation and fossilization of student movements and student politics. White student formations began as Christian 'ecumenical' movements and they also branched into the National Union of South African Students (NUSAS) formed in 1924 that was dominated by English-speaking white students who pursued liberal politics of protest; Afrikaans Studentebond formed in 1933 that were part of the broader Afrikanerization nationalism project; and South African Students Organization formed in 1968 that embraced black liberation thought in general and black consciousness politics that challenged the entire edifice apartheid colonialism (Heffernan 2015). White liberal students actively protested against particular actions of the apartheid government such as the 1968 decision to block the appointment of Archie Mafeje at UCT and against particular pieces of legislation, not targeting the very edifice of apartheid colonialism. This is why Richard Rathbone (1977: 108) wrote: 'Poor NUSUS was detested by government for being radical and detested by blacks for being insufficiently radical: in short the liberal dilemma'. Between 1968 and 1973, the 'black ethnic universities' became the real site of struggles particularly the University of the North (now University of Limpopo).

There were various reasons why these 'black ethnic universities' became a site of struggles. They were initially placed under the authoritarian Department of Native Affairs and were run by entirely white Vice-Chancellors together with entirely white university senates that were not critical of apartheid but were eager to sustain it (Nkondo 1976). As noted by Brown:

> At black universities, administrators generally assumed responsibility for suppressing protest that took place on their campuses. Protesting students were either expelled or suspended for an indefinite period of time, and consequently were forced to leave the university grounds – and often to abandon their studies. When students did not willingly obey the university's expulsion order and chose to remain on the campuses, the administrators

rarely hesitated before inviting the police onto their campuses to enforce their shaky authority.

(Brown 2010: 728–729)

The political consciousness of the black students reflected the harshness of the world outside the university. But the inside 'black ethnic universities' black politics, just like in outside society, was criminalized. By 1970 the students at the University of the North had fully embraced black consciousness thought and were speaking of 'liberation first before education' and were directly linking their struggle within the broader context of psychological liberation of black people (Heffernan 2015: 179). The university administrators responded with mass expulsions of students in 1972. These expulsions spread the Turfloop spirit to other campuses and black solidarity was expressed through the Alice Declaration where the oppressive politics practiced in 'Black Institutions of Higher Learning' was condemned strongly and this was followed by student protests at universities of Fort Hare, the Western Cape, Zululand and Durban-Westville (Heffernan 2015: 180).

However, what is commonly ignored in existing analysis of student protests is how the spirit of Turfloop (the spirit of black consciousness and protest) spread to Soweto and resulted in the Soweto Uprising of 1976. Heffernan captures how the expelled students from Turfloop spread to teach in schools in Soweto, spreading the spirit of protest and black consciousness, focusing mainly on the role of Onkgopotse Abraham Tiro, a former university student leader and firebrand who taught History and English at Morris Isaacson High School in Soweto (Heffernan 2015: 181). Black consciousness politics permeated the South African Students Movement (SASM) that was already active in Soweto. Tsietsi Mashinini passed through Tiro's tutorship and he became the leader of Soweto Students Representative Council (SSRC) that actively participated in the organization of June 1976 Soweto Uprising (Schuster 2004). This background is important because it genealogically links the Turfloop spirit, Soweto spirit and the current Rhodes Must Fall spirit as a continuum with ruptures and breaks in a living spirit of student protest.

The interesting and noticeable feature is the change of site of struggles from the previously black ethnic universities to the previously white-English and Afrikaans universities. Even though the protest began at the predominantly black TUT it captured the nation's imagination when it shifted to UCT, Rhodes University, Wits, University of Stellenbosch, University of Pretoria (UP), University of North-West (UNW-Potchefstroom campus), UKZN and UJ as well as the University of South Africa (UNISA) (Ndlovu-Gatsheni 2016a).

This is where transformation, Africanization and decolonization have been painstakingly slow. Of course, such universities as Cape Peninsula University of Technology (CPUT) and the Western Cape have also been rocked by student politics. The key reason being that a decolonization, which gets deep into epistemology, curriculum, pedagogy, institutional cultures, access, language, demographics and symbolic representation, is yet to take place in all South African universities.

The limits of transition and transformation of South Africa

Adam Habib (2013) described the South Africa compromise of 1994 as resulting in a 'suspended revolution'. He identified strong institutional constraints as well as a complex 'balance of forces' as key factors that resulted in the suspension of revolution (Habib 2013). This is an important intervention that enables a better understanding of the limits of the promises of a radical transition and transformation in the 1990s following the unbanning of political organizations and release of political prisoners and the notions of forgiveness, reconciliation and a 'new South Africa'. Resolution of student grievances, deracialization of society and decolonization of universities were among the causalities of suspension of revolution.

At one level, CODESA, which was meant to enable black and white people to find each other and the TRC aimed at breaking the long-standing practices of impossibility of co-presence through truth-telling and forgiveness, did result in suspension of open warfare and overt hostilities but did not deliver social, economic and cognitive justice (Mamdani 2015; Ndlovu-Gatsheni 2016b). The adoption of a new South African Constitution in 1996, which was meant resolve the paradigm of difference and bury the curse of a de-nationalized black majority, is today protected by those who benefitted economically from the transition and they are refusing any prospects of its amendment. The rainbow nation ideology that was a declaration of a new humanity of right-bearing citizens united into one nation that is culturally, racially and ethnically diverse but equally is unravelling as Mandela is experiencing posthumous public trial for failing to deliver on economic, social and cognitive justice.

The number of pieces of legislation and frameworks as well as commissions that have been rolled out so far in an endeavour to transform education in South Africa reveal serous limits if analysed from a decolonial perspective. For example the National Commission on Higher Education (1994) simply emphasized access and alignment of qualifications without a focus on epistemological change. The National Qualifications Framework (1998) emphasized adherence with international standards and training of students as a potential workforce for a global economy, revealing how the question of internationalization was privileged over decolonization. The National Plan for Higher Education (2001) openly emphasized a shift from access and transformation to adaptation to global knowledge-driven world (Kamola 2011: 121). What is clear from a close analysis of these policy frameworks is that the intended transition and transformation became entangled and captured between and betwixt powerful forces of human rights versus market-driven neoliberalism; internationalization/globalization versus indigenization; Africanization, and decolonization; as well as imperatives of rights versus imperative of justice (Ndlovu-Gatsheni 2016a).

To further reveal the limits and difficulties of transformation, Africanization and decolonization of South African universities, it is important to briefly reflect on three empirical examples. The first example is the Mafeje Affair (1968–2007), which is a case of exclusion during and after apartheid (Ntsebeza nd). During apartheid the state was blamed for having interfered with the appointment of Mafeje to a Senior Lecturer in Anthropology in 1968 but what boggles the mind and is hard to explain is why Mafeje was blocked twice in the 1990s when he expressed an interest in joining UCT. In 1990, Mafeje took initiative and indicated his willingness to join UCT only to be given a 1-year Visiting Senior Research Fellow, with a salary peaked at Senior Lecturer level for someone who has been a professor for over twenty years outside South Africa. The 1-year offer was explained as a result of 'the current financial circumstances', whatever that meant, and the peaking of the salary at senior lecturer was never explained, perhaps it was also due to 'the current financial circumstances' (Ntsebeza nd: 7–8). In 1993 Mafeje applied for the AC Jordan Chair in African Studies at UCT but a technicality was used to exclude him: that Mafeje had not advised the appointments office of his change of address when he left Namibia to go to Egypt (Ntsebeza, nd: 10).

The second is the Makgoba Affair (1994–1995). This example speaks directly to challenges of transformation and Africanization. Eddie Webster (1988: 3) argued: 'The Makgoba affair provides a deep and tragic insight into the South African transition. As with the rest of South Africa, black and white, are struggling to find a common project.' Malegapuru William Makgoba was appointed the first black Deputy Vice-Chancellor at Wits in 1994 and he began to champion the discourse of Africanization of the university, claiming that Eurocentric education was still the mainstay of teaching. As noted by Webster (1988: 2–3), Makgoba had 'entered a racially polarized campus' deeply entrenched 'in the ways of the old South Africa' where 'institutional change will take a long time'. Between 1995 and 1996, Makgoba found himself engrossed in a bitter struggle as his academic credentials were investigated and questioned, where he was accused of having embellished his CV, accused of being administratively incompetent and of tarnishing the image of the university (Makgoba 1997). James M. Statman and Amy E. Ansel (2000: 279) deployed the concepts of discursive ecology and hidden scripts to reveal:

> The Makgoba affair was profoundly unsettling in that it revealed and perhaps heightened the terrible racial, political and class-fault-lines suddenly found lying so close beneath the dominant discursive patina of reconciliatory rainbowism.

The then Vice-Chancellor of the university, R. W. Charlton (1996), indicated that the Makgoba Affair 'acted as lighting conductor for some of the tension s of society in transition' and somehow admitted that it was basically about transforming the university 'rather than the allegation convening Prof. Makgoba's managerial performance, his public statements, the accuracy of various versions of his CV, and his conduct in relation to the personal files of members of the staff who lodged complaints against him' (Charlton 1996: 3). Whatever the real truth behind the Makgoba Affair is, its entanglement in the politics of transformation is important and indicates the difficulties, tensions, contradictions and oppositions inherent in trying to actively advance Africanization in this case from the top. Makgoba eventually lost his position as a result this affair.

The third example is known as the Mamdani Affair (1995–1998). It is specifically about the challenges of curriculum change, particularly how 'Africa' is to be taught in a post-apartheid society and how to give content to a Centre for African Studies (Mamdani 1995a; 1998). The crisis began soon after Mahmood Mamdani was appointed as AC Jordan Chair in African Studies at UCT, particularly with regards to the introduction of a core of the foundation semester course of Africa that he crafted as 'Problematising Africa'. Mamdani's proposed course was worlds apart from 'versions of Bantu Education, Bantu Studies called African Studies' that was taught at UCT (Mamdani 1995b; 1998). The course was subject to contestation by a 'Working Group' that hastily designed another course that was said to be primarily about equipping students with learning skills necessary for students entering higher education rather than Africa as subject matter. Mamdani staged a one-man protest against this politics of curriculum making (Kamola 2011). Rhodes Must Fall emerged within this complex background to continue the decolonization struggle.

Aluta Continua: The Rhodes Must Fall movement

The Rhodes Must Fall movements broke onto the national stage like a tsunami that shocked the complacent national government and university leadership including some conservative academics. The students forcefully brought the idea of decolonization in a society that had sunk into capitalist neoliberal reality back into the public arena. Emerging two decades after the so-called democratic transition of 1994, Rhodes Must Fall became one of the most dramatic mass actions. While it emerged within a formerly white UCT, directly provoked by alienation cultures and offensive colonial/apartheid iconographies, it gave birth to other strands such as Fees Must Fall, which directly focused on material concerns of the students. The attack on colonial/apartheid symbols soon fanned out of Cape Town to the Howard Campus of UKZN and the culprit was a sculpture of King George V (Jansen 2017: 48).

The student themselves have depicted the Rhodes Must Fall as a revolutionary attempt 'from below to disrupt this unequal, racialised social and economic order. It rekindled and questioned the idea about the university in a postcolonial society' (Chinguno *et al.* 2017: 16). On the importance of the movement, this is what the student themselves wrote:

> One of its most important contributions is that it produced a new generation of post-apartheid activists and a new form of politics and claim-making driven by social justice and the need to address inequality, poverty, and unemployment in the broader society. It brought together, at its peak, various student formations from different ideological traditions and across diverse academic spaces to critique the state and the socio-economic order.

The movement brought back critical student movement to the fore and presented students with an opportunity to reclaim their position as the protagonists of transformation in society.

(Chinguno *et al.* 2017: 17)

Continuing the self-definition and self-understanding, the leading activists in the Rhodes Must Fall movements stated:

The Fees Must Fall movement on the other hand represents a rejection of the neoliberal education system and has forged new collective identities and an unprecedented process of collective learning. A collective identity-the 'Fallists' was forged through mobilization cutting across political and ideological, economic/class difference within the student movement. Drawing from our lived experience in the movement we define a fallist as an activist who rejects a hetero-patriarchal order and all forms of oppression and prejudice, drawing from intersectional lenses to understand resistance, and advocates for free and decolonized education without exclusion of others.

(Chinguno *et al.* 2017: 16)

What is also distinctive about the Rhodes Must Fall movements is that what had begun as a protest against the existence of a statue of Cecil John Rhodes at the centre of UCT soon gave birth to various formations that picked different but relevant issues that needed to be resolved within different institutions across the country. For example, while at UCT the nerve-centre of protest became colonial/apartheid iconographies, Wits became the key site of Fees Must Fall protests. One can, therefore, argue that there were different sites of decolonial struggles that were targeting diverse offensive immediate issues. At Rhodes University, the very name of the university became a rallying point for decolonial resistance – as the students wanted it immediately changed. TUT has always been a site of student struggles against high registration fees. At UNISA, perhaps because it is a Open-Distance e-Learning (ODEL) institution that charges reasonable fees, the students picked the labour issue of outsourced workers as its rallying point.

The activists who actively participated in the Fees Must Fall at Wits have collected and written down their experiences in a book entitled *Rioting and Writing: Diaries of the Wits Fallists* (Chinguno *et al.* 2017). It is one of the most important ways through which students have to take control of the narrative of the student movements and counter those narratives that seek to denigrate, caricature and delegitimize this important moment in South Africa.

Analytical speaking, there are two broad interpretations of the Rhodes Must Fall phenomenon. The first is the hostile neoliberal interpretation. Jonathan Jansen's book *As by Fire: The End of the South African University* (2017) symbolized the hostile neoliberal camp. But this camp also has another less hostile but still neoliberal interpretation represented by an edited volume entitled *Fees Must Fall: Student Revolt, Decolonization and Governance in South Africa* (2016) by

Susan Booysen. Unlike Jansen's outrightly hostile interpretation of the student movements, the edited volume by Booysen even included student voices. But what emerges from this work is the idea of a reformist movement that was provoked by poor state governance by the ANC and the emphasis that the students were 'rising against the liberators' rather than neo-apartheid and neoliberalism (see Booysen 2016). In the liberal interpretation of the Rhodes Must Fall phenomenon, there is a push for the use of the term 'transformation' and deep cynicism about the term 'decolonization'.

In the neoliberal interpretation, the preferred solutions include diversification and creation of cosmopolitan universities through simply increasing the number of under-represented demographic groups (Habib 2016). Curriculum change in the neoliberal interpretation entailed adding works of Africans without changing the scaffold of Eurocentrism. The pertinent language question is reduced to an issue of communication and instruction rather than dignity and identity restoration. The demand for decommissioning of colonial/apartheid iconography is interpreted to mean diversification of symbols to reflect diversity of society drawing from both Western and African traditions. It is the neoliberal perspective that has concluded that the Rhodes Must Fall movements' demand would result in the 'end of the South African university' (Jansen 2017).

There is a very disturbing intellectual arrogance cascading from the neoliberal interpretation of the demands of the students. The students are heavily criticized as a bunch of people who have misread the work of Steve Biko and Frantz Fanon (Jansen 2017). The decolonization as a rallying point is also caricatured as vague and meaningless. For example, Jansen argued:

> Decolonization, it is not clear, has become the radical replacement for that ANC keyword transformation. The word is supposed to do what the old one did not: namely, radically change society itself. But of course words do not change society. [. . .] Moreover, invoking the language of decolonization is best a distracter from the challenges of producing, acquiring, and using knowledge to advance our understanding of a complex world and to deeply transform our communities. These challenges have nothing to do with decolonization and everything to do with broken public schools, failing health-care system, and corrupt government.
>
> (Jansen 2017: 168–169)

Jansen (2017: 171) emphasized that decolonization was doing nothing other than 'replays of language and politics from the 1960s in a globalized century where interdependence is key to planetary survival'. This hostile neoliberal interpretation of Rhodes Must Fall is countered by the decolonial perspective (Comaroff and Comaroff 2012; Santos 2014; Ndlovu-Gatsheni and Zondi 2016). The decolonial perspective acknowledges the current epistemic and systemic crisis within which the Rhodes Must Fall emerged as a logical decolonial movement. This interpretation accepts that the student movement is a decolonial phenomenon driven by a combination of Steve Bantu Biko's black consciousness ideology and Frantz Fanon's decolonial interventions. What the students are demanding is the decolonization of the very idea of the university, its institutional culture, management style and epistemological foundations so as to attain cognitive justice (Santos 2014; Ndlovu-Gatsheni and Zondi 2016). More importantly, while the neoliberal interpretation of the student movements emphasizes the need for interdependency in a globalized world, the decolonial perspective highlights the mushrooming of such movements as 'Black Lives Matter' in the United States and 'Why My Curriculum Is White?' in the United Kingdom and many others in understanding the planetary decolonial insurrection.

Thus instead of adopting a hostile and dismissive attitude towards Rhodes Must Fall, it is important to note that these new intellectual student movements point to the need to rethink the future of university education within a context of possibilities that are radically different from the problematic neoliberal tradition. What was highlighted by Rhodes Must Fall was the centrality of the solidarity of students and the proletariat as fundamental stakeholders in the decolonization struggles. Building on what the students put on the table, it becomes possible to envision a university of the future and its key features. The first key feature is that of multilingualism. The second is ecologies of knowledges as defined by Santos (2007; 2014) or what Francis B. Nyamnjoh (2017) termed conviviality, which 'depicts diversity, tolerance, trust, equality, inclusiveness, cohabitation, coexistence, mutual accommodation, interaction, interdependence, getting along, generosity, hospitality, congeniality, festivity, civility, and privileges peace over conflict, among other forms of sociality' (Nyamnjoh 2017: 5). These ecologies of knowledge have to enable 'convivial scholarship' which is well defined by Nyamnjoh:

> A truly convivial scholarship is one which does not seek a priori to define and confine Africans into particular territories or geographies, particular racial and ethnic categories, particular classes, genders, generations, religions, or whatever other identity marker is ideologically en vogue. Convivial scholarship confronts and humbles the challenge of over-prescription, over-standardization, over-routinization, and over-prediction. It is critical and evidence-based; it challenges problematic labels, especially those that seek to unduly oversimplify the social realities of the people, places and spaces it seeks to understand and explain.
>
> (Nyamnjoh 2017: 5)

More importantly according to Nyamnjoh (2017: 6): 'Convivial scholarship does not impose what it means to be human, just as it does not prescribe a single version of the good life in a world peopled by infinite possibilities, tastes and value systems.'

The third feature of a university of the future is one that is socially responsive and banishes epistemicides, linguicides, culturecides, racism, sexism, patriarchy, tribalism, xenophobia and classism so as to become a home of everyone. Such a university has to be fully recapitalized to enable access even by those without capital and must be fully grounded in its context while remaining globally competitive.

Conclusions: from transformation to decolonization

The above analysis reveals how the discourse of transformation that was articulated in neoliberal terms of human rights and democracy became nothing but a lullaby aimed at keeping the victims of apartheid asleep within a neo-apartheid dispensation. Unless one accepts these core limits of transformation, it would be impossible to fully understand why university students have suddenly burst onto the political stage speaking the decolonial language of changing the very idea of the university from being a 'Westernized' institution into an 'African university'. The student are very specific that the decolonial change has to be realized in restoration of cognitive justice premised on the fact that African people have produced knowledge and that knowledge must be placed at the centre of the 'African university'.

The students are also pushing for the use of indigenous languages in universities. More specifically, students are demanding the implementation of 'the right to education' that was promised in the Freedom Charter of 1955. The students' emphasis is on quality, relevant, free and decolonized education in their life time. It is not surprising that the issue of alienating institutional cultures features prominently as a grievance in the student protests because political decolonization never succeeded in delivering epistemological decolonization, which was capable of containing cultural imperialism. University institutional cultures are deemed by student to be Eurocentric, anti-black, racist, sexist and patriarchal. Therefore what we are witnessing is rapture, not simply from transformation to decolonization but from the idea of South Africa to the South African idea, this time defined and shaped by descendants of the enslaved, colonized, racialized, dispossessed and dehumanized. They are loudly proclaiming that their lives matter and they were born into valid and legitimate knowledge systems that have been pushed out of the academy.

References

Ashby, E. 1964. *African Universities and Western Tradition: The Godkin Lectures at Harvard University*. London: Oxford University Press.

Asmal, K. 2001. *Manifesto on Values, Education and Democracy*. Pretoria: Department of Education.

Blyden, E. W. 1882. *The Aims and Methods of a Liberal Education for Africans: Inaugural Address Delivered by Edward Wilmot Blyden, L. L. D., President of Liberia College*, January 5, 1818. Cambridge, MA. 1882.

Booysen, S. 2016. 'Introduction'. In S. Booysen (ed.), *Fees Must Fall: Student Revolt, Decolonization and Governance in South Africa*. Johannesburg: Wits University Press, pp. 1–20.

Branch, A. and Mampilly, Z. (2015). *Africa Uprising: Popular Protest and Political Change.* Cape Town: HSRC Press.

Brown, J. 2010. 'SASO's Reluctant Embrace of Public Forms of Protest, 1968–1972'. *South Africa Historical Journal*, 62(94), pp. 728–729.

Brown, J. 2015. *South Africa's Insurgent citizens: On Dissent and the Possibility of Politics.* Johannesburg: Jacana.

Bundy, C. 2007. 'New Nation, New History? Constructing the Past in Post-Apartheid South Africa'. In H. E. Stolten (eds), *History Making and Present Day Politics: The Meaning of Collective Memory in South Africa.* Uppsala: Nordic Africa Institute, pp. 70–97.

Cesaire, A. 1972. *Discourse on Colonialism.* Translated by Joan Pinkham. New York: Monthly Review Press.

Charlton, R. 1996. 'Wits on A Survival Course'. *The Star*, 1 February.

Chatterjee, P. 2011. *The Politics of the Governed: Reflections on Popular Politics in Most of the World.* New York: Columbia University Press.

Chinguno, C., Kgoroba, M., Mashibini, S., Masilela, B. N., Maubane, B., Moyo, N., Mthombeni, A. and Ndlovu, H. 2017. *Rioting and Writing: Diaries of Wits Fallists.* Johannesburg: Society, Work and Development Institute.

Comaroff, J. and Comaroff, J. L. 2012. *Theory from the South or, How Euro-America Is Evolving Towards Africa.* Boulder, CO and London: Paradigm.

Cooper, B. and Morrell, R. eds. (2014). *Africa-Centred Knowledges: Crossing Fields and Worlds.* Oxford, UK: James Currey.

Davies, J. 1996. 'The State and the South Africa University System under Apartheid'. *Comparative Education*, 32(3), pp. 319–332.

Du Bois, W. E. B. 1903. *The Souls of Black Folk.* New York: Dover Publications.

Dubow, S. 2007. 'Thoughts on South Africa: Some Preliminary Ideas'. In H. E. Stolten (eds), *History Making and Present Day Politics: The Meaning of Collective Memory in South Africa.* Uppsala: Nordic Africa Institute, pp. 55–70.

Falola, T. 2001. *Nationalism and African Intellectuals.* Rochester, NY: Rochester University Press.

Fanon, F. 1968. *The Wretched of the Earth.* Translated by C. Farrrington. New York: Grove Press.

Gordon, L. R. 2000. *Existentia Africana: Understanding Africana Existential Thought.* New York: Routledge.

Grosfoguel, R. 2007. 'The Epistemic Decolonial Turn: Beyond Political-Economy Paradigms'. *Cultural Studies*, 21(2/3), March/May, pp. 211–226.

Habib, A. 2013. *South Africa's Suspended Revolution: Hopes and Prospects.* Johannesburg: Wits University Press.

Habib, A, 2016. 'Transcending the Past and Reimaging the Future of the South African University'. *Journal of Southern African Studies*, 42(1), pp. 35–48.

Halisi, C. R. D. 1999. *Black Political Thought in the Making of South African Democracy.* Bloomington and Indianapolis, IN: Indiana University Press, 1999, p. 4.

Harvey, D. 2012. *Rebel Cities: From the Right to the City to the Urban Revolution.* London: Verso.

Hayford, J. E C. 1911. *Ethiopia Unbound: Studies in Race Emancipation.* London: Sampson Low & Marton.

Heffernan, A. 2015. 'Black Consciousness's Lost Leader: Abraham Tiro, the University of the North, and the Seeds of South Africa's Student Movement in the 1970s'. *Journal of Southern African Studies*, 41(1), pp. 173–186.

Honwana, A. 2013. *Youth and Revolution in Tunisia.* London: Zed Books.

Jansen, J. 2017. *As By Fire: The End of the South African University.* Cape Town: Tafelberg.

Johnston, A. 2014. *South Africa: Inventing the Nation.* London and New York: Bloomsbury Academic.

July, R. 1987. *An African Voice: The Role of Humanities in African Independence.* Durham, NC: Duke University Press.

Juma, C. 2011. 'The African Summer'. *Foreign Policy*, 28 July. Available at: www.foreign policy.com/articles/2011/07/28/the_africa_summer (accessed 25 March 2016).

Kamola, I. A. 2011. 'Pursuing Excellence in a "World-Class African University": The Mamdani Affair and the Politics of Global Higher Education'. *Journal of Higher Education in Africa*, 9(1/2), pp. 121–142.

Luthuli, A. 2006. *Let My People Go: The Autobiography of Albert Luthuli.* Houghton: Mafube Publishing.

Magubane, B. 1977. 'The Poverty of Liberal Analysis: A Polemic on Southern Africa'. *Review*, 1(2), Fall, pp. 147–166.

Magubane, B. M. 1979. *The Political Economy of Race and Class in South Africa.* New York and London: Monthly Review Press.

Makgoba, M. W. 1997. *Mokoko: The Makgoba Affair: A Reflection on Transformation.* Lea Glen, FL: Vivlia Publishers.

Maldonado-Torres. N. 2012. 'Decoloniality at Large: Towards-Americas and Global Transmodern Paradigm (Introduction to Special Issue of 'Thinking Through the Decolonial Turn')'. *Transmodernity: Journal of Peripheral Cultural Production of Luso-Hispanic World*, 1(3), Spring, pp. 1–39.

Mamdani, M. 1992. 'Africa: Democratic Theory and Democratic Struggles'. *Economic and Political Weekly*, 27(41), 10 October, pp. 2226–2228

Mamdani, M. 1995a. 'A Reflection on Higher Education in Equatorial Africa: Some Lessons for South Africa'. *South African Journal of Higher Education*, 9, pp. 45–68.

Mamdani, M. (ed.). 1995b. *Teaching Africa at the Post-Apartheid University of Cape Town: A Critical View of the 'Introduction to Africa' Course in the Social Science and Humanities Faculty Foundation Semester.* Rondebosch: University of Cape Town.

Mamdani, M. 1996. *Citizens and Subjects: The Legacy of Late Colonialism in Africa.* Princeton, NJ: Princeton University Press.

Mamdani, M. 1998. 'Is African Studies to Be Turned Into A New Home for Bantu Education at UCT?' Centre for African Studies, Cape Town.

Mamdani, M. 2013. *Define and Rule: Native as Political Identity.* Johannesburg: Wits University Press.

Mamdani, M. 2015. 'Beyond Nuremberg: The Historical Significance of the Post-Apartheid Transition in South Africa'. *Politics and Society*, 43(1), pp. 61–88.

Maylam, P. 2005. *The Cult of Rhodes: Remembering an Imperialist in Africa.* Cape Town: David Philip.

Mudimbe, V. Y. 1988. *The Invention of Africa: Gnosis, Philosophy, and the Order of Knowledge.* Bloomington and Indianapolis, IN: Indiana University Press.

Mudimbe, V.Y. 1994. *The Idea of Africa.* Bloomington and Indianapolis, IN: Indiana University Press.

Ndlovu-Gatsheni, S. J. 2008. 'Black Republicanism, Nativism and Populist Politics in South Africa'. *Transformation*, 68, pp. 53–86.

Ndlovu-Gatsheni, S. J. 2013a. *Empire, Global Coloniality and African Subjectivity.* New York and Oxford, UK: Berghahn Books.

Ndlovu-Gatsheni, S. J. 2013b. *Coloniality of Power in Postcolonial Africa: Myths of Decolonization.* Dakar: CODESRIA Book Series.

Ndlovu-Gatsheni, S. J. 2015. 'Decoloniality in Africa: A Continuing Search for a New World Order'. *Australasian Review of African Studies*, 36(2), December, pp. 22–50.

Ndlovu-Gatsheni, S. J. 2016a. 'Why Are South Africa Universities Sites of Struggle Today?' *The Thinker: Pan-African Quarterly for Thought Leaders*, 4(70), pp. 52–61.

Ndlovu-Gatsheni, S. J. 2016b. *The Decolonial Mandela: Peace, Justice and the Politics of Life.* Oxford, UK and New York: Berghahn Books.

Ndlovu-Gatsheni, S. J. and Zondi, S. 2016. 'Introduction: The Coloniality of Knowledge: Between Troubled Histories and Uncertain Times'. In S. J. Ndlovu-Gatsheni and S. Zondi (eds), *Decolonizing the University, Knowledge Systems and Disciplines.* Durham, NC: Carolina Academic Press, pp. 3–24.

Neocosmos, M. 2010. *From 'Foreign Natives' to 'Native Foreigners': Explaining Xenophobia in Post-Apartheid South Africa: Citizenship and Nationalism, Identity and Politics.* Dakar. CODESRIA Book Series.

Ngugi wa Thiong'o. 1986. *Decolonizing the Mind: The Politics of Language in African Literature.* Nairobi: Heinemann Educational Publishing.

Nkondo, M. G. (ed.). 1976. *Turfloop Testimony: The Dilemma of a Black University in South Africa.* Johannesburg: Ravan Press.

Nkrumah, K. 1965. *Neo-Colonialism: The Last Stage of Imperialism.* London: Panaf.

Ntsebeza, L. (n). 'The Mafeje and UCT Saga: Unfinished Business'. Unpublished paper, University of Cape Town.

Nyamnjoh, F. B. 2017. *Drinking from the Cosmic Gourd: How Amos Tutuola Can Change Our Minds.* Bameda: Langaa Research & Publishing CIG.

Onimode, B. 1992. *A Future for Africa: Beyond the Politics of Adjustment.* London: Earthscan.

Owomonyela, O. 1996. *The African Difference: Discourses on Africanity and the Relativity of Cultures.* Johannesburg: Wits University Press.

Pratt, R. C. 1965. 'African Universities and Western Tradition – Some East African Reflections'. *The Journal of Modern African Studies*, 3(3), pp. 421–428.

Rathbone. R. 1977. 'Student Politics'. *The Journal of Commonwealth and Comparative Politics*, 15(2), pp. 98–120.

Rodney, W. 1972. *How Europe Underdeveloped Africa.* London: Bogle-L'Ouverture Publications.

Santos, B. de S. 2007. 'Beyond Abyssal Thinking: From Global Lines to Ecologies of Knowledge'. *Review*, xxx(1), pp. 45–89.

Santos, B. de S. 2014. *Epistemologies of the South: Justice Against Epistemicide.* Boulder, CO and London: Paradigm.

Schuster, L. 2004. *A Burning Hunger: One Family's Struggle Against Apartheid.* Athens, OH: Ohio University Press.

Statman, J. M. and Ansell, A. E. 2000. 'The Rise and Fall of the Makgoba Affair: A Case Study of Symbolic Politics'. *Politikon*, 27(2), pp. 259–290.

Tabata, I. B. 1959. *Education for Barbarism: Bantu (Apartheid) Education in South Africa.* London: Prometheus.

Wallerstein, I. 1991. 'Introduction: Why Unthink?' Immanuel Wallerstein (ed.), *Unthinking Social Science: The Limits of Nineteenth Century Paradigms.* Cambridge, UK: Polity Press, pp. 1–30.

Webster, E. 1998. 'Wits' Going On? Revisiting the Makgoba Affair'. *Southern Africa Report*, 13(2), March, pp. 1–7.

West, C. L. 1987. 'Race and Social Theory: Towards a Genealogical Materialist Analysis'. In M. Davis, M. Marable, F. Pfeil and M. Sprinker (eds), *The Year Left: Volume 2: Towards a Rainbow Socialism: Essays on Race, Ethnicity, Class, and Gender.* London: Verso, pp. 45–68.

Zizek, S. 2011. *Living in the End Times.* London: Verso.

10

CONCLUSION

African futures

At the centre of modernity emerged onto-epistemic struggles of who was 'modern', what does it mean to be human, who belonged to the future, what constituted knowledge, how society was to be organized and how power was to be conceived and configured. Under Euromodernity only the Europeans claimed to belong to the future. To sustain this monopoly of the future, Europeans not only colonized space, people and knowledge but more importantly time. Time became bifurcated into two – the pre-modern and the modern. To sustain this sense of time, Euromodernity invented such nomenclatures as indigenous, tribe, primitive and black as it drove towards distinguishing those who claimed to be modern (to be in the future) while actively working to confine other human beings to the past (primitivity/backwardness). Here was born a modern world in which those who had been pushed to the categories of indigenous, primitive, tribe and black, were questioned and rejected as human beings. Here was also born the painful reality of a people who became defined as a problem and a people who through such initiatives as colonialism were exiled from their knowledges, cultures, and even from themselves.

Building on the above strands of argument and what is contained in this book (Chapter 1 to Chapter 9), it becomes clear that the subject of epistemic freedom cannot make sense without addressing the key question of what it means to be human. This is the case because denial of being necessarily meant rejection of epistemic virtue. Euromodernity was fundamentally an attack on human freedom even though it claimed to contribute to advancement of human freedom. What the decolonization and deprovincialization struggles of today are grappling with is not just an epistemic issue cascading from crisis of reason but rather an onto-logical question emerging at the centre of dismemberment and dehumanization. Consequently, the cardinal crime of Euromodernity has been the invention and naturalization of the paradigm of difference, which instantiated a politics of alterity predicated on the notion of the unbridgeable distance between those who called themselves Europeans and those who became variously named as tribes, indigenous, primitive and black people. This emphasis on distance rather than connection was in reality a violation and distortion of human history.

Prior to Euromodernity, Africans always moved and settled in parts of what would later be claimed to be a unique and exclusive space called Europe. This is why such decolonial African scholars as Ali Mazrui (see Chapter 5 in this book) argued for the abolition of both the Red Sea and the Mediterranean Sea as boundaries separating Africa from Arabia and Europe respectively as they push for deprovincialization and decolonization of Africa. This remains a necessary decolonial struggle because Euromodernity concretized its discourse of distance through utilization of physical and non-physical features such as oceans, seas, rivers, mountains and many others to create boundaries and invent races. With these boundaries in place, colonial cartographies had succeeded in controlling how people related to one another not on their own terms. Before modern maps and modern boundaries, the world was limitless. Movement was free. Mobility was a way of life. Today, movement and mobility are called migration/immigration subject to regulation by Eurocentric international law and its replications as domestic laws. One has to be authorized to move. At another level, a combination biological and cartographical racism matured into cultural racism. At the linguistic level, Latin and Greek became the base for human languages and a base for the genealogy of such modern concepts as democracy.

It is within this context that this book posed the long-standing question of epistemic freedom as the essential base for other freedoms. Across nine chapters, the difficult challenge has been whether Africans could successfully launch themselves into the denied modern space and successfully create African futures within a modern world system structured by global coloniality. Global coloniality is a modern global power structure that has been in place since the dawn of Euromodernity. It commenced with enslavement of black people and culminated in global coloniality. Today global coloniality operates as an invisible power matrix that is shaping and sustaining asymmetrical power relations between the Global North and the Global South.

Even the current global power transformations which have enabled the re-emergence of a Sinocentric economic power crystallizing around China, and is predicated on the decolonial strategy of de-Westernization does not mean that the modern world system has now undergone genuine decolonization and deimperialization to the extent of being amenable to the creation of other futures. Global coloniality remains one of the most important and resilient modern power structures that constrain and limit African agency. Thus, a deeper analysis of the architecture and configuration of current asymmetrical global power structures entails a decolonial unmasking of imperial/colonial reason embedded in Eurocentric epistemology as well as grappling with the broader problem of Eurocentrism. It also demands the unpacking of the Cartesian notions of being and its relegation of African subjectivity to a perpetual state of becoming.

If we are to name the elephant inside the modernity house, the interconnected and intertwined issues of coloniality of power, knowledge and being as constitutive elements of global coloniality as a power structure continue to make it difficult for Africans to create their own futures. Therefore, contemporary struggles for epistemic freedom should directly and radically seek to attain cognitive and social justice. These could only be achieved when the dominant but exhausted knowledge system has been democratized if not allowed to fade away. Cognitive justice is an essential pre-requisite of social, economic, political and cultural justice. Thus, engagement with epistemic struggles of the twenty-first century in particular is invariably an enquiry into other ways of living that were not over-determined by discursive processes of capitalism, colonialism, racism, sexism and patriarchy.

What currently demonstrates that Euromodernity inscribed itself on the world through denying other human being a space in the present and the future is the African Union's Agenda 2063 which is still struggling to set Africans free to take charge of their history so as to launch themselves into a an African future of Pan-African unity, integration, prosperity and peace. Decolonization is that medium of placing the future into the hands of African people as drivers and dynamic forces operating within the global arena. Pan-Africanism then emerges as that decolonial ideological glue and framework for unity, self-reliance, integration, and solidarity, which embraces the African Diaspora (African Union 2013). Decolonization underscores the fact that such an African future will never be a game of chance or magnanimity of those who benefitted from colonialism and are benefitting from present global coloniality. It will be a product of present long struggles ranged against coloniality of power, coloniality of knowledge and coloniality of being as constitutive elements of global coloniality.

Thus, thinking deeper about the possibility of Africans creating their own futures, taking charge of their own destiny and mapping their own autonomous development trajectories reminds one of Karl Marx's arguments about how a people making history do so under circumstances they have not chosen. This is the situation within which Africans are struggling to create African futures. Global coloniality has never been an African choice. This means that for the African Union to realize its Agenda 2063, it has to struggle ceaselessly against and within the matrices of global coloniality and the present market fundamentalism. Capturing the future for Africans and all other people who experienced colonialism and who are today living under global coloniality entails fighting to create another world and to set afoot a new humanism. It is a search for meaning after centuries of been pushed to meaninglessness. A lot of daring to invent the future is needed. This is important precisely because, in a historical sense, the modern world system and its shifting global orders is largely a creation of Europeans and North Americans.

The British historian-cum-journalist John Keegan (2002) highlighted how the Europeans captured the present and the future through concrete sessions of planning, conspiring and inventions systems and orders. They concretely set down to work four times in the modern age. First, they met at the Peace of West-phalia in 1648 (after the Thirty Years War) to invent the modern nation-state.

Second, they met at the Congress of Vienna in 1815 after the Napoleonic Wars. Third, they sat in Paris in 1919 after World War I to consider Woodrow Wilson's Fourteen Points and to invent the League of Nations. And finally in San Francisco in 1945 after World War II to invent the United Nations Organization (UNO) (Keegan 2002:1). They have since met many times to discuss how to maintain the Eurocentric world system and to reactivate the global orders. What the European historian John M. Headley (2008) celebrated as 'the Europeanization of the world' is part of global coloniality. This Europeanization of the world entailed reducing African people to bystanders in the making of history. Thus the current epistemic struggles are partly meant to rectify the idea of a black people who were mere bystanders in human history while at the same time critiquing the Eurocentric idea and philosophy of history itself.

As colonial subjects for over 350 years, Africans were forced to play a role in the reproduction of a colonial future that was inimical to their aspirations. This is why it is possible to find some African people who have been so whitewashed mentally by colonialism to the extent that they speak on its behalf and mediate Eurocentric knowledge in their research and teaching in Africa. But can also find Africans who are highly conscious and cognizant of the debilitating effects of colonialism and coloniality. It is these Africans who spearheaded anti-slavery and anti-colonial decolonial struggles as part of their drive to create African futures. It is also these highly conscious Africans who directly countered European inventors of the modern world by also meeting in the twentieth century to question the reordering of the modern world in accordance with European imperatives and interests. These Africans set down to reorder the world in Africa's favour. They met at the First Pan-African Conference in London in 1900 where they critiqued the ongoing enslavement, conquest and colonization of Africa. Second, they met at the Second Pan-African Conference in 1921(in London, Paris and Brussels) to continue to counter European and American politics of making the modern world in Europe and North America's image, while continuing to exploit and dominate Africa and the rest of the non-European world. Third, they met at the Third Pan-African Conference in 1923 in London and Lisbon to continue to strategize and condemn what Europe was doing. Fourth, they met at the Fourth Pan-African Conference in 1927 in New York and continued to deepen Pan-African unity among the oppressed black people of the world. Finally, they met at the Fifth Pan-African Conference in Manchester in 1945 where they directly declared war on colonialism and demanded immediate decolonization of Africa (Nimako 2012). Later, they met at the All Africa Pan-African Conference in 1958 on the African soil, following the achievement of political independence by Ghana in 1957. They vowed to continue the decolonization struggle until the total decolonization of Africa.

These initiatives were taken by African people including those from the Diaspora to try and create another future free from direct colonialism and indirect global coloniality. Throughout the meetings, Pan-Africanism strongly emerged as the decolonial ideology that had the potential to carry African imaginations of the future and to directly European counter-worldview. Racism and colonialism were correctly identified as the key problems of the twentieth century (see Maldonado-Torres 2011; Ndlovu-Gatsheni 2013d, 2014c). What made the decolonial struggles difficult is that colonialism had already imposed colonial mindsets on the psyche of African people, which meant that they continued to reproduce coloniality as their future even after direct juridical colonialism has been dismantled (Ngugi wa Thiong'o 1986, Chinweizu 1987). This reproduction of coloniality amounted to what Frantz Fanon (1968) termed 'repetition without change' that was itself a product of pitfalls of consciousness. This was possible because colonialism was not simply a process of conquest, annexation, occupation, settlement, domination and exploitation. It entailed emptying 'the native's brain of all form and content' on top of committing epistemicides such as distorting, disfiguring and eventually destroying the history of the colonized (Fanon 1968).

It is therefore not surprising that one of the long-term consequences of these types of colonial interventions has been to make some Africans simply capitulate to the idea that what they can only do as part of making history is to adapt to a present and a future made for them by Europeans and North Americans. This is why it is very common to hear some African scholars arguing that globalization and neoliberalism are a reality to which African must quickly adapt to rather than resisting. Such arguments are not only a reincarnation of the defeatist Thatcherist–Reagomonics imperial discourse of 'There is No Alternative' (TINA) but is also born out of succumbing to the seductive aspects of Euromodernity, particularly its rhetoric of emancipation that hides its reality of coloniality.

However, having identified global coloniality as a major challenge limiting space for Africans to create African futures; decolonial theorists and activists did not fall into despair. They remained committed to the possibilities of 'another world'. 'Another World Is Possible' has actually become a slogan of the World Social Forum that is engaged in contesting and resisting capitalist-driven globalization that carries global coloniality. To create another world entails endless mobilization and consistent confrontation with the present structural and agential sources of social injustices, asymmetrical power structures, patriarchal ideologies, logics of capitalist exploitation, resilient imperial/colonial reason, and racist articulations and practices (McNally 2005; Santos 2008). Clearly, such an envisaged new world system and its new global orders cannot be realized without decolonization of power, knowledge and being. This is why it is pertinent for all those committed to fighting for better African futures to fully understand the constitution of the present and at the same time comprehend how the modern world system works.

Decolonization has to invent another way which the world works that is free from global coloniality. This is why this book highlighted the need for reconstitution of the 'global political' (see Chapter 4). As it stands today, global power structures, systems and orders are constitutively asymmetrical (Ndlovu-Gatsheni 2013a, 2013b). The world we live in today, within which Africa is struggling to create African futures, is made up of two core elements. The first is the modern world system that is traceable to the dawn of Eurocentric modernity.

The second element is global orders (Frank 1998; Nimako 2011). The modern world system is consistently proving to be resistant to deimperialization and decolonization. For instance, whenever it is confronted by anti-systemic forces, the world system responds in two ways. It either disciplines the anti-systemic forces violently or it accommodates them to its shifting global orders.

The shifting global orders are also consistently resistant to deimperialization and decolonization. The shifting of the global orders is an operative strategy of hiding the world system from anti-systemic forces and to present it as though it has changed. What links the modern world system and its global orders is called coloniality of power (Quijano 2000; 2007). Coloniality of power gave birth to a particular modern world system that Ramon Grosfoguel (2007) has characterized as a racially hierarchized, patriarchal, sexist, hetero-normative, Christian-centric, Euro-North American-centric, imperial, colonial and capitalist. Within this modern world system, coloniality of power exists as an entanglement of multiple and heterogeneous global hierarchies and hetararchies of sexual, political, epistemic, economic, spiritual, linguistic, aesthetic and racial forms of domination and exploitation (Grosfoguel 2007: 217).

Practically, coloniality of power's success depended on what Jack Goody (2006: 1) described as 'theft of history', that is, 'the take-over of history by the west' and the reconceptualization and representation of human history 'according to what happened on the provincial scale of Europe' and 'then impose upon the rest of the world'. This usurpation of human history by Europe and North America, unfolded in terms of colonization of space (cartography, conquest and settlement), colonization of time (bifurcating it into ancient and modern epochs), colonization of being (classification and racial hierarchization of human population according to race) and colonization of nature (subjecting it to the logic of capitalism and reducing it to a simple natural resource open for exploitation) (Ndlovu–Gatsheni 2013c).

In short, the inscription of coloniality of power not only resulted in the 'theft of history' but also in the theft of African future. African people became represented as bystanders in human history deserving to be civilized by Europeans and educated by Europeans within a world constructed and configured by Europeans. The present modern global power structure informed by coloniality has the United States of America and Europe at the apex. The emergence of new powers from the Global South such as China, Brazil, Russia, South Africa and India has not yet deeply shaken the dominance of the USA and Europe. At the subaltern bottom is Africa and its people (Ndlovu-Gatsheni 2014a; 2014b).

The challenging reality is that of the feasibility of African inventing their futures under and within conditions global coloniality. This is a structural straitjacket in which global coloniality exists to make sure the powerful Euro-North American powers remain powerful. This is evident from the panic the USA is revealing regarding competition from China. China's rise is provoking tremors down the spine of the USA to the extent that it is warning Africans to be aware of Chinese imperialism as though the USA is not an imperial power itself. The USA is trying hard to keep Africa as its theatre of economic operation free from Chinese influence. This is why Barack Obama, when he was still the president of the USA, invited 47 African leaders to the US-Africa Summit (4–6 August 2014). The event was meant to try and contain the influence of China through a deliberate articulation of the USA as a long-standing friend of Africa (see the Opening Remarks US-Africa Summit 2014).

A structural cul-de-sac hampered African leaders and their people's capacity to create African futures. Claude Ake (1981: 93) was correct when he highlighted that 'the nationalist movement which arose from the contradictions of the colonial political economy achieved independence, not economic independence'. The current book highlights the necessity of epistemic freedom as an essential pre-requisite for launching genuine African futures capable of delivering both epistemic and economic freedom. It is not clear whether African leaders and their people have managed to rise above the 'contradictions of the colonial political economy'. What is clear is that global coloniality produced a particular form of leadership in Africa – a petit-bourgeoisie that could not invent or even transform political, economic and social institutions inherited from colonialism 'into its own image' so as to 'become socially hegemonic' (Nabudere 2011: 58; Taylor 2014: 5).

Successfully balancing of internal and external imperative sustains African leaders in power. But interests of external forces often outweigh those of internal constituencies in African leaders' political calculations. Thus, they preside over postcolonial states that were not entrenched in African society but exist as 'a bureaucratic connivance' (Mafeje 1992: 31; Young 2012). Ralph Austen (1987: 271) clearly understood that the major economic problem facing African people is that of asymmetrical relationship between the 'role of the continent in the world and the degree to which that world [. . .] has penetrated Africa'. This is a perennial African problem that compromised any initiatives aimed at creating African futures particularly autonomous development. Ian Taylor (2014: 7) is also correct in arguing 'The external domination of Africa's economies and the pathologies of dependency that this engenders, constructed during the colonial period, have proven markedly resilient'. He is also correct that African economies have remained integrated into 'the very economies of the developed economies in a way that is unfavorable to Africa and ensures structural dependence' (Taylor 2014: 7).

What emerges poignantly from this analysis is the problem of structural dependence. The other is that of lack of state autonomy and 'a stable hegemonic project that binds different levels of society together' for the purpose of forging African futures (Taylor 2014: 7). In countries like Zimbabwe that have spearheaded a radical land reform programme, there exist 'intrinsically unstable personalized systems of domination' which crystallized around the former president Robert Mugabe and his wife (Taylor 2014: 7; Ndlovu-Gatsheni 2009). All these realities that were fundamentally informed by global coloniality need to be taken seriously as we grapple with the pertinent question of the possibilities of epistemic freedom and that of Africans' potential and indeed desire to create their own futures. This possibility is posed in the context of the discourse of an Africa that is rising economically. How sustainable is this discourse of Africa rising within a context of an un-decolonized world system and its mutating imperial global order? Is Africa not reproducing a diversified form of dependency by extending it to the East?

The entry of China, Russia, Brazil and India into the African market has boosted this sale of primary commodities. There is no change of the forms of integration of Africa into the ever-evolving capitalist economy, making the notion of 'Africa Rising' to exist as slogan trumpeted by benefitting global corporations. Such blocs as Brazil, Russia, India, China, South Africa (BRICS) are not about radical change of the world system and its global orders; they are about making neoliberalism work more efficiently in accordance with the long-standing discourse of free trade. Taylor is correct that for a proper economic decolonization there is need for thorough thought on the 'type of social system that will engender development and ensure broad improvements in the standard of living of the people' (Taylor 2014: 156).

What is happening currently in Africa is opposite to the advice of Amilcar Cabral for those leading Africa to avoid claiming easy victories and telling lies about Africa's economic and political successes. Today African leaders celebrate an economic growth that is premised on a problematic 'intensification of resource extraction through diversification of partners, while inequality and unemployment increase and deindustrialization continues apace' (Taylor 2014: 160). The narrative of 'Africa Rising' is blind to the problem of the new 'scramble' for African natural resources and the concomitant land grabbing that is articulated by advocates of neoliberalism as investment on land (Cotula 2013). Emerging powers from the Global South have joined the traditional Euro-North American powers and Multinational Corporations (MCs) in this new scramble for African natural resources. Global coloniality deliberately creates celebrations of these false starts as it protects and diverts attention of anti-systemic forces and formations from targeting the asymmetrical modern world system and its imperial global orders.

Throughout this book, what is consistently highlighted is how global coloniality is also sustained by a particular epistemology. African economic futures have remained trapped within the hegemonic Truman version of development, which is backed up by what Adebayo Adedeji termed the 'development merchant system' (DMS). DMS is driven by the Breton Woods Institutions (BWI), which finances the implementation of exogenous development agenda (Adedeji 2002: 4). At the centre of the DMS is what David Slater termed 'imperiality of knowledge' that is constituted by 'interweaving of geopolitical power, knowledge and subordinating representation of the other' (Slater 2004: 223). DMS maintains coloniality long after the dismantlement of administrative colonialism. It still approaches Africa as an space inhabited by a people 'shorn of the legitimate symbols of independent identity and authority' as well as a 'space ready to be penetrated, worked over, restructured and transformed' from outside (Slater 2004: 223). DMS exists as a consortium of IMF, WB, WTO, International Non-Governmental Organizations (IGOs) and MCs. They advance a 'Bretton Woods Paradigm' of African future that is amenable to global coloniality (Therien 1999: 723–742).

The fundamental question is, it possible to use the same knowledge system that created global coloniality to create African futures? The African Union Agenda 2063 articulates the need for a paradigm shift without necessarily elaborating on a clear epistemological and ideological foundation of such a change. The question of epistemology is very important because from the start the inscription of global coloniality commenced with

> a systematic repression, not only of the specific beliefs, ideas, images, symbols or knowledges that were not useful to global colonial domination, while at the same time colonizers were expropriating from the colonized their knowledge, especially in mining, agriculture, engineering as well as their products and work.
>
> (Quijano 2007: 169)

Epistemological colonization which amounts to colonization of the mind and imagination affected African 'modes of knowing, of producing knowledge, of producing perspectives, images and systems of images, symbols, modes of signification, over the resources, patterns, and instruments of formalized and objectivized expression' including intellectual and visual forms (Quijano 2007: 169). Having performed these epistemicides, the constructors and drivers of global coloniality, that included Christian missionaries, proceeded to make their own patterns of producing knowledge and modes of knowing to be the only legitimate and scientific ways of understanding the world. They mystified their own patterns of knowing and knowledge production. But they also tried to consistently place these Euro-North American-centric patterns 'far out of reach of the dominated' (Quijano 2007: 169).

When the Europeans decided to impart this knowledge on the colonized, they did so 'in a partial and selective way, in order to co-opt some of the dominated into their own power institutions' (Quijano 2007: 169). Consequently, they succeeded to a large extent in transforming 'cultural Europeanization' into 'an aspiration' of every African (Quijano 2007: 169). The long-term impact of this social engineering and epistemological process that was marked by epistemicides, displacements, expropriations and impositions invaded the core imaginary of the African psyche and culture to the extent that Africans today reproduce 'cultural Europeanization' without direct tutelage of Europeans. The challenge facing Africans is how to undo this imperial/colonial epistemological damage as part of their drive to create decolonial futures. They have to avoid the common trap of seeking solution to coloniality within coloniality (see Santos 2007: 78).

At the epistemological realm, Africans are still stuck in Eurocentric thought. They somehow breathe it on a daily basis because it is a major technology of domination. This is why the leading Egyptian economist and Marxist-decolonial thinker Samir Amin (1985) not only motivated for 'delinking' as part of enabling the Global South to escape from the constraints imposed by the world's economic system, but also highlighted the ubiquity and dominance of Euro-North American-centric conventional classical economic thought in all the African attempts to chart an autonomous economic trajectory for the continent. Even the Lagos Plan of Action was informed by this thought (Amin 1990: 58).

The African epistemological predicament is further compounded by the fact that there is increasing realization that Euro-North American-centric thought that has dominated the world for over 500 years has now reached an epistemic crisis – a form of exhaustion and irrelevance. Its promise to overcome all obstacles to human progress is today not taken serious because it has mainly succeeded in creation such modern problems as pollution of which it has no modern solutions (Escobar 2004: 230). This means that Africans can no longer rely solely on this epistemology in their endeavour to create African futures.

Even European scholars like Patrick Chabal (2012) made it clear that 'the social sciences we employ to explain what is happening domestically and overseas – are both historically and conceptually out of date' and he elaborated that the Euro-North American-centric 'theories are now obstacles to the understanding of what is going on in our societies and what we can do about it' (Chabal 2012: viii). His conclusion was 'The end of conceit is upon us. Western rationality must be rethought' (Chabal 2012: 335). The global financial crisis that hit Europe and North America from 2007 added to the questioning of the suitability of Euro-North American thought and epistemology in offering solutions to modern problems. The crisis in Euro-North American-centric thought is both a challenge and an opportunity. It means that Africans must take advantage and leverage their thought and theory together with that of the rest of the Global South. A space for another reason, logic, thought and epistemology is open, capable of enabling autonomy from traditional Eurocentric thought and epistemology that enabled global coloniality. Only a decolonized being can appreciate the value of indigenous and endogenous knowledge as ideal for the creation of African futures.

At the ontological level, Eurocentric modernity inaugurated the colonization of being through its social classification of human population according to race. While the processes of racialization took different forms and assumed different terms across different colonial spaces, the logic and purpose remained the same. This was followed by racial hierarchization of being according to race. White races claimed complete *being* for themselves and pushed African people into a perpetual state of *becoming* – a state of incompleteness (Ndlovu-Gatsheni 2013a; 2013b). This imperial reason was then used to consistently question the very humanity of African people in order to consign them to the status of inferiority. The overarching purpose of racial classification and racial hierarchization was to construct a system of social differentiation of those who could own slaves and those who would be enslaved, between those who could claim and own land and those who would be forced to work on it, a distinction in social category between those who could define others and those would always be subjects and objects of definition, as well as those whose lives were dispensable and those whose life is sacrosanct.

African subjectivity that emerged from these processes of racialization and inferiorization of blackness is one that has a diminished ontological density. It became a subjectivity that was said to be characterized by a catalogue of deficits and a series of lacks. Sabelo J. Ndlovu-Gatsheni (2013a) listed the deficits and lacks that were attributed to the African subject as ranging from lack of souls, writing, history, civilization, development, democracy to human rights and ethics. This gave birth to the colonial idea of Africans as the condemned people of the earth, the anthropos of the planet and the wretched of the earth.

What has compounded the phenomenon of coloniality of being is that the postcolonial state in Africa as an inherited institution continues to exert colonial-like brutalities on African people. The shooting of 34 black miners at Marikana by the South African police in 2012 confirmed Maldonado-Torres's (2007: 255) argument that black people endure 'hellish existence' in which 'killability' and 'rapeability' were a normal state of life. Across the world, the life of a black person is the cheapest (dispensable) (Magubane 2007). All this indicates that the problem of coloniality of being has a negative and disempowering bearing on the possibilities of African people creating their African futures. They cannot effectively create African futures if they have not regained their denied ontological density, which enables an escape route from imposed inferiority complexes.

To concretize decolonization and deprovincialization, Africans, and the rest of those who have been invented as black people, have to subvert the current colonial logics of familiarity and become 'strange' again for insurrectional purposes. Being 'strange' entails jumping out of colonial reduction into familiar 'natives'. Global coloniality is comfortable with familiarity. Its colonial matrices of power are effective on what is familiar. Only by turning into 'strangers,' will Africans become indifferent to Europe and successfully resist the long-standing idea of Europe as the centre of the world. This is a strategy offered by Himadeep Muppidi (2016). It entails being stranger to Europe while being neighbourly to each other. This strategy entails a return to the decolonial Bandung spirit:

> Bandung, looking through the eyes of an Achebe, is a feast, a coming together of postcolonial kith and kin. It is a festive gathering where Asia and Africa meet and look forward to meeting other Americas and other Europes. If Europe is not on the guest list, it is only because it is not yet willing to see itself as kith and kin to the once colonized. [. . .] A Bandung feast stages the times and places to come when European supremacy disappears from global politics. A Bandung feast is the social construction of another world, 'a world of our making'. [. . .] Bandung as a gathering is a feast of conversations – about what was and what might be in the world and not just in one's national home or in the regional neighbourhood.
>
> (Muppidi 2016: 33)

In these conversations, strategizing about epistemic freedom rather than shallow academic freedom must top our list. Epistemic freedom enables a tapping into the rich and inexhaustible wisdom and knowledge of the world as we break free from Eurocentrism. Such a decolonized world had to be predicated on '6-Ds': deimperialization, deracialization, detribalization, decorporatization, depatriachization and democratization.

References

Adedeji, A. 2002. 'From the Lagos Plan of Action to the New Partnership for African Development and from the Final Act of Lagos to the Constitutive Act: Wither Africa?' Unpublished Keynote Address Delivered at the African Forum for Envisioning Africa, Nairobi, Kenya, 26–29 April.

African Union, 2013. *Agenda 2063 Vision and Priorities: Unity, Prosperity and Peace*. Addis Ababa: African Union.

Ake, C. 1981. *A Political Economy of Africa*. Lagos: Longman Nigeria.

Amin, S. 1985. *Delinking: Towards a Polycentric World*. Translated by Michael Wolfers. London and Atlantic Highlands, NJ: Zed Books.

Amin, S. 1990. *Maldevelopment: Anatomy of a Global Failure*. Tokyo and London: United Nations University Press and Zed Books, p. 58.

Austen, R. 1987. *African Economic History: Internal Development and External Dependency*. Oxford, UK: James Currey.

Chabal. P. 2012. *The End of Conceit: Western Rationality after Postcolonialism*. London and New York: Zed Books.

Chinweizu, 1987. *Decolonizing the African Mind*. Lagos: Pero Press.

Cotula, L. 2013. *The Great African Land Grab? Agricultural Investments and the Global Food System*. London and New York: Zed Books.

Escobar, A. 2004. 'Beyond the Third World: Imperial Globality, Global Coloniality and Anti-Globalization Social Movements'. *Third World Quarterly*, 25(1), pp. 207–230.

Fanon, F. 1968. *The Wretched of the Earth*. New York: Grove Press.

Frank, A. N. 1998. *ReOrient: Global Economy in the Asian Age*. Berkeley, LA and London: University of California Press

Goody, J. 2006. *The Theft of History*. Cambridge, UK: Cambridge University Press.

Grosfoguel, R. 2007. 'The Epistemic Decolonial Turn: Beyond Political-Economy Paradigms'. *Cultural Studies*, 21(2–3), (March/May), pp. 211–223.

Headley, J. M. 2008. *The Europeanization of the World: On the Origins of Human Rights and Democracy*. Princeton, NJ and Oxford, UK: Princeton University Press.

Keegan, J. 2002. 'Book Review: Paris 1919 by Margaret McMillan'. *Washington Post*, 15 December.

Mafeje, A. 1992. *In Search of an Alternative: A Collection of Essays on Revolutionary Theory and Politics*. Harare: SAPES Books.

Magubane, B. M. 2007. *Race and the Construction of Dispensable Other*. Pretoria: UNISA Press.

Maldonado-Torres, N. 2007. 'On Coloniality of Being: Contributions to the Development of a Concept'. *Cultural Studies*, 21(2), March/May, pp. 240–270.

Maldonado-Torres, 2011. 'Thinking Through the Decolonial Turn: Post-Continental Interventions in Theory, Philosophy, and Critique – An Introduction'. *Transmodernity: Journal of Peripheral Cultural Production of Luso-Hispanic World*, 1(2), Fall, pp. 1–23.

McNally, D. 2005. *Another World is Possible: Globalization and Anti-Capitalism*. Winnipeg, MB: ArbeiterRing Publishing.

Muppidi, H. 2016. 'The Elements of Bandung'. In Q. N. Pham and R. Shillian (eds), *Meanings of Bandung: Postcolonial Orders and Decolonial Visions*. London and New York: Rowman and Littlefield International, pp. 23–36.

Nabudere, D. W. 2011. *Afrikology: Philosophy and Wholeness: An Epistemology*. Pretoria: Africa Institute of South Africa.

Ndlovu-Gatsheni, S. J. 2009. 'Making Sense of Mugabeism in Local and Global Politics: 'So Blair, Keep Your England and Let Me Keep My Zimbabwe'. *Third World Quarterly*, 30(6), pp. 1139–1158.

Ndlovu-Gatsheni, S. J. 2013a. *Coloniality of Power in Postcolonial Africa: Myths of Decolonization.* Dakar: CODESRIA Book Series.

Ndlovu-Gatsheni, S. J. 2013b. *Empire, Global Coloniality and African Subjectivity.* New York and Oxford, UK: Berghahn Books.

Ndlovu-Gatsheni, S. J. 2013c. 'The Entrapment of Africa within Global Colonial Matrices of Power: Eurocentrism, Coloniality and Deimperialization in the Twenty-First Century'. *Journal of Developing Societies,* 29(4), pp. 331–353.

Ndlovu-Gatsheni, S. J. 2013d. 'Decolonial Epistemic Perspective and Pan African Unity in the 21st Century'. In M. Muchie, P. Lukhele-Olorunju and O. Akpor (eds), *The African Union Ten Years After: Solving African Problems with Pan-Africanism and the African Renaissance.* Pretoria: Africa Institute of South Africa, pp. 385–409.

Ndlovu-Gatsheni, S. J. 2014a. 'What is Beyond Discourses of Alterity? Reflections on the Constitution of the Present and Construction of African Subjectivity', in S. Osha (ed.), *The Social Contract in Africa.* Pretoria: Africa Institute of South Africa, pp. 111–130.

Ndlovu-Gatsheni, S. J. 2014b. 'Global Technologies of Domination: From Colonial Encounters to the Arab Spring'. In E. Obadare and W. Willems (eds), *Civic Agency in Africa: Arts of Resistance in the 21st Century.* Oxford, UK: James Currey, pp. 27–48.

Ndlovu-Gatsheni, S. J. 2014c. 'Pan-Africanism and the International System'. In T. Murithi (ed.), *Handbook of Africa's International Relations.* London and New York: Routledge, pp. 21–29.

Ngugi wa Thiong'o. 1986. *Decolonizing the Mind: The Politics of Language in African Literature.* London: James Currey.

Nimako, K. 2011. 'Reorienting the World: With or Without Africa?' Working Paper: International Centre for Muslim and Non-Muslim Understanding, University of South Australia.

Nimako, K. 2012. Presentation at the International Summer School on Decolonizing Power, Knowledge and Being. Barcelona, Spain, July.

Opening Remarks by President Obama, available at: www.whitehouse.gov/us-africa-leaderssummit (accessed 22 January 2018).

Quijano, A. 2000. 'The Coloniality of Power and Social Classification'. *Journal of World Systems,* 6(2), (Summer–Fall), pp. 342–386.

Quijano, A. 2007. 'Coloniality and Modernity/Rationality'. *Cultural Studies,* 21(2–3), (March/May), pp. 168–178.

Santos, B. de S. 2007. 'Beyond Abyssal Thinking: From Global Lines to Ecologies of Knowledge'. *Review,* xxx(1), pp. 45–89.

Santos, B. de S. B. 2008. *Another Knowledge is Possible: Beyond Northern Epistemologies (Reinventing Social Emancipation: Towards New Manifestos).* London Verso.

Santos, B. de S. 2014. *Epistemologies of the South: Justice against Epistemicide.* Boulder, CO and London: Paradigm.

Slater, D. 2004. *Geopolitics and the Post-Colonial: Rethinking North-South Relations.* Malden, MA: Blackwell Publishing, p. 223.

Taylor, I. 2014. *Africa Rising: BRICS-Diversifying Dependency.* Oxford, UK: James Currey.

Therien, J. P. 1999. 'Beyond the North-South Divide: Two Tales of World Poverty'. *Third World Quarterly,* 20(4), pp. 723–742.

Young, C. 2012. *The Postcolonial State in Africa: Fifty Years of Independence, 1960–2010.* Madison, WI: The University of Wisconsin Press.

INDEX

Page numbers in **bold** indicate a table.

Quijano, Anibal 43, 62

'rainbow nation', Mandela's vision
106–107, 111–112, 214, 228, 233
Rancourt, Denis 85
Ranger, Terence Osborne 19, 149
Rastafarianism 47
Rathbone, Richard 231
Ray, Malcolm 175
Readings, Bill 188
reconstructing the political: African
humanism, leader adoption 96–97, 112;
Cabral's decolonial revolutionary theory
101–102; decolonial theory of life 94;
European conception elements 94–95;
fetishism of power 96; Jesus and Marx,
comparative teachings 93–94; Kaunda's
philosophy of humanism 99–101;
Lumumba's Pan-Africanism 97–99;
Mandela's non-racial inclusive
humanism 106–112; paradigms of war
and difference 95–96; Senghor's
philosophy of Negritude 102–106
Red Sea, Mazrui's abolition 126–127
re-humaning/humaning 76
re-humanizing/re-membering 76–77,
82–83
relation identity 47, **48**
rethinking thinking: African intellectual
challenges 25–26; decolonial process
23–24, 30–31, 86–87; gender constructs
and imposition 26–30; geography of
reason shift 24–25, 86
Rhodes, Cecil John 148, 189, 221
Rhodesia 173; see also Zimbabwe
Rhodes Must Fall movement: alienation
within universities 64; decolonial
attitude 78, 175, 189–190, 215;
epistemological decolonization 60;
formation factors 188–189, 222;
protest demands 222, 238–239; protest
politics and identities 224, 226, 229,
235–238
Richards, Howard 23–24, 87, 143, 175
Rodney, Walter 60, 180
root identity 47, **48**
Rwandan genocide 144

Said, Edward E. 22, 46, 86
Santos, Boaventura de Sousa: abyssal
thinking 3, 94, 124, 145, 204; cognitive
justice 4; ecologies of knowledge 238;
Eurocentric critical theory, changes to
7; 'impossibility of co-presence',
colonial legacy 145, 204, 227

Schatzberg, Michael G. 176
Schmitt, Carl 95
Seely, Stephen D. 72, 73–74, 77
Seme, Pixley Ka Isaka 212
Senegal 102–106
Senghor, Leopold Sedar 102–106, 121,
122
Shaka kaSenzangakhona 203
Shivji, Issa G. 26, 183
Sierra Leone 12–13, 120, 170–171
silencing of non-Western history 18–23
Slater, David 250
slave trade: Africa and the world economy
66; 'blackness', critical historic moments
45; Caribbean's 'nonhistory' 19, 46–47;
form of holocaust 118; Haitian
Revolution, challenging ethno-beliefs
21–22; post-abolition education 12–13;
syndrome of abolition 20
Slovo, Joe 110
Smith, Linda Tuhiwai 30, 85
Smuts, Jan, General 148
South Africa: Africanization and nationalist
objectives 211–213; Alexander's
national question issues 200–201; ANC
and liberation 108–109; Anglicization
and Afrikanerization 209–211, 213,
228; Bantucization 209; Bantu
Education for cheap labour 174, 230–
231; colonialism and native identity
115–116, 228; constitutionalism issues
214–215; Convention for a Democratic
South Africa (CODESA) 109–110,
154; democratic status threatened 133;
Fees Must Fall movement 189–190,
215; Freedom Charter (1955), adoption
206, 212, 213; idea to country 201;
identities and societal trajectories
204–206, 208–209, 213, 215–216,
227–229; Mandela's non-racial inclusive
humanism 106–108, 112–113, 214,
215; Mandela's presidency 111–112;
National Democratic Revolution
(NDR) 208; nation-building, liberal
ideals 206–207; 'New South Africa'
ideal 214, 228–229, 233; paradigm of
difference, continuing impact 226–229;
post-apartheid transition unfulfilled
189, 200, 215–216, 226, 233; pre-
colonial, settler's misrepresentation
201–203; re-humanizing movements
213–214; Rhodes Must Fall movement
175, 188–190, 215; Soweto Uprising
1976 232; transitional justice, ANC's
mission 109–111; Truth and

54867938R00154

Made in the USA
Columbia, SC
06 April 2019